DAYS *of* DECISION

RELATED TITLES FROM POTOMAC BOOKS, INC.

Divided America on the World Stage: Broken Government and Foreign Policy
—Howard J. Wiarda

Defiant Superpower: The New American Hegemony
—Donald E. Nuechterlein

Diplomacy Lessons: Realism for an Unloved Superpower
—John Brady Kiesling

DAYS *of* DECISION

Turning Points in U.S. Foreign Policy

MICHAEL J. NOJEIM AND DAVID P. KILROY

Potomac Books, Inc.
Washington, D.C.

Chapter 4, "The Korean War and the Cold War in Asia," is a revised version of "U.S. Foreign Policy and the Korean War," which was published in *Asian Security*, volume 2, issue 2, 2006.

Chapter 8, "The U.S. Opening to China and Detente," is reprinted from *Living Democracy, Custom Edition* (2007), by permission of Pearson Custom Publishing, a Pearson Education Company.

Library of Congress Cataloging-in-Publication Data
Nojeim, Michael J., 1960-
  Days of decision : turning points in U.S. foreign policy / Michael J. Nojeim and David P. Kilroy. — 1st ed.
      p. cm.
  Includes bibliographical references and index.
  ISBN 978-1-59797-526-1 (hardcover : alk. paper)
  1. United States—Foreign relations—20th century. 2. United States—History, Military—20th century. 3. Spanish-American War, 1898. 4. September 11 Terrorist Attacks, 2001. I. Kilroy, David P. II. Title. III. Title: Turning points in U.S. foreign policy.
  E744.N555 2011
  327.73009'049—dc22

                                            2010044686

Printed in the United States of America on acid-free paper that meets the American National Standards Institute Z39-48 Standard.

Potomac Books, Inc.
22841 Quicksilver Drive
Dulles, Virginia 20166

First Edition

10 9 8 7 6 5 4 3 2 1

For the turning points in our lives:
Jennette, Consuelo, Ciara, Liam, and *Catherine*

Contents

Acknowledgments

All books are collaborations and ours is no different. We wish to thank all those who helped us complete this project. Librarians Steve Shaw and Ollie Mayberry at Prairie View A&M University provided invaluable research assistance, as did the library staff at Nova Southeastern University and at Wheeling Jesuit University. Colleagues Kris Willumsen, Artemesia Stanberry, and Elizabeth Cohn commented on previous drafts of the text and provided useful and insightful commentary throughout the project. Our students, Lorne Senegal, Nicco Matthews, Carlton Singleton, and John Smith provided valuable comments on previous drafts and pushed us to write a book for university-level students that was accessible, useful, and timely. And our editors at Potomac Books, Hilary Claggett and Kathryn Neubauer, offered support and timely answers to all our questions. We would also like to acknowledge the contribution made by Michael Kilroy, who passed away before this book was completed. His keen intellect is present in revisions made to several of the chapters in this book—may he rest in peace.

Most of all we wish to thank our families for supporting us and enduring what can sometimes be a painstaking, all-consuming process.

List of Abbreviations

AIOC	Anglo Iranian Oil Company
ANZUS	Australia, New Zealnad, United States
ARVN	Army of the Republic of Vietnam
CIS	Commonwealth of Independent States
CPA	Coalition Provisional Authority
DefCon III	Defense Condition Three
DHS	Department of Homeland Security
DNI	Director of National Intelligence
EEC	European Economic Community
EXCOMM	Executive Committee
FEO	Federal Energy Office
ICBM	intercontinental ballistic missile
ICJ	International Court of Justice
IEA	International Energy Agency
IRBM	intermediate range ballistic missile
INR	Bureau of Intelligence and Research
JCS	Joint Chiefs of Staff
mbd	million barrels per day
MAAG	Military Assistance Advisory Group
MACV	Military Assistance Command, Vietnam

MAD	Mutual Assured Destruction
MOU	Memorandum of Understanding
MRBM	medium range ballistic missile
NATO	North Atlantic Treaty Organization
NEI	Netherlands East Indies
NIE	National Intelligence Estimate
NLF	National Liberation Front
NSC	National Security Council
NSA	National Security Advisor
NSA	National Security Agency
NVA	North Vietnamese Army
OAS	Organization of American States
OPEC	Organization of Petroleum Exporting Countries
OSS	Office of Strategic Services
PLO	Palestine Liberation Organization
PRC	People's Republic of China
RDF	Rapid Deployment Force
ROK	Republic of Korea
SAC	Strategic Air Command
SALT	Strategic Arms Limitation Talks
SAM	surface-to-air missile
SAVAK	National Information and Security Organization (of Iran)
SDI	Strategic Defense Initiative
SEATO	Southeast Asia Treaty Organization
SOFA	Status of Forces Agreement
START	Strategic Arms Reduction Talks
UNC	United Nations Command (in Korea)
UNSC	United Nations Security Council
WMD	weapons of mass destruction
WSAG	Washington Special Actions Group

Introduction

On a picture perfect day in late summer 2001, Americans' perception of the world and their place in it changed dramatically. Once seemingly immune to the often-random violence of terrorism, residents of the United States suddenly had to adjust to a world in which their personal security was no longer guaranteed. The September 11 terrorist attacks jolted Americans into facing the reality that they too were vulnerable to attack at any time and in any place. The 9/11 tragedy elevated national security and foreign policy to the top of the American political agenda to an extent that had not been seen since the early years of the Cold War. As was the case after the Japanese attack on Pearl Harbor in 1941, the 9/11 attacks compelled the people of the United States and their leaders to reexamine America's place in the world, and for that reason alone it constitutes a significant turning point in the history of American foreign policy.

This book examines twelve such case studies, or what we call turning points in U.S. foreign policy, from the Spanish-American War of 1898 to the 9/11 tragedy. We do not argue that these are the most important episodes in the history of U.S. foreign relations, nor do we claim that the cases we have identified here represent an exhaustive list. In addition to the cases we have identified for this book, there are numerous other critical moments between 1898 and the present that might justifiably be considered turning points. There are also many important episodes in the history of U.S. foreign relations prior to 1898 that fall outside the coverage of this book. Our rationale for choosing the case studies in this book rests on the following points: (1) each case study centers on a crisis moment or a profoundly new development that gives rise to an intense, and often condensed, period of debate and division regarding the existing and future direction of American foreign policy; these are the "Days of Decision" referred to in the title of the book. (2) These events drew foreign policy in from the margins of American politics where it so often resides and elevated it to the top of the national agenda. (3) The broad attention that these events engender placed the normally reclusive foreign policy bureaucracy into the "fish bowl" of public scrutiny and broadened the scope and intensity of the debate to include participants who might otherwise remain marginal to the process, including the press, special interest groups, and an aroused public opinion. And (4) in each case, the "Days of Decision" led to a significant redirection in the course of U.S. foreign policy.

The crisis or new development that anchors each chapter will be examined using four thematic questions as the common framework of analysis:

- What is the historical and political context for each event?
- What happened at the micro level?
- What happened at the macro level?
- In what ways is this event a turning point in U.S. foreign policy?

In addition to binding the case studies of this book together in a common analytical framework, this approach could also prove to be a useful heuristic for teachers and professors to help guide students' analyses of other significant events in U.S. foreign policy.

HISTORICAL AND POLITICAL CONTEXT

None of the events highlighted in this book occurred in a historical vacuum. As such, each chapter begins with an examination of the historical and political context leading up to the relevant turning point. The popular perception of events such as Pearl Harbor and 9/11 is that they were "bolts from the blue," totally unexpected developments that just happened to the United States. While there was certainly an element of surprise involved in most of the case studies examined in this book, the United States as a key player on the world stage played an integral role in shaping the climate in which crises such as Pearl Harbor and 9/11 occurred. The opening sections for each chapter thus provide the relevant context for each turning point.

For example, the Cuban Missile Crisis can only be understood within the context of the history of U.S. policy toward Cuba both before and after the Cuban Revolution and of the nuclear arms race between the United States and the Soviet Union. Similarly, the 1979 American hostage crisis in Iran has its roots in U.S. involvement in Iran going back to the 1950s. In order to understand the Iranian students' motives for taking American diplomats hostage in 1979, we must first comprehend their mindset, which was shaped by their memory of American meddling in Iran's domestic politics in the 1950s. We must therefore connect the main subject of analysis in each chapter to its historical antecedents if we are to give a full explanation of the event as a significant "Turning Point."

By providing this historical context, we seek to show how successive events can suddenly erupt in a crisis situation. Most of these turning points were triggered by a crisis, the definition of which involves a sudden, potentially catastrophic event that offers few policy options in a severely collapsed timeframe. Given the time and resource constraints on policy makers, given the vast network of relations and interests the United States must juggle around the world, and given the exceedingly complicated nature of global issues, it might be too much to hope for a U.S. foreign policy that can predict crises or one that always takes the initiative after careful and deliberate planning. Yet, as these case studies will show, U.S. policy makers are frequently surprised by fast-paced events for which they are often poorly prepared.

Consequently, readers might form the impression that nearly all of U.S. foreign policy is largely reactive in nature. However, by locating these events in their proper historical and political context, we can show that, while many of these events may have caught U.S. policy makers off guard, few were entirely unanticipated. For example, prior to the sinking of the *Lusitania*, U.S. Secretary of State William Jennings Bryan had sought unsuccessfully to prohibit American citizens from traveling on the ships of belligerent nations during World War I. In addition, the United States did in fact expect a Japanese attack in the 1940s, but Washington could not pinpoint when or where. And in discussions leading up to the American hostage crisis in Iran, President Jimmy Carter was acutely aware of the possibility of an attack on the U.S. embassy if he proceeded with his controversial plans to admit the hated and deposed Shah of Iran, Muhammad Reza Shah Pahlavi, into the United States for medical treatment. In some instances, such as the Tet Offensive or the launch of Sputnik, a crisis scenario resulted from media and public (mis)perceptions at odds with reality, or from political posturing in Washington. Some of the turning points occurred as a result of American initiatives, such as President Nixon's visit to China, while others were actively encouraged by the United States, such as the fall of the Berlin Wall. In all these cases, however, fast-paced events and new developments inspired a broad national debate over new policy initiatives.

MICRO LEVEL ANALYSIS

At the micro level, we "peel the onion" of the policy making process by looking inside the U.S. foreign policy bureaucracy. We explore the debates and divisions that occurred among key policy makers as they confront each turning point. Even though senior policy makers work for the same president, they often find themselves at odds with one another in counseling the president about the best option to choose. We believe it is imperative to demonstrate to students how the *substance* of American foreign policy is often the result of serious and profound disagreements among high-ranking officials who are engaged in what is a messy, even underhanded, policy making *process*. As the saying goes, no one wants to see how the sausage is made, but if we are to fully understand U.S. foreign policy we must look inside the manufacturing process. It is important to understand how the often-cacophonous debates and divisions among well-intentioned officials, who all want what is best for the country, sometimes result in confusing and muddled policy initiatives.

We therefore do not treat the government as a monolithic entity. Rather, the U.S. foreign policy making apparatus is a behemoth with many different wheels propelling it. Sometimes those wheels are pointed in different directions. In addition to divisions between the legislative and executive branches of government, there are numerous departments and agencies within the executive branch that are often at odds with each other. For example, as we show throughout the book, officials in the State Department often clash with those in the Defense Department, in part because of so-called turf battles. Furthermore, there are often heated debates among a group of people we refer to throughout the book as the foreign policy elite, many of whom hold no official government position but who for a variety of reasons are able to exert some influence on the foreign policy process. Examples addressed in this book include Woodrow Wilson's reliance on the advice of his close personal friend Col. Edward House during World War I, Lyndon Johnson's reliance on a group of elder statesmen, known as the Wise Men, for advice during the Vietnam conflict, and the pressure exerted by former Secretary of State Henry Kissinger as well as business tycoon David Rockefeller on President Carter, who went against his own instincts and permitted the Shah of Iran to enter the United States.

In terms of the debates and divisions that occur within the foreign policy community, a couple of examples here will suffice to illustrate the tenor of the book. In the 1890s, for instance, Americans debated in both the public and private spheres over how to respond to the Cuban insurrection in 1895. This reflected the broader, philosophical debate over what America's emerging role in the world should properly be. American victory over Spain in the War of 1898 appeared to settle the debate, albeit temporarily, in favor of an enlarged, activist American role in world affairs. The debate was resurrected in its most divisive form in the years between WWI and WWII as many Americans sought to disengage from world affairs almost entirely.

Another example of debate and division over foreign policy concerns the run-up to the Iraq War. U.S. officials vehemently disagreed over such things as the role of the United Nations (U.N.) and troop levels. But the debate was not confined to members of the foreign policy elite: Americans from all walks of life entered the fray, with tens of thousands staging antiwar demonstrations from coast to coast. The Iraq War itself has resulted in deep cleavages among Americans over the future direction of U.S. foreign policy.

More often than not, the president—alone in the end—settles these debates and divisions and must answer to history for his administration's conduct, whether wise or foolish. In some cases, we argue that the president's decisions resulted in foreign policy disaster, such as: (1) Franklin Roosevelt's missteps in handling relations with Japan; (2) Harry Truman's decision to allow Gen. Douglas MacArthur to expand the Korean War; (3) Lyndon Johnson's decision to escalate U.S. troop levels in Vietnam; (4) Jimmy Carter's decision to admit the Shah of Iran to the United States; and (5) George W. Bush's single-minded march to war against Iraq. In other cases, a president's decisions turned out quite favorably for U.S. policy and U.S. interests, such as: (1) Dwight Eisenhower's response to the Soviets' launch of the Sputnik satellite; (2) John F. Kennedy's handling of the Cuban Missile Crisis; (3) Richard Nixon's deft opening to China as well as his (and Henry Kissinger's) management of the October 1973 Arab-Israeli War; and (4) Ronald Reagan's pragmatic response to the transformation of the political climate in the Soviet Union in the 1980s. Regardless of the wisdom of these presidential decisions, however, a trend emerges throughout the course of the book, from the War of 1898 to the 9/11 tragedy, and that is the expansion of presidential and executive power in the arena of U.S. foreign policy vis-a-vis the other branches of American government. In chapters 1 and 2 we see the power of presidents William McKinley and Woodrow Wilson, respectively, somewhat constrained by Congress, but even in these early crises we can discern the beginning of the trend that would lead to what historian Arthur Schlesinger Jr. famously dubbed "the imperial presidency." At times, Congress tried to arrest this trend, as in 1973 when it passed the War Powers Act in the wake of the Vietnam War. Overall, however, the historic expansion of presidential power and prerogative in U.S. foreign policy in relation especially to Congress is undeniable.

MACRO LEVEL ANALYSIS

At the macro level, we analyze how these twelve case studies altered the big picture in domestic and world politics. We examine how these events led to changes in the overall direction of U.S. foreign policy, in the structure of the foreign policy bureaucracy, in world and regional politics, or in international alliances. Again, we offer several examples here to illustrate the point. For instance, the 1941 attack on Pearl Harbor and U.S. entry into World War II helped contribute to a major restructuring of the American national security bureaucracy: creation of the National Security Council, the Department of Defense, the United States Air Force, and the Central Intelligence Agency represent four of the biggest changes on this score. In addition, North Korea's 1950 attack on South Korea led to multiple policy reversals in Asia that were profound and long lasting. President Nixon's 1972 opening to China significantly altered the global balance of power in favor of the United States against its chief Cold War rival, the Soviet Union. And the fall of the Berlin Wall signaled the end of the Cold War and led to a major reorientation of global political structures and international institutions including the dissolution of the Warsaw Pact and the expansion of the European community to include formerly communist East European countries. The end of the Cold War also enabled the United Nations to demonstrate unprecedented unity during the 1991 Gulf War against Iraq.

TURNING POINTS

Each chapter concludes with a section that addresses how and why the event amounts to a turning point in U.S. foreign policy. The turning points are moments at which old or existing policies are scrutinized, debated, and evaluated and new initiatives are adopted or broad changes in policy take place. Many of these turning points fit into larger historical patterns and trends, which can be partially explained using what political scientists and historians sometimes call "mood cycle theory."

This approach posits that U.S. foreign policy experiences pendulum-like shifts between competing impulses that have been variously labeled extroversion vs. introversion, intervention vs. nonintervention, or internationalism vs. isolationism.[1]

The pendulum-shift model may serve as a useful tool in helping students fit important individual events into larger patterns which can then deepen and broaden their understanding of the conduct of foreign policy through the broad sweep of history. Given their complexity, of course, not all the turning points we examine in this book will fit nicely into a theoretical pattern devised by scholars. But throughout the book, we can identify instances where these turning points are part of larger historical shifts in the orientation of U.S. foreign policy. For instance, we observe that the War of 1898 was part of an emerging pattern of intervention, which at that time took the form of imperialism and helped transform the United States into a nascent colonial power. Then, in the aftermath of World War I, we see the pendulum shift back toward nonintervention in the form of vehement isolationism. The United States withdrew from world affairs, especially regarding any perceived political entanglements with European powers. During this period many Americans viewed Europe with suspicion and foreign policy makers sought to detach the United States from the dangers inherent in European power politics. The nonintervention impulse is evident at this time in Washington's promotion of treaties designed to make warfare illegal and by the passage of legislation that sought to enforce strict American neutrality. While the United States sought to keep itself free from any national security commitments in Europe or elsewhere around the globe at this time, it remained a player in the global marketplace. The United States has almost always played an active role in international *economic* relations, such as international trade and finance. But when it comes to foreign relations that involve political commitments that may lead to conflict or war, the United States has been of two minds.

Indeed, following Japan's attack on Pearl Harbor in 1941, the United States changed its mind about isolationism. This time the pendulum swung heavily back toward intervention as the United States had to literally fight its way back into Asia as well as Europe. The United States entered WWII a little more than two years after the war had started, which reflects the inherent tension in the American body politic between interventionist and noninterventionist impulses. But once U.S. entry did occur in 1941, the Americans tipped the balance in favor of the Allies and against Germany and Japan. Even before the war ended, the United States began planning for long-term interventionist commitments that included

American leadership of new international institutions, such as the United Nations and the World Bank, as well as new international security alliances, such as the North Atlantic Treaty Organization (NATO). Moreover, Washington's military campaigns on the Korean Peninsula in the 1950s and in Vietnam in the 1960s and early 1970s reflect the extent to which the pendulum had swung so heavily in favor of intervention in the thirty years following Pearl Harbor. So too did its actions in conjunction with the Soviets' launch of Sputnik as well as Moscow's stationing of nuclear missiles in Cuba.

However, by the early 1970s, the mood in America shifted yet again and so did U.S. foreign policy. After the tragic American experience in Vietnam, the pendulum swung back toward nonintervention, but this time the United States did not withdraw into an isolationist cocoon the way it had done after WWI. The United States did, however, take steps to curtail its overseas commitments. President Nixon announced that Washington would no longer send American troops to fight communists in far off places. Instead, he limited the American commitment in the struggle against communism to training local forces, especially as this pertained to the Global South. While the global diplomatic and security commitments of the United States remained quite extensive, Vietnam led to a wholesale rethinking in Washington regarding the use of American military force overseas. The so-called Vietnam Syndrome looms large in some foreign policy makers' decisions even today. The humiliating experience at the hands of the Iranian college students who took U.S. diplomats hostage in 1979 only served to reinforce the idea for some Americans that the United States should remain detached from world affairs. For many of those who rallied behind Ronald Reagan in the 1980 presidential election, however, the American experiences in Vietnam and during the hostage crisis appeared to offer a different lesson.

In the early 1980s the pendulum began to swing back in favor of intervention as the Reagan administration sought to "cure" America of its post-Vietnam apprehensions. While this shift may not coincide perfectly with the timing laid out by some mood cycle theorists, we cannot deny that it took place or that it was significant. For instance, Reagan not only launched one of the largest peacetime military buildups in American history, including a 500-ship naval fleet, he also intervened in hotspots around the world—he landed troops in Beirut, Lebanon, for what turned out to be a doomed peacekeeping mission; he used the military to dispatch the leftist government on the tiny Caribbean island nation of Grenada; he sent hundreds of millions of dollars in military aid to guerrillas fighting the Soviet invasion of Afghanistan; and he launched air strikes against Libya. With the fall of the Berlin Wall in 1989 and the end of the Cold War in 1991, however, many Americans expected a "peace dividend" with a reduction of military spending and a concomitant decline in U.S. global commitments. While the United States maintained an energetic foreign policy and its role as a world leader after the Berlin Wall fell—Washington sent U.S. forces to Somalia, Haiti, and the Balkans in the early 1990s—the decade was characterized by shrinking defense budgets and a general retraction of American commitments overseas.

Following the September 11, 2001, terrorist attacks, the pendulum has made its most recent swing, clearly in favor of intervention. President Bush sent the American military to conquer first Afghanistan and then Iraq as the United States became responsible for administering more than 67 million mostly Muslim people in two disparate, deeply divided countries, a challenge Washington has found unexpectedly difficult. While most observers would agree that the United States is now in a period of intervention, few can predict when this phase will end, even as opposition to the wars in Afghanistan and Iraq has risen. What makes this current period of intervention unusual is the nature of the enemy. Unlike WWI or WWII, when the United States made formal declarations of war against one or more sovereign countries whose defeat and unconditional surrender could be readily observed and recorded, the current conflicts are undeclared wars against an amorphous enemy(s) whose *behavior* (use of terror) is what we seek to defeat. The Bush administration's inability to establish clear-cut goals in Iraq and Afghanistan made it difficult to discern what the policy conditions for victory in such wars might be. The Obama administration has not had much better luck in its first two years either. It is not at all clear what the circumstances are that would bring an end to the current phase of American intervention. Neither is it clear if this current phase will see an escalation of U.S. military intervention in still other countries, with Iran and North Korea often mentioned as possible targets.

One thing we are certain about is that the debates and divisions over what direction and contours American foreign policy should take will endure. Witness the intense debate between Republican presidential candidate John McCain and then-Democratic candidate Barack Obama in the 2008 campaign. Witness further the heated public dispute between former Vice President Dick Cheney and President Obama in May 2009 over whether or not the United States should use torture or other heavy-handed tactics in its efforts to defeat such disparate enemies as al Qaeda in Afghanistan and Pakistan or the violent nationalist Baathist followers of Saddam Hussein in Iraq.

CHAPTER SUMMARIES

Following are brief synopses of the twelve case studies covered in this book. The book begins with the War of 1898 and ends with the attacks on 9/11 because this roughly one-hundred-year time frame is often the focus of analysis in history and political science courses covering U.S. foreign policy.

The turning point of chapter 1 is the sinking of the USS *Maine* in 1898. This chapter examines how that event triggered the Spanish-American War, which signaled America's arrival on the world stage as a Great Power. It marked the first time the United States obtained colonial holdings off the North American mainland.

The main event in chapter 2 is the 1915 sinking of the passenger liner *Lusitania* by a German U-boat, an event that triggered a process that would eventually result in America's entry into WWI and which set the stage for the coming "American century." The *Lusitania's* sinking helped shape the foreign policy debate between isolationists and internationalists and compelled the Wilson administration to make some fateful decisions concerning its policy of neutrality.

The turning point in chapter 3 is the Japanese attack on Pearl Harbor in 1941, which prompted America's entry into World War II. The emergence of the United States and the Soviet Union as victors from that conflict set the stage for the Cold War, a superpower rivalry that would dominate world affairs for the next half century. Pearl Harbor also led to fundamental changes in the national security bureaucracy in the United States.

In chapter 4 we discuss the debates and divisions among policy makers surrounding North Korea's surprise invasion of South Korea in 1950. The Korean War, which pitted the United States against communist China, led to the permanent extension of the Cold War into Asia and an expansion of U.S. security commitments to areas where Washington was initially reluctant to tread. The Korean Peninsula remains one of the few remaining regions in the world where Cold War tensions are still extant.

Chapter 5's turning point is the Soviet Union's 1957 launch of the Sputnik satellite. By highlighting the Soviet Union's capability to launch an intercontinental ballistic missile (ICBM), Sputnik caused fear and consternation throughout the United States as the American people suddenly realized their cities could now be held hostage to Moscow's nuclear arsenal. Not only did Sputnik signal the dawn of the Space Age, but it also triggered a massive escalation in the nuclear arms race between Moscow and Washington that caused the entire world to live for decades in the shadow of a nuclear holocaust.

Chapter 6's main event is the Cuban Missile Crisis. The crisis brought into focus the dangers of brinkmanship for policy makers in both the United States and the Soviet Union. Although the crisis inspired new thinking in Washington and Moscow regarding the prosecution of the Cold War that would help lay the foundation for detente in the 1970s, it also had the short term impact of emboldening the Kennedy administration to act decisively in combating the spread of communism, a factor that would have tragic consequences in Vietnam.[2]

Chapter 7 covers the 1968 Tet Offensive, a sophisticated military attack by communist forces during the Vietnam War. Tet compounded existing divisions in the United States regarding the efficacy of American involvement in Vietnam and led to a dramatic shift in U.S. policy from escalation to withdrawal. The failure of the United States to achieve its goals in Vietnam would lead to a fundamental reevaluation of America's global strategy of combating the spread of communism and in particular to the commitment of American military forces to conflicts in the developing world.

The turning point in chapter 8 is President Nixon's historic visit to China in 1972. By setting the stage for renewed relations with China, which had been frozen for more than twenty years, Nixon was able to "play the China card" against the Soviet Union. Friendly Sino-American relations not only increased America's influence throughout Asia, but also forced Moscow into closer ties with Washington, which further opened the door to detente.

In chapter 9, we examine the October 1973 Arab-Israeli War. While the Arabs and Israelis have fought many wars, this one stands out as a turning point in U.S. foreign policy because it almost led to a direct Soviet-American military clash and because it did lead to the Arab oil embargo, which shifted the international economic balance of power away from the United States and other oil *consuming* countries and toward Saudi Arabia and other oil *producing* countries. This war also forced Middle East politics to the top of the U.S. foreign policy agenda where it has remained almost uninterrupted ever since.

Chapter 10's turning point is Iran's 1979 Islamic Revolution. This event shattered the U.S. security system throughout the oil-rich Persian Gulf and precipitated the American hostage crisis at the U.S. embassy in Iran, one of the most humiliating experiences in U.S. foreign policy history. With the Shah of Iran's downfall, not only did the United States lose its greatest ally in the Persian Gulf, but it also gained an implacable foe in the Islamic Republic of Iran, which has been engaged in a sort of mini-cold war with the United States ever since.

Chapter 11's turning point is the fall of the Berlin Wall, which separated formerly communist East Berlin from democratic West Berlin. This event signaled an end to the Iron Curtain, a term coined by Winston Churchill in 1945 in reference to Soviet efforts to seal off Eastern from Western Europe. The fall of the Berlin Wall symbolizes the beginning of the end of the Cold War and the end of communist dictatorships throughout Eastern Europe and later the Soviet Union. The end of the Cold War left the United States struggling to find a new direction for its foreign policy in what George H. W. Bush dubbed the "new world order."

Finally, chapter 12 addresses the September 11, 2001, terrorist attacks on the World Trade Center in New York City and the Pentagon in Arlington, Virginia, across the Potomac River from Washington, D.C. Few turning points led to such sweeping changes in U.S. foreign policy as this one did. Two wars were launched—the invasion of Afghanistan in 2001 and the invasion of Iraq in 2003. The controversial Bush Doctrine of preemptive attack was developed. Another major reorganization of the national security bureaucracy occurred, the likes of which had not been seen since the aftermath of Pearl Harbor and World War II. And finally, the nation was riven over wide-ranging debates regarding such momentous issues as whether or not the country should go to war and whether or not the country should torture its suspected enemies.

We believe these "Days of Decision" are important for students of U.S. foreign policy to comprehend. The twelve turning points examined in this book represent condensed case studies of how U.S. foreign policy is made, of the forces that shape American decisions, and of the short- and long-term impact of policies adopted in Washington. During these most challenging of times, the more we understand about American foreign relations and the decisions officials make in that regard, the more we are able to comprehend their enduring implications. The turning points under review here not only helped to shape the course of U.S. foreign policy but they also had profound historical implications around the globe. The foreign policy of the world's lone remaining superpower, whether wittingly or not, leaves its imprint all over the world. We believe these case studies, by providing a greater understanding of the foreign policy process, will help students gain a greater understanding of the United States' place in the world.

One

THE SINKING OF THE *MAINE*
AND THE WAR OF 1898

"Remember the *Maine* and to hell with Spain" was a powerful rallying cry for jingoes who favored American intervention in the Cuban insurrection at the end of
the nineteenth century. For generations, American school children have been learning that the sinking of the USS *Maine* in Havana harbor in February 1898 inspired
an American declaration of war against Spain, resulting in the conflict that would
dramatically transform the United States' role on the world stage. While the latter
point is indisputable, why the United States went to war with Spain in 1898 and
what Washington hoped to achieve as a result are questions that are very much open
to debate. In fact, these issues have been and continue to be the subject of vigorous
debate among scholars of American foreign relations.

The War of 1898 marked a significant departure from two cornerstones of
nineteenth century U.S. foreign policy. After the Treaty of Ghent (1814) had
brought the War of 1812 with Britain to a conclusion, for much of the remainder
of the nineteenth century American leaders dutifully insulated the Republic against
potential conflict or alliance with the powers of Europe and concentrated American energy on continental expansion.[1] When that process was complete, however,
new debates and divisions about the future direction of American foreign policy
began to emerge. Even though the risk entailed in fighting the declining power of
Spain was, in 1898, limited, the war established the United States as a force to be
reckoned with by the Great Powers of Europe. No longer was Washington content

to limit itself to continental expansion; by defeating Spain, occupying Cuba, and acquiring the Philippines, Guam, and Puerto Rico, the United States took a very deliberate and visible step onto the world stage.

This departure from the nineteenth-century norm was neither as dramatic nor as unprecedented as it might appear. There were antecedents for this apparent sudden projection of American power. The massive growth of the American economy after the Civil War established the foundation for an increasingly aggressive foreign policy, manifested in the decades before 1898 in a more assertive application of the Monroe Doctrine and a growing commercial and strategic interest in the Pacific.[2] These were tentative steps, however, and ones on which there was often no clear consensus. While the war with Spain won far from universal support in the United States, the conflict created sufficient momentum to carry the day for those who advocated a broader American foreign policy over those who remained loyal to the ideals of George Washington's Farewell Address. Rather than representing a completely new departure, however, the new internationalism that characterized American foreign policy during and after the War of 1898 was in many respects consistent with the ideology of Manifest Destiny that had been integral to the process of continental expansion. Many Americans in the 1890s came to believe that "their nation was destined to lead humanity" in the march of progress, which they defined in terms of evolutionary theory, Anglo-Saxon identity, liberal Protestantism, and the core tenets of American republican government.[3] The sinking of the *Maine* was an invitation to undertake this new mission.

This chapter will begin with an examination of the major debates and divisions in American foreign policy in the run-up to the Spanish-American War, chief among which is the clash of views between a growing coterie of influential Americans who favored an imperial foreign policy and those intent on maintaining the isolationist foreign policy that had held sway since the early Republic. The chapter next turns to the Cuban insurrection against Spanish rule that began in 1895. It is against the backdrop of the debate over imperialism that the United States became increasingly drawn toward intervening in the Cuban conflict. The next section addresses the circumstances that led the United States to intervene in the crisis, the debates surrounding the nature of that intervention, and the consequences of the resulting War of 1898. The final section offers a brief examination of the implications of the American intervention in Cuba for the long- and short-term future of U.S. foreign relations.

MAJOR DEBATES AND DIVISIONS

The U.S declaration of war against Spain in April 1898 brought to an end a debate that had been at the forefront of American politics since the outbreak of an insurrection in Cuba in 1895. For three years Republicans and Democrats in Congress, and the public at large, had wrestled with the issue of whether or not the United States should intervene and, if so, in what capacity. The Cuban crisis was the dominant foreign policy issue during the successive presidential administrations of Democrat Grover Cleveland and Republican William McKinley, and in the fiercely contested presidential and congressional elections of that time period. The narrow debate over the U.S. response to the Cuban insurrection was symptomatic of a broader debate between imperialists and isolationists concerning America's role in the world.[4] This broader debate took center stage during negotiations over the terms of settlement with Spain following American victory in the War of 1898. Although the fate of Cuba had drawn the United States into the war, it was the capture and occupation of the Philippines that precipitated a decisive showdown between the imperialists and the isolationists.

Rise of Imperialist Sentiment in the United States

The late nineteenth century was characterized by fierce competition among the powers of Europe for territorial acquisitions in Africa and Asia. The era of new imperialism coincided with growing competition among industrializing nations for markets and resources and the rising importance of nationalism as a force in shaping the internal affairs of these nations. Industrial technology fueled the growing naval and military power of the imperialist states and limited the ability of non-industrialized societies to resist their seemingly insatiable demand for territory and resources. The emotive power of nationalism contributed to the intensity of the competition between imperialist states and made public opinion an important factor in the race for territorial acquisition, even in states where representative government was limited. In those countries where mass suffrage was introduced in the late nineteenth century, public opinion played a pronounced role in this imperialist surge. The internal dynamics created by industrialism and nationalism contributed to the civilizing mission that infused the imperialism of this period, particularly in the countries of Western Europe.

While a discussion of U.S. foreign policy in this period must be framed within the context of this imperialist surge, "American imperialism was not simply a copy of the European original."[5] There were important quantitative and qualitative differences in the American experience of empire. For a start, the U.S. experiment with formal imperialism was both short lived and territorially limited. After the War of 1898, the United States turned to less formal means of establishing hegemony in Central America and the Caribbean and of extending its influence across the Pacific. To a large extent this is a reflection of the fact that imperialism was a much more divisive factor in American politics than in Europe. In the 1870s and 1880s, as the Europeans engaged in competition for territory in Asia and Africa, sentiment for imperialism began to stir in some quarters of the United States. However, those who opposed imperialism, whether on ideological or practical grounds, remained a formidable force in American politics.

Notable figures like historian John Fiske and protestant clergyman Josiah Strong were among the most vocal proponents of a global civilizing mission for the United States. Fiske's writings on the existence of a racial hierarchy and the ascendant role of people of Anglo-Saxon descent in shaping world civilization were reflective of much of the pro-imperialist sentiment in nineteenth-century America. Strong echoed these sentiments in his widely read 1885 publication *Our Country: Its Possible Future and Its Present Crisis,* where he added the force of divine ordination to America's mission and wrote that God "is preparing mankind to receive our impress."[6] Such ideas were consistent with earlier, popular notions of Manifest Destiny and were representative of a broad body of opinion that subscribed to the belief that the United States was exceptional among the countries of the world. The influence of race, religion, and the mission to civilize are evident in the writings of naval historian Alfred Thayer Mahan, one of the most forceful and influential exponents of the imperial vision in this period. In his famous book, *The Influence of Sea Power on History* (1890), Mahan held up the British Empire and its powerful navy as a model for the United States. For Mahan, imperialism was not just ideologically desirable; it was imperative in an age when naval technology negated the security that geography had long afforded the United States.

Fiske, Strong, and Mahan were members of an elite social circle whose influence on public policy was disproportionate to their numbers. Although it is hard to gauge public opinion in this era before the advent of modern scientific polling, there is considerable evidence to indicate that only a small percentage of the general public paid any attention to foreign policy or adopted positions on foreign policy issues.[7] Thus the elite, who were vocal and active on these issues, came to constitute the "foreign policy public."[8] Although public opinion, stirred by the jingoistic yellow press, undoubtedly played a role in influencing the debate over American involvement in Cuba (see below), the framework for the debate had been established much earlier by ideas that emanated from this foreign policy elite. The ideas contained in the writings of Fiske, Strong, and Mahan found practical outlet in the activism of men like Henry Cabot Lodge, a member of the U.S. Senate (R-MA), and his close friend Theodore Roosevelt, who would serve as assistant secretary of the Navy in the first administration of President William McKinley. Both Lodge and Roosevelt were vocal public proponents of naval expansion and espoused the realist view that the United States must enter the race for empire or suffer the consequences that would result from an extension of European power in the Pacific or the Western Hemisphere. During the debate over Cuba, Lodge and Roosevelt were the chief advocates of what historians have dubbed "the large policy," arguing that the United States should not only go to war with Spain but that it should also avail itself of the opportunity to extend American influence in the Caribbean and the Pacific.

Lodge and Roosevelt were among the loudest voices calling for annexation of Hawaii in 1893 following the coup d'état of the Hawaiian monarchy by a revolutionary government led by American expatriate sugar growers. The bloodless coup was actively supported by the American minister to Hawaii and was quickly followed by a bill of annexation put before Congress by the lame duck Republican administration of Benjamin Harrison. However, before the treaty was taken up for ratification, Democrat Grover Cleveland ascended to the White House and, decrying the role played by the United States in the Hawaiian affair, immediately blocked annexation. Although Roosevelt and other imperialists praised the aggressiveness of Harrison and condemned what they saw as the weakness of Cleveland, the president was not alone in his concerns over Hawaiian annexation. Influential figures such as Carl Schurz, a German-born editor and politician, combined racial, ideological, and strategic arguments to build a case against expansion. Schurz and others contended that the annexation of noncontiguous territories such as Hawaii would undermine the political integrity of the United States by violating the anti-imperialist principles of republican government. Furthermore, the prospect of adding tropical states and people of alien races and religions caused alarm among segments of the white elite, many of whom also argued that the acquisition of far-flung territories would make the United States more difficult to defend.[9]

If "Hawaii demonstrated the absence of consensus on overseas expansion," the Venezuela crisis of 1895 served to underline the often-contradictory tendencies in American foreign policy in this period.[10] At issue was the disputed border between Venezuela and British Guyana, and British pressure on the Venezuelans to settle the border in its favor following the discovery of gold deposits in the region. The United States intervened calling for arbitration, but in effect pressing the British to back off their claim. Grover Cleveland's secretary of state, Richard Olney, justified Washington's intervention on the grounds that "the United States is practically sovereign on this continent and its fiat is law."[11] What became known as the Olney Corollary to the Monroe Doctrine demonstrated a clear intent on the part of the United States to pursue an assertive foreign policy in the western hemisphere. Cleveland rationalized the position in anti-imperialist terms, noting the U.S. obligation to ward off European territorial designs in the western hemisphere, but the Olney Corollary also contained a clear implication of American hegemony in the region.

THE CUBAN QUESTION

Cuba, just ninety miles off the coast of Florida, had long been an object of American interest when a rebellion erupted there against Spanish rule in 1895. An earlier rebellion lasting from 1868 to 1873 had excited considerable interest in the United States and brought the administration of President Ulysses S. Grant to the brink of intervention and annexation. Despite the enticing prospect of Caribbean ports and the logic of the Monroe Doctrine, Grant backed down in the face of pressure from Congress and the foreign policy elite, who feared the implication of acquiring a tropical territory with a mixed-race population and a culture deemed impossible to assimilate. At the outbreak of this second Cuban rebellion, American interest in events on the island was initially fairly limited. However, as the insurrection dragged on and the Spanish application of force received growing attention in American newspapers and in Congress, the passion of the American public was increasingly aroused and the debates of the Grant era resurfaced on Capitol Hill. By 1898 the country was in a state of "hysteria" and pressure for intervention was coming from a variety of sources.

From the outset the Cleveland administration adopted a cautious approach to the Cuban rebellion. The rebels, under the leadership of Gen. Maximo Gomez, were limited to the use of guerilla tactics, and there was some hope in Washington that the Spanish would quickly restore order on the island. American investments, primarily in sugar plantations, amounted to $50 million, and the prevailing view among these investors was that a speedy end to the fighting would best serve the interests of business. Senior pro-business politicians such as Senators Marcus Hanna (R-OH), Nelson Aldrich (R-RI), and Orville Platt (R-CT) gave voice to a noncommittal policy on the part of the United States. Cleveland shared the fears of these senators that American entanglement in Cuba would threaten the United States' "large pecuniary stake in the fortunes" of the island.[12] The Cleveland administration's initial response to the crisis was to invoke American neutrality laws. It was a position that was more important in appearance than in fact. Although Cleveland was clearly attempting to establish a policy of nonintervention, sympathy for the Cuban cause quickly grew to such an extent that this profession of neutrality did little to prevent a steady flow of arms from private sources inside the United States to the rebels. The inability of Washington to counteract the American filibustering in the Cuban conflict and the smuggling of arms was a constant cause of tension with Spain.

Mounting pro-Cuban sentiment in the United States reflected a variety of developing factors. From the beginning of the 1895 Cuban insurrection, imperialists among the foreign policy elite called for a more pro-active American response. Meanwhile a Cuban junta conducted a well-organized and effective lobbying campaign to push public opinion and sentiment in Washington toward a pro-Cuban and anti-Spanish policy. Finally, the plight of the Cuban people at the hands of tyrannical Spain became a cause célèbre among the yellow press, particularly the rival newspapers of publishing giants William Randolph Hearst and Joseph Pulitzer. Hearst is said to have dispatched the artist Frederick Remington to Cuba with the now infamous words, "You furnish the pictures and I'll furnish the war."[13] Although these forces developed from impulses that were often contradictory, American imperialism and nationalism on the one hand and Cuban nationalism on the other, they combined to shape public opinion in a manner that was increasingly at odds with the policies of the Cleveland administration. Nowhere was this more apparent than on the floor of the U.S. Congress.

Support for a pro-Cuban policy crossed party lines; both Republicans and Democrats endeavored to gain advantage from the issue in the lead-up to the 1896 elections. Efforts by Congress to push for recognition of the Cuban cause were blocked by Cleveland, but as the situation in Cuba deteriorated pressure to intervene mounted. In 1896 the Spanish government, led by Conservative Prime Minister Antonio Canovas, facing a mounting domestic crisis arising from the Cuban insurrection, dispatched Gen. Valeriano Weyler to the island with orders to bring a decisive military conclusion to the insurrection. Weyler's *reconcentrado* policy, designed to isolate the rebels by concentrating the civilian population in Spanish-controlled towns, proved disastrous both in terms of its ineffectiveness as a tool in winning the war and in terms of its impact on American public opinion. Weyler's tactics were widely denounced in the American press and on the floor of Congress as concrete evidence of the evils of Spanish tyranny. The populist wing of the Democratic Party under the leadership of William Jennings Bryan forcefully demanded that Washington take action to end the misery in Cuba and promote the cause of liberty in the face of oppression.

In the spring of 1896 Cleveland approached Spain about the possibility of mediating the conflict and floated a solution of autonomy for Cuba. Spain was racked by dissension, however, and the very future of the Spanish regency hung in the balance over the issue. Neither Canovas nor the man who would succeed him, the Liberal Party leader Praxedes Mateo Sagasta, could afford to alienate nationalist elements and invite the possibility of widespread political unrest in Spain by admitting defeat in Cuba or seeming to cave in to American pressure. The Spanish position was clear: Cuba was an internal Spanish affair and any effort by the United States to intervene would be interpreted as a threat to Spanish sovereignty. Nonetheless, pressure for intervention continued to mount in step with the deteriorating situation in Cuba. The lurid reports of atrocities reported in the yellow press and recounted in Congress, were confirmed by Fitzhugh Lee, the special envoy dispatched by Cleveland to report firsthand on affairs in Cuba. Lee painted a pessimistic picture and put an end to hopes Cleveland might still have entertained that Spain could restore order on the island any time in the near future. Faced with the reality of Lee's assessment, in December Cleveland warned Spain that, issues of sovereignty aside, if the situation in Cuba continued to deteriorate the United States might be driven to intervene by "higher obligations, which we can hardly hesitate to discharge."[14]

Within a year of the rebellion's outbreak, the United States shifted slightly from a policy of nonintervention to probing the Spanish on the issue of arbitration. Cleveland's December statement, though, appeared to promise intervention unless Spain demonstrated its ability to restore order on the island. Cleveland was a lame duck president when he made this statement so it now fell to his successor, Republican William McKinley, to decide on a future course of action for the United States. McKinley, who defeated the populist challenge of William Jennings Byran in the 1896 election, entered the White House with a pro-business reputation, often seen as an explanation for his initial caution with regard to Cuba. But the momentum toward intervention that had begun under Cleveland gathered speed under McKinley. Although McKinley decried the impact of "jingo nonsense," he quickly came to terms with political pressure arising from the Cuban crisis. Prominent Republicans such as Elihu Root and Henry Cabot Lodge warned that failure to take action on Cuba could have disastrous consequences for the party. Root raised the ominous specter of "the elevation of Silver Democracy to power," a reference to the populist movement, if the president were to engage in "fruitless attempts to hold back . . . the momentum of the people bent upon war."[15]

The Cuban Revolution became the dominant foreign policy issue in the McKinley administration to a large extent because it had "explosive potential as a domestic issue."[16] Congress was set to debate a resolution drafted by Sen. James Cameron (R-PA) calling for good offices to secure Cuban independence, and as the war in Cuba dragged on with no resolution in sight, Americans with economic interests on the island became progressively more concerned. Hearst and Pulitzer competed for copy on the latest Spanish outrages, particularly where the lives and property of American citizens were concerned, and in so doing continued to stoke the fires of public opinion. Reports in late 1896 of the murder of rebel leader Antonio Maceo at the hands of Spanish forces who he had approached under a flag of truce were widely reported and inspired anti-Spanish demonstrations in towns and cities across America.[17] McKinley, however, also had to deal with the international dimension of the Cuban revolution. When he took office rumors were circulating that one or more of the European powers might choose to intervene in support of Spain; certainly the major powers were keeping a watchful eye on the United States and the position it adopted with regard to Cuba. The Cuban crisis provided another test of the Monroe Doctrine, which Secretary of State Richard Olney had so forcefully restated during the Venezuela crisis.

McKinley therefore had to balance a variety of concerns in formulating a Cuban policy, not least of which was the fact that an influential wing of his own party remained cool to the idea of American intervention. Though he was open to counsel from within his cabinet and from influential members of Congress, McKinley was very much in charge of the formulation and direction of the Cuban policy of his administration and he chose initially to follow a policy of cautious engagement. The president publicly stated that the United States wants "no wars of conquest" while at the same time he urged Congress to appropriate funds for the relief of the victims of reconcentrado and informed the Spanish of U.S. concerns regarding the excesses of the Weyler policy.[18] McKinley was not, however, in a hurry to commit the United States any further. The ideal solution would be a settlement that could satisfy the growing sentiment in the United States for the rebel cause without a breach of U.S.-Spanish relations. McKinley briefly entertained the idea of purchasing Cuba from Spain but came to rely instead on the hope that the Spanish government would concede autonomy to the rebels. When Canovas's reform agenda of 1897 failed to entice the rebels to the negotiating table, McKinley appointed Stewart Woodford U.S. envoy extraordinary and minister plenipotentiary to Spain in an effort to push for further concessions.

Woodford's arrival in Spain coincided with the collapse of the Conservative government and the accession to power of Sagasta and the Liberals. The new Spanish government took the dual steps of recalling the controversial Weyler and issuing a more comprehensive reform program based on the Canadian model of political autonomy within the British Empire as a compromise solution for Cuba. Cautious engagement appeared to be paying dividends and McKinley publicly lauded Spain's initiatives. However, he still left the option open for American intervention in "the near future" if these initiatives failed to bear fruit, noting that America might be compelled to "end the war by imposing a rational compromise between the contestants."[19] Hopes for such a compromise occurring without American intervention quickly faded as the rebels made clear their intention to settle for nothing less than complete independence. The Sagasta government was facing an angry backlash from nationalists in Spain for the limited concessions it proposed, so the likelihood of a negotiated settlement appeared remote in the extreme. With McKinley on record as committing the United States to playing some role in resolving the crisis in Cuba, a military and diplomatic stalemate between the rebels and Spain left little room for anything else but an escalation of American involvement.

Although the Sagasta reforms temporarily quieted public agitation in the United States over Cuba, riots in Havana in January 1898 heightened fears of anarchy on the island and led to a resurgence of congressional interest. Fears for the safety of American citizens in Cuba prompted McKinley to dispatch the USS *Maine* to

Havana harbor. The *Maine's* arrival in Havana coincided with the public release in the United States of a private letter written by the Spanish minister in Washington, Dupuy de Lome, in which he characterized McKinley as "a weak bidder for the admiration of the crowd" whose Cuba policy reflected his desire to placate jingoes in his party.[20] The de Lome letter had come into the possession of the Cuban Junta who eagerly passed it on to the press. Its publication succeeded in fueling anti-Spanish sentiment and energizing momentum for American intervention in Cuba. Although Washington and Madrid endeavored to smooth over the controversy with the resignation of de Lome and the solicitation of an apology, there was a flurry of congressional activity including resolutions in both the House and Senate calling on the administration to release consular reports on the reconcentrado policy and the status of Cuban autonomy. The McKinley administration was well aware that these reports highlighted the failure of the Sagasta reforms and the devastating impact of the reconcentrado policy and as such would provide ammunition for interventionists. By giving his tacit support to these resolutions, the president "had taken an important step toward war."[21]

Fast on the heels of the de Lome crisis came the sensational sinking of the *Maine*. The American public responded with shock to the news of the deaths of 264 sailors, but this mood quickly gave way to anger. The *Maine* disaster provided the first tangible link for many Americans between the United States and events in Cuba. The perception that the United States had been attacked sparked an upsurge of patriotic sentiment and contributed to a shift in emphasis away from Cuban independence and toward war with Spain. It was a critical moment in the unfolding crisis. All indications are that the McKinley administration, cognizant of the importance of Cuba as a domestic political issue, was moving toward intervention. The *Maine* incident did not cause the United States to declare war on Spain, but it contributed greatly to creating the environment in which such a declaration became possible. The Senate Foreign Relations Committee held a special closed-door day-long session on the incident and the general mood in Congress was "intense and threatening."[22] There were several theories about what had caused the *Maine* to sink, but the most popular theories, widely disseminated in the American press, involved Spanish mines or torpedoes. Although McKinley deferred taking action until a U.S. naval board investigation was complete, his decision to ask Congress in March for a $50 million appropriation for national defenses was a clear indication that his policy of cautious engagement was giving way to direct intervention.

By the time the naval board's bulky report reached Washington in March 1898 with its conclusion that a Spanish mine had sunk the *Maine*, the nation was already primed for intervention.[23] The mood in the United States had changed perceivably since the beginning of the year and as the conclusions of the Navy report were made public, momentum for war appeared unstoppable. Pressure for intervention had become an increasingly bipartisan issue and even the conservative pro-business wing of the Republican Party had shed its early skepticism on the issue. One of the most influential pro-business Republicans, Sen. Redfield Proctor (R-VT), undertook his own fact-finding mission to Cuba and upon his return in March delivered a speech to Congress that set the Cuban rebellion in terms that appealed to the essence of American exceptionalism.[24] The central issue for the United States in Cuba, according to Proctor, was neither "the barbarity practiced by Weyler nor the loss of the *Maine* . . . but the spectacle of a million and half people, the entire native population of Cuba, struggling for freedom and deliverance from the worst misgovernment of which [he] ever had knowledge."[25] The Proctor speech, coming as it did from a senior senator with no history of jingoism, added huge moral weight to an interventionist cause already gathering momentum after the *Maine* disaster.

THE DECISION FOR WAR

The impact of the *Maine* tragedy severely restricted McKinley's room for maneuver. Up to the beginning of 1898 he had pursued a policy of cautious engagement that charted a middle path between those in the United States who favored American intervention in Cuba and those who opposed such a move. McKinley had moved slowly from urging a Spanish resolution to the problem to endorsing autonomy for Cuba. Like his predecessor, he had staved off pressure to recognize the belligerency or publicly endorse independence. McKinley's policy was aided by the iron grip over the House of Representatives exercised by Speaker Thomas B. Reed (R-ME), who displayed little enthusiasm for a more proactive U.S. policy toward Cuba. However, in the charged atmosphere of the spring of 1898 Reed could no longer rein in the interventionists in Congress and McKinley was compelled to increase the pressure on Spain. The McKinley administration drafted an ultimatum urging Spain to call an armistice in Cuba, open negotiations with the insurgents with possible American arbitration if required, and provide relief for the reconcentrado population. If these conditions were not met by October, the United States reserved the right to intervene. McKinley meanwhile prepared to address Congress.

Both the Spanish and American governments made some final efforts to resolve the crisis short of war. Although the lines of communications were often unclear, the United States probed for Spanish concessions through the official channel of Woodford and the unofficial channel of Archbishop John Ireland, working through both the Vatican and the Catholic government of Austria. Such channels bore little fruit. Although there was considerable sympathy among the monarchs of Europe for the plight of the Queen Regent, Maria Christina, the European powers saw little value in aiding Spain, particularly if it meant antagonizing the rising power of the United States. Spain, for its part, despite significant nationalist pressure on the Sagasta government not to give in to American pressure, willingly abandoned the disastrous reconcentrado policy and, forty-eight hours before McKinley was due to address Congress, Madrid called a cessation of hostilities in Cuba. However, by this point it was too late. The rebels would settle for nothing less than complete independence while Madrid offered nothing more than limited autonomy. The president faced mounting pressure to outline a strategy for breaking the deadlock.

On April 11, 1898, President McKinley went before Congress and asked for the power "to take measures to secure a full and final termination of hostilities between the Government of Spain and the people of Cuba," including the use of military force.[26] Consistent with McKinley's general conduct of foreign policy, his war message was vague and couched in terms designed to leave him some degree of flexibility, even to the extent of prolonging negotiations. Notably absent from his address was any commitment to the recognition of Cuban independence, thus leaving the United States a free hand to determine the fate of the island in the event of war. The fact that McKinley had consistently pursued a nonrecognition policy toward the Cuban rebels indicates an expectation on his part that war with Spain would be for broader reasons than to secure Cuban independence. McKinley, though, ever the cautious politician, left it to Congress to find meaning in his words during the subsequent ten days of debate. Eventually the Senate and House co-sponsored a joint resolution demanding that Spain relinquish sovereignty over the island and authorizing the president to use force in the event that Spain refused. However, the addition of the Teller Amendment—named for its sponsor, Sen. Henry M. Teller (R-CO)—pledging that the United States would not assume sovereign control over Cuba—contrasts sharply with the absence of such a commitment in McKinley's war message and highlights the fact that, although there was broad consensus for war, there was no common vision supporting the goals of armed intervention.

McKinley's address to Congress and the subsequent war resolutions were met with public outrage in Spain. Few Spanish officials were under any illusions about Spain's chances of victory in a conflict with the United States. Yet the patriotic backlash against American action, together with the determination of the Cuban rebels to hold out for complete independence and the failure of Madrid to entice meaningful European diplomatic intervention on its behalf, left the Spanish government little option but to accept war. In fact, there were those in Spain who saw defeat at the hands of the United States as the only honorable way of resolving the Cuban crisis, which for so long had hung like an albatross around the country's neck. Few Spaniards, however, anticipated the devastating ease with which the United States inflicted defeat on Spain or the eventual extent of Spanish territorial losses in the conflict. American technological superiority was a decisive factor in the war, and it was particularly telling in the naval arena. Not only did the United States completely destroy a Spanish fleet outside Santiago harbor but, in the biggest surprise of the war, Cdre. George Dewey, following a contingency plan drawn up two years prior, sailed into Manila Bay and in short order wrested control of the Philippines from Spain in a surprisingly easy naval victory.[27]

Although lack of organization among American ground forces highlighted a serious flaw in war preparations, these decisive naval victories laid the foundation for American victory in little over three months of fighting. John Hay, who at the time was the U.S. ambassador to Great Britain, captured the ebullient mood of the country in his now famous description of the conflict as a "splendid little war." The war was a coming out party for a rising power and it helped to heal old fractures in American society dating from the Civil War and more recent ones arising from what Richard Hofstadter termed the "psychic crisis" of the late nineteenth century. According to Hofstadter's thesis, the pressure arising from immigration, labor and agrarian unrest, economic depression, and a host of other internal factors inspired a war to restore a national order.[28] While there can be little doubt that the war inspired a new spirit of nationalism in America, victory over Spain raised a whole new set of questions about American identity.

AFTERMATH: THE USS *MAINE* AND THE WAR
OF 1898 AS A TURNING POINT

The military triumph over Spain presented the United States with the opportunity of joining the ranks of the imperial powers. The war and its aftermath could be interpreted as a historical shift in the mood of U.S. foreign policy toward what is called "extroversion."[29] The extroverted turning point associated with the Spanish-American War is most conspicuous in the triumph of the imperialists. While the Teller Amendment prevented American annexation of Cuba, no such stipulation applied to Puerto Rico, Guam, and the Philippines, the other territories captured from Spain. A furious debate now ensued between the imperialists and anti-imperialists, but while the former had been thwarted during the Hawaiian crisis of 1893, they were not to be denied now. Indeed, arguably the most telling sign that the Cuban crisis had transformed the national scene was the absence of significant controversy accompanying Congress's decision to annex Hawaii in July 1898, at the height of the war with Spain. McKinley made noises about Hawaiian annexation in 1897, but he was able to achieve this without expending any political capital only in the patriotically charged climate of the following summer. Imperialism was suddenly ascendant and it was personified by the larger than life figure of Theodore Roosevelt, whose exploits with the all-volunteer Rough Rider regiment at San Juan Hill in Cuba elevated him from the margins of American politics to the status of national hero. The escalation of the Cuban crisis had suddenly thrust imperialists like Roosevelt and Lodge to center stage. The apparent ease of American victory over Spain strengthened the case of those who claimed that the United States was destined to become a world power.

The McKinley administration quickly determined that Spain should surrender Cuba and Puerto Rico following the cessation of hostilities. This was in keeping with the express wishes of Congress and the spirit of the Monroe Doctrine that gave a degree of international legitimacy to American actions. The thornier issue of what to do with the Philippines was deferred until treaty negotiations began. The United States had several options. The conquering American fleet could sail out of Manila Bay and leave the archipelago under Spanish control or, alternatively, Washington could throw its support behind Emilio Aguinaldo and the Filipino independence movement. The first idea was discounted largely because the war had been couched in terms of a struggle against Spanish tyranny while the latter was given very little serious consideration, with McKinley ultimately concluding that independence would result in "misrule over there worse than Spain's was."[30] McKinley and his advisors toyed with the idea of keeping only a portion of the islands, perhaps just Luzon with the strategically valuable Manila Bay, or maybe even relinquishing control of the islands to a third power. The president feared the political backlash that might result from not gaining some strategic advantage from Dewey's victory and strategic disadvantage that would result from a stronger power than Spain acquiring the territory. Ultimately "the issue came down to an all-or-nothing choice" and McKinley elected to opt for "outright colonial possession."[31]

McKinley famously informed a group of Methodist ministers visiting the White House in 1899 that he reached his decision regarding the Philippines after several nights of contemplation during which he "prayed [to] Almighty God for light and guidance" and, thus divinely inspired, he concluded that the United States had an obligation to "uplift and Christianize" the Filipinos.[32] This providential sense of mission was wholly consistent with the spirit of Manifest Destiny and American exceptionalism and helped to reinforce the imperialist mood spreading throughout the country. It also echoed the racially infused logic of Fiske and Strong and the Great Power imperialism favored by Lodge and Roosevelt. The importance attached to Manila reflected the influence of naval strategists like Mahan, who advised the president on the Naval War Board. In sum, all the arguments made earlier in the century for American empire were now found in the motives guiding American policy toward the Philippines after the War of 1898. Under the terms of the Treaty of Paris signed with Spain in December 1898, Spain ceded not only Puerto Rico and the Philippines to the United States, but also the Pacific island of Guam. The United States chose to embrace imperialism.

However, organizations like the Anti-Imperialist League bore testimony to the existence of dissent against this new direction in U.S. foreign policy. The failure of these anti-imperialists to muster sufficient support to block the annexation of the Philippines underlined the shift in momentum that had taken place over Cuba. The anti-imperialist lobby included numerous high-profile figures such as Carl Schurz, Grover Cleveland, William Jennings Bryan, Mark Twain, and Andrew Carnegie, but their motives were as disparate as their backgrounds and they rarely presented a united front. During the debates over the Treaty of Paris, anti-imperialist arguments about the dangers posed to the sanctity of the American Republic by a policy of imperialism appeared anachronistic in contrast to the energizing power of imperialism. Indeed the contrast between aging anti-imperialists such as Schurz on the one hand and youthful imperialists like Roosevelt on the other lends credibility to the concept that the transformation of American foreign policy in this period reflected in part a generational shift.[33]

Certainly there would be no turning back from the new direction of U.S. foreign policy. Although the Philippines would be the last formal colony acquired by the United States, the same logic that led to the decision to annex the islands would guide American foreign policy through the early decades of the twentieth century. In the Caribbean and Central America the United States took on the role of regional hegemon, forcefully exerting its influence at the expense of the European powers and the regional republics. In the Pacific, too, the United Sates now sought to exert greater influence, a path that would set it on an ultimate collision course with the era's other new power, Japan (see chapter 3). Washington's decision to go to war in 1898 and the subsequent annexation of the Philippines represent a blending of "the ideological and cultural sources of [American] identity with the practical exigencies of international relations," which would become an enduring pattern of American foreign policy throughout the subsequent century.[34] The War of 1898 also presaged the emerging power of the executive branch in American politics, a development that became fully apparent with elevation to the presidency of Theodore Roosevelt in 1901. Roosevelt's hero status earned him a place on William McKinley's reelection ticket in 1900, and when the president was assassinated soon after being returned to office, the former Rough Rider and champion of the imperialist cause found himself in the Oval Office. Under his leadership the Monroe Doctrine would be transformed from a passive to an aggressive canon, the United States would force through the construction of the Panama Canal, effectively turning the Caribbean into an American lake and making the United States a two-ocean power, and the United States would assertively stake out a place for itself on the world stage. The age of America as an insular state impervious to the lure of Great Power politics had vanished as surely as if it had gone down to the bottom of Havana harbor with the USS *Maine*.

Two

THE *LUSITANIA* CRISIS AND U.S. ENTRY INTO WORLD WAR I

The sinking of the Cunard liner *Lusitania* by a German U-boat on May 7, 1915, caused shock and outrage throughout the United States. Despite the fact that the *Lusitania* was a British ship and that the United States had adopted a policy of neutrality at the outbreak of WWI, long after the guns had been silenced Americans could still remember "the exact details of what they had felt and done when they first heard the news" of the *Lusitania*.[1] The sinking of the *Lusitania* shocked Americans out of the detachment they had felt toward events in Europe since the war had begun in August 1914. Of the nearly twelve hundred people who went down with the ship, one hundred and twenty four were American citizens; the war was no longer a distant affair. While some people in the United States, such as former president Theodore Roosevelt, were outraged to the point of favoring a declaration of war against Germany, for most Americans the tragedy highlighted the necessity of staying out of the increasingly destructive conflict. Rather than propelling America toward war, the *Lusitania* incident sparked a vigorous debate on the future of American neutrality and the most effective means by which the United States could preserve its traditional policy of avoiding entanglement in the affairs of Europe.

This chapter examines that debate and explains how the United States veered from its chosen path of neutrality toward entry into the war. The chapter begins with an examination of the debate between isolationists and internationalists that permeated the U.S. foreign policy process during the first fourteen years of the twentieth century. This debate is reminiscent of the debate over America's expansionism in the late nineteenth century, which was discussed in chapter 1. The next section addresses the U.S. response to the outbreak of the war in Europe in 1914 and Washington's struggle to observe a policy of neutrality in the face of British and German violations, the most infamous being the sinking of the *Lusitania*. From there we turn our attention to President Wilson's increasingly expansive vision of a role for the United States in ending the war in Europe and the triumph of his internationalist agenda with American entry into the war in 1917. The final segment deals with the immediate and long-term implications of U.S. involvement in the war and of Wilson's efforts to reshape the world order on the basis of his own ideological precepts.

ISOLATIONISM VERSUS INTERNATIONALISM

The War of 1898 marked the arrival of the United States as a major power on the world stage (see chapter 1). In the two decades after the defeat of Spain, however, the United States chose to limit the focus of its foreign policy to the western hemisphere and the Pacific region. For many Americans the implications of American victory in 1898 were not immediately apparent and the mood of the country remained relatively insular in the early twentieth century. The influential journalist Walter Lippman later recalled that, despite being well read and well educated, it was not until the outbreak of WWI that he took an interest in foreign affairs and came to realize the consequences of the War of 1898.[2] For the foreign policy elite, the limited scope of American foreign policy in the first two decades of the twentieth century represented a conscious effort to avail of the fruits of the United States' new found power without abandoning the country's traditional policy of avoiding entanglements with Europe. Preserving American exceptionalism required avoiding contamination by the politics of the Old World.

Balancing America's growing interests outside the western hemisphere with its self-imposed isolation from Europe proved increasingly difficult, however, in the years leading up to WWI. The emergence of the United States as a Pacific power after 1898 and efforts to open the door to American trade and investment in China brought Washington face to face with the imperial powers of Europe and the rising power of Japan, all anxious to carve out spheres of influence at the expense of China's crumbling Manchu dynasty. At the dawn of the twentieth century the American economy, having experienced massive growth in the late nineteenth century, was poised to challenge the global economic dominance long enjoyed by the major European powers. The very strength of American economic power inspired a shift in U.S. policy after 1900. The United States was a latecomer to the Great Power struggle over China and, rather than seek to muscle its way in on traditional imperialist terms, Washington played to its strengths, turning to free trade as a means to secure access to the potential riches of Asia. In 1899 and again in 1900, Secretary of State John Hay sent a series of notes to the capitals of Europe calling for free and open trade for all nations throughout China. The "Open Door" notes, while initially of only limited effectiveness in China, marked a new departure in U.S. foreign policy. From 1900 on the United States came to rely increasingly on its economic might and what many historians refer to as 'informal empire' to secure its interests overseas.

The expanding tentacles of American economic interests overseas increasingly brought the United States into direct conflict with the interests of the European powers. During William Howard Taft's administration, American efforts to establish economic protectorates in Latin America and East Asia, and even as far afield as West Africa and Ottoman Turkey, often met stiff opposition in Europe. Taft's policies, dubbed "dollar diplomacy" by the press, presaged a broader expansion of American interests overseas involving a host of agencies, from tourists to missionary groups to investors. These developments were symptomatic of the expansion of international capitalism and the growth of new technologies in transport and communications, and contributed to the shrinking of the geographic and cultural distance between North America and Europe. Meanwhile, there were those among the foreign policy elite who believed the United States should embrace the opportunity to take a place among the Great Powers of the world. As president, Theodore Roosevelt initiated a U.S.-arbitrated settlement to the Russo-Japanese War of 1904–1905, for which he won the Nobel Peace Prize, insisted on U.S. participation in a conference in Algeciras, Spain, in 1906 to settle a Franco-German dispute over Morocco, and, in the same year, led the Great Powers in convening the Second Hague Peace Conference in the Netherlands. The crowning emphasis of the arrival of the United States as a world power was Roosevelt's dispatch of the "Great White Fleet," comprised of the U.S. Navy's most modern and imposing ships, on a grand tour of the world in 1907.

Roosevelt of course had his critics who charged him with overstepping the bounds of traditional American foreign policy rooted in Washington's Farewell Address and in the Monroe Doctrine. For his part Roosevelt would become highly critical of his immediate successors in the White House, Taft and Woodrow Wilson, both of whom he charged with failing to recognize the role the United States had to play as a Great Power on the world stage. After his failure to recapture the White House as the Progressive candidate in the 1912 election, however, Roosevelt, with his expansive view of U.S. foreign policy, became to a large extent a marginal figure in American politics. Isolation from Europe remained a major theme in American foreign policy on the eve of WWI, its depth evident in the concerted effort of the United States to avoid embroilment in the conflict for three years. However, the transformation that had taken place in the American economy and the country's relationship with the outside world in the previous quarter century made the continuation of isolation extremely difficult, a reality that became increasingly apparent with each passing year of the conflict. As it became ever more difficult for Americans to ignore developments in Europe, a broad division began to form pitting those who favored continued isolation against proponents of a greater international role for the United States. While the initial impetus for the debate between the isolationist and international camps was Washington's response to the war, the future of America's role in international affairs quickly emerged as the dominant issue at stake.

U.S. NEUTRALITY AND WORLD WAR I

Broadly speaking the American public initially responded to the outbreak of the war in Europe with disbelief at the extent of the destruction and bloodshed. The bloody fighting in Europe appeared to many Americans "to provide spectacular confirmation of traditional beliefs in the moral separation between America and Europe and ample justification for continued isolation."[3] Most Americans were relieved to be separated from the carnage by the Atlantic Ocean and once the initial shock of the outbreak of hostilities wore off, the mood of the country eased into one of general detachment from the war. The prompt decision of the Wilson administration to declare neutrality was wholly consistent with the sentiment of the vast majority of Americans. There did not appear to be any reason at the outbreak of the conflict for the United States to become involved.

Woodrow Wilson's call in 1914 for Americans to be "impartial in thought as well as in action," reflected his fear that hyphenated Americans, through their bonds to the "old country," might imperil American neutrality.[4] While there certainly was sympathy for the German cause in the German-American community, and hostility to Britain on the part of many Irish-Americans, the evidence appears to be clear that the vast majority of Americans remained impartial. A November 1914 nationwide survey of newspaper editors conducted by *Literary Digest* found that two thirds of the respondents expressed favoritism toward neither side in the conflict. Of the remaining third the vast majority favored the Allies, with sympathy for the Central Powers confined to small areas of the West and Midwest with large German communities.[5] If there was a bias in the United States it was largely an east coast bias that favored Britain, but as would become apparent, it was disproportionately evident among those charged with making American policy. However, as long as the outcome of the conflict appeared to bear little relevance to the United States, the policy of neutrality was politically unassailable.

Defining Neutrality

At the outset of the war the Wilson administration embraced strict neutrality. Secretary of State William Jennings Bryan quickly pushed for a ban on loans to all belligerent powers and the State Department embraced the 1909 Declaration of London as the basis of its neutrality. The Declaration of London represented the fruits of a conference at which Britain, Germany, and the United States had agreed to certain clarifications of maritime law pertaining to neutral rights in wartime. By August 1914, however, only the United States had ratified the declaration, making it a precarious foundation upon which to base U.S. wartime policy. Free from constraint by the declaration, the European powers engaged in wholesale violations of the terms hammered out by delegates to the conference only five years earlier. The preservation of American neutrality rested on the Wilson administration's response to these violations. It proved to be an extremely difficult challenge as the United States found itself in the paradoxical situation of becoming increasingly drawn into the conflict in Europe in an effort to preserve its neutrality.[6]

Given the eventual decision of the United States to enter the war on the Allied side, it is somewhat ironic that it was Britain that initially posed the greatest threat to American neutrality. Germany was at the outset willing to accept the Declaration of London as the basis of American neutrality, but for Britain to do so ran contrary to London's grand strategy of isolating Germany from the outside world and cutting off its lifeline to international trade. British dominance of the seas from the beginning of the war kept the German fleet moored in the North Sea, thus making easy pickings of the German merchant marine by the Royal Navy. However,

Germany could still conduct trade with the outside world through neutral neighbors and, with the exception of contraband, goods could still reach Germany or its neighbors on the ships of neutral states. On August 20, 1914, the British cabinet approved an Order in Council designed to close this loophole in its encirclement of Germany by granting the Royal Navy powers not traditionally sanctioned by international law to impede neutral trade with Germany. The British strategy, which included a broad definition of contraband, opposition to the practice of continuous voyage, and the indiscriminate mining of the North Sea, presented a very serious challenge to the U.S. policy of strict neutrality.

The Wilson administration's response to British interference with American trade and contravention of the established rules of maritime law would prove critical to the future role of the United States in the war. The war created "complex problems for which there were few guiding precedents in American history."[7] One obvious parallel, however, was the War of 1812 when British violations of American neutrality resulting from London's grand strategy to cripple Napoleonic France brought the two countries to blows. Wilson was cognizant of the events of 1812 and looked on then-President James Madison, a fellow Princeton man, as a kindred spirit and a "peace loving" man.[8] Wilson interpreted the U.S. declaration of war on Britain in 1812 as a mistake foisted on Madison by an excited public who failed to appreciate that Britain represented the cause of civilization against the despotism of France. The evidence is strong that Wilson saw the war in 1914 in a similar light, only this time it was Germany that posed a threat to civilization. Many of Wilson's closest advisors shared his views in this regard and their pro-British bias would increasingly shape the administration's response to the challenges posed by the war in Europe.

While Wilson was genuinely committed to the cause of peace, he nonetheless came to see the strict neutrality outlined by Secretary of State Bryan at the start of the war as incompatible with American interests that were increasingly entwined with the Allied cause. As a result the Wilson administration would demonstrate a willingness to apply neutrality in way that would not prove detrimental to the Allied war effort.[9] Rather than lodge an official diplomatic protest against British interference with legitimate American commerce, Wilson, trusting that Britain would do the right thing, chose to pursue a more discreet path by empowering U.S. Ambassador Walter Hines Pages to address grievances on a case-by-case basis with British Foreign Secretary Sir Edward Grey. Page, arguably the most Anglophile of

Wilson's appointees, showed considerable willingness to accommodate British efforts to effect its strategy against Germany. British officials were soon convinced that there was little danger of a serious breach in relations with the United States, and so rather than abate, the Royal Navy's efforts to curb neutral commerce with continental Europe increased as the year progressed. Pressure from disgruntled merchants finally convinced the Wilson administration to file a formal diplomatic protest but when it came it was "mild and in places almost apologetic."[10] Meanwhile in October, Wilson modified the ban imposed on loans to belligerent powers and as a consequence France and Britain were able to secure an increasing line of credit in the United States. In contrast with the largely effective British impediments against American trade with the Central Powers, U.S. trade with Britain and France, facilitated by this new line of credit, grew dramatically. The result was a mutually beneficial trade boom with the Allies. At best American policy as it evolved through the course of 1914 could be seen as "benevolent neutrality;" at worst it had become decidedly un-neutral.[11]

The pro-British direction of American foreign policy was at odds with a body of opinion in the United States that favored stricter neutrality. In late 1914 German-Americans generated significant support for bills in both the House and Senate banning all arms sales to Europe. The proposed legislation was designed to counteract the growing reality that the Allies were the chief beneficiaries of the continuation of such sales. The Wilson administration worked with Anglophile Republicans such as Sen. Henry Cabot Lodge to kill the legislation, decrying the pro-German sentiment behind the measures. Secretary Bryan, the leading isolationist in the Wilson administration, took a prominent role in having the embargo legislation tabled in early 1915 on the grounds that by harming Britain it would indirectly favor Germany. However, a good deal of support for the embargo actually came from rural Republicans and Democrats representing constituencies without large German populations. Such support reflected a small but increasingly coherent constituency favoring the emergent political cause of isolation resulting from the fusion of traditional ideas of American exceptionalism with populist suspicion of the profiteering that war allowed.[12] This emergent isolationist constituency would provide a base of support for the embargo measures of late 1914 and early 1915.

On the other side of the political spectrum, conservative Republicans such as Lodge, Rep. Augustus Peabody Gardner (R-MA), Theodore Roosevelt and former Secretary of War Henry Stimson questioned the logic that America was protected by its ocean frontiers and pressed the Wilson administration to adopt measures toward greater military preparedness. All these men believed that the outcome of the war would have very important repercussions for the United States and they were united in their support for an Allied victory. Wilson rejected the preparedness campaign as unnecessary and contrary to the interests of the United States as a disinterested bystander capable of carrying the torch of peace. This time Wilson was able to call upon populist Democrats and progressive Republicans to support the administration's efforts to defeat the broader campaign for military preparedness on Capitol Hill. Wilson, however, did sanction an increase in naval appropriations in 1915, but even here he faced opposition. The populists and progressives very nearly succeeded in adding an amendment to the naval appropriations bill that called for the reduction of new battleship production on the grounds that militarism was contrary to traditional American values and ideals.

Although the twin issues of preparedness and the embargo generated considerable debate on the floor of the House and Senate, most Americans remained detached and remote from the war and the issues it generated. After the initial shock and interest that had greeted the outbreak of the conflict, concern for events in Europe began to wane in 1915. "By January, newspaper coverage of the war had shrunk to a few front-page columns in the New York dailies and passing references in many papers in the interior of the country."[13] It took the sinking of the *Lusitania* to shatter this mood of complacency and bring the reality of the war home to Americans for the first time. Many of the assumptions on which Americans previously viewed the war in Europe suddenly became open to question; it could no longer be safely assumed that the United States was immune from the ravages of the conflict.

The Sinking of the *Lusitania*

The sinking of the *Lusitania* was symptomatic of an escalation in the conflict that would have profound consequences for the United States. Faced with the tightening grip of what was in effect a British blockade, Germany responded by deploying submarines or U-boats, then a relatively experimental technology, against British shipping in the Atlantic. The early successes of this new tactic, combined with Britain's retaliatory Order in Council of March strengthening the blockade, convinced Berlin to expand the scope of the U-boat campaign. It was a campaign that was complicated by the increasingly blurred definition of contraband and the rapidly eroding foundation of the traditional rules of maritime law. Submarine technology, dependent as it was on the element of surprise, was incompatible with long-practiced rules of search and seizure whereby belligerent ships were required to fire a shot across the bow of a merchant ship suspected of trading in contraband and to safeguard the lives of the crew before sinking offending vessels. The German submarine campaign inspired Allied countermeasures such as the arming of merchant ships, the illegal use of neutral flags as cover and the carriage of contraband in passenger ships that further contributed to the erosion of the law of the sea.

While Britain's decision to restrict further neutral commerce with the March Order in Council inspired only muted protest from Washington, Wilson immediately responded to the German declaration of submarine warfare by vowing to protect U.S. lives and property and by informing Berlin that it would be held "strictly accountable" for violations of neutral rights.[14] With U.S. neutrality now assailed from both sides of the conflict in Europe, Wilson was sending out mixed signals. While Germany was put on notice that any infringement of American neutrality would have serious consequences for relations between the two countries, Britain was given considerable leeway to test the boundaries of American patience. Wilson's initial statements in response to the German U-boat campaign gave the president little room for maneuver in the wake of the *Lusitania* tragedy. In contrast to the much less dramatic British violations of American neutrality and the informal protests from Washington that they inspired, the *Lusitania* incident, and as a consequence the broader U-boat campaign, was embroiled from the beginning in the explosive issues of morality, national honor, and prestige.

The attack on the *Lusitania* was an unprecedented act and it inspired an emotive response in the United States. In addition to being a great human tragedy, it was arguably "one of the biggest public relations disasters of all time," causing irreparable damage to Germany's image in the United States.[15] As a consequence, British propaganda such as the Bryce Report, a lurid recounting of German atrocities in Belgium published shortly after the *Lusitania* incident, found fertile ground in the United States. However, while some Americans called for retaliation and many more became increasingly sympathetic toward the Allies, most Americans were alarmed by the prospect that similar events in the future might suck the United States into the conflict. In the somber atmosphere of May 1915, many newspaper editors across the country issued calls for banning travel by U.S. citizens on belligerent ships.[16]

The Wilson administration was divided on what response to take. Secretary of State Bryan favored sending a formal diplomatic protest to Berlin, while at the same time emphasizing Washington's intention to remain neutral and balancing the German note by similarly protesting the British blockade. Bryan also favored banning American citizens from traveling on belligerent ships. Ambassador Page and Col. Edward M. House, Wilson's closest advisor on issues of foreign policy even though he held no official post in the administration, favored sending an ultimatum to Germany. While there was widespread support across the country for holding Germany accountable, the public was leery of any action that would risk American entry into the war. President Wilson shared this general sentiment and the policy of his administration reflects an effort to straddle the increasingly contradictory camps of neutrality on the one hand and the forceful protection of American interests on the other.

On May 13 Wilson issued a note condemning Germany's role in the *Lusitania* incident and calling for an apology, reparation, and a guarantee from Berlin that no similar incidents would occur in the future. When Germany responded with only regret and contended that the *Lusitania*, in contravention of international law, had been carrying contraband, there followed a series of heated diplomatic exchanges through the summer of 1915 that ended with an American note on July 8 stating that another attack on a passenger ship would be interpreted in Washington as "deliberately unfriendly."[17] At this point Secretary of State Bryan, citing what he believed was Wilson's increasingly intemperate handling of the crisis and the danger this posed to American neutrality, submitted his resignation. His replacement, Robert Lansing, was much more favorably disposed to the president's position and, like Wilson, House, and Page, was predisposed to favor the Allied cause.

The *Lusitania* crisis came to a head on August 19 when a German U-boat sank the British liner *Arabic*. Although there were only two American casualties among those killed, Wilson's note of August 8 left him little room for maneuver, particularly given the vociferous criticism he faced from Theodore Roosevelt and the nationalist wing of the Republican Party who charged that "professional pacifists" were directing U.S. foreign policy.[18] Any further official protest would likely have to come in the form of an ultimatum, so Wilson chose instead to instruct Lansing to issue the strongest possible protest informally to Count Johann von Bernstorff, the German ambassador to the United States. Wilson achieved a major diplomatic victory when the Germans, recognizing the danger of war with the United States, responded with the *Arabic* pledge granting impunity to passenger liners from submarine attack. Berlin insisted, however, that in return Washington put greater pressure on Britain to observe the rules of international law and the rights of neutral states.

The *Arabic* pledge, by satisfying American honor while at the same time pre-serving neutrality, temporarily quieted those critics of Wilson who believed he had not responded forcefully enough to the *Lusitania*. Wilson appeared to have achieved his stated goal of maintaining "peace with honor." In reality, however, as 1915 drew to a close the notion of American neutrality was strained almost to the limit. The sinking in September of the Italian liner *Ancona* by an Austrian U-boat, with the loss of twenty-seven American lives, illustrated the precariousness of the *Arabic* pledge. The submarine campaign was clearly eroding the spirit of American neutrality. Colonel House concluded that public anger made it "increasingly dif-ficult to refrain from drastic action" and Lansing was convinced that mounting tensions with Germany made it imperative that the United States do nothing to "endanger our friendship with Great Britain, France, or Russia."[19] While Berlin became increasingly frustrated by what it saw as American passivity in the face of British violations of neutral rights, London interpreted U.S. policy to mean that the Royal Navy's tactics posed no threat of a breach with Washington. With the Wil-son administration unwilling to challenge the British stranglehold on trade with Europe, the option of unrestricted submarine warfare, even with its attendant risks of war with the United States, remained very much on the table as far as Germany was concerned.

THE TRIUMPH OF INTERNATIONALISM

At the beginning of 1916 Wilson appeared to have successfully steered the Unit-ed States through the submarine crisis and maintained American neutrality, even if that neutrality was clearly benevolent toward the Allies. There were still critics who took issue with Wilson's handling of foreign policy. Nationalist Republicans charged that the crisis and "national humiliation" that followed the *Lusitania* in-cident were products of Wilson and Bryan's "pacifism," while populist Democrats renewed calls in early 1916 for a ban on travel on belligerent ships and progressives in both parties cited the dangerous "jingle of the bloody dollar" as grounds for reviving the issue of an arms embargo.[20] For the most part, however, the president's handling of foreign policy enjoyed majority support on Capitol Hill and in the country at large, and efforts to revive the embargo and other isolationist measures never gathered any significant momentum in 1916.

With the submarine crisis apparently resolved, Wilson sought to press the role of the United States as mediator in the European conflict. Since the outbreak of hostilities Wilson had perceived the possibility of American mediation, given the fact that the United States had no role in the origins of the war and seemingly had nothing to gain from the outcome. It was a role wholly consistent with the philosophy of American exceptionalism. Wilson told an audience in Chicago in 1916 that mediation was "the task that is assigned to the United States" involving the "ideal figure of America holding up her hand of hope and of guidance to the people of the world." However, as the U.S. stake in the outcome of the conflict became clearer, so too did the benefits of what Wilson called "peace without victory."[21] In early 1915 House had traveled to Europe, ironically on board the *Lusitania*, as Wilson's special emissary to mediate a restoration of the status quo, arms reduction, and the establishment of free trade. Although politely received, the first House mission was uniformly rebuffed in the capitals of Europe. In 1915 all the major belligerents still held out hope of a victory resulting in spoils inconsistent with the antebellum status quo. By 1916, however, the war reached a high point of destruction and bloodshed and the growing significance of American trade to the eventual outcome of the conflict meant that the United States was in a much stronger position to promote mediation. A new mediation initiative was given added impetus as Wilson came to realize in the wake of the *Lusitania* crisis "that peace in Europe was the only way to keep the United States out of war."[22]

In January 1916 House left for Europe again, traveling first to London and then to Berlin and Paris before returning to the British capital in February. House went to Europe convinced in his own mind that a German victory would have disastrous consequences for the rest of Europe and for the United States. He made little more headway than he had the previous year in convincing the belligerents to accept an American brokered peace settlement. Instead House, without first consulting with Wilson, issued a joint memorandum with British Foreign Secretary Grey that unabashedly pledged American sympathy for the Allied cause. The House-Grey Memorandum of February 22, 1916, stipulated that Wilson would summon a peace conference at a moment acceptable to Britain and France and that if Germany refused to attend or proved unreasonable in negotiations the United States would join the war on the Allied side. This bizarre memorandum reflected

House's pro-British sentiment and his conviction that the prospect of a resumption of the German U-boat campaign made American entry into the war inevitable. For Grey, the document was useful in that it kept Wilson and his peace plans at bay until the Allies' situation improved. While the memorandum inspired hope in Washington for an American brokered peace, it soon became apparent that the French and British were not interested in negotiating a settlement as long as Germany held the territorial advantage in Europe. When Wilson backed away from House's commitment, the initiative, never likely to succeed in the first place, foundered. The House-Grey memorandum, nonetheless, clearly illustrated the public shift in U.S. policy toward the Allies that had begun in the wake of the *Lusitania* disaster.

Two weeks before the publication of the House-Grey memorandum, German-American relations once again entered crisis mode following Berlin's announcement of a submarine campaign against armed merchant ships. Although populist Democrats in Congress sought to safeguard against a new crisis with Germany by proposing legislation limiting the travel of Americans on such ships, Wilson refused to support any legislation that amounted to an "abatement of right" on the part of the United States.[23] The crisis that populists feared would threaten American neutrality came on March 24 when a German U-boat torpedoed the French steamer *Sussex*. The attack on the *Sussex* violated Germany's earlier *Arabic* pledge and resulted in the Wilson administration's ultimatum that Germany either end its submarine campaign against passenger ships and merchantmen or the United States would break diplomatic relations with Berlin. Anxious to avert American entry into the war, Germany agreed to abide by traditional rules of search and seizure in its submarine campaign while at the same time implying that it would not rule out a resumption of the campaign if Britain failed to moderate its violations of international law. While the *Sussex* pledge represented another short-term diplomatic victory for Wilson, as long as his administration was unwilling to hold Britain to a similar standard, Germany was always likely to resort to submarine warfare as a means of breaking the deadlock in Europe.

The League of Nations

The *Sussex* pledge appeared to have taken the edge off the crisis in Europe and pushed foreign policy issues into the background as the campaigns began for the 1916 presidential election. The one exception was Wilson's increasingly vocal support for the concept of a league of nations. The idea of an international organization designed to create stability in the world and avoid conflicts like the one then raging in Europe had its origins before WWI but won many new converts as the crisis deepened. It was an idea that appealed to elements on both sides of the political spectrum and it now came to form the centerpiece of Wilson's peace strategy. In May 1916 Wilson addressed the League to Enforce Peace, a non-partisan organization headed by former president William Howard Taft, in which he contended that isolationism was a thing of the past and that the United States had a vested interest in the outcome of the war and in the future of Europe. The president called for a new diplomacy based on "a common order, a common justice, and a common peace."[24] Wilson was essentially laying out the agenda of progressive internationalism that was becoming the focal point of his foreign policy, and which would eventually be articulated in his famous Fourteen Points.

The speech to the League to Enforce Peace, given just three weeks after the first anniversary of the *Lusitania* tragedy, represented an important new departure for Wilson's foreign policy. In the space of twelve months, "the United States had prepared itself economically and intellectually for a crucial role in the European conflict."[25] The progressive role envisaged by Wilson, however, was not one necessarily shared by the more conservative League to Enforce Peace or one that appealed to the belligerent powers. For both the British and the conservative internationalists the idea of a peace short of Allied victory and the implication that all the powers would work together to reorder the world was not acceptable. Instead men like British Foreign Secretary Grey and Republican leaders such as Roosevelt and Lodge envisaged a *Pax Atlantica*, whereby the Anglo-Saxon powers would form a partnership following the defeat of Germany and establish a post-war order based on their terms. While Wilson's progressive vision won over many converts in his own party and on the left in general, isolationists in the Republican Party became increasingly alarmed by his agenda. Opposition to U.S. membership in a league of nations, a goal Wilson had written into the 1916 Democratic Party platform, began to coalesce into a sizable isolationist bloc in Congress. Conservative internationalism was largely muted during the presidential campaign and the League to Enforce Peace was essentially sidetracked by Wilson's appropriation of the idea of the League of Nations. Ironically, Wilson's narrow victory over his Republican challenger, Charles Evans Hughes, increased the likelihood of American participation in a post-war League of Nations but "dimmed the prospect of bipartisan support" for such an eventuality.[26]

Wilson's evolving internationalist vision was rooted in American exceptional-ism and in the mind of the president it drew moral strength from the fact that the United States was not a party to the carnage in Europe. He had campaigned on the slogan "he kept us out of war" and his reelection provided a mandate for the policy of "peace with honor." Mediation remained a key goal of the Wilson administra-tion, only now it was reinforced by an emerging American vision of the post-war world. Immediately after the election, in December 1916, Wilson dispatched a note to each of the belligerent powers asking them to state their conditions for the termination of the war. The move excited considerable opposition from isolation-ist Republicans such as Sen. William Borah (R-ID) who criticized Wilson's efforts at peacemaking as the first step toward growing entanglement in European affairs. In Europe, the initiative made no headway among warring factions still hoping for military victory. Wilson did not abandon the idea of a negotiated peace and in a January 1917 address to the U.S. Senate he called upon the warring factions to embrace "peace without victory." Once again isolationist opposition was aroused by Wilson's pledge that the United States would play a role in maintaining the peace and in the politics of the post-war world. Meanwhile, all the European powers politely ignored the man they came increasingly to see as a "self righteous phrase-maker."[27]

Wilson's phrases were immaterial to the realities of war as far as the major combatants were concerned. At the same time, however, the European powers were acutely aware that U.S. commerce and potential military power could make the decisive difference in the conflict. Germany was faced with a quandary at the be-ginning of 1917: either resume unrestricted submarine warfare and run the risk of U.S. entry into the conflict, or face a slow, grinding defeat at the hands of an enemy who controlled the seas and had access to America's resources. After much inter-nal debate, Kaiser Wilhelm II sided with his naval and military commanders over the objections of his civilian chancellor, Theobald von Bethmann Hollweg, and decided to run the risk that a resumption of the U-boat campaign might contrib-ute to the defeat of Britain before the United States decided to enter the war. The German announcement of the resumption of the submarine campaign on January 31, 1917, essentially reneged on the earlier *Arabic* and *Sussex* pledges, and thus left Wilson with little room to maneuver. However, even though Wilson now spoke of Germany as "a madman that should be curbed," he still hoped that "peace with honor" could be preserved.[28] Although Wilson announced the severance of diplomatic relations with Germany, it would be two more months before the United States entered the war.

Despite his outrage over the German decision and the decidedly pro-Allied sentiment that had increasingly influenced the policy of his administration since 1915, Wilson sought to keep the United States from entering a war he believed represented all that was wrong with European Great Power politics. For a while it appeared that the policy of "armed neutrality," whereby American merchants were permitted to mount guns on their ships, might provide an alternative to war. However, by the end of February momentum toward war was mounting rapidly. The interception and publication of the infamous Zimmerman telegram, a German effort to recruit the aid of Mexico in the event of war with the United States, set off a frenzy of nationalist protest in the United States. A "wave of editorial indignation swept from coast to coast" and large segments of the press called for war.[29] Nationalists were increasingly critical of the administration and Theodore Roosevelt, playing on a phrase Wilson had coined in support of peace, berated Wilson as a man who was "too proud to fight." As German attacks on American shipping in the Atlantic increased, Wilson's range of options shrank quickly and finally on April 2 he went before Congress to seek a declaration of war.

In his address to Congress, Wilson emphasized that the United States was a reluctant belligerent "thrust" into war against its will with no selfish goals or hidden agenda. He called upon the United States to lead the fight against autocracy and aggression and to "make the world safe for democracy" and avert future wars by joining like-minded nations in a "concert of purpose" to secure "the principles of peace and justice in the life of the world."[30] Once in the war, Wilson would formalize these goals in the Fourteen Points, outlining a vision based on free trade, anti-imperialism, and collective security. Wilson's war aims represent an enormous departure from the guiding parameters of American policy in 1914, which limited the U.S. interests to the Western Hemisphere and East Asia and militated against any involvement in the affairs of Europe. In 1917 the United States assumed a leadership role in world affairs that it has arguably never relinquished.

AFTERMATH: THE *LUSITANIA* AND U.S. ENTRY
INTO WWI AS A TURNING POINT

U.S. entry into WWI in 1917 ultimately proved to be the deciding factor in a conflict that had been stalemated for three years. Fresh American troops and unlimited

American supplies tipped the balance in the Allies' favor and forced Germany to accept an armistice in November 1918 or face the prospect of certain defeat. Although Wilson was careful to distance American goals from those of Britain and France by referring to the United States as a co-belligerent rather than an ally, there was no escaping the fact that for the first time in its history, American troops had fought in a war in Europe and Washington had entered the fray of European power politics.

The sinking of the *Lusitania* may have not been the *casus belli* that led directly to U.S. entry into WWI, but it undoubtedly contributed to a transformation of the public mood in America that made this eventuality possible. Prior to the *Lusitania* tragedy, American interest in WWI was focused firmly on the issue of neutrality and how best to maintain it. There was no solid political foundation upon which support for U.S. involvement in the war could have been built. After 1915, vocal support for American entry into the conflict grew and continued to gather steam as German deprivations against merchant and civilian ships continued and the crisis in U.S.-German relations was exacerbated by the Wilson administration's uneven interpretation of neutrality law in favor of Great Britain. It was against this backdrop that support for isolationism and neutrality slowly eroded, and Wilson's evolving vision of a new world order based on American stewardship began to take shape.

Although Wilson was greeted as a conquering hero in London and Paris in 1919, his vision of a world remade in America's image was to receive a much frostier reception at the Paris Peace Conference. With Germany and the other losing powers not invited to the conference, and Soviet Russia facing united Western commitment to a policy of non-recognition,[31] the Big Three of Britain, France, and the United States were free to shape the peace settlement as they saw fit.[32] Britain's David Lloyd George and France's George Clemenceau were anxious to punish Germany and achieve as many of their original goals as they could without completely alienating the United States, a country to which they were now heavily indebted both financially and militarily. Wilson, for his part, was willing to compromise on many of the principles outlined in the Fourteen Points as long as he secured support for the League of Nations, which in his mind, once properly constituted, would resolve any weaknesses in the peace agreement.

Wilson's willingness to compromise in Paris was in marked contrast to his inflexibility in the face of domestic criticism of the Treaty of Versailles. Republicans, already angry at Wilson for excluding them from the Paris negotiations and for campaigning on the war in the 1918 mid-term elections, were particularly opposed to Article X of the Covenant of the League of Nations which required member states to commit troops if called upon by the League. Internationalists like Senator Lodge were willing to support the treaty if such offending clauses were modified. However, "irreconcilable" isolationists such as Senator Borah opposed the treaty in its entirety. To make matters worse Wilson faced opposition within his own party from Irish-Americans who were angry at what they saw as Wilson's failure to press Britain to address the issue of Irish self-determination. Wilson rejected the critiques put forward on Capitol Hill and set out on a national speaking tour to generate support for the treaty. The effort broke his health and the failure of his support-ers in the Senate to muster enough votes to ratify the Treaty of Versailles broke his spirit. He spent the last months of his presidency in seclusion and died shortly after leaving office, deeply embittered by what he saw as the Senate's betrayal of America's commitment to the post-war world.

Ultimately the United States would conclude separate peace treaties with each of the Central Powers. The failure of the Senate to ratify the Treaty of Versailles marked a victory for the isolationists and, with the election of Republican President Warren Harding in 1920, America's flirtation with Great Power politics in Europe appeared to be over. Throughout the 1920s and 1930s the United States retreated into isolation from Europe and avoided political commitments that might involve it in future world wars. In the 1920s economics became the focus of U.S. policy and Washington made a concerted effort at that time to facilitate American trade, investment, and access to raw materials overseas. The onset of the Great Depression in 1929 plunged the United States further into isolation as the country's energy went into resolving the domestic crisis.

Meanwhile, Wilson's vision of a stable post-war world, where free trade, de-mocracy, self-determination, and the League of Nations combined to secure the peace, never materialized. In addition to the flaws of the Treaty of Versailles, most notably the punitive measures taken against Germany, there was little chance that this vision could ever materialize without the participation and support of the country that had promoted it in the first place. The European nations were only half-heartedly committed to Wilson's ideals and, without American participation, the League of Nations, the institution upon which all else depended as far as Wil-son was concerned, failed when faced with serious challenges by Japan's occupation of Manchuria in 1931 and Italy's invasion of Ethiopia in 1936. The failure of the United States and the Great Powers in Europe to embrace Wilson's vision of a post-war order, or to replace it with a workable alternative, created a power vacuum in the interwar years. Furthermore, the Great Depression created a political environment that gave rise to extremist regimes in Germany and Japan that were only too willing to fill that vacuum. Having retreated into isolation, the United States sought to prevent a recurrence of the events that had brought the country into WWI by passing a series of Neutrality Acts beginning in 1935. As the next chapter highlights, it took the Japanese assault on Pearl Harbor to shake the United States out of its slumber. By the 1940s, President Franklin Delano Roosevelt, who had earlier served as Wilson's assistant secretary of the Navy, revived Wilson's ideals and enshrined them as the goals of the United States after WWII. This time there would be no retreat into isolation, as Wilsonian idealism became a dominant theme in American foreign policy for much of the remainder of the twentieth century.

Three

THE ATTACK ON PEARL HARBOR
AND WORLD WAR II

More than any other event in American history, the December 7, 1941, Japanese attack on Pearl Harbor propelled America's unequivocal entry onto the world stage. From it, the United States plunged into WWII. From it, the United States settled its internal debate between isolationism and internationalism. And from it, the United States has forever a reminder of the catastrophe that could befall an unprepared country.

Pearl Harbor brought U.S. foreign policy into focus more clearly than it had been in years. Through the 1920s and 1930s, U.S. foreign policy was inconsistent. Policy makers tried to navigate between the two competing tendencies that long-characterized American sentiments, isolationism and internationalism (see chapter 2). Although the isolationists held the upper hand at this time, from December 7, 1941 onward, after Japan's bombs rained down from the Hawaiian sky and its torpedoes penetrated Pearl Harbor's shallow waters, Americans were of one mind: achieving total victory in WWII, including Japan's unconditional surrender. The illusion that the Atlantic and Pacific Oceans, buffering the country's eastern and western flanks, could act as a security blanket now lay exposed as a chimera.

This chapter examines the renewed debate between the isolationists and the internationalists and how Pearl Harbor, and U.S. entry into WWII, gave the upper hand in that debate to the internationalists. Next the chapter examines the debate among the foreign policy elite about how to deal with Japan's rising power in the East: some wanted to take a conciliatory approach while others favored a more aggressive stance. Then the chapter addresses the actual attack and decisions surrounding it. Finally, the chapter concludes with a discussion of the changes the attack on Pearl Harbor led to in U.S. foreign policy and in world politics.

DEBATES AND DIVISONS: ISOLATIONISM VS.
INTERNATIONALISM REDUX

As with other eras of U.S. foreign policy covered in this book, there was considerable debate within the United States over what U.S. foreign policy should be as war spread throughout Europe and Asia in the late 1930s and early 1940s. Prior to the attack on Pearl Harbor, these debates focused on two overlapping areas, one broad and the other specific. The broad debate dealt with the isolationist vs. internationalist impulses. The second debate dealt specifically with what to do about Japan, a rising power in Asia and the Pacific. How should the United States, the other rising power in the region, deal with Japan's aggressive moves? Should it try accommodation or confrontation? We begin by revisiting the isolationist vs. internationalist debate, but this time in the context of the specter of WWII.

Isolationism vs. Internationalism

During the period between WWI and WWII (1919–1939), most Americans, both the elites and the masses, were vocal about not getting involved in overseas squabbles, especially pertaining to Europe, which was treated with a "benign remoteness,"[1] but also including Latin America and Asia.[2] During this time, Americans held Europe in no small manner of contempt, disdaining the continent's political machinations. With its constant bickering that often erupted into horrific bloodshed, Europe was seen as incorrigible; many Americans, in their hopeful ignorance of the continent, wished to keep the United States far removed from Europe's quarrels.[3]

As the novelist John Dos Passos said, the United States' main *raison d'être* was as a rejection of Europe. Given its violent and imperialist tendencies, Americans felt a sense of moral and political superiority toward Europe.[4] Never mind that the United States engaged in its own brand of expansionism through territorial conquest, first in North America during the nineteenth century as it spread westward across the continent, then in the Caribbean and the Pacific after the War of 1898 (see chapter 1).

Americans were embittered toward Europe in the wake of WWI as they "had lost their lives [but] Europe was still a mess."[5] Many Americans believed that the

United States was manipulated into entering the war by Great Britain and by profiteering munitions makers (see below). WWI's legacy, therefore, was a virulent strain of isolationism. Michael Roskin calls this period of acute withdrawal the "Versailles paradigm," which he named after the peace treaty that brought WWI to an end in 1918.[6] Immediately after WWI, Congress reduced military appropriations and insisted on bringing the troops home.[7] Moreover, the Senate refused to ratify U.S. membership in the League of Nations despite President Woodrow Wilson's tireless campaign. Led by conservative Sen. Henry Cabot Lodge, opponents objected to Article X of the League's charter, which could effectively compel U.S. entanglement in many overseas disputes. Since Wilson would not compromise on Article X, the Senate refused to ratify U.S. membership in the League. The League's impotence in preventing WWII (1939–1945) can be explained in part due to the United States' failure to play a leading role in the organization.[8]

Meanwhile, the United States initiated the infamous Kellogg-Briand Pact (1928), which tried to prevent war simply by declaring it illegal. All major nations of the world, including Germany, Italy, and Japan, signed the treaty. In the United States, Senator Borah, a staunch isolationist, shepherded the treaty through the Senate, which at that time was heavily isolationist, with few dissenting votes. But the Pact had no teeth to it and only served to underscore the lack of will on the part of the United States to play a leadership role in world affairs. The United States did not want to get involved in overseas disputes and it thought that this treaty would guarantee that. But the treaty "did more harm than good" because it freed the United States from shouldering the responsibility of achieving world peace, even as that peace was increasingly threatened.[9]

In the 1920s and 1930s, liberal isolationists opposed intervention overseas on human rights grounds while conservative isolationists opposed foreign intervention on the grounds that the United States should not sacrifice its blood and treasure to fight other peoples' battles. But by 1939, as WWII began, the isolationist movement "was purged of its nonconservative elements."[10] Isolationists began referring to themselves as America Firsters, after a group formed primarily by conservatives called the America First Committee, which argued against U.S. participation in overseas squabbles, although they did not object to the United States engaging in international trade. Opposed to the America Firsters was the Committee to Defend America by Aiding the Allies, whose chair was William Allen White, the editor of the Emporia (Kansas) *Gazette*. The Committee to Defend America supported all forms of aid to the Western democracies short of war, although some of its members began to call for U.S. military involvement by 1940.

Throughout the 1930s, the world got uglier and the danger crept closer to American shores. Japan conquered Manchuria in 1931, Adolf Hitler rose to power in Germany in 1933 and then seized the demilitarized Rhineland in 1936, Italy's Benito Mussolini invaded Ethiopia in 1935, the Spanish Civil War broke out in 1936, and Japan launched an invasion deep into China in 1937.[11] And what was the American response to all these ominous developments? It strengthened its commitment to isolationism. Indeed, isolationism gained momentum in the 1930s. Both political parties felt pressured by their constituents to remain disengaged from world affairs because "opposition to war was one of the most popular and pervasive features of American society."[12] FDR, campaigning before his first election in 1932, renounced his internationalism in order to curry favor with the voters and with influential Americans, such as the media tycoon, William Randolph Hearst.[13] Even after Japan's 1937 invasion of China, the United States remained committed to a foreign policy that relied on "settlement by consent, rather than by coercion," and which tried to make foreign policy based on "morality and neutrality alone."[14] Despite the onset of world war in 1939, the campaign platform of both political parties in 1940 was characterized by an overwhelming anti-war sentiment.[15]

Buttressed by the Neutrality Act of 1935 (and its subsequent revisions), isolationism in the United States had peaked. Also known as the Arms Embargo Act, the Neutrality Act was a product of Sen. Gerald P. Nye's (R-ND) congressional investigation into the role of munitions makers in WWI. The investigation discovered that arms manufacturers, scorned by Nye as merchants of death, had bribed politicians and skipped out on paying taxes. The Neutrality Act sought to limit the sway of the arms industry by placing an embargo on the sale of military weapons to any country engaged in hostilities. The Act did not distinguish between aggressor and aggressed nations, so its effect was to punish victim and victimizer alike. Worse, the act sometimes had the unhappy consequence of aiding the aggressor country at the expense of the aggressed as happened in the case of Italy's 1935 invasion of Ethiopia—the Act prohibited the sale of weapons to Ethiopia in order to defend itself, but it did not prohibit the sale of oil to Mussolini's invasion forces, which he needed in order to fuel Italy's military machine.[16] The Act was made more inflexible with amendments in 1936 and 1937. The list of embargoed material was expanded, U.S. trade with belligerent countries was curtailed, and travel by U.S. citizens on ships of countries at war was also limited. Congress was safe in doing this insofar as the American people supported the sentiments expressed through the Act. A Gallup poll showed that 94 percent of Americans wanted the country to remain out of the "European mess."[17]

Whatever interest Americans did have in foreign affairs was dominated by economic considerations, which were influenced by the catastrophic effects of the Great Depression. Americans were willing to engage overseas, but only for commerce, even if that included trade with Germany and Japan, the two countries that appeared increasingly threatening to most Americans. American investment in Germany had increased by more than 40 percent in the late 1930s and the United States remained Japan's chief supplier of weapons-grade oil well into 1940.[18]

By late spring 1940, Hitler's armies crushed Denmark, Norway, the Netherlands, Belgium, and even France in quick succession. Moreover, Japan threatened British, French, and Dutch colonies in Asia and by extension American holdings in the Philippines, Guam, and elsewhere.[19] Isolationist sentiments began to lose their luster as Americans awakened to the necessity of global participation.

Yet U.S. foreign policy remained confused and inconsistent. On the one hand, Congress repeatedly strengthened the Neutrality Acts. FDR repeatedly proclaimed his promise not to involve the United States in any "foreign" wars. While he was personally opposed to the Neutrality Acts, he signed them into law anyway because he felt he could not stand up to the "isolationist cyclone" that was sweeping the Congress and the American people.[20] Even though a majority of Americans favored relaxing the arms embargo, powerful isolationist senators, including Robert La Follette Jr. (R-WI), Gerald Nye (R-ND) and Hiram Johnson (R-CA), led opposition to revision, arguing that repeal of the arms embargo would effectively constitute a commitment to military intervention.[21]

On the other hand President Roosevelt's sympathies clearly favored aiding the British. He was not alone: a Gallup poll in 1940 found a majority of Americans supporting aid to Britain even if it risked plunging the United States into the war.[22] As such, various steps were being taken to give aid to Great Britain, such as the controversial destroyer deal[23] and a series of economic sanctions against Japan.[24] Furthermore, President Roosevelt and other top U.S. officials began to use declaratory rhetoric in their speeches and essays designed to prepare the American people for possible war with Germany and Japan, but with little success. In his "Quarantine the Aggressor" speech in 1937 (after Japan invaded China), FDR spoke against isolationism and tried to warn the country of the impending danger, but he was met with a tidal wave of resistance and criticism.

Debate continued, but by late 1941 (just before Pearl Harbor), the isolationists had finally lost their bid. History's events left Americans little choice but to gear up for war. The isolationist senators' attempt to prevent the arms embargo from being lifted was defeated in November 1940. Between May 1940 and December 1941, public opinion supporting "peace" as opposed to supporting action to bring about the downfall of the Axis powers declined from 64 percent to 32 percent.[25]

FDR sensed the momentum shifting his way as he denounced the isolationists as "ostriches in our midst."[26] In December 1940 he began discussing what later became known officially as the Lend-Lease program and he made his famous speech referring to America as the "arsenal of democracy."[27] He also succeeded in convincing the Congress to go along with his plans to strengthen U.S. defense capabilities. Congress imposed the first-ever peacetime draft in 1940 and renewed it the following year (by the slimmest of margins, 203–202), two years into the start of WWII and only three months before the attack on Pearl Harbor.[28] FDR also succeeded in getting passed a much larger defense bill, which included plans for building a two-ocean navy. He then set about convincing Congress to lend material support to more than thirty countries, which came officially in March 1941 when the Lend-Lease Act was passed, which enabled FDR to direct war material, including battleships and tanks, to the British, the Soviets, the Chinese and dozens of other countries fighting Germany and Japan. Lend-Lease enabled FDR to aid the Allies while claiming that the United States adhered to its policy of neutrality. He framed support for the Act as the best opportunity for keeping America out of the war, not getting it in one.

The point here is that Americans, both the elite and the masses, were already inching away from isolationism a couple of years prior to the attack on Pearl Harbor. Isolationism was "steadily losing ground" even before Japan bombed Pearl Harbor.[29] Aggressive moves by Germany in Europe and by Japan in Asia, together with FDR's skillful public pronouncements, increasingly convinced a majority of Americans that withdrawal and nonparticipation was no longer the best approach to protecting the United States. Still, it took a catastrophe of Pearl Harbor's magnitude to bring about America's full entry in the war.

As such, the attack on Pearl Harbor can be seen as the main event that definitively tipped the balance toward internationalism and away from isolationism, transforming the latter into an unpopular, minority-held viewpoint. Important public figures previously wedded to the isolationist position began to change their tune. Wendell Willkie, the Republican presidential candidate in 1940, came around to internationalism as he expressed support for some new kind of international collective security organization like the League of Nations. He even wrote a book, the title of which, *One World* (1943), suggested the impossibility of the United States remaining aloof any longer.[30] New York Gov. Thomas Dewey, who would become the 1944 Republican presidential candidate, also swung to the internationalist camp.[31] By 1943, the Republican Party, which was more heavily stacked with isolationists than was the Democratic Party, adopted the Mackinac Charter, which expressed support for U.S. participation in post-war international organizations.[32] Even that old isolationist stalwart, Sen. Robert A. Taft (R-OH), called for a new approach to foreign policy that included "some kind of association of nations to maintain the peace of the world."[33] By winter 1943–1944, public opinion showed a majority of people believing in U.S. participation in a world body for peace.[34]

Ironically, by the 1944 presidential elections, both parties were stumbling over each other to present their internationalist credentials to the American people when just a few years back, they stumbled toward the electorate from the opposite direction. By 1944, each side chided the other for having been isolationist not so long ago. In the end, the 1944 elections amounted to a serious rebuke of the isolationists. Even though Dewey, the Republican with the internationalist credentials, lost to FDR, he ran a much stronger race than his isolationist Republican counterparts running for Congress: many old-time Republican isolationist stalwarts, including Senator Nye, lost their reelection bids.[35] The election showed that the United States was overcoming its allergy to internationalism and collective security organizations.

The Debate Over Japan

The War of 1898 (see chapter 1) announced the rise of the United States while Japan's victory in the 1905 Russo-Japanese War signaled Tokyo's bid to Great Power status.[36] U.S.-Japan relations were thus complicated by the competing interests of two rising powers, especially in the Philippines and China. U.S. policy makers had to debate how best to manage this increasingly tense relationship. This task was complicated by European colonial holdings in East Asia. On the one hand, the United States resisted coming to the aid of Britain, France, and Holland in Asia because it did not want to provoke the Japanese and because it did not want to be seen as defending colonialism. On the other hand, the United States did not want Japan to seize these areas and use the valuable resources there to strengthen its war-making capacity.

Everyone agreed on the basic U.S. foreign policy goals, namely restraining Japan's increasingly aggressive behavior, keeping the region at peace, maintaining advantageous economic ties in the region (including with Japan until a certain point), and keeping the United States out of a war. The problem was how to accomplish these goals using two different approaches, one that relied on diplomatic carrots and the other that utilized diplomatic sticks. Carrots are rewards for good behavior while sticks are punishments for bad behavior. And for the first several decades of the twentieth century, U.S. foreign policy makers had great difficulty in finding the proper mix of carrots and sticks vis-a-vis Japan.

American officials had to contend with two divergent schools of thought regarding Japan. First were the accommodationists, led early in the century by President Theodore Roosevelt (1901–1909). Accommodationists wanted to use diplomatic carrots to reach an understanding with Japan regarding interests in Asia. For instance, they solicited Japan's help in restricting immigration to the American West Coast. And after President Theodore Roosevelt recognized Japan's control over Korea in 1905, Tokyo reciprocated by recognizing U.S. control over the Philippines.[37]

When Japan, in clear violation of its treaty obligations, launched a brutal invasion of Manchuria in 1931, all President Hoover's administration (1929–1933) did was issue an ineffectual statement condemning Japan's actions. Hoover's secretary of state, Henry L. Stimson, called for bolder action but Hoover opposed, arguing that developments in Asia did not threaten Americans' freedom.[38] Hoover agreed only to a statement by Stimson asserting that the United States refused to recognize Japan's acquisition of territory by military conquest: this became known as the Stimson Doctrine. With public opinion backing him, Hoover refused to apply any harsh diplomatic sticks, such as military or economic sanctions.[39] Ultimately, however, the Japanese conquest of Manchuria put Japan and the United States on a collision course that both countries spent the next ten years unsuccessfully trying to avoid.

Initially under FDR, U.S. policy toward Japan remained in the form of "inaction and nonprovocation" whereby Secretary of State Cordell Hull would only lecture Japanese diplomats about the principles of foreign affairs and good behavior.[40]

Hull tilted toward the accommodationist school of thought, always urging Roosevelt to take a more temperate tack with the Japanese. So too did Chief of Naval Operations Adm. Harold Stark and Army Chief of Staff Gen. George Marshall, but for different reasons. While Hull urged moderation because he feared a tougher stance might spoil chances for more temperate leaders to emerge in Japan,[41] the military chiefs opposed inciting Japan because neither the army nor the navy was prepared for a two-front war, which was an increasing possibility.[42]

Opposed to these accommodationists were the confrontationists who wanted to deal with Japan more aggressively by using diplomatic sticks, particularly trade sanctions. President William Howard Taft (1909–1913) and his Secretary of State Philander C. Knox were the first to stake out this position but it was not until FDR's later administrations, with Roosevelt himself acting as the crucial pivot point, that the confrontationists gained significant ground against the accommodationists.[43]

In 1940 FDR strengthened the hand of the confrontationists in his administration when he appointed Henry L. Stimson secretary of war and Frank Knox secretary of the navy.[44] Stimson and Knox joined Treasury Secretary and Roosevelt-intimate Henry Morgenthau Jr. and Interior Secretary Harold L. Ickes in calling for a more aggressive approach to Japan. Secretary of State Hull opposed them, arguing that free trade was the correct path to peaceful relations. Hull worried that tough sanctions against Japan might provoke Tokyo into taking drastic actions.[45] Stimson, Knox, Morgenthau, and Ickes thought that trade sanctions, especially an oil embargo, might so cripple Japan as to render it incapable of perpetrating further acts of aggression.[46] These competing positions on Japan reflected the tension and confusion within FDR's administration as well as the American populace at large. Ultimately, Hull lost this debate as increasingly stringent trade sanctions were applied to Japan.

In July 1939 the United States canceled its commercial treaty with Japan, enabling it to place a trade embargo on metals that could be used in military production. After Japan moved into northern Indochina in 1940, the United States tried to tighten the screws a little bit more by extending the embargo to all scrap metals.[47] Finally, by July 1941, the United States placed a total embargo on trade with Japan, including vital oil shipments. The oil embargo was a response to Japan's seizure of southern Indochina and its daily bombing of Chungking, the Chinese capital.[48] FDR punctuated these severe trade sanctions with an executive order freezing all Japanese assets in U.S. financial institutions.

48 DAYS *of* DECISION

From Japan's perspective, the American moves were a belligerent attempt to cripple it and keep it weak in the Pacific, where it believed it was freeing other Asians from European colonialism and at the same time halting the spread of communism, something for which Tokyo thought the United States ought to be grateful. Japanese leaders feared that the embargo, especially when it came to oil, would lead to Japan's collapse in less than two years since the Imperial Navy, indeed the entire Japanese economy, depended on raw materials from the United States. The situation became especially acute as Japan observed increasing cooperation and joint naval operations between the Europeans and the Americans in Asia, which made Japan feel encircled by hostile powers.

This brought Tokyo's choices into clear relief: it could either acquiesce to U.S. demands to quit the region, endure the sanctions through extensive scrimping, or launch a defiant war and seize even more areas in Asia that were rich in resources in order to replace those lost to the American trade sanctions.[49] Japanese officials believed the longer they waited, the worse off their position would be. In particular, "the oil gauge influenced the time of decision" of Japan's war planners.[50] That is why the oil-rich Netherlands East Indies (NEI) and Malaya were targeted at the same time as Pearl Harbor.[51] Furthermore, Japan felt compelled to expel the United States from the Philippines, Guam and Wake Island and the British from Singapore in order to secure the transport routes for its vital material.

Although he did not intend for it, FDR's use of these diplomatic sticks backed Japan into a corner from which it came out fighting. This became increasingly likely by mid-October 1941 when Japan's moderate government fell and was replaced by the militant hardliners who had orchestrated the China invasion. From this point forward in Japan, "war came first, diplomacy second."[52] Ultimately, the embargo failed because it did not change Japanese policy and because it failed to prevent Japan from attacking.[53] The stick the United States began to apply, in the form of trade sanctions, "turned out to be the most potent American weapon and it supplied, contrary to Washington's intentions, the single strongest push toward war."[54]

THE JAPANESE ATTACK ON PEARL HARBOR

By early 1941, U.S. policy makers expected a Japanese attack. American intelligence officials had broken the Japanese codes and were worried about a surprise attack on Pearl Harbor as early as January 1941, which is when Japan actually did start planning the attack. But since no such attack materialized, officials turned their attention to other possible targets, including the Philippines and elsewhere in East Asia.[55] Further, U.S. officials discounted Pearl Harbor as a target because they believed: (1) that the U.S. military did not present much of a threat to Japan; (2) that Japan did not have the ability to simultaneously attack in East Asia as well as at Pearl Harbor;[56] and (3) that Pearl Harbor, with its shallow waters, was safe from torpedo attack. As it turned out, U.S. officials were only partially correct: Japan did attack in East Asia but in tandem with an attack on Pearl Harbor. The multi-pronged assault was possible in part because Japan had devised a technique that enabled its torpedoes to attack in Pearl's shallow waters.

Japan launched the attack on Pearl Harbor because its immediate goal was to cripple the Americans' Pacific Fleet and thus render the United States unable or unwilling to contest Japan's moves in the Asia-Pacific region. In this regard, the attack was a spectacular success, but only in the short term. The attack fleet, including six aircraft carriers, bombed all the military bases on Hawaii and many of the ships anchored at Pearl Harbor, destroying nearly every plane on the ground, sinking or severely damaging twelve battleships and killing 2,403 Americans. The battleship *Arizona* was sunk, accounting for more than 1,100 dead alone.[57] With the U.S. Pacific Fleet essentially neutralized, the United States was unable to play any significant role in the Pacific War for more than six months, so Japan was free to conquer Southeast Asia and the southwest Pacific region as well as penetrate deep into the Indian Ocean.

But American military capacity was only delayed, not destroyed. The attack failed to destroy any of the three aircraft carriers Japan mistakenly hoped were stationed in Hawaii. That these carriers, plus submarines, were what remained of the bulk of the Americans' Pacific Fleet meant that the United States was forced to rely on those ships to fight its Pacific War, which turned out to be a good idea because the United States used these weapons to great effect in halting, then reversing, Japan's advances in the Pacific. Further, the Americans were able to salvage and redeploy all but five battleships.

Adm. Isoroku Yamamoto, Japan's chief architect of the attack, said the move would probably give Japan no more than a year of freedom of action in the Pacific before the mighty U.S. industrial machine recovered. Even though Japanese military planners knew that they would probably lose a long, all-out war with the Americans, they felt that to wait any longer meant Japan would grow weaker while the

United States grew stronger. Still, Yamamoto said, "I fear we have awakened a sleeping giant and have instilled in him a terrible resolve." Yamamoto made that comment upon learning that the Japanese message to Washington ending negotiations and effectively declaring war reached the Americans *after* the attack had begun and not before as was intended, thus enraging the Americans who perceived it as a surprise attack.

The day after the attack, a furious President Roosevelt made his famous speech declaring that December 7 would be "a day that will live in infamy." Less than an hour later, Congress voted overwhelmingly to declare war on Japan.[58] The country launched a massive arms-production drive and the United States turned the engines of war hot. As American presidents are wont to do, FDR framed the war as an epic struggle of good vs. evil and freedom vs. tyranny. The surprise nature of the attack helped matters in this regard because it gave Americans a rallying cry. Moreover, the attack united a deeply divided country and paved the way for the Allies to adopt their inflexible position toward Japan: total victory that would lead to Japan's unconditional surrender.

AFTERMATH: PEARL HARBOR AND WORLD WAR II
AS A TURNING POINT

Pearl Harbor helped prompt yet another shift in U.S. foreign policy, but this time the pendulum swung from the introversion and withdrawal that isolationists engineered in the wake of World War I (see chapter 2) back toward extroversion and involvement in world affairs to an extent not previously known in the United States. The nature of this extroverted shift is characterized by a broad national consensus that saw a confrontational United States that sought total victory and a U.S. foreign policy that sought to reshape both international and domestic institutions and structures.

On January 1, 1942, less than a month after the attack, the signatories to the Declaration by United Nations created the Grand Alliance of twenty-five nations dedicated to defeating the Axis. The widespread popular support with which this Declaration was received in the United States illustrates the transforming effect Pearl Harbor had upon American thinking. The country's total participation as a full-fledged and formal ally in WWII stands in sharp contrast with its meager presence in WWI, when the United States was willing only to refer to itself as an "associated power." The attack brought focus and clarity to U.S. foreign policy where previously there was none. No longer did President Roosevelt feel the need to strike a balance between isolationists and internationalists: virtually everyone was an internationalist now. And no more did FDR have to navigate between the accommodationists and confrontationists in his administration: now, virtually everyone was a confrontationist. Indeed, before the attack, FDR's doubts and inconsistencies revolved around a "negative question," namely how to restrain Japan and prevent American entry in the war.[59] But after the attack, FDR's focus was on a singular and clearly defined objective: to completely and totally win the war. Therefore, Pearl Harbor is connected to Japan's unconditional surrender and to dominance over Japan's future and much of the rest of the Pacific for decades to come.

Divisions and disunity in the country seemed to instantly fade away. Arthur Krock reported in the *New York Times* that

national unity was an instant consequence . . . for national unity—which has been a distant and unattained goal since and before Hitler invaded Poland in 1939—seemed visibly to rise out of the wreckage at Honolulu.[60]

Krock later observed that even labor and industry "cohered."[61] Groups known for their internationalist views, such as the Committee to Defend America and the Council for Democracy, either dissolved or merged because they felt their job of persuasion was finished. Moreover, isolationist groups, such as America First and the Christian Front, dissolved "because their job was now hopeless" since the country was thrust into a total global war effort.[62] Renowned American philosopher Ralph Barton Perry observed, "the Great Debate" between isolationists and internationalists was settled.[63] One of Pearl Harbor's immediate effects, therefore, was to "shatter the inter-war isolationist front."[64]

Pearl Harbor also exposed a high degree of latent racism against the Japanese. That racism not only led to calls for wiping out the entire Japanese nation but also played a role in the U.S. decision to drop nuclear bombs on Nagasaki and Hiroshima, which forever left a "wound to human consciousness."[65] Moreover, only seventy-four days after Pearl Harbor was attacked, FDR issued an order giving the government authority to round up tens of thousands of Americans of Japanese descent and place them in what FDR himself called "concentration camps."[66] FDR's action was backed by Congress without a dissenting vote, and applauded by most Americans.

Pearl Harbor's most far-reaching impact however, was recognition by the United States of the need to break with its isolationist past, its willful ignorance of world events, and its tradition of refusing to join international collective security organizations like the League of Nations. Pearl Harbor convinced the country that it could no longer survive in a cocoon, with thousands of miles of water acting as a protective shell. For the first time since the War of 1812, Americans started to realize that events overseas had serious consequences at home.[67] According to Dulles:

> The assault on Pearl Harbor drove home, with compelling force, the lesson being so laboriously learned from the rising conflict with Germany in the Atlantic. Its tremendous emotional impact united the country almost overnight in a final realization that the United States, part of a world community with which its own destiny was inextricably interwoven, could not escape direct participation in the war because of its geographical position.[68]

Pearl Harbor convinced the American government and the American people of the necessity of staying engaged in world affairs in order to forestall the rise of new threats to American interests. John C. Zimmerman suggests "the shadow of Pearl Harbor has lurked behind every major American foreign policy decision since 1941."[69] In fact, the Truman Doctrine, and each following presidential doctrine during the Cold War (1947–1991), all of which were designed in one way or another to contain and confront Soviet communism, bear Pearl Harbor's imprint. Ironically, Pearl Harbor's legacy was a period of U.S. activism and interventionism designed to achieve the same goals that the previous decades of isolation and withdrawal had failed to do, namely protect U.S. interests in world affairs.[70] So it is important to recognize here that, even though the United States may experience mood shifts in U.S. foreign policy, it may do so within the context of achieving the same goals from one cycle to the next.

Pearl Harbor convinced the United States it must assume a leadership role in world affairs. That meant taking the lead in forming collective security organizations like the United Nations and the North Atlantic Treaty Organization. President Wilson tried to teach the country that lesson after WWI, but his message failed to take. Only after Japanese torpedoes sent American ships to the watery depths in Hawaii was the lesson finally learned. This lesson was helped along considerably by Sen. Arthur H. Vandenberg (R-MI), the old-hand isolationist, who was thoroughly converted to internationalism in the wake of Pearl Harbor. Vandenberg, who had assumed leadership of the isolationists after Borah died, said his newfound convictions regarding international cooperation and collective security "took firm hold on the afternoon of the Pearl Harbor attack. That day ended isolationism for any realist."[71] Vandenberg's January 1945 speech announcing his dramatic about-face had far-reaching consequences for the future of U.S. foreign policy.[72] Influenced by his nephew, Hoyt Vandenberg, who was a general in the Air Corps (later the Air Force), Vandenberg's speech was favorably received because he was able to blend his newfound support for an internationalist-oriented collective security organization with his staunch nationalist credentials. This from the man who had been a favorite presidential candidate of the isolationist wing of the Republican Party as recently as 1940![73]

Roosevelt and Secretary of State Cordell Hull's efforts to create an international security organization were influenced by President Wilson's failure to get the United States to accede to the League of Nations. They did this by ensuring that the United Nations, the League's successor, had an executive body, the U.N. Security Council (UNSC), with five permanent members, including the United States, who could veto U.N. resolutions. When Roosevelt died in 1945, Harry Truman took over and he was no less internationalist-minded. Under the Truman administration, not only did the United Nations come into creation, but so too did other significant international collective security apparatus, such as the Marshall Plan for reconstructing war torn Europe and NATO, which was the first binding peacetime military alliance the United States ever joined.[74] And there was very little popular or congressional opposition because the way had been cleared by "molders of public opinion [who] were almost unanimous in favor of the United States playing its full part in this new movement for collective security."[75] The Senate voted 89–2 in favor of the United Nations and approved the NATO treaty by a vote of 82–13.

Pearl Harbor was also a turning point insofar as it led to substantial changes in the United States' national security bureaucracy, notably in the area of intelligence (other chapters, especially chapter 12, show this to be a recurrent theme). The attack revealed flaws in the U.S. ability to acquire, decipher, catalog, and then properly interpret vast amounts of information, some of it genuine, some of it fraudulent. And while U.S. intelligence sources were able to decode most Japanese messages (this proved a critical factor in helping the Americans win the Pacific War) the timing of the delivery as well as the target of the delivery was sometimes compromised. Consider the challenge just before the Pearl Harbor attack: "In the handling of coded messages, there was inevitably a delay—from interception of the message at the intercept station through transmission to the decoding center in Washington, determination of priority in handling, assignment for full decoding, assignment for translation and the actual translation, to final delivery to the approved list of recipients."[76]

Furthermore, important intelligence often went unshared because various agencies and officials feared a leak or that the Japanese might discover that the United States had broken their codes. In fact, intelligence officials even withheld information from President Roosevelt and between May and November 1941 army intelligence had stopped sending messages to the White House altogether.[77]

The failure of intelligence services to discover the attack on Pearl Harbor led to the establishment of the Office of Strategic Services (OSS) in June 1942 in the midst of WWII. President Truman abolished the OSS after the war and replaced it with the National Intelligence Authority, composed of the Secretaries of State, War, and Navy, as well as a personal military advisor. He also created a new organization called the Central Intelligence Group, which was headed by General Vandenberg.

By 1947 the Central Intelligence Agency (CIA) was designated the successor to the post-Pearl Harbor intelligence gathering structures and organizations. It was created by the National Security Act of 1947, a landmark piece of legislation that significantly strengthened the president's powers in foreign affairs and national defense while fundamentally reorganizing U.S. national security. In addition to creating the CIA, the National Security Act also created the Office of the Secretary of Defense, the Air Force and the Joint (military) Chiefs of Staff (JCS). It also created the National Security Council (NSC), which is the successor to the National Intelligence Group. Historically, the NSC's membership has consisted of the president, vice president, secretary of state, secretary of defense, the CIA director, and the president's national security advisor who usually acts as coordinator between the NSC's members. A 1949 amendment replaced the War Department with the Department of Defense, under which all the military services (army, air force, navy, marines, and the coast guard) are organized.

Pearl Harbor also provided the impetus for developing more sophisticated signals intelligence capabilities to aid in electronic eavesdropping. Government officials instituted methods that would ensure greater cooperation between signals interceptors and the code breakers in the Army, the Navy, and the Federal Bureau of Investigation, plus increased collaboration with British signals intelligence efforts.

In addition, Pearl Harbor is indirectly responsible for the creation of the National Security Agency (NSA), an organization so secretive that even its budget is classified. The NSA was established by presidential directive in 1952 and is responsible for constructing U.S. spy codes and for breaking the codes of friend and foe alike. Headquartered at Fort Meade, Maryland, it has incredibly sophisticated electronic eavesdropping capability.

Four

THE KOREAN WAR AND THE
COLD WAR IN ASIA

If Japan's 1941 attack on Pearl Harbor helped to silence the debates over U.S. foreign policy, then North Korea's 1950 invasion of South Korea helped resurrect them. Truman's handling of the Korean War set the stage for a return of serious debates and divisions as his Republican critics in Congress attacked him so severely that they contributed to one of the lowest approval ratings for any president in the modern era.

Although it is sometimes called the "Forgotten War" because Americans pay so little attention to it, the Korean War is nevertheless a pivotal event in U.S. foreign policy because it prompted policy reversals throughout East Asia. These reversals were influenced by developments on the field of battle in Korea where the U.S. military experienced one of its greatest achievements and one of its worst defeats, all while under the command of Gen. Douglas MacArthur, the larger-than-life charismatic hero of WWII fame. MacArthur's incredible and masterfully planned Inchon landing was followed only a few weeks later by the longest forced retreat in U.S. military history. With these and other battlefield developments came numerous policy shifts. The policies that emerged had far-reaching global impacts that endured for decades. The Korean War helped deepen the worldwide competition between the United States on the one hand and China and the Soviet Union on the other. It was the first major armed conflict of the Nuclear Age and the Cold War. The Cold War was an ideological and strategic competition between the United States and the Soviet Union. It was called "Cold" because the Americans and Soviets never fought each other directly on the battlefield (although their proxies did in places like Korea, Vietnam, and Afghanistan). It was a "War" because it was an ideological competition insofar as the United States'capitalist and democratic system confronted the Soviet Union's socialist and communist system. It was a strategic competition as these two nuclear-armed superpowers engaged in a global contest for allies and influence.

After achieving some notable victories in the first years of the Cold War, it now looked as though the United States was losing its struggle with the Soviet Union.[1] For several reasons, 1949 was a difficult year for the Truman administration, especially its chief diplomat, the powerful but embattled Secretary of State Dean Acheson. First, Acheson was attacked for remaining loyal to an old State Department colleague, Alger Hiss, who was convicted in January for lying about his communist affiliations. The Hiss case was a part of the now infamous Red Scare that swept through much of the country in the late 1940s and early 1950s. Fueled by the outrageous rhetoric and unsubstantiated charges of a political opportunist, Sen. Joseph McCarthy (R-WI), anti-communist panic sowed the seeds of suspicion and derision everywhere. From Hollywood to Washington, D.C., thousands of innocent lives were ruined as they got caught up in a political whirlwind where accusation and innuendo sufficed as judge and jury. Once the Korean War started, "McCarthyism" received a boost as it merged with "serious critics" of Truman's foreign policies, such as Sen. Robert Taft (R-OH).[2]

Second, the Soviet Union detonated a nuclear explosion in August 1949, thus ending the short-lived American monopoly on nuclear weapons. News of the Soviet Union's entry into the Nuclear Age contributed to a sense of doom across the country. Third, Republicans in Congress blamed the Truman administration for "losing" China when it fell to Mao Zedong's communists in October 1949. Chiang Kai Shek's Nationalist regime, which was allied with the United States during WWII, withdrew in defeat to the island province of Formosa (present-day Taiwan) where it set up a rival government as an alternative to the communists who now controlled China's mainland. Defense Department officials wanted to aid Chiang but Acheson and other State Department diplomats worried that assisting the defeated and discredited Nationalists would upset allies in Asia and Europe. Although the Truman administration refused to recognize the communists, Acheson argued there was little that could be done to aid the Nationalists. Republicans in the Free China lobby in Congress complained bitterly that Truman and Acheson had not done enough to prevent China, the world's most populous country, from joining the communist Soviet Union, the world's largest country. When China and the Soviet Union signed a Treaty of Friendship in February 1950, the foreign policy elite feared that the great Asian landmass risked coming under the complete domination of communist influence. Such was the political context in which the Truman administration found itself.

It is against this backdrop that this chapter examines U.S. foreign policy and the Korean War. We begin with a discussion of North Korea's surprise attack and how it compelled policy reversals on the part of the Truman administration. We then delve deeply into the debates and divisions surrounding several controversial foreign policy decisions that Truman made during this period, including debates about military tactics and strategy, the so-called Great Debate about America's role in world affairs, and Truman's decision to fire General MacArthur. We conclude with a look at how the Korean War radically altered the United States' national security policy, especially insofar as East Asia is concerned.

NORTH KOREA'S SURPRISE ATTACK

When North Korea launched its invasion of South Korea on June 25, 1950, Acheson was blamed for the invasion, his critics citing a foreign policy speech he gave only six months earlier, which specifically excluded South Korea (as well as Formosa and Indochina) from the area of vital American interests in Asia. Even though Acheson's speech reflected the prevailing wisdom of the foreign policy elite, including General MacArthur and the rest of the military hierarchy, he was held responsible by his critics because they believed the speech was interpreted by North Korean leader Kim Il Sung as a green light to invade.[3] Acheson excluded South Korea as vital to U.S. interests because U.S. strategic policy at that time focused on maintaining a strong American presence in Europe as well as in several island countries throughout Asia, such as Japan and the Philippines. South Korea was part of the Asian mainland and the United States had neither the interest nor the resources to cover it under the Americans' emerging strategic umbrella. In fact, 45,000 U.S. troops in Korea, left over from WWII, were withdrawn by June 1949.

But fast-paced battlefield developments led to several policy reversals by the Truman administration. The first such reversal came only days after the initial invasion as Truman and Acheson quickly decided that South Korea was an American vital interest after all. In successive order, Acheson convinced Truman to direct that weapons from Japan be delivered to the reeling South Koreans (as well as to the Philippines and parts of Indochina), that General MacArthur, who was Supreme Allied Commander in Japan, be given broad discretion to use his air and naval forces to evacuate some 2,000 U.S. nationals from South Korea, and that the Navy's Seventh Fleet be placed under MacArthur's command and stationed between Communist China on the mainland and Nationalist China on the island of Formosa.[4] Truman and Acheson feared that North Korea's invasion was a prelude to the communist Chinese attacking Formosa. The Seventh Fleet was, therefore, to act as a buffering deterrent, although to China it looked more like a provocation and a prelude to an American thrust onto the mainland.

This represented yet another policy reversal insofar as the United States now proclaimed that it would use force to keep Formosa from falling to China even though only a few months earlier the Truman administration expected and accepted that China would retake the island.[5] Truman saw Chiang's Nationalist government as the "world's rottenest," comprised of "corrupt bloodsuckers."[6] But Truman signaled a change in policy with the Seventh Fleet's redeployment, and by August 1950 Truman had completely reversed himself when he accepted General MacArthur's advice to send U.S. military advisors and assistance to Formosa.[7]

On June 30, and in response to MacArthur's dire assessment that South Korea would fall to the communists without U.S. combat forces, Truman ordered U.S. ground troops into battle declaring, "We have met the challenge of the pagan wolves."[8] In just five days, Truman reversed U.S. policy regarding Korea by making what he called the "toughest decision" of his presidency.[9] Suddenly, U.S. soldiers were fighting, killing, and dying for a piece of land that Acheson only six months earlier had declared outside U.S. defense interests.

The reasons for this decision were clear, at least to Truman, Acheson, and just about everyone else in the upper echelons of the Truman administration. Although North Korea launched the invasion, it was seen as only a puppet whose Soviet masters in Moscow pulled the strings. Such a blatant breach of international peace and security, coming so soon after the lofty ideals of collective security were codified in the United Nations, could not go unpunished. Truman saw the attack as a direct challenge to the United Nations' efforts of achieving international peace through collective security by having many countries come to the aid of a single country, such as South Korea, that was threatened by aggression. His decisions thereafter were geared toward upholding the United Nations' principle of collective security, as well as the sixteen-country military alliance that the United Nations authorized in its Security Council Resolution, calling on the international community to use any means necessary "to repel the armed attack and to restore international peace and security" in the region.[10]

But Truman's reasons extended beyond the idealism expressed in U.N. resolutions. He likened North Korea's attack to Hitler's moves in Europe during the 1930s and vowed not to make the same mistake Britain and France did when they gave only a tepid response to Hitler. So, it was America's strategic interests in Europe and elsewhere, and not credibility in Korea, that compelled Truman to fight. If the United States did not respond forcefully in Korea, then the Soviets would take that as a sign of weakness and challenge U.S. interests elsewhere. This type of thinking later came to be known as the "Domino Theory." Truman put it best when he said, "If we let South Korea down, the Soviets will keep right on going and swallow up one piece of Asia after another," which would cause collapse all the way to Europe.[11] Hence, Truman could not allow other "dominoes," such as Europe and Japan, both possessed of a mighty industrial capacity, to fall to the communists. Korea thus became a central bulwark of the Truman Doctrine of containment, i.e., checking the expansion of communist influence around the globe. If he held up that domino, others would be safe.

Moreover, Truman had domestic political reasons for reacting so forcefully to the invasion. He and his administration were being bludgeoned by Republicans in Congress and by the conservative press for being soft on communism. By reacting decisively and forcefully in Korea, Truman was able to quell, but only for a time, his domestic critics. Even though Senator Taft objected to the fact that Truman committed American troops to Korea without consulting Congress, he nevertheless supported Truman's decision, at least initially.

DEBATES AND DIVISIONS: TACTICS AND STRATEGIES
But while there was agreement on who was behind this attack and unity on what the initial response was to be, this unity quickly fell by the wayside as serious debates and divisions at the tactical and strategic level emerged. Differences over how to fight the war became so grave that Truman relieved MacArthur as Supreme Commander of the United Nations Command (UNC) forces, thus ending the general's military career.[12] These debates on tactics fed into the broader, strategic debates gripping the whole country, not just the foreign policy elite. These disputes in-

cluded the so-called Great Debate about the overall direction of U.S. foreign policy, and the debate—between Truman, Acheson, and the military service chiefs on the one hand and General MacArthur and his congressional allies on the other—over whether the Korean War should be fought as a limited war or as an all-out attempt at total victory.

Policy Debates Over Tactics

The war went badly for the UNC during late summer 1950 as its troops were boxed into the southern tip of the Korean Peninsula, in the Pusan area. But by August, the troops had regrouped and planned a counterattack under their new, highly capable general, Matthew B. Ridgway. Meanwhile, from his Tokyo headquarters, MacArthur was planning a daring counter-offensive based on an amphibious landing at the port city of Inchon.

Even though MacArthur made his WWII reputation in part by conducting successful amphibious assaults, most in the military hierarchy opposed his plan to launch a counter-offensive at Inchon, for several reasons. First, they argued that Inchon was too far north of the main battle line down near Pusan and hence would have little battlefield significance. Second, and more important, the harbor at Inchon was wholly unsuitable for an amphibious assault. With the second highest tides in the world that could easily shipwreck vessels, the military's JCS believed such a landing was suicidal. So they sent Army Chief J. Lawton Chiles and Adm. Forrest Sherman, Chief of Naval Operations, to Tokyo to talk MacArthur out of his plan and to recommend the landing occur at a point further south, in more hospitable waters. But MacArthur was a gambler, prone to taking bold risks. And his confidence and charisma were infectious. He argued that since no one, including the enemy, would believe such a landing at Inchon could succeed, that is precisely why it would succeed. Instead of Chiles and Sherman convincing MacArthur to change his mind, MacArthur convinced them to change theirs. Because of his larger-than-life reputation, his previous record, his self-assured confidence, and also because of the American practice of giving great leeway to commanders in the field, MacArthur was given the go-ahead to plan the landing at Inchon.

There were only two days each year when the tides at Inchon were just right, making a landing possible. September 15 was one of those days and it was fast approaching. With a little luck and superb execution, the Inchon landing was a smashing success.[13] It was one of the most daring, incredible maneuvers by an

American general perhaps since General Washington crossed the Delaware River. Mac-Arthur had done it again and just in time to meet up with Ridgway's forces, which were breaking out of the Pusan perimeter. Effectively surrounded and with their supply-lines cut off, the battle-weary North Koreans were beating a hasty, messy retreat behind the 38th parallel, the international borderline between North and South Korea. They scattered throughout the countryside as UNC forces mauled them badly.

So the rout was on, or so it appeared and the next major decision that had to be debated was whether or not to cross the 38th parallel (preliminary discussion had actually begun before the Inchon landing). Although the initial U.N. resolution called only for turning back North Korea's invasion and restoring the international border at the 38th parallel, MacArthur's successful Inchon landing, together with Ridgway's momentum, made it irresistible for U.S. policy makers to overstep their U.N. mandate. Here we see battlefield developments leading to yet another policy shift. This is called mission creep and it often ends in disaster, as this one did.

Since some at the State Department supported crossing the 38th parallel while others opposed, its official position became a watered down compromise that basically reserved judgment until the military situation on the ground stabilized.[14] Acheson supported crossing the 38th parallel in part because the Soviets hinted that they would not get involved.[15] But George Kennan, a highly respected State Department official and the primary influence behind the containment policy, consistently urged caution.[16] However, since Kennan had left his position on the State Department's influential Policy Planning Staff in August, his objections held less sway. Another State Department official, Charles Bohlen, an expert on Soviet affairs, also urged caution but he softened his objections under the weight of so many countervailing voices in both the State and Defense Departments.

Nearly everyone else, including a unified Defense Department, Republican and Democratic leaders in Congress and members of the liberal and conservative press agreed on sweeping past the 38th parallel to conquer North Korea, dissolve its communist government and unite it with the South under American influence. Moreover, South Korean leader Syngman Rhee insisted on crossing. Rhee was a considerable force in South Korean politics, so the United States felt compelled to deal with him.[17] Although he was U.S.–educated and a staunch anti-communist, he was no democrat. South Koreans chafed under his tyrannical rule, but he was popular with some Koreans and with many in the U.S. Congress. Rhee threatened to send his Republic of Korea (ROK) forces across the border even if the UNC did not.

Truman favored crossing the 38th parallel as well. He believed in the biblical command that a punishment must always follow a sin.[18] North Korea's sin was to invade South Korea and so it must now be punished. In addition, Truman saw a chance to shore up his political fortunes. Conquering North Korea would silence his Republican critics in Congress who were constantly criticizing him for allowing communism to spread in Asia. In fact, Sen. William Knowland (R-CA) said that a failure to cross the 38th would constitute "appeasement" of the Soviet Union, a term he used to deliberately tie Truman to the disastrous diplomacy prior to Hitler's conquest of Europe.[19] Since congressional elections in November were fast approaching, a dramatic victory in Korea would surely boost his party's electoral chances.

So too was the military hierarchy in favor of continuing north. The 38th parallel was an artificial border, dreamed up by U.S. and Soviet negotiators in the 1940s as they agreed on how to divide their spheres of influence in Korea. It had no geographical characteristics that made it a natural border. Moreover, the JCS worried, halting the UNC's advance would give the enemy the respite it needed to regroup and launch another attack from the North whenever it chose to.

Not surprisingly, MacArthur favored crossing. Any concerns the JCS had about getting too close to China's border were dismissed by MacArthur who convinced the military hierarchy that China would not enter the war. Not only did MacArthur hold China's military in low regard, he also believed that Beijing had let pass its best opportunity to enter the war: when the North Koreans had the UNC and ROK forces boxed in at Pusan. Now that the North Koreans were retreating in defeat, MacArthur was convinced that China would not dare to enter the war. Besides, Truman, Acheson, Defense Secretary George Marshall, and the JCS were more concerned about how the Soviets would react than the Chinese. And who could deny MacArthur after his spectacular success with the Inchon landing? So MacArthur received orders from Marshall to "feel unhampered" in crossing the 38th parallel.[20]

Shortly after this decision was made in Washington, it was given diplomatic window dressing with a new U.N. resolution passed on October 7, 1950 authorizing a new mission to forcibly establish a united, democratic government "in the sovereign state of Korea," with any reference to North or South pointedly omitted.[21] On the same day, UNC forces crossed into North Korea. The Truman administration had made yet another about-face on its policy, this time repudiating containment and instead adopting a new policy of forcible "liberation" and rolling back communism.[22] With the recent military successes and the policy changed accordingly, MacArthur confidently predicted that the war would be over soon and that the troops would be home by Christmas. Neither Acheson nor MacArthur took seriously China's warnings against UNC forces crossing the 38th. MacArthur thought China's military incapable and Acheson discounted the warning, which was delivered by India's Ambassador to China, K. M. Panikkar, who Acheson derided as unreliable and sympathetic to the communists. Truman disregarded China's warning as well: his narrow vision of China as only a Soviet client prevented him from comprehending China's genuine national security interests. Although Truman believed that punishment follows sin, he did not consider that trouncing North Korea and expelling its forces from South Korea was punishment enough. Moreover, Truman was blinded to the fact that China saw *his* actions as a transgression for which the United States deserved punishment. So he convinced himself that China would not feel threatened as UNC forces approached within miles of China's border.[23]

But China *was* threatened, fearing that the American thrust would revive anticommunist elements in China.[24] Concerned about what can be called the communist version of the Domino Theory, Mao feared U.S.–sponsored anti-communist forces running amok throughout Asia. After an initial foray by Chinese soldiers momentarily slowed the UNC's advance, Chinese forces mysteriously disappeared. MacArthur thought Mao was bluffing but it appears the Chinese were issuing a warning not to come any closer and giving the UNC time to take stock. Instead, MacArthur charged ahead, thus precipitating the very thing he was so sure would not happen: hundreds of thousands of Chinese "volunteers" poured across the border. By November, MacArthur's troops were routed by waves of Chinese troops.[25] MacArthur was completely wrong about China's intentions and capabilities but he took credit for exposing the Chinese as aggressors. Nevertheless, his forces, which only a few weeks earlier accomplished an amazing military feat, were forced into the longest retreat in U.S. history, some 300 miles. Instead of the troops coming home for Christmas, MacArthur conceded that he faced "an entirely new war."[26] Crossing the 38th parallel was the most costly decision of the war: four-fifths of American casualties occurred *after* crossing.[27]

This incredible turn of events on the battlefield forced yet another policy shift by the Truman administration. Although the latest policy, changed from containing communism to rolling it back, was officially only a couple of weeks old, the bleak battlefield situation forced the Truman administration to summarily jettison that new policy. Suddenly, administration officials worried about evacuating the peninsula altogether. MacArthur was instructed to fight a rearguard action for as long as he could while considering withdrawing to Japan.[28] At the same time, diplomats in Washington probed for a diplomatic solution.

But now it was China's turn to shift policy in accordance with its fortunes on the battlefield. Mao demanded that foreign troops withdraw from Korea, that Formosa be reincorporated into China, and that Beijing be given China's UN seat.[29] Faced with this dire military situation, we come now to the most serious debate at the tactical policy level, which pitted MacArthur and his congressional allies against Truman, Acheson, and the military hierarchy in Washington. The dispute boils down to Truman's desire for limiting the war to the Korean Peninsula set against MacArthur's desire to widen the war to include Chinese and possibly Soviet targets.

Both sides had convincing reasons for their position. Truman, Acheson, Marshall, and the JCS did not want to risk breaking apart the coalition of UNC forces fighting the North Koreans (and now the Chinese). Although Americans were doing the majority of the fighting and dying, the whole operation was based on the United States receiving diplomatic cover from a U.N.-sanctioned military action. But if the war expanded to include targets inside China, many allied countries would withdraw their support. Of greatest concern were European powers, such as Britain and France. Without their support, collective security—the rationale on which the action was predicated—would crumble. Moreover, in convincing Truman to limit the war to Korea, Acheson argued that the United States could not afford to get drawn into an all-out war on the Asian landmass, that the greatest threat to U.S. interests was the Soviet Union's challenge in Europe, and that fighting the North Koreans and the Chinese was like fighting the "second team," which would only drain American strength in Europe.[30]

However, General MacArthur, supported by Truman's Republican critics in Congress, argued that limiting the war would mean that the communists, who had a huge advantage in manpower, could bleed the UNC in an endless war of attrition. In February 1951, Congressman Joseph Martin (R-MA) gave a speech saying, "If we are not in Korea to win, then this administration should be indicted for the murder of thousands of American boys."[31] Senator Taft argued that, if the reason for limiting the war was to prevent China's entry, then that policy had obviously failed, so acknowledge the reality and deal with it forcefully. MacArthur chafed under the restrictions placed on his bombing targets: he expressed his frustrations publicly when he complained to the media about the unprecedented and "enormous handicap" under which he was forced to operate.[32] He sent cables to Washington, urging officials to adopt a more aggressive war policy. He recommended bombing China's war-fighting industries in Manchuria, accepting Chiang's long-standing offer of 33,000 Nationalist troops to augment UNC forces, and imposing a naval blockade on China.[33] Acheson and the European allies opposed expanding the war to China and believed that using Chiang's forces would contribute little militarily while further antagonizing China. Truman delayed decision on these matters to the extent that none of these options were formally adopted, although he did order a trade embargo against China.

Moreover, MacArthur was at odds with Truman and Acheson over strategic policy. He did not agree that Europe was the prime region to meet the communist challenge, arguing instead that Asia and in particular Korea was where the West should make its ultimate stand against communism. While Truman, Acheson, and even the military brass at the Pentagon tried to keep the reigns on MacArthur between December 1950 and March 1951, the debate spilled into the public sphere in such a way as to make it look like a military challenge to civilian control over foreign policy. MacArthur's bellicose public declarations against China in March 1951 torpedoed Truman's plan to issue a new peace proposal.[34] Truman could not abide what he considered a direct challenge to his authority as Commander-in-Chief, so he fired MacArthur, but only after receiving assurance from the unanimous approval of the JCS.

A firestorm greeted news of MacArthur's dismissal. A president—whose popularity ratings were in the basement—had abruptly dismissed a larger-than-life war hero. There were demonstrations burning Truman in effigy and calls for MacArthur's reinstatement. Outraged members of Congress condemned Truman as a fish, a pig and a traitor.[35] House Minority Leader Joseph Martin and Senator Taft discussed possible impeachment procedures against Truman. MacArthur, after receiving a hero's welcome with a ticker-tape parade, was given the rare opportunity to address a joint session of Congress where he defended his position for expanding the war, elaborating on his famous dictum that "there is no substitute for victory."

Like many Americans, MacArthur was mystified by limited war, which was largely alien to the American mentality. MacArthur condemned limited war as even worse than surrendering to the enemy on its terms. Limited war to him was nothing more than appeasement and "doomed to disaster."[36]

In private, Truman called the speech "a hundred percent bullshit."[37] Mac-Arthur toured the country giving speeches and even gathering steam for a presidential run. Congress held hearings designed in part to give MacArthur a stage from which to criticize the Truman administration's policy of limited war. While Mac-Arthur gave impressive testimony, the hearings turned into a long, drawn-out affair that worked to the advantage of the Truman administration. As official after official testified at the hearings, the public gradually came to recognize that the military hierarchy, including Secretary of Defense George Marshall and Chairman of the Joint Chiefs of Staff Omar Bradley, respected WWII heroes in their own right, unanimously opposed MacArthur and supported Truman's policy.

The debate began to shift with the testimony of all the military officials who presented a unified chorus singing the virtues of limited war. The argument was ultimately settled when General Bradley uttered the famous phrase that engaging in an all-out war with Chinese forces on the Asian mainland would be "the wrong war, at the wrong place, at the wrong time and with the wrong enemy."[38] It also helped to mollify congressional critics when administration officials, while giving their testimony, tilted toward a closer relationship with Chiang on the island of Formosa.

Divisions Over Principles and Strategies: The Great Debate

Those congressional hearings actually signaled the final salvo in what is called the Great Debate, which occurred along the old isolationist vs. internationalist fault lines. Beginning in the fall of 1950 and lasting until the spring of 1951, the Great Debate had two key components: the role of Congress in making U.S. foreign policy and the extent of U.S. commitments overseas. We begin with the first component of the Great Debate.

Throughout U.S. history, there has been tension between the executive and legislative branches over making and conducting foreign policy. Congress has the constitutional authority and duty to declare war and also to pass laws funding the military. Prior to Korea, presidents rarely committed troops to such dangerous, far-flung operations without a declaration of war or some other kind of congressional authorization. However, Truman tended to make decisions regarding foreign policy without consulting, or even informing, Congress. When Truman committed American ground troops to fight in Korea, he probably overstepped his constitutional authority because he did not obtain a formal congressional declaration of war or even a milder authorization in the form of a congressional resolution supporting his actions *ex post facto*. Instead Truman referred to the conflict in Korea as a "police action" and not as a war. As a police action, Truman did not have to bother with the nuisance of first obtaining congressional approval.[39] But, to be sure, this was a war by any stretch of the imagination. The United States alone lost nearly 34,000, while Korean and Chinese losses were staggering: as many as four million Koreans (from both sides, including civilians) were killed and an estimated 360,000 Chinese were killed with hundreds of thousands more wounded.[40]

If referring to Korea as a police action gave Truman more freedom to maneuver vis-a-vis Congress, he paid for it in other ways. After China's dramatic entry turned the tide against the UNC, the war became increasingly unpopular and Truman's approval ratings plummeted. By early spring, 1951, as the war ground to a stalemate with mounting casualties on both sides, Senator Taft began calling it Truman's War to underscore the fact that Korea was Truman's wholly owned policy blunder, that Congress was excluded, and that Truman deserved the blame for this terrible slugfest. Taft complained that Truman had violated the Constitution by unilaterally committing the United States to battle without getting congressional authorization. Such attacks on Truman contributed to his widespread unpopularity. While a July 1950 poll found 77 percent of the public approved of Truman's decision to commit ground troops the month before, by March 1952 Truman's approval rating plunged to less than 30 percent, making him one of the least popular presidents since WWII.[41]

But Truman's actions in Korea were not all that raised Congress's ire during the Great Debate. On December 19, 1950, Truman announced that more U.S. troops would be sent to Western Europe to shore up NATO's defenses. Members of Congress, especially Truman's Republican critics who had no love for Europe in the first place, questioned Truman's authority to unilaterally order a massive overseas troop buildup. Congressional resolutions were introduced attempting to curtail the president's ability to commit troops overseas.

The Republicans' quarrel with Truman's decision to increase troop deployments in Europe dovetailed with the second component of the Great Debate, namely the extent to which the United States should make overseas commitments. Bolstered by their electoral gains in November 1950, Republicans increased their attacks on Truman and Acheson.[42] Shortly after his reelection, a defiant Taft openly questioned the U.S. commitment to Europe when he opined, "Is Europe our first line of defense? Is it defensible at all?"[43] Then, the day after Truman announced more troops for Western Europe, former President Herbert Hoover, who had earlier questioned the wisdom of America's ever-expanding overseas commitments, gave his famous "Gibraltar" speech, in which he called on the United States to withdraw into a defensive fortress-like shell. Hoover opposed the growing U.S. commitments in both Europe and Asia. Even some Democrats, like Joseph P. Kennedy, former U.S. ambassador to Britain and father of the future president, questioned the wisdom, and cost, of trying to contain communism anywhere it might pop up.

Truman and his allies in the foreign policy elite derided these born-again isolationists. Acheson ridiculed them and compared them to the dull-witted farmer who yanks his crops up every morning to see how well they had grown the night before.[44] Truman's former Secretary of War Robert Patterson called Hoover's words "the counsel of discouragement, despair, and defeat."[45] Even some Republicans from the party's more moderate, eastern wing questioned the wisdom of their peers in the Great Debate. New York Gov. Thomas Dewey, who had lost to Truman in 1948, condemned Hoover's "Gibraltar" speech, saying it amounted to national suicide that would make us "the loneliest people on earth."[46] And Senator Taft's own father, former President and Supreme Court Chief Justice William Howard Taft, contradicted his son's reservations about defending Europe.[47]

In the end, Truman and Acheson came out of the Great Debate battered but intact. First, Congress's attempt to pass legislation curtailing executive war powers won only limited support. All that could be mustered was a watered-down Senate resolution, passed on April 4, 1951, approving the new troop deployments but also calling on the president to consult with Congress before sending any more troops overseas. Such resolutions are unimpressive challenges to the president since they express only the sense of the Senate and carry no actual force of law. Second, the Great Debate, whose urgency was hastened by the Chinese onslaught in Korea, was losing steam as the issue was, yet again, decided on the battlefield. By early spring 1951 Ridgway's forces, having recovered from the initial shock of China's entry, were now making new progress on the ground, beating back several furious Chinese offensives.

Nevertheless, the seemingly endless war and deadlocked peace talks hurt Truman's popularity.[48] Truman acknowledged his unpopularity when he declined to run for reelection. So the Democrats fielded Adlai Stevenson as Truman's would-be successor. The Republicans painted Stevenson as soft on communism, calling him "Adlai the appeaser." In fact, Stevenson had firm anti-communist credentials, but that mattered little since no one from the Democratic Party would have been able to beat the Republicans' standard-bearer, WWII Gen. Dwight D. Eisenhower. A poll taken two months before the 1952 presidential election showed 67 percent of voters believing that Eisenhower could handle the Korean problem better than Stevenson with only nine percent thinking the opposite.[49] The Democrats might have had a chance against Senator Taft, who initially appeared to be the Republicans' choice. But Eisenhower, who was serving as NATO Commander, opposed Taft's isolationist tendencies. He returned from Europe to run for president because he did not want Taft to win the White House and then pull the United States out of NATO and Europe. Although the Korean War played a small role in the election, Eisenhower issued a campaign promise to "go to Korea." He did not specify what he would do or what his policy was, but his immense popularity was enough for most voters. Plus, he had the distinct advantage of not being Truman.

After his victory, and before he was sworn in, Eisenhower did in fact go to Korea. But the policies he adopted once he was inaugurated differed from Truman's only in degree and not in kind. There was considerable continuity, in policy and personnel, between the two administrations.[50] With the help of some Democrats in Congress, Eisenhower was able to push back the Taft isolationists in the Republican Party.[51] Unlike previous Republican presidents, Eisenhower made clear from Inauguration Day that there would be no shirking of international responsibilities and commitments.[52] Like Truman, Eisenhower was no isolationist. Like Truman, Eisenhower adopted a policy seeking a diplomatic solution based on restoring the original border at the 38th parallel. And also like Truman, Eisenhower would not give in to China on certain negotiating points including voluntary prisoner exchange, China's demand for a seat at the United Nations, and China's desire to reincorporate Formosa under its rule.

The major difference between the two administrations is that Eisenhower, and his hawkish Secretary of State John Foster Dulles, were more willing to consider the use of nuclear weapons to break the stalemate. Because of his popularity, Eisenhower was less susceptible to pressure from Congress, thus giving him more freedom than Truman to try different approaches.[53] Although Truman also considered using nuclear weapons in Korea, Eisenhower and Dulles were much more willing to break the taboo surrounding nuclear weapons when they engaged in diplomatic brinkmanship in which they gave the impression that they would risk military escalation rather than concede points at the bargaining table.[54] And diplomatic brinkmanship was backed by a nuclear weapons policy called massive retaliation. Even if the Soviets attacked using only conventional weapons, the United States threatened to retaliate using the full complement of its nuclear arsenal.

Eisenhower and Dulles had popular support for this more aggressive approach: a March 1953 poll revealed 56 percent of Americans willing to employ tactical nuclear weapons if the truce talks once again broke down, while only 23 percent opposed.[55] By May, the JCS unanimously recommended using nuclear weapons against China as well as North Korea if the talks failed. Eisenhower also continued the stepped-up bombing of North Korean targets, which Truman ordered during his last weeks in office out of frustration with the stalled talks. Eisenhower also ordered the Seventh Fleet away from Formosa, thus implying that Chiang might attack China from Formosa. This forced China to redirect some of its forces toward Formosa. Ironically, all this signaled an expansion of the war, just as MacArthur had been arguing.

By spring 1953, after further Chinese offensives had ground to a halt, the parties finally reached agreement. A ceasefire could have been reached more than a year earlier except for disagreement on a single issue, prisoner exchanges. Both Truman and Eisenhower insisted that Chinese and North Korean prisoners of war (POWs) would not be forcibly returned if they did not want to be. This was unacceptable to the communists because it would amount to a huge propaganda defeat for them. But agreement on this issue was finally reached when the communists conceded to most of the American demands regarding POWs, so long as remaining disputes were settled by a third party. Eisenhower hailed the truce, declaring that "the collective resolve of the free world can and will meet aggression" anywhere.[56]

Many observers insist that Eisenhower's open willingness to use atomic weapons is what succeeded in bringing the communists back to the negotiating table. However, the historical record casts doubt on that assertion. Rather, it appears that Stalin's death in March 1953, together with an exhausted China and North Korea, were the key factors behind moderating the communists' position.[57]

AFTERMATH: THE KOREAN WAR AS A TURNING POINT

How was the Korean War a turning point in U.S. foreign policy? From a long-term historical perspective, the Korean War coincides with a period that is characterized by an active, extroverted U.S. foreign policy that began around the time of Japan's attack on Pearl Harbor (see chapter 3). While part of that active, even interventionist phase of U.S. foreign policy, it is a turning point because it led to significant reversals and other shifts in U.S. foreign policy.

First, at the regional level, recall that Korea was not considered a strategic prize by either policy planners in the State Department or military strategists in the Defense Department. With the outbreak of hostilities, however, the United States quickly decided to intervene with its own combat troops, thus committing itself to the indefinite military defense of South Korea. Indeed, to this day, the United States has a bilateral security alliance with South Korea. By 1980 the United States had provided $6 billion in non-military aid to South Korea.[58] Today, South Korea is an economic dynamo with a budding democratic tradition whereas North Korea remains a closed country that suffers from periodic famines. Tens of thousands of U.S. troops are stationed along the demilitarized zone that separates North and South Korea. This tense border region remains the last bastion of the Cold War conflict. During the Clinton administration, serious consideration was given to launching air strikes against North Korea's suspected nuclear weapons facilities. But the two countries reached an agreement that precluded an attack. However, North Korea broke that agreement and now openly proclaims it possesses nuclear weapons. The stakes on the Korean peninsula are now higher than ever as the Obama administration struggles to find a way to confront the newest addition to the nuclear weapons club, even as North and South Korea have engaged in bloody skirmishes along their border.

Second, recall that U.S. policy toward Chiang Kai Shek and the Nationalist Chinese on Formosa was to keep Chiang at arms length since China was expected to quickly reassert its sovereignty over the wayward island. But the war prompted the United States to inject itself between mainland China and Formosa, thus preventing China from reacquiring Formosa. At the MacArthur hearings in Congress, Secretary of Defense Marshall proclaimed that Formosa must never be allowed to fall to communist control. The result was decades of bitter relations and recriminations between China and the United States. As with South Korea, the United States signed a security alliance with Taiwan (the new name for Formosa) and helped arm Taiwan with billions of dollars worth of state-of-the-art weapons. Taiwan still has not been reincorporated into China and has instead grown into a wealthy, modern country that is independent in all but name only. Taiwan, which also has a budding democratic tradition, thus remains an island unto itself and is on the verge of officially declaring its independence. China has repeatedly threatened to use military force against Taiwan if Taiwan does that.

Third, the Korean War prompted a policy reversal regarding Indochina, in particular Vietnam. With the domino-theory mentality gaining ground since 1950, the United States changed its policy regarding giving aid to the French colonialists in Vietnam. Before Korea, Acheson agreed to only modest financial help for the French, but less than a year after the Korean War ended, the United States was underwriting about 80 percent of France's war in Indochina.[59] Soon thereafter, the first American military personnel were sent to Vietnam thus embroiling the United States in Indochina for two decades (see chapter 7).

Related to this, the Korean War also brought Japan and the United States closer when Tokyo and Washington signed a Mutual Defense Treaty in 1951. The treaty ensured U.S. influence in Japan for years to come. Thousands of U.S. military troops were stationed throughout Japan as the United States extended its strategic umbrella over the island country.

On the global level, the Korean War prompted a policy reversal regarding military expenditures. Truman's first Secretary of Defense, Louis Johnson, was appointed in large part to oversee cuts in defense expenditures. However, shortly before the war, a controversial joint State-Defense Department report called NSC-68 used stark language in recommending significant increases in the military budget. State officials Kennan and Bohlen had reservations about massive defense expenditures.[60] But North Korea's attack vindicated NSC-68: in September 1950, Truman formally signed NSC-68 as the new U.S. policy, which committed the United States to spending one-fifth of its GNP on the military to wage global war.[61] U.S. armed forces increased from 1.5 million to 3.5 million, air forces were rapidly increased and modernized, and new airfields were constructed in the Middle East and North Africa. Military expenditures quadrupled immediately after Korea and, over the next twenty years, NSC-68 became the "field manual" for waging the Cold War.[62]

Aside from these policy reversals, the Korean War was a turning point for other reasons as well. For instance, the War led to the increased militarization of U.S. foreign policy whereby global challenges facing the United States were seen as soluble by the application of military force. Not only did the United States use force in Korea and Vietnam, but Korea confirmed for the U.S. foreign policy elite the need to intervene militarily to fight communism around the world. U.S. troops (or their proxies) were deployed in 1958 in Lebanon under Eisenhower, in 1961 in Cuba during the Bay of Pigs fiasco under President Kennedy, and in 1965 in the Dominican Republic under President Lyndon Baines Johnson (LBJ).

Korea also prompted the United States to either create or significantly strengthen a series of collective security alliances that, taken together, amounted to a set of global commitments designed to forcefully confront and contain communism around the world. For instance, in Europe, Korea prompted the rapid fortification of NATO, making it a true "working alliance."[63] The United States quickly built more strategic air bases in Europe and bolstered its troop deployments there. Greece and Turkey joined the alliance in 1952, and Acheson changed his mind and now favored rearming West Germany. Moreover, the United States concluded a series of multilateral collective security treaties that effectively tied the United States to many other countries around the world. For instance, the ANZUS alliance includes Australia, New Zealand, and the United States. And the original members of the 1954 Southeast Asia Treaty Organization (SEATO) included not only the United States, Australia, and New Zealand, but also France, the United Kingdom, Pakistan, the Philippines, and Thailand.

Finally, on the domestic level, the Korean War strengthened the power of the executive branch over the legislative branch, especially in times of war or international crises. Despite Congress's complaints, Truman's unilateral decisions intensified the trend toward establishing the supremacy of the executive in foreign policy making. It also confirmed the supremacy of civilian control over the military. Even though Truman was reluctant to fire General MacArthur unless he had the support of the entire Joint Chiefs of Staff, and even though MacArthur was overwhelmingly popular in Congress and among the public at large, Truman's decision to relieve the general was necessary to preserve the constitutional prerogatives of the civilian commander-in-chief.

Five

THE SPUTNIK CRISIS AND
THE NUCLEAR AGE

On October 4, 1957, the Soviet Union launched a 184-pound sphere called Sputnik into orbit around the earth. By the standards of today's satellite technology, Sputnik was the epitome of primitive; its sole capability was the transmission of a continuous "beep-beep" picked up by certain airwave frequencies on earth. Nonetheless, the launch of Sputnik was greeted with both awe and fear in the United States. *Time* magazine captured the public mood with an editorial titled "Red Moon Over the U.S.," referring to the "chilling beeps" of the Soviet satellite.[1] Sputnik inspired a period of national soul searching in the United States as a public debate ensued regarding the relative strengths of Soviet and American scientific and technological capabilities. For the Soviet Union, Sputnik was undoubtedly one of the great propaganda coups of the Cold War, but to many American observers, it was also a serious portent of the future of the strategic military balance between the rival superpowers. Sputnik provided dramatic evidence of the Soviet Union's ability to successfully construct and launch an ICBM, the delivery system of the future for nuclear weapons and capable of reaching targets inside the United States from launch sites in Russia.

The launch of Sputnik led to a multiplicity of concerns in the United States. The Soviet Union's stunning achievement "created a crisis in confidence for the American people."[2] Critics blamed the Eisenhower administration for falling asleep at the wheel and allowing the Soviets to get a head start in the race for control of space, while at the same time opening a technology gap and, most alarmingly, a

missile gap, over the United States. The Soviet satellite appeared to signal a serious setback for the United States in the Cold War struggle and led to widespread
calls for a dramatic American response. While there was considerable political and
public pressure for a demonstrable American reaction, President Dwight Eisenhower had reason to doubt the worst projections of his alarmist critics and was also
constrained to act by his fiscal conservatism. He encountered significant resistance
to his efforts to downplay Sputnik, however, and eventually he was compelled to
take action beyond the limits of what he thought was necessary. The Sputnik crisis
and the political debate it spawned would have lasting consequences for the United
States in the fields of education, science, space exploration, strategic defense, and
military spending. The missile age had begun and American foreign policy had to
adjust accordingly.

This chapter opens with an examination of the major developments in U.S.
foreign policy during the first term of Eisenhower's presidency, with a particular
focus on the increasing importance of nuclear weapons and missile technology in
the Cold War. The next section addresses the impact of the 1957 Sputnik launch
and the debates and divisions it inspired both in Washington, D.C., and the country at large. Of particular importance here is the debate over whether or not Sputnik served as evidence that the Soviet Union had opened a lead over the United
States in missile development and over Eisenhower's resistance to calls for a sweeping American response. After outlining the American response to Sputnik, the final
section will examine the long- and short-term implications of this dramatic turning
point in the history of U.S. foreign policy.

THE NUCLEAR AGE

In the 1952 presidential election, Republican Dwight D. Eisenhower won a resounding victory over his Democratic challenger Adlai Stevenson. For many Americans, Eisenhower, the victorious commander of Allied armies in Western Europe
during WWII, was the perfect man to lead the United States out of the morass of
the Korean War and through the fog of crisis that had enveloped the country since
1949. As was discussed in chapter 4, the American public had been hit with a series
of shocks that appeared to constitute direct threats to the country's security and that
gave the Cold War the potential to become hot at any moment. The 1940s ended
with the double blow of the "loss of China" to communism and the successful
Soviet testing of an atomic bomb, both of which in turn contributed to the national

paranoia of McCarthyism. The 1950s began with the deployment of American forces in the Korean conflict amid fears that the communist monolith was on the move. President Harry Truman bore the brunt of public anxiety and his approval ratings plummeted below 30 percent during his last months in office, a trend that proved to be a major disadvantage to his fellow Democrat Stevenson.

When Eisenhower succeeded in establishing a ceasefire in Korea, he defused a conflict that at one point threatened to snowball into a much larger war. Recall that one of the keys to the success of Eisenhower's disengagement from Korea was the use of brinkmanship against the Chinese. The veiled threat to employ nuclear weapons against China was an early taste of the New Look defense policy of the Eisenhower administration. Eisenhower was appalled by the massive increases in military spending during the Truman administration and he vowed to remove this albatross from around the United States' neck by cutting conventional forces and placing greater emphasis on nuclear weapons. As Secretary of State John Foster Dulles noted, the United States would rely on the threat of massive retaliation rather than conventional warfare to tackle the threat of communism. The goal was to give the United States greater diplomatic leverage with the Soviet Union while at the same time reducing the burden of military spending on the American treasury. In the now famous phrase of Secretary of Defense Charles E. Wilson, the New Look offered the American taxpayer "more bang for your buck."

The New Look enabled Eisenhower to bring fiscal constraint to American defense spending and the successful use of brinkmanship in Korea appeared to offer a recipe for diplomatic leverage in future crises. At the same time, however, a Soviet counter initiative matched the growing reliance by the United States on nuclear weapons and the nuclear arms race gathered increasing momentum as the decade wore on. Thus when the United States tested its first hydrogen bomb in 1954, obliterating Bikini Atoll in the South Pacific with a bomb hundreds of times more powerful than the ones used against Japan to end WWII, it took the Soviet Union only a matter of months to match the feat with its own successful H-Bomb test. Even though these tests made abundantly clear the massive destructive power of thermonuclear bombs and the catastrophic consequences that would result from World War III, the belief prevailed in both Moscow and Washington that such weapons must be good for something and nuclear weapons development increasingly took on its own peculiar logic.[3] Soon after entering office, President Eisenhower placed a priority on developing missile technology and long-range delivery systems for nuclear weapons as an alternative to the dependence on strategic air power. The Soviets too began to move away from more conventional delivery systems for their nuclear arsenal and gave increasing priority to the development of missile technology. In the 1950s, nuclear firepower became the primary yardstick for measuring power in the Cold War struggle between the United States and the Soviet Union. It was an area of competition, however, that for reasons of national security was shrouded in secrecy. Each side, therefore, depended heavily on projections and estimates of their enemy's future capabilities to make key decisions about weapons production.

In 1955, Eisenhower approved of the development of an American satellite program called Vanguard but made a conscious decision to separate the new project from the U.S. military missile program. The goal was to have the launch of Vanguard coincide with the end of the International Geophysical Year in 1958, a twelve-month cooperative venture between scientists from both sides of the Cold War divide. The administration hoped that by separating Vanguard from the development of ICBMs and IRBMs (intermediate range ballistic missiles), the United States could establish the principal that "outer space was international space" and not another venue for Soviet-American competition.[4] The Eisenhower administration offered the public position that by demilitarizing space it was opening a venue for peaceful scientific purposes. Such public declarations, however, masked some hidden motives. Work on Vanguard began in 1956, the same year that the United States dispatched the first U-2 spy planes on intelligence-gathering missions over the Soviet Union. Eisenhower recognized the provocative nature of these flights and was anxious to find other, less volatile means to gather intelligence. The American president hoped that Vanguard would establish the principle of "Open Skies" in space and allow for unobtrusive intelligence gathering through satellite technology.

At the 1955 Geneva Summit with Soviet leader Nikita Khrushchev, Eisenhower had proposed to the Soviet Union an Open Skies initiative that would allow the Soviets and Americans to openly engage in aerial reconnaissance of each other's defenses. The summit was the first meeting between Soviet and American leaders since WWII and signaled a possible thaw in relations between the Cold War enemies, facilitated by Stalin's death in 1953 and the hint of reform in the Soviet Union that came with Khrushchev's accession to power. Both the American and Soviet leaders came to Geneva unsettled by the prospect of nuclear war and Eisenhower saw in Open Skies a more reliable means toward arms control than the proposal then being floated for ground inspections. Khrushchev interpreted Eisenhower's proposal as a propaganda ploy and a mask for American intelligence gathering and so, not surprisingly, he rejected the plan. In many respects Khrushchev was correct. The Soviets had better intelligence on American nuclear installations and so Open Skies would have proven particularly advantageous to the United States. In light of the Soviet Union's rejection of the plan, Vanguard and the principle of Open Skies in space took on greater significance for Eisenhower.

Vanguard, however, always took a back seat to the development of military missiles and was a victim of the competition, exasperated by Eisenhower's general emphasis on fiscal conservatism, for funding between various missile programs. The very decision to place Vanguard under the control of the U.S. Navy drew resentment from the Army and Air Force, highlighting the stiff, and often bitter, competition among the military branches for funding for lucrative missile projects. Given the United States' ability to place missiles in Europe, the Eisenhower administration gave priority to developing IRBMs over ICBMs. Thus, IRBM projects such as the Air Force's Thor, the Army's Jupiter, and the Navy's Polaris missiles took priority over Vanguard. Approval was also given to each branch of the military to work simultaneously on ICBM projects, thus leading to even greater budgetary pressure. By 1957 Eisenhower became concerned that redundancy in missile production engendered by inter-service rivalry was straining the $38 billion military spending budget ceiling he had imposed, and in the months before Sputnik he pressed the Defense Department to scale back some of these expensive programs. The development of nuclear weapons and the means to deliver them nonetheless remained a priority for the Eisenhower administration.

The Geneva Summit had briefly provided a window of opportunity for detente in Soviet-American relations. At Geneva, the Soviets did agree to finally sign a WWII peace treaty with Austria and assent to the central European nation's neutralization and both sides put out feelers for strategies to end the arms race. However, the Soviets refused to give ground on the issues of German unification and reform in Eastern Europe. Within a year of the Geneva meeting, the well of Soviet-American relations was poisoned once again. With the United States preoccupied with containing the fallout from the Suez Crisis, involving a joint British-French-Israeli military expedition in response to Egypt's decision to nationalize the Suez Canal, the Soviet Union in the fall of 1956 sent tanks into Budapest to crush Hungary's effort to withdraw from the Warsaw Pact. While the Eisenhower administration was justifiably horrified by the repression of Hungary's uprising, the United States too had been busy securing friendly governments in regions deemed vital to American interests with CIA-led coups toppling left-leaning governments in Iran and Guatemala in 1953 and 1954 respectively. Meanwhile, French withdrawal from Indochina in 1954 left the embers of another conflict in the global struggle between capitalism and communism smoking dangerously (see chapter 7). Given this volatile global climate, deterrence and not detente took precedence in U.S.-Soviet relations and nuclear weapons were central to each superpower's strategy in this regard. The logic of continuing the arms race was given further impetus by the fact that the Soviet Union found in missile production one of the few ways it could successfully compete with the United States.

THE POLITICS OF SPUTNIK

The launch of Sputnik in October 1957 proved to be the final nail in the coffin of the early attempts at detente and reversed any momentum toward arms reduction that had been generated at Geneva in 1955. Public reaction in the United States was at first somewhat muted, but interest in the consequences of Sputnik increased as the enormity of the Soviet achievement became clear. While regional daily newspapers in the United States the day after Sputnik gave priority to the opening of the World Series and the school integration crisis in Little Rock, by week's end magazines such as *Time* and *Newsweek* bleakly trumpeted "man's greatest achievement since the atomic bomb."[5] Soon editorialists nationwide were lamenting that the Soviets had gained an upper hand over the United States in the field of technological and scientific development and fear mounted among observers that the Soviet Union was ahead in the race to build an ICBM. Reaction in official circles was more measured but "the press assumed that Sputnik meant Soviet superiority, and the press pushed the panic button."[6]

The scale of the public reaction to Sputnik proved a political bonanza for the Democratic Party. Democratic efforts to unseat Eisenhower in the 1956 presidential election had been easily pushed aside and so the Democrats were anxious to seize upon something to help them in the mid-term elections of 1958 and the presidential election of 1960. Thus while the Eisenhower administration sought to play down Sputnik by insisting that the United States was never in a space race with the Soviets, Sen. Henry M. Jackson (D-WA) called Sputnik "a devastating blow to the prestige of the United States."[7] Partisanship was certainly a factor in sounding the alarm bell, but the sense of crisis created by the Soviet satellite extended far beyond the realm of party politics. The perception of Sputnik as a shocking setback for the United States in the Cold War struggle was quite pervasive. Nuclear physicist Edward Teller told a television audience that the United States had lost "a battle more important . . . than Pearl Harbor," and *The Reporter* magazine echoed this theme by claiming that Sputnik "is to Pearl Harbor what Pearl Harbor was to the sinking of the *Maine*."[8] Historian John Lewis Gaddis continues, "as a revelation of an unexpected threat, the shock of Sputnik rivaled only that of Pearl Harbor and Korea."[9]

In the aftermath of Sputnik, Eisenhower's approval ratings began to drop for the first time since entering the White House in 1953. According to polls conducted by Gallup, Eisenhower's approval ratings dropped twenty-two points from 79 percent in January 1957 to 57 percent by November.[10] Critics charged the Eisenhower administration with having placed budgetary restraint ahead of the country's defense needs and thus failing to remain ahead of the Soviet Union in the race to build an ICBM. Sputnik's success appeared for the first time to put the United States within range of Soviet missiles and thus vulnerable to a Soviet nuclear strike. If the Soviets were to launch an ICBM at the United States the warning time would only be thirty minutes and, while the Eisenhower administration had done a great deal to strengthen the U.S. Strategic Air Command (SAC), there was no defense against a ballistic missile strike. The perception that the United States had been caught off guard was compounded by official intelligence estimates on the eve of Sputnik that the Soviets were three to four years away from developing an ICBM. The appearance of an intelligence breakdown would make it very difficult for Eisenhower to assuage fears that Sputnik signaled the opening of a Soviet missile gap over the United States.

Another concern of Eisenhower's critics was the ideological victory Sputnik represented for the Soviets. The Soviet satellite added weight to Khrushchev's boasts about the achievements of communism and confrontational assertions such as his infamous "We will bury you" statement, made to Western journalists in Moscow just a month after Sputnik. Not content to just score symbolic points from Sputnik, Khrushchev also sought to extract political and strategic advantage from the satellite's launch. The appearance of Soviet missile superiority that Sputnik helped to create was a critical factor in Khrushchev's decision in the fall of 1958 to increase pressure on the West to abandon West Berlin. Khrushchev's efforts "to extract political advantages from the demonstration of long-range missile capability that [Sputnik] provided" exasperated the missile gap crisis in the United States and placed significant pressure on the Eisenhower administration to match the Soviet achievement.[11]

While the Soviets basked in the success of Sputnik, many Americans feared that this apparent setback for the United States exposed deep flaws in their society. A poll conducted in the wake of Sputnik found that 67 percent of respondents held the view that the American people "have been too smug and complacent about our national strength," while 69 percent believed "our schools have put too little stress on science."[12] Former Rep. Clare Boothe Luce (R-CT) contended that Sputnik exposed "a decade of American pretensions that the American way of life was a gilt-edged guarantee of our national superiority," while a *New York Times* editorial reproached the American people for having become "too self-satisfied, complacent, and luxury loving."[13] In addition to the controversy over the missile gap, Sputnik prompted widespread calls for educational reform, defense reorganization, and a reinvigoration of American commitment to prove the Western way of life superior to communism. Sputnik wounded America's national pride and damaged much of the self-confidence that Eisenhower had helped to restore to the American people since the Korean War. Pressure now mounted on the president to restore that self-confidence.

Eisenhower was determined to remain calm in the face of the tempest created by Sputnik. During a press conference on October 9, the president downplayed the significance of the Soviet satellite and the notion that America was losing the technology race. However, what Eisenhower had hoped would be a reassuring demeanor was interpreted by many critics as a sign that the president was out of touch and not fully cognizant of the far-reaching implications of Sputnik. The White House recognized that public relations were a critical aspect of the Sputnik crisis; the challenge was in crafting a message that could convey what the president knew about relative American and Soviet strength without appearing complacent in the face of what many Americans perceived as a serious threat to American security and prestige. Eisenhower fully understood the military implications of Sputnik and his desire to downplay its significance would be vindicated in the long run. U-2 reconnaissance flights provided sufficient intelligence on Soviet installations to counteract mounting claims by the president's critics of the existence of a missile gap. Meanwhile, Eisenhower's confidence in American strategic air defenses as a deterrent to Soviet aggression and in the progress of U.S. ballistic missile and satellite programs was well placed. However, Eisenhower failed to fully grasp the depth of public anxiety in the wake of Sputnik, seriously undermining his ability to effectively communicate on the issue. As a consequence of "insufficient understanding" of American fears in the wake of Sputnik, the president "responded in ways that made them grow."[14]

Eisenhower's efforts to reassure the American people were dealt a further blow by the launch of Sputnik II in November 1957. Larger than its predecessor and with a thrust of 500,000 pounds, Sputnik II added significantly to the perception of advanced Soviet ICBM capability. Sen. Stuart Symington (D-MO) contrasted the Soviet Union's apparent ability to launch an ICBM with projections that the United States was still two years away from matching this feat.[15] Such projections added weight to the growing chorus of critics who called for bold initiatives from the White House and to those who had contended from the beginning that the New Look did not provide sufficiently for U.S. defense.[16]

The American Response

Eisenhower responded to this crisis in confidence in his presidency with a series of "chin-up" speeches addressing the American people directly on television, the new broadcast medium of the day. In his first address on November 7, the president pledged to the American public that he was on top of the situation. Such vague reassurances, however, did little to counteract claims by the missile gap exponents that within three years the Soviets would have a stockpile of 3,000 ICBMs. In his memoirs, Eisenhower reminisced that such assertions (and the missile gap in general) were "nothing more than imaginative creations of irresponsibility."[17] As noted above, Eisenhower's confidence was based on solid intelligence. However, he was reluctant to share this intelligence for fear of compromising the U-2 as a reconnaissance tool. Furthermore, even though the Kremlin was well aware that such flights were taking place, going public with this information would embarrass the Soviets and might spark a major international incident. As a military man, Eisenhower felt confident in his own judgment about security and defense and he took exception to press suggestions that his reluctance to act in accordance with his critics' suggestions was motivated by partisanship. This explains why "Eisenhower's reassurances, until very late in the game, were general and personal, not detailed and comprehensive."[18]

Eisenhower's second "chin-up" speech focused on the issue of science and society. This was an area where he readily admitted a lack of expertise and was willing to defer to experts, particularly in the area of space, which, in his mind, was the arena where Sputnik had the greatest impact. Eisenhower appointed MIT President James Killian chair of the President's Science Advisory Committee where Killian would act as the conduit between the president and the scientific community. Thus, Killian a played an important role in shaping the White House response to Sputnik. In his address to the nation on science and society, Eisenhower conceded that Sputnik highlighted deficiencies in American science and education and promised to remedy the situation. However, as with defense, he eschewed a hasty, and potentially wasteful, response in favor of more gradual long-term change.

Pressure on the White House continued to mount, however, as Senate hearings on Sputnik opened on November 27, 1957, chaired by Majority Leader Lyndon Baines Johnson (D-TX). The hearings opened a new phase in the "post Sputnik hysteria."[19] Democrats smelled blood and Eisenhower's fiercest critics, who had long believed that his emphasis on balancing the budget endangered national security, were determined to take advantage of the momentum that Sputnik created. The news for the White House went from bad to worse as an attempted launch of Vanguard in December ended in a very public failure as the missile burst into flames after rising just four feet off the launching pad. The signing of the Paris Agreements whereby the United States' NATO allies agreed to the deployment of IRBMs in Europe failed to deflect from the public humiliation of the Vanguard failure, particularly as the first U.S. IRBMs were not set to become operational until 1958. In contrast to Eisenhower's flagging fortunes, Khrushchev ended 1957 on the cover of *Time* magazine, named Man of Year for his achievement in leading the Soviet Union into space. Noted political scientist Hans J. Morgenthau added his voice to the chorus of gloom in the United States, characterizing Sputnik as a "national failure," and predicting that it could mark the beginning of the United States' decline as a world power.[20]

Such dire forecasts received new stimulus in December 1957 when portions of the government-commissioned Gaither Report were leaked to the press. Coming as it did, hot on the heels of Sputnik, the Gaither Report was an aftershock possibly more intense than the original quake. The Gaither Committee had been established in the spring of 1957 by the Eisenhower administration to investigate issues pertaining to civil defense and the need for fallout shelters. Instead, the committee focused its attention on the issue of deterrence as the surest defense against nuclear attack. The committee's final report, much of which was written by Paul Nitze, author of NSC-68 (see chapter 4) and former head of the State Department's Policy Planning Staff in the Truman administration, stressed the vulnerability of SAC and U.S. nuclear defenses and called for marked increases in U.S. defense spending. Portions of the report were leaked to Chalmers Roberts at the *Washington Post*, whose alarmist interpretation of the committee's conclusions contributed to a heightened sense of alert in the public mind.[21] The Gaither Report created a political storm and led to widespread calls for increased military spending on Capitol Hill. The report highlighted that, with a GNP only a third the size of the United States', the Soviet Union was nonetheless matching the United States in heavy industry and defense spending. Future trends appeared to favor the Soviet Union in both areas. The report offered specific recommendations for increases in American missile capability by speeding up the production of ICBMs and the timetable for deploying IRBMs in Europe, for protecting defenses by dispersing strategic air bases and reinforcing missile launch sites, and for civil defense by constructing fallout shelters. The cost to the American taxpayer was estimated at $44 billion over five years. The Gaither Report bore a marked similarity to the National Security Council's 1949 NSC-68 report, both in terms of the massive spending increases it entailed and the atmosphere of crisis in which it was issued.[22]

The economic austerity component of Eisenhower's New Look policy, which was constructed on the logic of turning back the soaring defense spending of the United States that had been set in motion by NSC-68, came under increasing pressure after the release of the Gaither Report. Momentum for defense spending was given a further boost with the publication of the results of a private study by the Rockefeller Brothers Fund that echoed the findings of the Gaither Committee. These reports added significant momentum to the efforts of the Democratic opposition and leaders in all three branches of the military to pressure the White House into revising its defense spending priorities. Eisenhower, however, was relatively unimpressed with the Gaither Report and, unlike many of his critics, he refused to draw a connection between Sputnik and the committee's findings.

Eisenhower had long separated the issue of space rockets on the one hand and ballistic missiles intended for war on the other, and he was confident that his administration was already doing all that was necessary in both areas before Sputnik. As far as Eisenhower was concerned, neither Gaither nor Sputnik was relevant to the "real problem of strategic deterrence."[23] In his mind deterrence was a matter of judgment and not an issue of projections, whether based on perceptions of Soviet capability provided by Sputnik or the statistics compiled by the Gaither Committee. Eisenhower remained confident that as long as the United States had sufficient power to deter a Soviet attack, there was no justification to increase weapons spending just to keep pace with the Soviets. Instead of matching the Soviets in every field, the United States should concentrate on its strengths and measure them against Soviet weaknesses. In this way the United States could reap both strategic and economic benefits. To overspend unnecessarily, Eisenhower feared, might undermine the United States' ability to afford those programs that were truly essential to secure the nation's defenses.

The year 1958 began with the White House on the defensive as Democrats prepared an aggressive attack on the president's policies on space and defense with the opening of what the press dubbed "the Sputnik Congress." Just two days before Eisenhower was due to deliver his State of the Union Address to Congress, Lyndon Johnson gave a major speech on the issue of space. Johnson, who had an eye on the 1960 presidential campaign, gained considerable publicity on the issue of space through his Senate hearings on Sputnik, which continued to ensure that the issue remained very much in the news. A parade of witnesses echoed the committee chairman's dire warnings about the implications of Sputnik, including high-ranking army officers who took issue with the spending priorities of the Eisenhower administration. In his January speech, Johnson contended that Soviet control of space represented a much greater threat to American security than any "ultimate weapon" they might develop.[24] Johnson's speech implied that space was the next great arena for Soviet and American competition, something the Eisenhower administration had long sought to avoid. Building a rocket engine with one million pounds of thrust and developing manned missile systems were just two of seventeen recommendations that Johnson's committee published in its findings as the hearings on Sputnik came to a close in late January. Some of the committee's other recommendations included strengthening SAC, accelerating missile production, and reorganizing the Department of Defense. It was space, however, that increasingly captured the imagination of the American public, and it was Johnson who seemed to grasp the issues of the future, while to many observers Eisenhower appeared mired in the past.[25]

The president nonetheless remained consistent in his response to Sputnik and the issue of space played little significance in his State of the Union address. Instead,

Eisenhower answered his critics by offering further reassurances about U.S. deterrent capacity and promising moderate increases in defense spending to speed up development of both ICBMs and IRBMs. He also offered moderate increases in spending on scientific education and placed significant emphasis on reorganizing the Pentagon in order to address the issue of inter-service rivalry, a problem that was raised repeatedly during Johnson's Sputnik hearings. Eisenhower's proposals still failed to satisfy those critics who believed the president's fiscal conservatism was clouding his judgment. An editorial in the *New Republic* challenged the effectiveness of Eisenhower's agenda on the issue of science and education, bemoaning "that the preference for dollars-over-minds that dominated the nation's thinking for so long before Sputnik is still very much with us."[26]

Johnson's success in focusing public attention on space, together with the contrasting fortunes of the Vanguard and Sputnik programs, made a successful launch of an American satellite imperative for the Eisenhower administration. Only the successful launch of an American satellite could fully assure the American public that the Soviet Union was not surpassing the United States in the vital areas of science and technology. Vanguard, however, continued to be plagued by technical problems and surprisingly it was the U.S. Army's Explorer, funded somewhat reluctantly by the Eisenhower administration as a backup to Vanguard, which became the first American satellite in space on January 29, 1958.[27] This initial triumph was followed two months later by another successful launch when Vanguard finally made it into space. With American satellites in orbit, a significant amount of the pressure that Eisenhower had been under since the previous November was lifted. The press and the public embraced the Explorer and Vanguard launches as a sign that the United States was no longer languishing in second place behind the Soviets. Americans took pride in the fact that the U.S. satellites were more complex and more scientifically productive than their Soviet counterparts. This opening gambit by the United States in the history of space exploration brought to an end "the national agony resulting from Sputnik" and effectively silenced the president's critics on the issue.[28] More than anything else, however, Explorer I and Vanguard I had an immense psychological impact on the American people.

AFTERMATH: SPUTNIK AS A TURNING POINT
The Sputnik launch in 1957 elevated the interrelated issues of space exploration and missile technology from relative obscurity to the top of the American political

agenda. The American press and public were enthralled by this scientific break-through, yet there was also a sense of deep disquiet regarding the deficiency in American technology that Sputnik appeared to highlight. Sputnik contributed to a mood of uncertainty over the future security of the United States. Critics of the Eisenhower administration's defense policy were alarmed by what they saw as the United States' failure to keep pace with Soviet missile production. Despite intense public and political pressure to respond forcefully to Sputnik, Eisenhower was constrained by his commitment to fiscal conservatism and was secure in the knowl-edge that actual intelligence regarding Soviet capabilities told a different story as compared to the alarmist projections of a missile gap making the rounds on Capitol Hill and on the editorial pages of the nation's newspapers. So intense was the po-litical pressure, however, that Eisenhower was forced to adopt some new initiatives with regard to space exploration and missile production that would have profound implications for the United States and the world.

The successful launching of American satellites in early 1958 led to an intensi-fication of the debate over the future of the U.S. space program. One of the central features of this debate was the issue of creating a space agency to direct the Ameri-can space effort. Should such an agency be under civilian or military control? What should be the extent of American space exploration? Should the interests of science or competition with the Soviets shape the American agenda in space? Eisenhower was concerned that a competitive space race with the Soviets could lead to over-spending and for this reason he favored making the United States' goals in space general in nature rather than focused on reaching specific targets. Avoiding compe-tition with the Soviets and the budgetary implications such competition entailed was a decisive factor in the president's decision to place the new space agency under civilian rather than military control. The creation of the National Aeronautics and Space Administration (NASA) in 1958 is one of the most visible responses of the Eisenhower administration to Sputnik. Although resented by the military estab-lishment as a civilian intruder competing for already limited funds, NASA won immediate approval from the American public and press. Contrary to Eisenhower's expectations, however, its establishment heightened public expectations and led to widespread calls for a trip to the moon. Not only was Eisenhower's view of space colored by fiscal restraint, but also, the president saw the space program in practical terms rather than in terms of its propaganda value. While a successful lunar expedi-tion may prove politically popular, Eisenhower saw little value in such a venture

from a national security perspective. The president actually went farther than he
wished to go when he approved the concept of a NASA lunar probe and hinted
at future manned space flight. But such ventures helped to shield attention from
the ongoing efforts of the ARPA (Advanced Research Projects Agency), originally
created by the Pentagon to oversee military missile development, but which the
president now directed to develop military spy satellites.[29]

The Eisenhower administration followed the passage of the National Aeronautics and Space Administration Act by successfully securing other legislative initiatives in the summer of 1958. Eisenhower used the Sputnik crisis to help push
legislation through Congress reorganizing the Department of Defense for the first
time since its creation in 1947, an issue he had long seen as of critical importance.
The most significant elements of this legislation involved changing the role of the
joint chiefs of staff with a view to reducing inter-service rivalry and centralizing
management of weapons development in the Pentagon under a new director of
defense research and engineering. Passage of the National Defense Education Act
(NDEA) in August represented the administration's response to calls for reform
in the nation's education system and specifically for increased funding in science
and technology. The NDEA exemplifies Eisenhower's proportionate response to
Sputnik.[30] The president's critics believed that Sputnik exposed a crisis in American
education that required a massive injection of federal spending to secure a long-
term fix. Eisenhower, on the other hand, saw such spending as the real problem and
favored a more limited agenda, spending $1 billion over four years on a range of
programs promoting science, technology, and language and area studies at all levels
of education. After four years Eisenhower believed the responsibility for streamlin-
ing American education for the space age should revert to the local level. Despite
the moderate nature of the Eisenhower reforms, the legacy of Sputnik would have
long-term implications for American education. "Sputnik provided a political catalyst that created a large infrastructure for basic research [in higher education] that
remains a market advantage for the United States in the world economy."[31]

The White House's success in passing these legislative reforms did not quiet
those critics in Congress and the press who continued to maintain that Eisenhower's defense policy was enabling the Soviets to open a missile gap over the United
States. Prior to the launch of Sputnik, Eisenhower had endeavored to cap defense
spending at $38 billion annually. The political fallout from Sputnik and the Gaith-
er Report saw the budgets for 1958 and 1959 climb to over $40 billion and the

administration tacked on additional supplemental spending bills in response to requests from each military branch. These supplemental bills, totaling $2.9 billion, fell far short of the $10 billion requested by the armed services and, as Senator Symington eagerly pointed out, did not match spending increases recommended by the Gaither and Rockefeller reports.[32] While a large portion of this additional spending went into producing the B-52 bomber aircraft, the majority was earmarked for missile-related programs. Eisenhower reluctantly agreed to increase production and deployment of first generation IRBMs but he resisted pressure for a rapid expansion in production of second-generation ICBMs. Instead, he put money into more deliberate, longer-term projects for developing solid-fuel ICBMs while relying on IRBMs as an interim, stopgap measure. In the face of the national outcry that followed Sputnik, Eisenhower felt compelled to embrace initiatives "with which he was not wholly comfortable."[33] However, these initiatives, while they exceeded both what the president thought was strategically necessary and financially prudent, enabled him to avoid even more excessive spending increases called for by some of his critics.

Nonetheless, the missile gap remained a political flashpoint for the duration of Eisenhower's presidency. The publication of two books in 1958, *New York Times* military correspondent Harry Baldwin's *The Great Arms Race* and retired army chief of research and development Gen. James G. Gavin's *War and Peace in the Space Age,* helped to reignite public concern over the missile gap. Both took issue with the defense strategy of the Eisenhower administration as a contributing factor to the crisis. Even as late as 1960 critics, such as analyst Albert Wohlstetter writing in *Foreign Affairs,* spoke of the damaging consequences of "our deep pre-Sputnik sleep."[34] Ironically, American spy satellites, the technological consequence of Sputnik that Eisenhower put greatest stock in, ultimately revealed the relative weakness of Soviet missile capabilities in 1960–1961 and exposed the missile gap as a fiction. Sputnik had essentially created the precedent of Open Skies in space and thus intelligence gathered by American reconnaissance satellites was not nearly as politically sensitive as information garnered from U-2 spy planes. Therefore while Sputnik had initiated the missile gap controversy, it also created a precedent for the means to eventually end it. Eisenhower's skepticism regarding the missile gap and his measured response in the face of widespread criticism were both vindicated in the end.[35]

For many Americans the historic steps taken by Neil Armstrong on the surface of the moon in 1969 served as the ultimate exclamation point to the U.S. response to Sputnik. By 1969 the shock of Sputnik was a distant memory and so too was the furor it had helped to generate over the issue of the missile gap. But while fears of the Soviet Union bypassing the United States in weapons production and techno-logical innovation had long since evaporated, the shadow cast by nuclear missiles had not. Indeed, in the post–Sputnik years the Soviet Union and the United States built up formidable ballistic missile stockpiles and developed new weapons tech-nology that made the nuclear arsenals of the 1950s appear quaint by comparison. The intense competition to gain leverage in the Cold War struggle by deploying these new weapons brought the world to the brink of nuclear war in 1962 during the Cuban Missile Crisis (see chapter 6). Eisenhower, who struggled to maintain a balance between what he saw as the strategic and economic benefits of nuclear weapons on the one hand and the tremendous momentum toward overproduction of ballistic missiles in the aftermath of Sputnik on the other, left the White House with deep misgivings about the direction American defense policy had taken during his presidency. In his farewell address to the American people, Eisenhower warned about the dangers of what he famously called "the military-industrial-complex" for the future of American government. The Cold War fostered an environment of perpetual crisis in the United States that gave considerable economic and political power to those charged with procuring and producing the weapons deemed neces-sary to secure the nation's defense. Eisenhower had done much to temper the worst excesses of the process but ultimately the nuclear arms race took on a logic and energy all of its own.

Six

THE CUBAN MISSILE CRISIS AND
THE BRINK OF NUCLEAR WAR

On October 14, 1962, American U-2 spy planes flying high over Cuba photographed the construction of a Soviet missile base near San Cristobal in the western part of the island. Two days later the U-2 photographs were put in the hands of President John F. Kennedy, opening a thirteen-day period that defined his presidency and sparked a crisis that brought the world to the brink of nuclear war. A measure of the seriousness of this crisis can be found in the fact that, as one scholar notes, "no episode in the history of international relations has received such microscopic scrutiny from so many historians."[1] In the now famous phrase of then–U.S. Secretary of State Dean Rusk, the United States and the Soviet Union, the world's two nuclear superpowers, came "eyeball to eyeball" in the fall of 1962. The nuclear saber rattling that both powers had engaged in since the early 1950s was put to the ultimate test and, fortunately for the world, the two adversaries backed away from nuclear conflagration.

The Cuban Missile Crisis would prove to be a critically important turning point in U.S. foreign policy during the Cold War. The gravity of the crisis reflects the intersection of myriad issues that characterized superpower competition during the Cold War. The Cuban Missile Crisis was most obviously the climactic event of the first phase of the nuclear arms race, but it also highlighted such critical areas of tension in U.S.–Soviet relations as Third World rivalries, the divergent ideological agendas of the two powers, the impact of domestic political considerations on each side's foreign policy, and the influence of the personalities of U.S. and Soviet leaders.[2] Both the Soviet Union and the United States would be compelled to make adjustments in their approach to world affairs in the wake of this crisis and the implications of the Cuban standoff would be felt through the end of the Cold War almost three decades later.

This chapter begins with an examination of U.S.-Cuban relations in the years leading up to the Cuban Missile Crisis. After Fidel Castro took control in 1959, relations between Cuba and the United States quickly deteriorated as Havana reached out to the Soviet Union and first Eisenhower and then Kennedy resolved to remove the new Cuban leader from power. The next section addresses the circumstances surrounding the Soviet decision to send military assistance to Cuba and the debate within the Kennedy administration and the country at large concerning an appropriate U.S. response, prior to the realization that this assistance included offensive nuclear missiles. From here we turn our attention to the standoff between the United States and the Soviet Union that ensued following Washington's discovery of these weapons and the crucial debate within the executive committee (ExComm) established by Kennedy to deal with the crisis. In the final section we examine the short- and long-term consequences of the successful U.S. blockade of Cuba that resolved the crisis and averted nuclear war.

THE UNITED STATES AND CUBA

The Spanish-American War of 1898 had clearly established U.S. hegemony in the Caribbean (see chapter 1). The subsequent adoption of the Roosevelt Corollary of 1907 replaced the old passivity of the Monroe Doctrine with a determination that the United States would be proactive in warding off rival powers from interfering in the affairs of Central America and the Caribbean. For five decades American dominance in the region had gone virtually unchallenged and during this period no country was of greater importance to the United States than Cuba. Under the terms of the 1903 Platt Amendment, Cuba became a virtual protectorate of the United States and remained so until FDR relinquished that role in 1934 as part of his Good Neighbor Policy. The United States nonetheless maintained its naval station at Guantanamo Bay and continued to exert considerable control over Cuban affairs. Lying just ninety miles off the coast of Florida, Cuba was of obvious strategic importance to the United States. In addition, American investors enjoyed considerable economic influence there, with dominant or near dominant roles in such vital industries as utilities, sugar, and mining. The United States supplied 65 percent of the island nation's imports and purchased 74 percent of Cuba's exports.[3] But the dramatic change in Cuba's government with the accession to power of the revolutionary forces of Fidel Castro in January 1959 proved to be a jarring blow to the complacency of U.S.-Cuban relations.

Castro's rise to power was paved by the corruption and ineptitude of the U.S.-backed regime of Fulgencio Batista, who himself had come to power through a military coup in 1952. After initially embracing Batista as a stalwart anti-communist ally, the failings of his regime led the Eisenhower administration to increasingly regard him as a liability. At the same time, however, Washington harbored grave misgivings about Fidel Castro's mounting challenge and the anti-American ideology of his 26th of July Movement. As a result, the Eisenhower administration stuck with Batista until his ouster became inevitable, and in the eyes of many Cubans the United States became tainted with the sins of that regime. Thus, although Washington immediately recognized the new regime after Castro came to power, the seeds of a crisis in U.S.-Cuban relations were already sown. Castro's accession to power and subsequent developments in Cuba would challenge the Monroe Doctrine "more powerfully than at any other time in the twentieth century."[4]

This challenge to traditional U.S. hegemony in the region was made all the more ominous by the close ties Castro would develop with the Soviet Union. Although conservatives in the Republican Party voiced early concerns that Castro was a tool of Moscow, the Eisenhower administration initially maintained an open mind on the new regime despite its anti-American rhetoric. However, by the end of 1959 the tentative diplomacy that characterized the new relationship between Havana and Washington had failed to assuage either side's suspicions of the other. Meanwhile, concerns were increasingly raised in Congress and the American press about the sanctity of the Monroe Doctrine in the face of the Castro regime's growing ties with the Soviet Union.

Cuban-American relations quickly deteriorated. Castro's suspicions of the United States and the influence of communists, such as Raul Castro and Che Guevara, within his inner circle laid the foundation for Havana's first overtures to Moscow. For Nikita Khrushchev and the Soviet leadership, Cuba represented a gilt-edged opportunity to score a victory in the global struggle with the United States to win the hearts and minds of the developing world and to do so right in the middle of the United States' historic sphere of influence. Castro's economic policies, driven as much by Cuban nationalism and hostility to "Yanqui imperialism" as they were by communist ideology, raised concerns in Washington as well as hackles among American investors. As a result of Castro's apparently abrupt shift to the left, American rhetoric and policy toward Cuba took on an increasingly hostile tone and the sum of all these developments drove Havana and Washington even further apart. With Castro increasingly less malleable to U.S. diplomatic efforts, the Eisenhower administration began to explore different strategies to deal with this growing threat to its interests in the Caribbean.

Washington had a model for action against Cuba in the overthrow of the leftist governments of Muhammad Musaddiq in Iran in 1953 (see chapter 10) and of Jacobo Arbenz in Guatemala in 1954. Both were toppled by CIA-inspired coups. Despite the now common perception that "the CIA intervention [in Guatemala] was a massive overreaction to a minor irritant," to Cold Warriors in the Eisenhower administration such as Secretary of State John Foster Dulles and his brother Allen Dulles, who headed the CIA, the ouster of Arbenz proved the value of covert operations.[5] The use of CIA covert operations was one dimension of Eisenhower's New Look strategy and the Dulles brothers in particular embraced it as a proactive, and relatively cheap, tool in the increasingly global struggle against the spread of communism. The success of the Guatemalan and Iranian operations made the use of covert operations an almost irresistible model for dealing with regimes that posed a threat to American strategic interests in various parts of the world. It is hardly surprising therefore that once Castro was assessed to pose such a threat, the Eisenhower administration quickly embraced covert operations as the best means to restore its influence in Cuba.

Kennedy and Cuba

Once Washington determined that Castro must be overthrown, there was so much certainty in the legitimacy of such a move that it would prove virtually impossible to check the momentum of the CIA's plans for a covert operation in Cuba. Those who favored action against Cuba viewed an assault on the Castro regime in terms of "taking back the patrimony of 1898 and James Monroe."[6] By the time JFK was elected in 1960, the CIA's plans for action against Cuba were well underway but to a certain degree the plan had lost some of its covert status by then. Kennedy himself bears much of the burden for both the mounting public evidence of impending action against Cuba and for the political momentum that made such action virtually inevitable. Kennedy made Cuba a major campaign issue in 1960 and attacked the Eisenhower administration for being soft on communism in Latin America. During his now famous televised debates with his Republican opponent Richard Nixon, Kennedy even went so far as to endorse the idea of covert U.S. action to topple Castro. Once in office Kennedy began immediately to explore options for overthrowing Castro, including offering his support to the CIA's on-going covert operations. The new president saw Cuba as the first line of defense against the spread of communism in Latin America and a vital battleground in the global struggle against the Soviet Union. As one historian notes, "standard Cold War assumptions helped to fuel a burning desire in Kennedy to oust Castro."[7]

Kennedy took office determined to explode the myth cultivated by Republicans since Truman's presidency that Democrats were soft on communism. His propensity to appear tough in the foreign policy arena was enhanced by his own understanding of history and the parallels he saw between the international crisis of the 1930s that spawned WWII and the state of world affairs in the early 1960s.[8] Two of the most common markers Kennedy would repeatedly use during his presidency to frame his foreign policy were the appeasement of Nazi Germany and the Japanese attack on Pearl Harbor. Cuba became the focal point of Kennedy's foreign policy both in terms of his desire to project himself as a man of action and in terms of the convergence in one place of the many "positions and assumptions" that appeared to the president to make the world such a dangerous place.[9] Kennedy's near obsession with Cuba was also a reflection of the domestic political climate. From the moment he entered the White House, JFK faced a mounting chorus for action against Castro emanating from the foreign policy elite on Capitol Hill, in the press, among the increasingly vocal Cuban exile community, and from American businessmen angered by Castro's nationalization policies. His room for maneuver on the issue was further limited by his own public pronouncements on Cuba during the presidential campaign.

Kennedy's Cuba policy was anchored by the CIA's covert operations program that he had inherited from Eisenhower. The president gave his support to CIA plans for launching an invasion of the island using U.S.-trained Cuban émigrés and relied exclusively on the agency's intelligence estimates to determine the feasibility of the plan. However, he was concerned that any U.S. effort to oust Castro must be free from the stamp of U.S. involvement. Kennedy's mounting concern over Cuba must be set in the context of his alarm at the tone of Khrushchev's 1961 speech declaring Soviet support for "wars of national liberation," a phrase interpreted in the United States as a euphemism for communist revolution.[10] Destroying the Castro regime was therefore just one part of a larger strategy of defeating Castroism in Latin America. While the Kennedy administration did place some hope in the Alliance for Progress, with its emphasis on evolutionary capitalism, as a bulwark against communism in Latin America, covert operations remained the weapon of choice against regimes perceived to be already well on the way to embracing communism. The irony here is that part of the rationale for using covert operations against Castro was that the Cuban regime posed a direct threat to American efforts to foster reform as an alternative to social revolution in Latin America.[11]

Kennedy's skepticism about the possible fallout from a U.S-sponsored invasion of Cuba was never strong enough to convince him to give serious consideration to shelving the project. The president "sought deniability of an American role" but nonetheless allowed the project to proceed.[12] Thus it was with JFK's assent that 1,400 CIA-trained commandos landed at the Bay of Pigs in western Cuba on April 17, 1961, hoping to spark a general uprising against Castro. But the Bay of Pigs invasion was a disaster from the outset. Castro's forces, armed with fairly accurate intelligence of the impending assault, quickly killed or captured the invaders. Much has been said about the failure of the Kennedy administration to provide air support but there were enough additional flaws in the plan, including a serious overestimation of the level of discontent on the island, to undermine its chances for success.[13] Kennedy's anger with what he perceived to be the misleading advice he received from the CIA seriously damaged his trust in the intelligence community. Publicly, however, the president took full responsibility for the Bay of Pigs disaster. But this did little to alleviate the criticism he now faced from Republicans and Cuban exiles who blamed him personally for the failure of the invasion. The Bay of Pigs fiasco cast a very long shadow over the administration of the young president. Now more than ever Kennedy had to prove to his detractors that he was capable of tough, forceful action and Cuba came into even sharper focus as the testing ground of the president's mettle.

PRELUDE TO THE CRISIS

While the Bay of Pigs debacle weakened Kennedy, it had the opposite effect on Castro's regime and also encouraged Moscow to become more deeply involved in Cuba. In fact, Khrushchev, sensing that the Kennedy administration was particularly vulnerable, sought to exert pressure on the United States in strategically vulnerable areas such as Cuba, Southeast Asia, and Berlin. Khrushchev began to equate Soviet aid to Cuba with the relationship the United States had with countries on the rim of the Iron Curtain such as Italy, Greece, and Turkey. The presence of American Jupiter missiles in Turkey was a particularly galling reminder to the Soviet premier that earlier Soviet claims of strategic nuclear advantage or even parity with the United States were pure fiction. The only "missile gap" that existed in 1962 was firmly in the United States' favor. Cuba represented an opportunity for Khrushchev to reassert the kind of momentum the Soviet Union had enjoyed in the Cold War struggle in the wake of Sputnik (see chapter 5). American vulnerability after the Bay of Pigs appeared to offer the perfect opening.

Just eight weeks after the Bay of Pigs, Khrushchev and Kennedy came face to face at the Vienna Summit. The primary issue on the agenda in Vienna was the ongoing crisis over the divided city of Berlin, but recent developments in Cuba loomed large over the proceedings. Khrushchev's bellicosity at Vienna, where he threatened to sign a separate peace with East Germany, thus calling into question the future of West Berlin, reignited the Berlin crisis. Kennedy, anxious to avoid a second major setback following the disastrous Bay of Pigs operation, responded by sending a clear message that the United States would not be pushed around. Ultimately Khrushchev backed down and endorsed the building of the Berlin Wall, creating an enduring symbol of the bankruptcy of Soviet communism (see chapter 11). While much of the credit for this apparent American victory belongs to back channel diplomatic negotiations, it was the Kennedy administration's tough talk and the preponderance of American military might that appeared to have forced the Soviet Union's hand.[14] The success of American saber rattling in the ensuing crisis over Berlin did little to enhance the notion that diplomacy and not force was the way forward in the superpower struggle.

Kennedy's success in standing up to Khrushchev over Berlin failed, however, to erase the Bay of Pigs nightmare for the president. Rather than backing away from his desire to oust Castro from power, Kennedy doubled his commitment to effecting regime change in Cuba. According to one historian, "Kennedy's attitude toward Cuba after the Bay of Pigs fiasco became a matter of personal dignity and honor, almost a vendetta."[15] For the can-do Kennedy administration, the failure of covert operations in Cuba was a mistake that had to be corrected. The administration adopted a three-track approach toward this end. First, the president encouraged the Joint Chiefs of Staff to develop contingency plans for military action against Cuba and to begin military and naval maneuvers in the Caribbean. Until the conclusion of the missile crisis, the Kennedy administration kept the door open to the option of direct military intervention in Cuba. Second, the administration took steps to isolate Cuba economically and politically by encouraging trade restrictions and using its influence to oust Cuba from the Organization of American States (OAS). Finally, the president approved clandestine operations to foment internal unrest against the Castro regime. Under the leadership of Edward Landsdale, an Air Force brigadier general who had played a leading role in American counterinsurgency efforts in South Vietnam in the late 1950s, a program designed to destabilize the Castro regime, dubbed Operation Mongoose, was launched in 1962. The White House, and particularly Attorney General Robert Kennedy, took a direct interest in planning and implementing Mongoose, which the administration hoped would trigger a revolt in Cuba without appearing to have the stamp of American involvement so evident in the Bay of Pigs debacle.[16]

Kennedy's Cuba policy succeeded only in convincing Castro that desperate measures were required to counteract what was clearly U.S. intent to destroy his regime.[17] It is against this backdrop that Castro accepted Khrushchev's offer of assistance in the form of nuclear weapons. Castro's willingness to invite Soviet assistance as a counterweight to American power reflects his conclusion that U.S.-Cuban relations could not be made any worse than they already were and that only a dramatic show of force could deter a U.S. invasion. For Khrushchev the rationale behind the decision to deploy nuclear missiles just ninety miles from the coast of Florida is more complex. Moscow was less certain than Havana about the prospect of a U.S. invasion, but at the same time the Soviet Union could not appear to be lax in its defense of communist allies. Khrushchev's 1961 speech in support of "wars of liberation" that had so alarmed Kennedy was made partly with a view to counteracting Chinese efforts to supplant the Soviet Union as the leading supporter of revolutionary communist movements around the world. Stalin's death in 1953 left Mao Zedong feeling less constrained to follow Soviet leadership and the government in Beijing had since increasingly challenged the assumption of Moscow's preeminence among the world's communist nations (see chapter 8). Thus, in the same way that South Vietnam came to be viewed in Washington as a litmus test of American resolve (see chapter 7), the Kremlin feared that failure to save Castro might seriously damage its leadership claims in the communist world.

As important as this issue was, however, by itself it is not sufficient to explain why Khrushchev would be willing to take such an extraordinary risk. While the

Soviet leader might publicly dismiss the Monroe Doctrine as a tool of U.S. imperialism, he and his advisors were well aware that direct military aid to Cuba, let alone the installation of nuclear weapons, represented a direct provocation of the United States in its own backyard.[18] The expected advantages for the Soviet Union of such a move, therefore, had to be considerable. The key to understanding the Soviet Union's decision lies in the missiles themselves. Under Operation Anadyr, the Soviets dispatched 50,000 military personnel backed up by tactical nuclear weapons and surface to air missiles (SAMs) to defend Cuba in the event of an American invasion. However, the crux of the crisis lay in Moscow's decision to send twenty-four medium range ballistic missiles (MRBMs) and sixteen IRBMs capable of striking cities in the heart of the United States. This was clearly an effort to equalize the increasingly apparent Soviet deficiency in the strategic nuclear arms race and to recapture some of the momentum the Soviet Union had lost in the Cold War struggle since the late 1950s.

Since Sputnik the United States had opened a clear gap in the construction of ICBMs which, together with IRBMs such as the U.S. Jupiter missiles in Turkey, put the Soviet Union in a very weak strategic position vis-a-vis the United States. The missiles in Turkey were particularly galling to the Soviets and the concept of equalization figured prominently in the Kremlin's rationale for the Cuban deployment. Furthermore, Khrushchev demonstrated a predilection for brinkmanship and for using nuclear weapons to cut overall military spending costs, mirroring in both respects the earlier priorities of the Eisenhower administration. The missiles in Cuba might serve the dual purpose of providing the Soviet Union with leverage in places such as Berlin while freeing money for Khrushchev's domestic priorities. Khrushchev's decision was based on the assumption that Kennedy was too "intelligent" to allow the Cuban missiles to provoke thermonuclear war and that therefore the risks could be easily managed.[19] Ultimately though, Khrushchev failed to adequately consider how Kennedy might interpret this bold move and thus he stumbled into a crisis that would prove to be a "colossal mistake."[20]

Khrushchev's intention was to carry out the entire installation operation without detection, keeping it secret until after the mid-term elections in the United States and then presenting the missiles in Cuba as a fait accompli to Kennedy when the two leaders met at the U.N. General Assembly in November. That gave the Soviets just four months from the decision to deploy to complete the whole operation without being detected by American intelligence. Even were this operation not to be carried out under the nose of the United States, this was a tall order indeed. The Soviets took extensive precautions to conceal their efforts. But Cuba was already under heavy CIA, State Department, and U.S. military surveillance and it was only a matter of time therefore before the heavy cargo traffic between the Soviet Union and Cuba aroused suspicion in the United States.[21] Throughout the summer American intelligence began to compile a picture of increasing Soviet activity in Cuba, from the sudden presence of large numbers of Soviet personnel in July to the deployment of SAMs in August. However, while these reports were cause for considerable anxiety in Washington, American intelligence consistently underestimated the scale of the Soviet operation. Furthermore, although the prospect of the Soviets deploying strategic missiles in Cuba was a nightmare scenario for American leaders, "virtually no one thought they would be so foolish."[22]

The Debate Over Cuba

John McCone, who had replaced Allen Dulles as director of the CIA after the Bay of Pigs fiasco, was one of the few major figures in Washington who feared the Soviet buildup in Cuba might involve plans for strategic missiles. McCone, the lone Republican on the National Security Council, urged the White House to step up aerial surveillance of Cuba and to consider contingency plans, including invasion, in the event the Soviet strategic missiles were deployed on the island. Although officials such as Robert Kennedy and National Security Advisor McGeorge Bundy were leery about provoking the situation, the president became sufficiently alarmed to ask the Defense Department to explore the pros and cons of various options, from a naval blockade to a full-scale invasion, to compel the removal of missile sites in Cuba.

While reports of Soviet missile activity started to circulate among the Cuban exile community in Florida, in Washington Sen. Kenneth Keating (R-NY) began sounding alarm bells about developments on the island. In fact Keating was one of the first people in Washington to publicly claim the existence of Soviet missile installations in Cuba. The source of Keating's information remains somewhat of a mystery, but it seems likely to have been either his contacts within the Cuban community or his close friend CIA Director McCone, all of whom shared a desire to prompt the Kennedy administration into more assertive action. In the run up to the mid-term elections Keating's withering assaults against the White House's apparent lack of concern over the potential existence of Soviet missiles in Cuba, made both on the floor of the Senate and directly to the media, were proving politically embarrassing. While publicly the Kennedy administration downplayed the severity of the situation, privately the issue was coming to be seen as increasingly critical.

By the beginning of September, however, there was still no concrete evidence that the Soviets were planning to install anything more than SAMs in Cuba. While McCone was convinced that the only reason for the Soviets to install an extensive air defense system was to protect strategic missiles, most other administration officials clung to the belief that the SAMs were solely to defend Cuba from air assault. The Soviets had a track record of installing SAMs in other client states, such as Egypt and Indonesia, and in any case the deployment of strategic missiles remained too inexplicable a risk for most American officials to countenance. Given that the chief alarmists McCone and Keating were both Republicans, it was tempting to conclude that the strategic missiles charge was politically motivated to damage the Democrats in the run up to the mid-term election. The White House's reluctance to fear the worst was compounded by private assurances sent directly from the Kremlin that the Soviet Union did not intend to install ballistic missiles in Cuba. Republican pressure continued to mount, however, with a number of prominent senators, such as Karl Mundt (R-SD) and Barry Goldwater (R-AZ), echoing Keating's consistent criticism of the administration's Cuba policy. On September 4 Kennedy briefed a congressional delegation on the situation, contending that there was no hard evidence of Soviet strategic missiles and that up to this point Soviet activity in Cuba appeared to be of a defensive nature only. The president then issued a public statement declaring that the deployment of Soviet strategic missiles in Cuba would pose a serious threat to American security, the implication being that the defensive weapons already installed did not.[23]

Keating and other critics of the administration's Cuba policy ensured that Cuba remained firmly in the public eye. In an effort to counteract his critics and appear firm on the issue, Kennedy followed up his September 4 statement nine days later with the assertion that, while no invasion of Cuba was planned, the United States would take military action if Castro allowed Cuba to become a base for Soviet offensive weapons. The president would soon come to regret this remark as it seriously hindered his room for maneuver once the existence of such weapons became apparent. Meanwhile, pressure on the White House continued to grow. On August 31 *Time* magazine published an article based on anonymous intelligence sources warning about the aggressive nature of the Soviet buildup in Cuba and on the same day Senator Keating offered a detailed intelligence briefing to members of the press on the floor of the Senate.[24] Kennedy's new hardline rhetoric did little to placate his critics but it did succeed in alarming Khrushchev and the Soviet leader moved quickly to dispatch additional tactical nuclear weapons to Cuba as the only viable means of counteracting a large-scale U.S. invasion. The Soviets continued to deceive the Kennedy administration up to the moment of discovery in the hope that once installed the United States would have little option but to accept the missiles as an accomplished fact. The mounting sense of crisis in the United States and the increasingly forceful language of the president, however, now appeared to cast doubt on the efficacy of Soviet calculations. In Moscow, Khrushchev "began to wonder whether he had made a terrible mistake."[25]

As the volume of press coverage continued to grow and a stream of alarming observer reports flowed in from Cuba, McCone pushed vigorously for more U-2 over-flights. Secretary of Defense Robert McNamara, among others, however, feared that increased U-2 activity might spark another international incident, like the one that followed the capture of Gary Powers after the U-2 he was piloting was shot down over the Soviet Union in 1959. McCone's voice remained a lonely one, even within the intelligence community where perceptions of Soviet thinking tended to trump the growing body of evidence on Soviet activities in Cuba. Nonetheless, "anxiety levels were increasing" and there was sufficient activity in Washington to counteract the notion that when the missiles were discovered it did not come as a complete surprise to the Kennedy administration.[26] McNamara began to discuss contingency plans for invasion or air strikes with the JCS in the event that the United States was faced with Soviet strategic weapons in Cuba. The administration's growing sense of urgency is evident in McNamara's request that the JCS have their plans in place by October 20. Publicly, however, the administration continued to play down the crisis. When Keating charged on October 10 that six Soviet IRBM sites were under construction in Cuba, Bundy went on television to assert that it was highly unlikely that either the Cuban or Soviet governments would assent to such action.[27]

THE MISSILE CRISIS

The now famous October 14 U-2 flight over Cuba proved what few people in Washington had wanted to believe, the existence of Soviet strategic nuclear weapons just off the coast of the United States. The U-2 flight provided incontrovertible photographic evidence of three MRBM sites near San Cristobal along with evidence of more extensive strategic missile operations on the island. On October 15 the CIA shared this evidence with Bundy who, waiting a day in order not to disrupt the president's campaign schedule, presented the pictures to Kennedy on the morning of October 16. The subsequent thirteen days constituted, without question, one of the most serious crises of the Cold War. As noted earlier, it is also one of the most intensely studied episodes in the history of U.S. foreign relations and the process of decision making during this nail-biting period has been dissected and analyzed from a considerable variety of angles by political scientists and historians.[28] While the outcome of the crisis is obviously of great significance, it is important to understand how the key players in the drama arrived at the decisions they did and how those decisions ultimately defused the crisis.

Pivotal to understanding the U.S. response to the Soviet missiles in Cuba are the deliberations of a large group that Kennedy gathered together immediately upon learning the news. Known as ExComm (the Executive Committee of the National Security Council), it was comprised of prominent officials from the defense, intelligence and diplomatic community, as well as key figures from within the White House. ExComm met almost continuously throughout the crisis. While its membership fluctuated somewhat over those crucial thirteen days, its key figures included McNamara from the defense department, Maxwell Taylor of the joint chiefs of staff, McCone from the CIA, Dean Rusk and George Ball from the state department, White House advisors Bundy and Theodore Sorenson, Robert F. Kennedy (RFK) from the justice department, and of course President Kennedy himself. ExComm provided an open (or as some critics would later charge, chaotic) forum where the president could field advice from a variety of perspectives. The importance of all the advice JFK drew from the accumulated wisdom of ExComm, however, "paled in comparison to Robert Kennedy's" counsel.[29] RFK was one of the few ExComm members who did not come from within the foreign policy community, yet over the course of the crisis he emerged as the key figure in the committee's deliberations. The president, still smarting from the Bay of Pigs, trusted nobody as closely as he did his own brother. RFK, who like his brother was very conscious of the Kennedy administration's place in history, was intensely protective of the president, and was determined to shield him from another foreign policy disaster, especially in this instance where the stakes were so dramatically high.

President Kennedy was perplexed by Khrushchev's motives and early in the crisis appeared to be more concerned with what he perceived to be the Soviet leaders' audacity than he was with the firepower now in place in Cuba. Kennedy felt betrayed by earlier Soviet assurances about Cuba and, while he never downplayed the significance of this development for U.S. national security, he did see this latest challenge from Khrushchev as a personal test of his leadership.[30] JFK's deeply personal response to the crisis contributed to his sense of belligerency early in the proceedings of ExComm. His initial inclination therefore was to favor the advice of the hawks on the committee whose proposals ranged from invasion to air strikes (either surgical or general) or a combination of the two.

Diplomacy as a stand-alone option received little serious consideration and the only major alternative to military action raised in the early sessions of ExComm appeared to be a blockade or quarantine of Cuba. The JCS, meeting separately during a break in ExComm deliberations on October 16, promoted the option of massive air strikes against a broad range of military targets in Cuba as the only means of effectively disabling the Soviet threat. Although some key players, including RFK, inched toward support of air strikes, consensus within ExComm proved elusive on the opening day of deliberations. Some ExComm members, such as Taylor, saw the missiles as a direct threat to the global balance of power, while others, such as McNamara and the president himself, tended to view the crisis in political rather than military terms. Despite the hint of panic evident in these early deliberations, ExComm was not pressed to take immediate action because, as yet, no one outside of its members knew that the United States had discovered the missiles. The committee was also fortunate in that some of the ideas now under consideration had been explored in the months before the crisis and "this accelerated the process of evaluating their strengths and weaknesses."[31]

Over the course of the next two days, as more advisors entered the process, the range of options expanded and then narrowed again. Returning from his honeymoon in France, CIA Director McCone, fearing that immediate military action might quickly escalate, argued in favor of giving Khrushchev an ultimatum before ordering air strikes. Meanwhile, U.S. Ambassador to the United Nations and former presidential candidate Adlai Stevenson proposed a purely diplomatic track, even suggesting in a memo to the president that the United States should offer its missiles in Turkey in exchange for the removal of Soviet missiles from Cuba, advice the Kennedy brothers initially rejected as defeatist.

ExComm now narrowed its focus to two options, air strikes or a blockade. Blockade advocates, such as former U.S. Ambassador to the Soviet Union Llewellyn

Thompson, argued that while air strikes would force Khrushchev to respond in kind, the blockade allowed for the political dimension of the crisis to be explored while giving the Soviets time to consider their options. The blockade also shifted the onus to the Soviet Union to make the next move. Having appeared on October 16 to be close to endorsing air strikes, President Kennedy now supported the blockade. The advice of his brother, who himself had initially favored air strikes, proved critical in JFK's shift in opinion. RFK repeatedly voiced concerns during ExComm deliberations that unannounced air strikes amounted to committing another Pearl Harbor and he was determined that his brother would not go down in history as the Tojo of the Cold War.

The Blockade

While President Kennedy began to prepare the ground for the implementation of the blockade, he instructed his brother to build a larger consensus in ExComm for this course of action. Although hawks on the committee, such Chief of the Air Staff Gen. Curtis Le May, dismissed the blockade as appeasement, Kennedy was now convinced that air strikes would lead to Soviet counteraction, perhaps in Berlin, leading in all likelihood to a general escalation.[32] The White House began to prepare the ground for going public on the missiles by bringing its closest allies and key members of Congress into the loop and preparing diplomatic notes for such important forums as the United Nations and the OAS explaining the rationale behind American action. Concerns were raised in ExComm that a blockade was technically an act of war and in order to diminish the likelihood of provocation, U.S. actions must appear consistent with international law. Secretary of State Dean Rusk's ability to secure unanimous OAS support for the blockade, therefore, added a veneer of legality to the initiative. On Monday, October 22, eight days after the U-2 flight, President Kennedy went on national television to announce the implementation of a quarantine of Cuba until the Soviet Union withdrew its missiles from the island. Kennedy told a shocked nation that Soviet actions were "provocative and unjustified" and that the United States could not accept this situation if "our courage and our commitments are ever to be trusted again by friend or foe."[33]

Kennedy's October 22 speech ushered in the most tense and dramatic stage of the Cuban Missile Crisis. Its effort to legitimize the blockade aside, the United States had no way of predicting how the Soviet Union, or Cuba for that matter, would react to the move. The initial indications were not encouraging. While the

Pentagon ordered the U.S. military to Defense Condition Three (DefCon III), which is the highest level of alert for U.S. forces short of war, Khrushchev condemned American actions as "banditry" and informed the Cubans, whose military stood on high alert, that the Soviets would not back down.[34] Although the Americans and Soviets both took a hard line in public, after October 22 Khrushchev and Kennedy each began to explore possibilities for compromise that would allow for a peaceful resolution of the conflict. Such a resolution was only possible if each of the two superpowers could claim some measure of success from the standoff. Striking such a delicate balance required the simultaneous conduct of public and private (or back channel) diplomacy, a diplomatic high-wire act where even the slightest misstep could prove fatal.

The lack of a direct line of communication between the White House and the Kremlin led to the employment of some unorthodox lines of back channel communication. For example, Robert Kennedy recruited journalists Frank Holeman and Charles Bartlett, both Kennedy family friends, to deliver messages to KGB agent Georgi Bolshakov communicating that the president was determined to have the missiles removed but he did not intend to invade Cuba and that a deal, possibly involving the Jupiter missiles in Turkey, might be worked out.[35] RFK himself met secretly with the Soviet Ambassador to the United States, Anatoly Dobrynin, in an effort to lay the groundwork for a settlement. Publicly President Kennedy continued to take a tough position, warning of the danger of nuclear war and hinting that the Soviets had underestimated the will and resolve of the United States, but at the same time he called upon the Soviet leader to demonstrate prudence and avoid taking steps that might escalate the conflict.[36] Khrushchev appeared to get the message and on October 26 he dispatched a note to Kennedy indicating his willingness to withdraw the missiles in return for a U.S. guarantee not to invade Cuba. Khrushchev also agreed to U.N. Secretary General U Thant's proposal, inspired by Adlai Stevenson, that until the final resolution of the crisis Soviet ships would stay out of the quarantine zone on the understanding that the U.S. Navy would refrain from intercepting them.[37]

Before the White House had a chance to fully digest this apparent concession, however, a second, more belligerent communication arrived from Khrushchev on October 27, demanding U.S. withdrawal of its missiles from Turkey in exchange for the removal of Soviet missiles from Cuba. These conflicting notes caught the administration off guard and inspired a spirited debate within ExComm over how to respond. Most of the committee members were oblivious to the back channel negotiations and the fact that Kennedy had essentially put the issue of the Jupiter missiles on the table. When Stevenson had raised the possibility of a trade at an ExComm meeting on October 26 he was met with angry resistance and earned the rebuke of the president. McCone and the other hawks on the committee adamantly opposed a trade, arguing that it would seriously weaken America's pledges to its NATO allies while appeasing Soviet aggression. Kennedy, cognizant of how an appearance of intransigence might damage U.S. standing in world opinion, was however not willing to risk war over missiles in Turkey that were essentially obsolete. He was prepared to make a deal but only without publicly opening himself up to charges of appeasement.

Faced with the dilemma of conflicting messages from Khrushchev, the members of ExComm agreed that the president should embrace the first letter and ignore the additional terms of the second. Kennedy duly dispatched a note to the Kremlin indicating his willingness to lift the quarantine and pledge not to invade Cuba in return for withdrawal of Soviet offensive missiles from Cuba. After the main ExComm meeting broke up, President Kennedy met with select members, including RFK, McNamara, Sorenson, Bundy, Rusk, and Thompson, essentially leaving the hawks out of the loop. The result of this furtive meeting was to suggest that Robert Kennedy inform Dobrynin that while the United States might be willing to remove the missiles from Turkey after the resolution of the crisis, it would not make them part of an explicit trade for the missiles in Cuba. Kennedy and his inner circle also formulated a backup plan (which as things turned out was never implemented) to prompt U.N. Secretary General U Thant to propose the missile trade as a U.N.-inspired resolution to the conflict and thus allow the United States to embrace a peaceful resolution without appearing to be giving in to Soviet demands. Kennedy had essentially decided upon his course of action and taken the decision on how to resolve the crisis out of the hands of ExComm.[38] The disparity between Kennedy's overt and covert offers of resolution illustrates his deep concern with how U.S. policy would be perceived both at home and abroad. Domestic opinion and the confidence of American allies required that the White House appear resolute in the face of Soviet provocation, but to the rest of the world it was imperative that the United States not appear intransigent or, worse still, trigger happy.

Khrushchev embraced this opportunity to extricate himself from a crisis that had escalated far beyond the point he had envisioned when he made the decision to deploy. On October 28 Khrushchev dispatched a message to Kennedy accepting the terms laid out in his letter of the day before. To make sure that there was no confusion this time, the Soviet leader ordered that the letter be read over the airwaves of Radio Moscow. Both leaders now moved quickly to bring the crisis to a speedy conclusion. Kennedy, ignoring the grumblings of ExComm hawks such as Le May who continued to endorse military action, agreed to a Soviet compromise of U-2 over flights as a means of verification when Castro refused to allow inspectors into Cuba. Khrushchev for his part had to placate his furious Cuban ally, who rejected the Soviet leader's argument that the U.S. non-invasion pledge represented a victory for communism. The world issued a collective sigh of relief as the leaders of the two superpowers cautiously stepped back from the brink of nuclear war.

AFTERMATH: THE CUBAN MISSILE CRISIS AS A TURNING POINT

The Cuban Missile Crisis marked the intersection of a series of Cold War developments dating back to the 1950s. Key among these was the broad adoption by the United States of the tactic of covert operations and John F. Kennedy's obsessive desire to use this tactic to overthrow the Castro regime in Cuba. Washington's efforts to oust Castro opened the door for Khrushchev to place offensive nuclear missiles in Cuba. Nonetheless, despite the fact that Kennedy's Cuba policy helped provoke the crisis, the president deserves a great deal of credit for promoting a resolution that did not entail a resort to military action and the threat of nuclear escalation that this entailed.[39] While the traditional view of Kennedy's handling of the crisis emphasizes a "calibrated dissection of alternatives" resulting in "the merger of politics and force as an instrument of policy," the tape-recorded sessions of the ExComm meetings reveal a far less cohesive process of decision-making.[40] There was an element of luck involved in the final outcome. The prospect of U.S. military action remained pronounced right up to October 28 and Soviet records indicate that Moscow was prepared to use force to defend the island. Incidents like the shooting down of a U-2 spy plane over Cuba on October 27 had the potential to ignite the fuse of conflict. Ultimately, however, fear of nuclear war on both sides, particularly for Khrushchev and Kennedy, outweighed all other considerations. When each leader finally came to realize that the other shared this view, the door to a settlement was opened.

Both Kennedy and Khrushchev emerged from the Cuban Missile Crisis with a sense of empathy for the enemy that was clearly absent in their relations leading up to the affair. This was evident in the commencement address Kennedy delivered at American University in June 1962, in which the president called upon the American people to see beyond the evils of communism and recognize the humanity of their counterparts in the Soviet Union.[41] To avoid the danger of the communication errors so evident during the crisis, the two sides agreed to the installation of a "hot line" between the White House and the Kremlin. But in probably the clearest indication that the Cuban Missile Crisis had a positive influence on Soviet-American relations, the two nuclear superpowers signed the Partial (Nuclear) Test Ban Treaty (PTBT) in 1963 marking the first concrete step to arrest the momentum of the nuclear arms race. Under the terms of the PTBT, the United States and the Soviet Union agreed to prohibit the testing of nuclear weapons in the atmosphere, at sea, or in space. By bringing the superpowers to the brink of nuclear war, the Cuban Missile Crisis had highlighted the dangers of the unrelenting nuclear arms race and created for the first time a climate where a brake on the process became possible.

These positive short-term benefits, however, must be measured against longer-term consequences that appear to have done more damage than good to U.S.-Soviet relations and the politics of the Cold War in general. Although Khrushchev could claim to have saved Cuba from American invasion, the Chinese were emboldened in their challenge to Soviet leadership that they continued to portray as soft in dealing with the West. Meanwhile, Soviet hardliners saw only defeat in the withdrawal of the missiles and now pushed for more military spending. Soviet expenditures on strategic nuclear weapons increased at the expense of domestic spending on consumer goods and agriculture, exactly the opposite of what Khrushchev had hoped the Cuban gamble would achieve. For many Soviet hardliners the PTBT was little more than a breathing space during which time the Soviet Union could play catch up. Expansion of Soviet production and deployment of ICBMs and nuclear submarines was a clearer indication of the future of the Cold War than the PTBT. The last hope that the Cuban Missile Crisis might dramatically alter Soviet Cold War policy died when Khrushchev was ousted from power in 1964 and replaced by Leonid Brezhnev, who through the remainder of the 1960s demonstrated none of his predecessor's inclination for compromise. One of the many charges leveled against Khrushchev by those who drove him from power was his "recklessness and adventurism in Cuba."[42]

Kennedy, on the other hand, was able to bask in the glow of what most observers counted as an American victory in the Cold War struggle. To be sure, Cuban

Americans, for whom the non-invasion guarantee exacerbated the anger they felt for Kennedy after the Bay of Pigs, did not see it that way. Also for those Americans who saw the Monroe Doctrine as a cornerstone of American foreign policy, Kennedy's guarantee amounted to a betrayal of "the sacred text."[43] To the majority of Americans, and most observers around the world, Kennedy emerged from the Cuban Missile Crisis as a strong and forceful leader. It was an image the White House had been careful to construct by keeping the Turkish missile deal secret from all but the closest of the president's advisors and micro-managing media coverage in wake of the crisis.[44] Kennedy's tragic assassination just over a year after the conclusion of the missile crisis helped to immortalize his image as a tough, decisive president and White House advisors such as Sorenson and Arthur Schlesinger Jr. perpetuated the legend in their memoirs.

Although Kennedy's determination to appear tough had been critical in resolving the crisis, this tactic served to undermine the role of diplomacy in resolving future Cold War disputes. The president's sabotage of Adlai Stevenson in the media as an appeaser for suggesting that the Turkish missiles be used as a bargaining chip, the very thing that proved critical to the success of Kennedy's back channel diplomacy, was designed to contrast the chief executive's "nerve and wisdom" with the diplomat's weakness and fear.[45]

The Cuban Missile Crisis put to rest the sense of insecurity and self doubt in the United States that had followed Sputnik (see chapter 5). The Soviet threat, which loomed so large over the previous five years, suddenly diminished as Americans once again felt confident in the superiority of American military power to promote their interests around the world. The apparent American victory over the Soviets in the missile standoff helped to shift the national mood from uncertainty to assertiveness in the Cold War struggle. With diplomacy largely discredited, "force and toughness" became paramount in the making of U.S. foreign policy.[46] Both the Soviet Union and the United States came to see "military credibility as more important than its non-military counterparts."[47]

The very real danger of nuclear war that the Cuban Missile Crisis entailed also had important consequences for American defense policy. While nuclear weapons lost their appeal as offensive weapons and became increasingly instruments of deterrence, a new emphasis on military strategy was placed on the use of limited war. Vietnam would prove to be the testing ground for this evolving strategy. Defense Secretary McNamara wanted to show in Indochina that the United States could achieve its objectives without the threat of nuclear weapons and thus avoid the kind of stark choices that were necessary during the missile crisis. The self confidence that the Cuban Missile Crisis created within the Kennedy administration, most of the key figures of which were kept on by Kennedy's successor in the White House, Lyndon Johnson, was a critical factor in the decision-making process that led the United States ever deeper into Vietnam as the decade wore on. Many of these veterans of the missile crisis believed they had found the formula for managing the Cold War in America's favor. The proximity of the Cuban Missile Crisis and the Vietnam debacle, the subject of the next chapter, represents the short road it takes to travel from confidence to arrogance.[48]

Seven

THE TET OFFENSIVE AND
THE VIETNAM WAR

"The American Embassy is under siege; only the besiegers are American."[1] These are the words of CBS News correspondent Walter Schanke reporting from Saigon on January 31, 1968. Earlier that morning a small cadre of communist insurgents had seized the new U.S. Embassy building in South Vietnam's capital as part of a broad, well orchestrated assault against urban centers and strongholds of that country's pro-Western government. The embassy raiders were all dead within five hours of the beginning of their assault but their success in breaching the most important symbol of American security in Vietnam was a dramatic prelude to a stunning series of events known as the Tet Offensive. Timed to coincide with the Tet holidays marking the lunar New Year, the South Vietnamese insurgents, backed by regular army units from communist North Vietnam, launched a series of offensives throughout the country aimed at ending the stalemate in their decade-long struggle against the government of South Vietnam and its ally, the United States. Their targets were all locations understood to be firmly under the control of the government of South Vietnam and U.S. forces. Over the course of several days in late January and early February, six of South Vietnam's major cities, thirty-six regional capitals, and a host of district capitals and hamlets came under assault. The inherent contradiction of American forces besieging their own embassy was mirrored by the larger spectacle of American forces and the Army of the Republic of Vietnam (ARVN) fighting to recapture territory that for two decades the United States government had touted as an impenetrable bulwark against communism in Southeast Asia.

While historians continue to debate the meaning and significance of the Tet Offensive, there is a broad consensus that it marks a defining moment in the long and tragic history of American involvement in Vietnam. Nothing was the same after Tet in either Vietnam or the United States. The communist offensive challenged many of the long held assumptions of American military and political leaders with regard to Vietnam and it had a profound impact on media and public perceptions of the war in the United States. Tet appeared to contradict in the most dramatic terms the U.S. government's optimistic public assessments regarding American prospects for victory in Vietnam.[2] In the wake of Tet many Americans, including leading figures in the foreign policy elite, began to question not just the progress of the war, but the very logic of U.S. involvement in Vietnam. Tet brought into the open a host of issues that had been slowly festering behind closed doors, not just with regard to Vietnam, but concerning many basic assumptions about American foreign policy during the Cold War. The Tet Offensive marked the end of American military escalation in Vietnam and ushered in a slow, torturous process of withdrawal. It also marked the beginning of a period of profound transformation in American foreign policy, as the country's leaders gradually came to terms with the reality that there were limits to the scope of American power.

This chapter opens with an examination of the history of U.S. involvement in Indochina from 1945 to the beginning of overt American military intervention in 1964.[3] This opening section addresses the increasing commitment of successive American presidents to maintaining Vietnam as the line of containment against the spread of communism in Southeast Asia. The next section examines the circumstances surrounding the United States' escalating military commitments in Vietnam after 1964 and the debates and divisions over the war within the United States as a whole and also inside the Johnson administration in particular. From there we turn our attention to the Tet Offensive and the dramatic impact it had on the U.S. war effort in Vietnam. The final section addresses the impact of Tet on both American involvement in Vietnam and on U.S. foreign policy during the Cold War in general. We examine how Tet contributed to a shift in foreign policy skewed heavily against the use of force overseas.

THE UNITED STATES AND INDOCHINA

The roots of American involvement in Vietnam are inextricably linked to the transformation of the world in the wake of WWII. The United States had waged that war as an anti-imperialist struggle and the administration of Franklin Delano Roosevelt embraced the cause of anti-colonialism in the Atlantic Charter of 1941.[4] American rhetoric gave hope to anti-colonial nationalists around the world, including Ho Chi Minh and his Vietminh movement that had received American assistance in its struggle against Japan's occupation of Indochina. Japan had invaded the French colony of Indochina in 1941 and the French authorities in the region had willingly collaborated with Tokyo's designs in Southeast Asia. The Vietminh were the focal point of opposition to the Japanese occupation, thus clearly establishing their credentials as the standard bearers of Vietnamese nationalism. Ho and the Vietnamese communists thus emerged as the latest incarnation in a long history of Vietnamese struggles against outside invaders, from the Chinese who first invaded Vietnam in 111 B.C. to the French who took control in 1858 to the Japanese during WWII. With Japan's defeat in 1945, the Vietminh occupied Hanoi and declared the establishment of the Democratic Republic of Vietnam. On September 2, Ho Chi Minh, quoting from the American Declaration of Independence, declared Vietnamese independence and appealed directly to the United States for recognition of the new nation.

Despite some sympathy from American officials on the ground in Vietnam, Ho's appeal for recognition fell upon deaf ears in Washington. Anti-colonialism as a principle of American foreign policy was linked to the post-war "one world" vision of the Roosevelt administration, where capitalism and democracy triumphed over all other ideologies. However, the new administration of Harry Truman faced a bipolar Cold War struggle between American liberal capitalism and Soviet communism where the positives of nationalism and the evils of colonialism were no longer so clearly discernable. Indochina, where national liberation and social revolution were intertwined, exemplified more than any other region of the world the complications and contradictions that the Cold War raised in terms of Washington's position on colonialism.[5] The U.S. response to Ho Chi Minh's appeal was further complicated by broad geopolitical concerns. While French collaboration with Japan during WWII had angered many officials in Washington, the post–war climate in Europe proved decisive in the U.S. decision to support the reestablishment of French control in Indochina. Although Washington harbored doubts about French policy in Indochina, the United States' need to secure the full support of Paris for the task of containing the Soviet Union in Europe outweighed these concerns.[6] The U.S. goal to reconstruct Japan as the centerpiece of a new liberal capitalist order in

East Asia also influenced American policy toward Indochina. The spread of communism in this region threatened access for Japan to the markets and raw materials of Southeast Asia, thus undermining American reconstruction efforts.

With these concerns in mind, the United States chose to ignore Vietnamese independence claims and instead supported French efforts to restore its colonial authority in Indochina. War subsequently broke out between French forces and the Vietminh in late 1946. Although the United States backed French colonialism over Vietnamese communism, Washington was at the same time anxious to distance itself from the taint of European imperialism in Asia, so American financial support for the French war effort was initially funneled through metropolitan France under the guise of post-war reconstruction aid.[7] By 1950 the French war effort appeared to be stalling, however, and the United States became increasingly alarmed about the future of Southeast Asia. In the aftermath of the "fall of China" to Communism in 1949 and the outbreak of the Korean War the following year (see chapter 4), Washington had come to see French success in Vietnam as critical to the containment of communism in Southeast Asia. The United States began to directly fund the flagging French war effort while at the same time seeking a more active role in the conduct of the war. Fearful about the future viability of French colonial rule in the region, the United States also encouraged Paris to institute reforms in Indochina that would enable viable regional anti-communist alternatives to emerge. Washington was thus quick to recognize the French puppet government of Bao Dai, the playboy descendant of Vietnam's imperial house. French reforms, however, were largely superficial and did little to counteract the growing strength of the Vietminh.

Despite considerable American investment in support of France, the situation in Indochina was becoming considerably more problematic for the United States by the time Truman vacated the White House.[8] The war had become internationalized with the United States openly supporting France and both the People's Republic of China and the Soviet Union providing assistance to the Vietminh. The Eisenhower administration nonetheless embraced existing U.S. policy toward Indochina and, if anything, sought to apply it more vigorously. Eisenhower and his Secretary of State, John Foster Dulles, firmly embraced the Domino Theory, which held that if Vietnam fell to communism then its neighbors would fall like a row of dominoes. While U.S. support for the French still to some extent reflected concerns over the future of Europe, by 1952 Indochina had become an area of geostrategic significance in its own right. Soviet and Chinese support for the Vietminh was extensive enough to warrant legitimate American concerns regarding a broader communist agenda in Southeast Asia.[9]

Despite extensive U.S. support for France, victory over the Vietminh proved elusive.[10] Soviet and Chinese assistance greatly increased the effectiveness of Vietminh forces in Indochina, but perhaps the greatest strength of Ho Chi Minh and his followers was their popularity relative to the French colonial regime. Meanwhile, as French casualties mounted, public support for the war in France began to erode and pressure for a negotiated settlement gathered momentum. The end came for France in the spring of 1954 at the Battle of Dien Bien Phu, where a Vietminh force of close to 50,000 surrounded 16,500 French troops. During the two-month siege of Dien Bien Phu, the Eisenhower administration toyed with the prospect of direct U.S. intervention. While there was some support in American military circles for using American air power, and even tactical nuclear weapons, to lift the siege and save the French, Eisenhower and Dulles rejected unilateral American action. There was little public support in the United States for joining another conflict in Asia, particularly so soon after the protracted and costly Korean conflict. Instead Eisenhower and Dulles began to plan for possible future multilateral intervention or "United Action" in Indochina, involving Britain, France and regional allies such as Thailand and Australia.[11] Meanwhile the battle raged on at Dien Bien Phu and on May 7, 1954 the French garrison finally surrendered, bringing the First Indochina War to an end.

The Republic of (South) Vietnam

Even before the defeat at Dien Bien Phu, the French government, over American objections, had agreed to put the issue of Indochina on the agenda for a major international conference in Geneva scheduled for April 1954. Despite the fact that the Vietminh were in a very strong position both politically and militarily in Vietnam, local realities counted for little in Geneva as the major powers dominated the proceedings.[12] Both the Soviets, who were hoping to appease Paris and undermine French support for U.S. policies in Europe, and the Chinese, who feared the prospect of American intervention in Southeast Asia, persuaded the Vietminh to accept the partition of Vietnam at the 17th parallel. Under the terms of the Geneva Accords, Indochina was divided into four parts, Laos, Cambodia, and North and South Vietnam. The partition of Vietnam was designed to be temporary, with the

Vietminh in control in the north, the pro-French regime of Bao Dai in power in the south and elections to be held within two years to determine the future of a united Vietnam. The United States, which was deeply concerned that Ho Chi Minh and the communists had won a strong foothold in Vietnam, refused to associate itself with the Indochinese settlement reached in Geneva. Instead the focus of American policy now turned toward nation building in South Vietnam and the 17th parallel became the line of containment in Southeast Asia.

With France gone, the South Vietnamese government under recently installed Ngo Dinh Diem now became the major vehicle of U.S. policy in the region. Head of State Bao Dai had appointed Diem, an anti-communist Catholic with legitimate nationalist credentials, to the post of Prime Minister shortly after the Geneva settlement. The Eisenhower administration immediately threw its support behind Diem in an effort to establish a non-communist regime in South Vietnam that would serve as a bulwark against communism in Southeast Asia.[13] American aid began to pour into South Vietnam and in 1954 Eisenhower dispatched a CIA team to Saigon charged with conducting covert missions aimed at undermining the communist regime in the north. American support proved crucial in allowing Diem time to consolidate his narrow base of support and in 1955 he declared himself President of the Republic of (South) Vietnam. With American support, Diem rejected the validity of the Geneva Settlement and refused to conduct the election mandated by that agreement. As the pace of the disintegration of the European empires in Africa and Asia increased in the latter half of the 1950s, the U.S. goal of building a viable, independent, non-communist South Vietnam took on increasing significance. It was vital not just to the security of Southeast Asia, but in the larger struggle between the Soviets and Chinese on the one hand and the United States on the other to win the hearts and minds of people in the developing world. As one historian notes "the experiment of nation building (in South Vietnam) tapped the wellsprings of American idealism and took on many of the trappings of a crusade."[14]

After the date for national elections came and went and it became increasingly clear that Diem was determined to crush all opposition in South Vietnam, former Vietminh fighters and others opposed to Diem launched an insurgency against his regime. This challenge to its client state prompted Washington to increase its support for the Saigon government and by the late 1950s South Vietnam had become the fifth largest recipient of U.S. aid worldwide. Between 1955 and 1961, military assistance accounted for 78 percent of all American aid to South Vietnam and by

1960 there were almost 2,000 U.S. civilian and military advisors in the country.[15] The United States created the Military Assistance Advisory Group (MAAG) to assist in the organization, training, and equipping of the Army of the Republic of Vietnam. However, the ARVN was trained and outfitted to fight a conventional war and thus had little success in combating the guerrilla campaign launched against the Diem regime in 1957. Communist guerrillas assassinated hundreds of South Vietnamese government officials in 1957 and 1958 and the insurgency gathered strength throughout South Vietnam. In 1959 the government of North Vietnam, which had wavered in the hope that nationwide elections might still be held, began supporting the insurgency and a year later the National Liberation Front for South Vietnam (NLF) was formed to orchestrate the growing military and political campaign to overthrow Diem. Despite the fact that the NLF was not exclusively communist, it was dubbed the Vietcong (Vietnamese communists) by the Diem government and Washington shared Saigon's conviction that an NLF victory translated into the fall of Vietnam to communism.

The mixed results in South Vietnam of American military assistance were mirrored in the areas of economics and politics. Rather than invigorating the South Vietnamese economy, the huge volume of American aid only succeeded in creating a cycle of dependency. Meanwhile, despite the urgings of his American advisors, Diem rejected the principles of representative democracy and instead cultivated his own brand of authoritarianism, which he labeled "personalism." The United States, however, was prepared to overlook his shortcomings as long as he remained steadfastly anti-communist. Washington too often interpreted mounting unrest in South Vietnam as the work of outsiders and northern agents and failed to recognize Diem's complicity in the growing crisis. The blind support that the United States gave to Diem's regime reflected its reflexive fear of communism and its determination to "immunize" the developing world against this threat. The victory of Fidel Castro in Cuba in 1959 (see chapter 6) heightened Western notions of vulnerability at a critical juncture in Vietnam and contributed to what in hindsight appears to be a myopic vision of the situation in Southeast Asia.[16]

During the last year of the Eisenhower administration the situation in Cuba—along with crisis developments in Berlin and Laos—also had the effect of reducing the priority of South Vietnam in Washington and thus increasing the tendency to accept the status quo. John F. Kennedy entered the White House in early 1961 in an atmosphere of crisis and he was determined to demonstrate resolve in standing up to what he perceived to be challenges to both his own personal credibility and to the security of the nation, particularly after the Bay of Pigs disaster. Preserving South Vietnam and defeating the insurgency were part of the broad message of strength that the Kennedy administration wished to project. Although he only initially endorsed small increases in military aid to South Vietnam, Kennedy embraced and expanded a CIA counterinsurgency program that had been launched in 1960. In addition to CIA efforts to undermine the NLF, the new strategy included leading covert operations with the ARVN against North Vietnam and arming Hmong tribesmen in Laos to attack the Ho Chi Minh trail, the jungle road along which supplies moved from North Vietnam to rebel forces in the south. Kennedy also activated a Special Forces unit, the Green Berets, with specialized training in counterinsurgency. Meanwhile, Vice President Lyndon Johnson flew to Vietnam on a fact-finding mission and the president put together a Task Force to discuss U.S. options, including the possibility of military intervention, in Vietnam.

A report written by National Security Advisor Walt Rostow and Kennedy's personal military advisor Gen. Maxwell Taylor would prove critical in shaping the future of American involvement in South Vietnam by opening the door for direct American military engagement in that country's widening war. In the face of deteriorating conditions in South Vietnam, Rostow and Taylor recommended increasing American support in the form of material aid and advisors to bolster the Diem regime. They also recommended sending to South Vietnam a "logistic task force" of several thousand men ostensibly to help with flood relief in the Mekong Delta but in reality to bolster the ARVN's military campaign. Despite his misgivings about an open-ended escalation, Kennedy endorsed the Rostow-Taylor report and, as a result, American military assistance to South Vietnam doubled between 1961 and 1962. The number of U.S. "advisors" in South Vietnam jumped in the same period from 3,000 to 9,000 and MAAG was replaced by the Military Assistance Command, Vietnam (MACV) with a corresponding shift in emphasis from training the ARVN to influencing the direction of the war. Despite his misgivings about military engagement, Kennedy's decisions in 1961 marked a major step toward the United States assuming responsibility for the war.[17]

The war nonetheless continued to go badly for the ARVN and the government of South Vietnam, and counterinsurgency measures proved ineffective in counteracting the increasing effectiveness of the NLF. Ultimately, the corruption and unpopularity of the Diem regime proved to be the Achilles Heel of U.S. policy in

South Vietnam. Diem continually ignored American pleas for meaningful political reforms and by 1962 his government was reduced to a family oligarchy increasingly unresponsive to the broader needs of the country. However, many American officials both in Saigon and Washington had come to see Diem as essential to the U.S. cause in Vietnam and were wont to interpret all challenges to his regime as communist inspired. Thus, in a pattern that would only become more pronounced as American involvement in Vietnam increased, the American Embassy in Saigon and MACV papered over many of the more disturbing signs of impending chaos and instead sent back to Washington optimistic reports about the military and political situation in South Vietnam. President Kennedy was complicit in this pattern of deception as the White House even resorted to putting pressure on the *New York Times* to recall its correspondent, David Halberstam, whose reports portrayed the Diem regime as deeply corrupt and the ARVN as woefully inept.[18]

Halberstam was not alone in his criticism. Senate Majority Leader Mike Mansfield (D-MT), once a strong Diem supporter, returned from a fact-finding mission to report widespread corruption and political deterioration throughout South Vietnam. As official evidence of Diem's shortcomings mounted, many senior U.S. officials began contemplating the prospects for a change in government in South Vietnam. The future of the Diem regime rested increasingly on decisions made in Washington.[19] Dramatic scenes in Saigon that summer of Buddhist monks engaging in self-immolation eroded the last vestiges of support for Diem in the United States. The macabre suicides made front-page news across the United States and heightened public and media scrutiny of American policy in Vietnam. Diem's heavy handed and insensitive response to mounting protests from Buddhist monks and student activists made it increasingly difficult for Washington to portray him as a champion of freedom and democracy in Southeast Asia.

For a number of years American officials in Saigon had been cognizant of, and sometimes complicit in, plans for a coup by ARVN officers. After Maxwell Taylor and Secretary of Defense Robert McNamara reported that an improvement of the political situation might reduce the NLF insurgency within two years to "little more than organized banditry," the Kennedy administration washed its hands of Diem and the U.S. Ambassador in Saigon Henry Cabot Lodge was encouraged to make it known to ARVN officers that the United States would not stand in the way of a coup attempt that might succeed.[20] In the early morning hours of November 1, 1963, ARVN troops surrounded the presidential palace in Saigon and by the end of the day Ngo Dinh Diem was dead and the regime in which the United States had invested so much came to an end. Less than a month after the Saigon coup, John F. Kennedy was assassinated in Dallas, Texas and so responsibility for U.S. policy in post-Diem Vietnam fell to his successor Lyndon Baines Johnson.

THE MAKING OF TET

The U.S. role in Vietnam was transformed dramatically in the Johnson era. Under the previous three administrations American involvement in Vietnam was limited to supporting first the French and then the South Vietnamese in their wars against communist insurgency. Under Johnson the United States would take on the lion's share of the military burden. Johnson's presidency is inextricably linked with the military quagmire in which the United States found itself in Vietnam and there can be no doubt that there were key moments during his tenure in office when he could have chosen a different path. In many respects, however, his Vietnam policy was simply a logical extension of the successive escalations of American commitment under the previous three administrations. Truman and Eisenhower had both passed on a deepening crisis in Vietnam and Kennedy also "bequeathed to his successor a problem imminently more dangerous than the one he had inherited."[21] Diem's overthrow failed to produce political stability in South Vietnam and the country slid further into chaos as leading ARVN officers competed against each other for control of the state. Meanwhile, the NLF, backed by North Vietnam, stepped up its campaign in the hope of precipitating the complete collapse of South Vietnam.

Johnson, however, was determined to save South Vietnam and thus he never questioned the basic assumptions about the region that had become embedded in American foreign policy during the three preceding administrations.[22] In addition to the danger of falling dominoes, Johnson was concerned that withdrawal from Vietnam would undermine American credibility in the eyes of its allies and embolden the Soviet Union and China in the worldwide struggle between communism and capitalism. Johnson also worried about the impact his appearing to be soft on communism in Southeast Asia might have on support among deeply anti-communist Southern Democrats for his ambitious domestic agenda. He was cognizant of the risks involved in getting sucked deeper into Vietnam and this is reflected in the gradual process of escalation and the limited nature of American goals during his tenure in office. His Vietnam policy was a contradictory mix between his determination to avoid "a full scale commitment in Vietnam, risking both his Great Society [program] and the war with China and Russia," and his commitment to preventing a communist victory in South Vietnam.[23] Although he would commit American forces to Vietnam, the conduct of the war would be as much influenced by domestic and international politics as it was by events on the battlefield. It was from this enigmatic stew that the Tet Offensive of 1968 would draw its great significance.

Johnson initially approached the deteriorating situation in South Vietnam cautiously, with a basic commitment to continue existing policies but to apply them more efficiently.[24] However, the insurgency continued to gather strength and so Johnson and his advisors began to explore new options to alter the direction of the conflict. Secretary of Defense Robert McNamara now began to push the idea of taking military action against North Vietnam. Striking North Vietnam would send a message to Hanoi that the United States would not tolerate a communist victory in South Vietnam, while at the same time disrupting North Vietnam's logistical support for the NLF. A second coup at the beginning of 1964 highlighted the continuing instability of South Vietnam and by the spring of that year McNamara and other senior officials in the Johnson administration concluded that striking the North represented the best way forward in terms of arresting the deteriorating fortunes of the South.[25] The pretext for that action came in August when the USS *Maddox* was fired upon on two separate occasions by North Vietnamese gunboats while lying in international waters in the Gulf of Tonkin off the northern coast of Vietnam.[26] The Gulf of Tonkin affair would provide the grounds for American military action against North Vietnam and in the process open the door to a broader American military commitment in Vietnam.

Johnson and the Cycle of Escalation

The Johnson administration responded to the attack on the *Maddox* by ordering immediate retaliatory bombing raids against military and economic targets in North Vietnam. At the same time the White House drafted a proposed congressional resolution granting the president broad discretionary powers to employ military force in Vietnam. The resulting Gulf of Tonkin Resolution secured unanimous support in the House of Representatives and won the approval of all but two members of the U.S. Senate. It greatly expanded the president's war-making powers as it authorized LBJ to take "all necessary measures to repel any armed attacks against the forces of the United States and to prevent further aggression" in Vietnam. One of the two dissenting senators, Wayne Morse (R-OR), referred to passage of the resolution as "a historic mistake" and predicted that the country would come to regret the Senate's decision to circumvent the Constitution by giving the president a free hand to use force in Vietnam.[27] By waiving its constitutional prerogative to declare war, Congress essentially presented Lyndon Johnson with a blank check for military action and paved the way for an escalating commitment that would result in military stalemate in Vietnam and bitter divisiveness at home.

Johnson did not choose to use his new power to escalate immediately. His firm response to the Gulf of Tonkin affair had won him widespread domestic approval but he was anxious not to appear too hawkish in the run up to the 1964 presidential election, particularly as one of his electoral strategies was to portray his Republican challenger Barry Goldwater as an irresponsible warmonger intent on widening the war in Vietnam. After securing re-election in a landslide victory, however, Johnson dramatically transformed the U.S. commitment in Vietnam by initiating regular bombing of North Vietnam. While some members of the administration, most notably Under Secretary of State George Ball, expressed grave doubts about American escalation in Vietnam, the majority favored more forceful action as an effective means of convincing North Vietnam to end its support for the insurgency or face destruction. With the South Vietnamese government in crisis and the NLF growing in strength, escalation appeared to be the only alternative to accepting defeat in Vietnam. There was general agreement in the administration that withdrawing from Vietnam would undermine American credibility around the world and make Johnson vulnerable to domestic critics. The American public, however, remained apathetic about Vietnam and few U.S. allies shared Washington's concern about the consequences of a communist victory in Vietnam. Ultimately, "Johnson was not forced into war by the exigencies of domestic or international politics," rather, the decision to escalate was based primarily on administration perceptions of the consequences of the fall of South Vietnam.[28]

The purpose of American military intervention was always limited to the goal of preserving South Vietnam as an independent, non-communist nation. Johnson was determined to avoid a wider war and, although the Pentagon and the JCS did explore such contingencies, the U.S. military strategy was based on the principle of containment rather than the goal of rolling back communism in Southeast Asia. Once the initial military commitment was made, however, a series of complications and contradictions would gradually emerge. While the Johnson administration would publicly promote the idea that bombing North Vietnam would precipitate a negotiated solution to the conflict, the plans drawn up by the Pentagon and MACV were clear from the beginning that air power alone would not suffice and that American ground forces would be needed in Vietnam.[29] The logic of American military intervention was to bolster South Vietnam and persuade Hanoi and the NLF to back down, but the consequences of bombing North Vietnam and the eventual introduction of American troops into the conflict proved otherwise. The NLF and North Vietnam responded in kind to Washington's application of greater force and as the political situation in South Vietnam continued to deteriorate the United States found that it had to carry more and more of the burden of the conflict.

Perhaps the greatest weakness of the Johnson administration's intervention in Vietnam was the manner in which it was conducted. In building support for American intervention, Johnson shrouded his Vietnam policy in "deceit and obfuscation."[30] The president and his advisors shielded important details about the nature and scope of American intervention and, perhaps most damagingly, continued to tout progress and stability in South Vietnam when the reality was otherwise. This can be explained in part by the president's desire to maintain public and congressional support for his domestic agenda but it also reflects the fact that many administration officials shared the view widely accepted at the height of the Cold War that foreign policy issues were too complex and too important to be left to an indifferent and ignorant public and a divided and unwieldy Congress.[31] This pattern of deception would come back to haunt the Johnson administration as the lack of transparency in its public rhetoric would ultimately magnify the significance of the 1968 Tet Offensive.

A succession of coups continued to undermine South Vietnam's political stability and by early 1965 the country's viability appeared to be in doubt. Key administration officials such as National Security Advisor McGeorge Bundy, Maxwell Taylor (by then-U.S. ambassador in Saigon), and Robert McNamara all advised Johnson in January that the only alternative to defeat in Vietnam was an expanded bombing campaign against the north. The United States had reached, in Bundy's words, "a fork in the road" with one path leading to escalation and the other to negotiation. Bundy concluded that only the former path presented a viable means of saving South Vietnam as an independent non-communist state. An NLF attack on a U.S. base in Pleiku in South Vietnam's central highlands in February was quickly followed by reprisal attacks against North Vietnam. Within forty-eight hours of these initials raids, the United States launched Operation Rolling Thunder, a sustained bombing campaign that from 1965 to 1973 would result in the United States dropping three times the tonnage of bombs on North Vietnam that had been dropped on Europe, Asia, and Africa through the entire course of WWII.[32]

Once started, Operation Rolling Thunder had a built-in philosophy of escalation that was quickly fulfilled. Shortly after American B-52s began raining bombs on targets across North Vietnam, Johnson authorized the dispatch of two marine battalions to protect the American air base at Danang in response to a request from General William Westmoreland, recently appointed commander of MACV. Once American ground forces had been introduced it would prove very difficult to resist the temptation to introduce more troops to arrest the declining fortunes of South Vietnam. Within a month of the arrival of the marines in Danang, Westmoreland, with the backing of the JCS, pressed the president for two additional divisions for offensive operations in the Central Highlands. Despite warnings from Ambassador Taylor of the potential for ever increasing commitments and high casualty rates, in April Johnson agreed to introduce 40,000 additional troops into South Vietnam. At this point Johnson stopped short of approving Westmoreland's call for using U.S. forces in offensive combat operations. Instead the White House emphasized the strategy of "depriving [the enemy] of victory" in an effort to enable the new military regime in Saigon, headed by ARVN General Nguyen Van Thieu and Air Vice Marshall Nguyen Cao Ky, to restore stability in South Vietnam.[33] The United States had nonetheless reached a new level of commitment in Vietnam from which it would prove increasingly difficult to step back.

The scale and scope of U.S. military intervention in Vietnam was inextricably linked to the fortunes of the Republic of (South) Vietnam. In order for the American commitment to remain limited, the government of South Vietnam had to reverse the trend of the war and recapture the momentum from its communist enemies. When this did not happen, U.S. air power and ground forces became the only barrier between South Vietnam's collapse and a subsequent communist victory. The government of South Vietnam and the ARVN became increasingly dependent on their American allies and allowed more and more of the burden of war to shift to U.S. forces with each successive escalation. The White House, however, continued to mislead Congress and the public regarding both the level of American commitment in Vietnam and progress being made in the war. Despite the administration's positive spin, the 1965 escalation encountered critics both at home and abroad. Prominent Democratic senators such as Mike Mansfield, Frank Church (D-ID), and George McGovern (D-SD) voiced concerns that were echoed on the editorial pages of a small number of prominent newspapers. The antiwar movement, though still only in its embryonic stage, captured public attention with a large number of teach-ins and student protests on college campuses across the country in 1965. U.S. escalation met with criticism from members of the non-aligned movement and on the floor of the United Nations General Assembly. Even American allies such as Canada and Great Britain expressed misgivings about the new direction of American policy in Vietnam. Although officially the administration tended to be dismissive of this criticism, the president instituted a temporary halt to the bombing of North Vietnam in May and issued a call for peace talks in an effort to counteract this trend. The White House recognized that such talks were impossible as long as Hanoi refused to accept the legitimacy of the South Vietnamese state.

The bombing halt had more to do with the administration's media strategy than any meaningful attempt to halt the process of escalation in Vietnam. The White House was intent on convincing the American public that Hanoi was the aggressor and that the United States was willing to discuss peace if North Vietnam ceased its aggression. Johnson's public statements on the war were "designed to allow the American people and America's allies abroad to face the future with some confidence" and to mask Washington's deepening commitments in Vietnam.[34] Lacking a clear strategy, the administration's confidence that it could achieve its goal through force was based largely on the assumption that the vast military firepower at its disposal would overwhelm the enemy. When North Vietnam and the NLF refused to back down, the United States simply applied more pressure. The number of U.S. troops on the ground in South Vietnam jumped from 185,000 at the end of 1965 to 480,000 by the end of 1967 and the bombing campaign was expanded in this same period to include targets in South Vietnam and along the Ho Chi Minh Trail. After initially limiting U.S. troops to defensive actions, Johnson soon turned the conduct of the war over to General Westmoreland who was determined to take the offensive against the enemy. Westmoreland and the military were confident that American technology such as helicopter gunships, napalm bombs, and chemical defoliants such as Agent Orange would enable the United States to successfully employ a strategy of search and destroy against the insurgents. The military's confidence was based on the assumption that victory was inevitable. This attitude was reflected in reports about the situation on the ground in South Vietnam that ended up on the president's desk.

North Vietnam and the NLF responded to the greater application of American force with an escalation of their own. With aid from the Soviet Union and China, Hanoi began to ship more men and supplies down the Ho Chi Minh trail and deployed regular troops of the North Vietnamese Army (NVA) against American forces along the demilitarized zone. While U.S. forces were able to prevent the collapse of South Vietnam, they were unable to strike a decisive blow against the NVA and NLF. The conflict in South Vietnam quickly became a war of attrition in which U.S. forces, fighting without identifiable front lines, began to measure success by deploying a body count of enemy dead. These figures were often distorted, however, as the lines between civilian and combatant casualties were sometimes blurred and statistics were frequently padded as they moved up a chain of command anxious for good news. Meanwhile Americanization of the conflict tended to marginalize the ARVN and shunted the government of South Vietnam into a supporting role, which tended to undermine its credibility in the eyes of many Vietnamese. Despite the fact that elections in 1967 gave a veneer of legitimacy to the Thieu/Ky regime, the paper-thin margin of victory and the climate of instability in which the election took place highlighted the serious weakness of the government in Saigon. Despite millions of dollars of aid and thousands of civilian personnel dispatched to South Vietnam, Washington found that "progress in the critical area of nation building . . . was even more limited than on the battlefield."[35]

Domestic unrest intensified as the United States became increasingly bogged down in Vietnam. While American tactics appeared to make little headway in breaking the enemy's will, mounting American casualty rates (the figure had reached 14,000 dead by late 1967) soon began to take a political toll back in the United States. The general apathy that had greeted American intervention in 1965 contrasted sharply with the increasing disquiet over Vietnam in 1967. At the start of that year, polls showed that 37 percent of Americans believed U.S. intervention had been a mistake; by the end of the year that figure had risen to 45 percent.[36] While only a minority of that 45 percent favored immediate withdrawal, the Vietnam War was beginning to generate a level of opposition unprecedented in U.S. military history.[37] Growing disquiet over the war on Capitol Hill mirrored this shift in public opinion. Of particular concern to the Johnson administration were the proceedings of the Senate Foreign Relations Committee and public pronunciations of its liberal chairman J. William Fulbright (D-AR). Fulbright, at the President's request, had guided the Gulf of Tonkin Resolution through Congress in 1964 but later came to feel misled as Johnson had assured him that he had no intention of leading the United States into a wider war in Vietnam. Fulbright's Senate Foreign Relations Committee hearings on Vietnam in 1966, watched on television by millions of Americans, raised serious concerns about American policy in Southeast Asia and proved particularly embarrassing to the Johnson administration. In the same year, Fulbright published *The Arrogance of Power,* which offered a damning critique of the U.S. war in Vietnam.

By 1967 Johnson found himself losing traction with other key Democrats and administration supporters such as Robert Kennedy and Martin Luther King Jr. who both came out publicly against the war. Many mainstream liberals began to join the chorus of critics on the left who equated the Vietnam War with a broader critique of American globalism and, although it still only represented a minority of Americans, the growing and visible antiwar movement was beginning to exert considerable pressure on the White House. Cracks began to appear within the administration, as long time critics of Johnson's Vietnam policy such as George Ball quietly resigned and key architects of that policy such as Robert McNamara began to doubt the wisdom of continuing the process of escalation. By 1967 McNamara had come to question whether the United States could achieve its goals through military means in Vietnam and he was increasingly concerned that the bombing of North Vietnam was eroding the goodwill and support of American allies around the world.

Rather than reevaluate his Vietnam policy in the face of this mounting criticism, Johnson chose instead to fight back against his detractors. McNamara, at odds with military commanders in the United States and Saigon, would find himself increasingly marginalized in the administration as the president chose instead to side with administration hawks such as Bundy and Secretary of State Dean Rusk and to meet General Westmoreland and the JCS halfway in their request for more troops and an intensification of the bombing campaign. The White House also began a major public relations campaign to shore up support for the Vietnam War. Johnson, who encountered protests and demonstrations wherever he went, was convinced that the antiwar movement was primarily the work of communist agitators and he pressed the CIA and the FBI into action, gathering intelligence on various antiwar groups and monitoring the activities of leading activists. In an effort to counteract the visibility of the antiwar movement, the White House sponsored prowar rallies and gave a platform to groups that espoused support for the war. General

Westmoreland was brought home from Vietnam in November 1967 for a round of speaking engagements and press conferences designed to highlight American progress and the prospects for future success. Westmoreland repeatedly claimed to see "light at the end of the tunnel" in Vietnam and he confidently asserted "we have reached an important point when the end comes into view."[38] Such rhetoric failed to turn the tide of skepticism toward the war in the United States and within two months would prove deeply damaging to the administration's ability to maintain its course in Vietnam.

THE TET OFFENSIVE

The White House continued to push this positive assessment of the situation in Vietnam right up to the beginning of the Tet Offensive. Although Johnson sided with the hawks in his administration, discrepancies between the CIA's assessment of the military situation in Vietnam and the military's positive analysis gave the president some cause for concern. However, to embrace the CIA's estimated strength of the NLF, which was essentially double the military's assessment, would constitute an acceptance that the insurgency was genuinely popular and that the United States was an occupying power propping up a puppet government. The military's figures were much more consistent with the White House's perspective that the NLF was a front for North Vietnamese aggression against the popular government of South Vietnam, thus legitimizing the U.S. presence in Vietnam.[39] To some extent the administration became trapped by its own political rhetoric. Maintaining anything other than a uniformly positive assessment of the situation in Vietnam might embolden the enemy and erode the willingness of the South Vietnamese to continue fighting. The positive assessment, therefore, became a necessary prerequisite for victory. Thus, Vice President Hubert Humphrey returned from Vietnam shortly before Tet to announce, "we are making progress," while reporters at a military briefing in Saigon were informed "the Vietcong has been defeated."[40]

While such claims were clearly overstated, there is no doubt that U.S. intervention had made it difficult, if not impossible, for the NLF/NVA to win the war. By the beginning of 1968 the war had become a bloody stalemate where both sides believed that applying more pressure would lead to a decisive breakthrough but each side underestimated the staying power of the other.[41] The Tet Offensive represented a major gambit on the part of North Vietnam and the NLF, the goal of which was two-tiered. In the best-case scenario it would result in a decisive victory leading to the collapse of South Vietnam and the withdrawal of American troops. At the very minimum, Hanoi hoped it would halt the process of U.S. escalation and the bombing of North Vietnam and force the United States to the negotiating table. The plan centered on a series of diversionary tactics, designed to draw U.S. and ARVN forces away from urban centers and other secure areas in South Vietnam, the centerpiece of which was a large buildup of NVA troops around the U.S. base at Khe Sanh in the far northwestern corner of the country. Westmoreland welcomed Khe Sanh as the long awaited opportunity to strike a decisive blow against the enemy in a conventional battlefield setting and so he quickly committed large numbers of troops to reinforce the base. Both Westmoreland and President Johnson interpreted Khe Sanh to be North Vietnam's attempt to replicate Dien Bien Phu and they were determined to avoid a defeat similar to the one that had driven France from Indochina fourteen years earlier. Johnson became obsessed with the potential for a showdown. From the White House, he kept constant track of events unfolding at Khe Sanh. As one historian has noted, the president's obsession with Khe Sanh may have reflected his growing mistrust of the reports he received from Westmoreland and the JCS on the situation in Vietnam.[42]

The diversionary tactics of the NLF/NVA succeeded in leaving the real targets of the offensive vulnerable to attack. Coming at the beginning of Vietnam's most important holiday, the offensive caught both the United States and the government of South Vietnam off guard. U.S. intelligence had indicated heightened enemy activity around urban centers and U.S. strongholds over the previous several weeks, but this activity was generally interpreted as a diversionary tactic for the offensive at Khe Sanh. In addition, U.S. military commanders in Vietnam believed that NLF/NVA losses had been too high in 1967 to enable them to launch an attack on the scale of Tet. The element of surprise gave all the initiative to the communists during the first hours and days of the offensive, but the ARVN and U.S. forces recovered quickly and were able in a short time to drive back the enemy from the ground it had gained in the initial assault. In the process, the United States and the ARVN inflicted heavy casualties on the NLF/NVA. Only in Hue, the former imperial capital of Vietnam, did the NLF/NVA hold on for any considerable length of time. It took three weeks of some of the bloodiest fighting of the war for U.S. forces to recapture Hue and when they did much of the once-majestic city lay in ruins. In purely military terms Tet was a clear victory for the United States and South Vietnam, but in terms of the political will of the former and the political stability of the latter, the damage from the events of February 1968 would prove irreparable.

Tet sent "shock waves" across the United States as "television accounts of bloody fighting in Saigon and Hue made a mockery of Johnson and Westmoreland's optimistic end of year reports."[43] The massive communist offensive belied earlier claims of imminent American victory and widened an already-expanding credibility gap between the government's assessment of the situation and other evidence from Vietnam. Tet raised doubts about the claim that the United States was protecting the legitimate and popular government of South Vietnam from outside aggression, as it appeared that the NLF enjoyed widespread support and perhaps it was the United States that represented the outside aggressor. For many Americans, Tet brought home in vivid detail the brutality of the conflict and highlighted contradictions in the U.S. role in the war. People were perplexed to hear an American officer explain that "we had to destroy it in order to save it" when asked why the United States was bombing a Vietnamese village. Meanwhile searing television images such as the shooting of an unarmed NLF prisoner in the head by the Saigon police chief muddied the water in terms of who represented the force of good in the conflict. Tet provided a massive boost to the antiwar movement but probably more significantly it eroded the confidence of Middle America in the administration's Vietnam policy. In the weeks following Tet the number of Americans who believed that intervention in Vietnam was a mistake topped 50 percent for the first time, and by the end of the year 78 percent of Americans polled believed that the United States was not making any progress in the war.[44] Walter Cronkite, the dean of American television journalism, captured the mood of the country when he editorialized that the United States was "mired in a stalemate" and that to continue to believe the optimists was to fly in the face of the evidence. "Cronkite's stark evaluation was a turning point in America's reaction to the Tet attacks, just as Tet marked a turning point of the U.S. experience in Vietnam."[45] Johnson is reported to have conceded, "if I've lost Cronkite, I've lost America."

JCS Chairman General Earle Wheeler and General Westmoreland both argued that NLF/NVA losses had been so great during Tet that for the first time since entering the war, U.S. forces in Vietnam enjoyed a significant battlefield advantage, which the generals were anxious to press home. However, when the story broke in the *New York Times* that Westmoreland now sought 206,000 additional American troops, it "hit the American public with almost as much impact as the Tet attacks themselves."[46] Secretary of Defense Clark Clifford, who was only just transitioning into the post following the resignation of Robert McNamara, captured the dilemma facing the administration when he noted that to the American people claims that Tet was a defeat for the NLF/NVA just did not appear compatible with the additional troop request. The White House faced mounting pressure from Congress and the public to find a way *out* of Vietnam, not to send more American troops *in*. Sen. Robert C. Byrd (D-WV) raised "serious concerns" about the future of U.S. involvement in Vietnam during congressional briefings with the president, while Sen. Joseph Clark (D-PA) wrote a damning report entitled "Stalemate in Vietnam" for the Senate Foreign Relations Committee in which he referred to the Vietnam War as a "cancer" in American society.[47] As if to underscore America's growing disillusionment with Vietnam, the $3.6 billion-a-year price tag for the war precipitated an economic crisis in 1968 that finally brought the United States' post-WWII prosperity to an end. According to *Newsweek* the White House now had no option but to reexamine its plans for Vietnam, declaring that in the wake of Tet, "a strategy of more of the same is intolerable."[48]

While Johnson remained publicly militant, he had lost faith in the advice of the military and he became increasingly influenced by the advice of those who favored a revision in the existing policy. After conducting a broad Pentagon review of Vietnam policy, Secretary of Defense Clifford recommended that the president reject the military's call for additional troops and instead, shift toward a defensive strategy aimed at laying the groundwork for negotiations. Johnson received similar advice from a group of distinguished former government officials, foreign policy experts, and military men that he had begun consulting in the months before Tet. Dubbed the "Wise Men" by the press, the group included members of the foreign policy elite, such as former Secretary of State Dean Acheson and ex-JCS Chairman General Matthew Ridgway, a hero of the Korean War who had supported the Vietnam War up to this point. The majority of the Wise Men now, however, counseled de-escalation either unilaterally or through negotiations. Johnson backed away from the idea of sending additional troops and began to push for the ARVN to carry more of the burden for the war in Vietnam, a policy that would become known as "Vietnamization" under his successor Richard Nixon. The President also embraced Secretary of State Rusk's proposal for a bombing halt as a prelude to opening negotiations with North Vietnam, thus allowing the White House to undercut its critics and regain some moral high ground on the issue of Vietnam.

While Johnson was not yet willing to admit defeat in Vietnam, his decision not to escalate in the wake of Tet marked an important new departure. By turning down Westmoreland's request for more troops, the president implicitly recognized that the United States could not win the war at an acceptable military price. Some of the heaviest fighting of the conflict took place in 1968, yet by the end of that year the United States had achieved little more than "a favorable stalemate" and the government of South Vietnam was as vulnerable to collapse as it had been in 1965.[49] Johnson's own political future suddenly came into doubt when Eugene McCarthy, running as a grass roots antiwar candidate, made a surprisingly strong showing in the New Hampshire Democratic primary. When Robert Kennedy joined the race for the Democratic nomination as an antiwar candidate a month later, the president was compelled to make an effort to regain the initiative by shifting the emphasis in Vietnam from victory to peace. On March 31, 1968, Lyndon Johnson gave a national television address in which he announced a limitation on the bombing of North Vietnam and his willingness to open negotiations with Hanoi. The president then shocked the nation by announcing his decision not to seek re-election. By falling on the sword of the policy of gradual escalation Johnson was conceding that, "a limit to American commitment had been reached."[50] American military involvement in Vietnam would continue for another five years, but Johnson's March speech clearly marked the end of a policy that dated back to the Truman administration.

AFTERMATH: THE TET OFFENSIVE AS A TURNING POINT

After March 1968, U.S. policy in Vietnam shifted from escalation to de-escalation and withdrawal. Although the United States hoped to preserve South Vietnam while disengaging U.S. forces from the conflict, the dominant concern in Washington now became damage limitation. The Tet Offensive was the key turning point in shaping U.S. policy in Vietnam. Through four presidential administrations, from Truman to Johnson, escalating American commitments in Vietnam had been accepted as a major plank of U.S. policy in Southeast Asia. While a small but vocal antiwar movement began to take shape in the months after Johnson's major escalation in 1965, American involvement in Vietnam enjoyed broad bipartisan support through 1967. Although significant cracks were starting to emerge in the political consensus in the months before Tet, it was the scale and scope of the communist offensive in South Vietnam in January 1968 that destroyed the foundations on which U.S. policy in Vietnam was based. White House claims that victory was in sight and that South Vietnam represented a viable bulwark against communism in

Southeast Asia now no longer appeared to hold water. From a military standpoint, Tet exposed the Vietnam War as a quagmire from which the United States could not extricate itself.

The war had torn asunder the broad domestic consensus on which U.S. foreign policy during the early Cold War had securely rested and had done serious damage to the United States' reputation in the eyes of many of its allies. Withdrawal now became imperative but in order to avoid any further erosion of U.S. standing in the eyes of both its allies and its enemies, it had to be done in a way that would avoid the impression of American defeat. The process of withdrawal would prove just as complicated and protracted as the process whereby the United States became drawn into Vietnam in the first place. Peace talks between the United States and North Vietnam began in Paris in May 1968 but immediately bogged down as neither side was fully willing to meet the other's preconditions for negotiation. While they continued to engage each other diplomatically for the next five years, both sides also continued to seek a battlefield advantage that would strengthen their negotiating position. Thus even while the United States was endeavoring to extract its ground forces from Vietnam, it persisted to employ extensive air power in an effort to make Hanoi more pliant at the negotiating table. Ultimately that strategy would prove futile and in the end it served only to exacerbate the domestic and international fallout from the war.

For Johnson the decision to halt escalation in 1968 did not immediately translate into an acceptance of withdrawal. The president's advisors were divided on what steps to take next. Rusk and Rostow, on the one hand, counseled that the president should increase military pressure using existing forces in order to begin negotiations from a position of strength, while Clifford and chief negotiator Averill Harriman favored making concessions that would enable the United States to withdraw as soon as possible and thus limit the damage to America's broader global interests. Johnson initially wavered, but following the violent scenes that shocked the nation during the Democratic Convention in Chicago and facing pressure from his own party to do something to boost the sluggish presidential campaign of Vice President Hubert Humphrey, the president called a bombing halt in October 1968 in order to jump start the peace talks.[51] Negotiations stalled, however, as the South Vietnamese refused to embrace a process they feared would end in the demise of their state. In a preview of the philosophy of subterfuge that would permeate his presidency, Richard Nixon's campaign secretly encouraged the South Vietnamese government to hold out for a Republican victory in the November election hinting that his administration would be less willing to make concessions to North Vietnam. Nixon beat Humphrey in a landslide after promising the American people that he had a secret plan to end the war in Vietnam while at the same time emphasizing that his administration would only accept "peace with honor." Although new National Security Advisor Henry Kissinger promised that the president would not repeat the mistakes of the past, the new administration nonetheless ended up employing many "methods that had been tried before and found wanting" and like Johnson, Nixon found that extricating the United States from Vietnam on his terms would prove exceedingly difficult.[52]

Nixon was determined not to be the first American president to lose a war and he and Kissinger were adamant that withdrawal must occur on American terms and must not damage the United States' status as a superpower. Nixon believed that his reputation as a militant anti-communist would convince North Vietnam that it must meet the United States' terms for peace—that is, the preservation of South Vietnam—or face serious military consequences. His model for success in Vietnam was Eisenhower's threat to use nuclear force against China to extract the United States from the Korean War. Nixon and Kissinger also turned to Great Power diplomacy to improve the United States' position in Vietnam. They planned to use improved relations with the Soviet Union and the People's Republic of China (see chapter 8) to gain leverage with North Vietnam while all the time holding out the use of military tactics that had been explicitly avoided during the Johnson administration. Nixon, however, repeated the mistake of his predecessors in that he seriously underestimated the enemy and its will to win.

One of Nixon's first acts in Vietnam was to approve the secret bombing of NLF/NVA bases in Cambodia, just across the border from South Vietnam. This was done in part to relieve pressure on American forces and in part to send a message to Hanoi (what Nixon liked to call "the mad man theory") that the new president was capable of acting in a manner his predecessor had not been. Nixon and Kissinger did indeed explore the possibility of striking a "savage blow" at North Vietnam, a plan codenamed "Duck Hook," but abandoned it in the face of potential public backlash. As it was, public reaction to Nixon's incursion into Cambodia would have far reaching implications. Although Nixon responded to public criticism by denouncing doves in Congress as "new isolationists," an implicit reference to the appeasement of fascism in the 1930s, he did announce the beginning of the phased withdrawal of U.S. troops from Vietnam. Nonetheless, Nixon's claim to have a comprehensive plan for peace met with skepticism from a large segment of the American public, including the antiwar movement which was enjoying a revival of interest following the Cambodia incursion. By widening the war into Cambodia Nixon inspired a backlash on Capitol Hill that saw Congress seek to reassert its authority by terminating the Gulf of Tonkin Resolution and prohibiting funding for the use of American combat forces outside of South Vietnam. The shooting death by the Ohio National Guard of four students protesting the secret war in Cambodia on the campus of Kent State University inspired a further wave of protests across the country, highlighted by a huge march in Washington, D.C., that culminated in the encirclement of the White House.

Nixon adopted a siege mentality and dramatically increased illegal government surveillance of and destabilization tactics against the peace movement. The President's obsession with antiwar protestors reflected the extent to which the peace movement limited the White House's freedom of action in Vietnam.[53] Nixon's public relations campaign to garner support for his policies did succeed in removing some of the movement's teeth and buying him time to find an acceptable solution to the Vietnam dilemma. The President appealed to the "great silent majority" of Americans to mobilize behind his efforts to secure "peace with honor." This appeal to Middle America followed his decision to embrace Vietnamization, the practice of shifting the burden of the war back to the government of South Vietnam and the ARVN begun under Johnson, as part of a larger policy of limiting the role of U.S. ground forces in Asia. By providing funding and support for the ARVN and continuing the bombing campaign, "Vietnamization raised the possibility of perpetual war at an acceptable cost."[54] There is certainly no doubt that phased withdrawal of American troops bought the White House some breathing room to find a way out of Vietnam and the "silent majority" would enthusiastically throw its support behind the president's re-election bid in 1972.

Ironically, however, before the election, Vietnam would indirectly inspire actions on the part of Nixon that would ultimately destroy his presidency. In the spring of 1971 the White House, facing a barrage of bad press following a disastrous ARVN raid into Laos and the high profile trial of Lt. William Calley for his part of the infamous massacre of South Vietnamese civilians in the village of My Lai, reacted angrily to the *New York Times* publication of leaked secret defense department documents exposing a history of government duplicity regarding Vietnam. Nixon subsequently approved the creation of a clandestine group known as "the plumbers" to prevent future leaks, a practice that would lead directly to the Watergate scandal and the president's subsequent resignation.

Meanwhile fighting and negotiations continued simultaneously with both sides seeking momentum in the former in order to gain leverage in the latter. Nixon's room to maneuver, however, became increasingly limited as his plan for peace made little progress. His decision to push for a breakthrough at the negotiating table by ordering a Christmas bombing blitz of North Vietnam in 1972 caused widespread condemnation and led to calls in Congress to cut off funds for South Vietnam. Eventually the United States had to threaten South Vietnam that it would end its support for the war and conclude a separate settlement with North Vietnam in order to convince Saigon to agree to a peace settlement that was largely favorable to the communist government in Hanoi. To the end Nixon and Kissinger continued to make secret commitments in order to secure their agenda, this time promising Saigon that the United States would respond with full force to any North Vietnamese violation of the proposed treaty.

The Paris Peace Accords were officially signed in January 1973 and the chief negotiators for the United States and North Vietnam, Henry Kissinger and Le Doc Tho, were nominated for the Nobel Peace Prize. However, while the Paris agreement did mean peace for the United States, it did not signal the end of the war in Vietnam. As the Watergate scandal enveloped the White House, Congress began to reduce American funding for the ARVN and the government of South Vietnam. Reduced American aid left the Saigon regime teetering on the brink of collapse and at the beginning of 1975, North Vietnam began the final offensive of a conflict that had begun thirty years earlier. Congress stood firm in the face of appeals by Nixon's successor, Gerald Ford, that the United States had an obligation to fund South Vietnam's desperate defense and on May 1, 1975, Saigon fell to communist forces.

Even before American involvement in the Vietnam War had come to an end, the far-reaching implications of this conflict for U.S. foreign policy had started to become evident as the consensus that had prevailed since WWII was shattered.[55] A significant minority of Americans had come to question the motives behind the post-1945 internationalist agenda and the manner in which American power was employed in world affairs. Hence, we begin to see a return to a retrenchment in foreign policy, especially pertaining to far flung overseas adventures. A chastened Congress began to question the growth of executive power which had been so evident during the Vietnam conflict and which can be seen as part of the historical trend in U.S. foreign policy, especially since Teddy Roosevelt's presidency in the early 1900s. Accordingly, Congress passed the War Powers Act in 1973 requiring the president to inform Congress within forty-eight hours of any decision to deploy American military forces in harm's way abroad and obliging the withdrawal of those forces within sixty days unless Congress approved otherwise. Nixon's decision to normalize relations with the People's Republic of China and pursue detente with the Soviet Union (see chapter 8) reflected the realization that communism was not monolithic and that Great Power diplomacy was a necessary tool for managing a volatile world now that the limits of American power had been so clearly exposed. The Nixon Doctrine foreshadowed the United States' reluctance to deploy combat troops overseas, and Congress over the course of three decades would repeatedly frustrate efforts of the executive branch to employ force in various locations around the world, from Angola to Nicaragua.

"For over two decades the specter of Tet helped to define and limit America's behavior" as the country continued to debate the lessons of Vietnam, in particular when and how the United States could and should use force in pursuit of foreign policy goals.[56] For much of the remainder of the 1970s the general consensus among the foreign policy elite was that American intervention in Vietnam had been a mistake and that the use of force in future endeavors entailed a serious risk of quagmire. What became known as the Vietnam Syndrome would make most post-Vietnam presidents think twice before even considering the deployment of U.S. forces overseas. However, Ronald Reagan's election in 1980 ushered in a moderate revision in this line of thinking. Reagan and the conservative wing of the Republican Party sought to recast the war as a noble effort in a positive cause, but despite military interventions in Lebanon and Grenada as well as an air raid against Libya, the Reagan administration was unable to guide the United States completely out from under the shadow of Vietnam. George H. W. Bush claimed to have kicked the Vietnam Syndrome with the successful liberation of Kuwait from Iraqi occupation in 1991 (see chapter 11), but Bill Clinton clearly felt its effect when he was forced to withdraw American troops from a failed peacekeeping and nation-building mission in Somalia in 1994. In the aftermath of September 11 (see chapter 12) the country once again embraced force as a legitimate tool of American foreign policy, but as the original goals of U.S. military intervention in both Afghanistan and Iraq have proved elusive, "the specter of Tet" hovers ominously close to the surface of American politics.

Eight

THE U.S. OPENING TO CHINA
AND DETENTE

This chapter traces the diplomatic breakthrough that occurred between the United States and China in the 1970s. President Richard Nixon's historic visit to China in 1972, the first for any sitting American president, followed by President Jimmy Carter's 1978 declaration officially recognizing the People's Republic of China (PRC), significantly altered the balance of power in the Cold War between the Soviet Union and the United States. By playing the so-called China card, Nixon and his National Security Advisor (and later Secretary of State), Henry A. Kissinger, outmaneuvered the Soviet Union, forcing Moscow into a diplomatic dance based on detente that was highly advantageous to U.S. interests. Nixon and Kissinger deftly used a combination of public and secret diplomacy to shepherd one of the greatest turnabouts in U.S. foreign policy. This was all the more remarkable because it occurred in an area that was seemingly locked in a permanent vise of mutual suspicion and animosity for more than twenty years.

The United States has always had an interesting relationship with China, occasionally swinging from one extreme to another. On the one hand, Americans look upon China and its ancient civilization with great admiration and wonder. On the other hand, they see China as a mortal threat, which is how U.S. foreign policy makers viewed China after Mao Zedong's communist forces defeated Chiang Kai Shek's Nationalist forces in 1949 (see chapter 4). Sino-American relations deteriorated rapidly thereafter. The United States refused to recognize Mao's communist regime on the mainland and instead gave diplomatic recognition to Chiang's regime, which had withdrawn in defeat to the island province of Formosa, later called Taiwan. Whenever communist China threatened to forcibly reunite Taiwan with the mainland, the United States rattled its saber in return, threatening to match China's use of force with its own.

This chapter begins by examining the harsh political and diplomatic context that contributed to so much animosity between Beijing and Washington and how domestic politics in both countries made it difficult to improve relations. Next we examine developments in both China and the United States that led both sides to consider changing their approach toward one another. The chapter then discusses how Nixon and Kissinger used a combination of public and private diplomacy to pull off the breakthrough visit, which held the entire world in its grip. Next the chapter examines how President Carter built on Nixon's historic visit by opening formal diplomatic relations with China, a move that caused far more debates in the United States than Nixon's initial opening. Finally, we examine how this new relationship amounts to a turning point as it fundamentally altered the balance of power in both regional and world politics.

A FROZEN RELATIONSHIP

As chapter 4 chronicles, Sino-American relations went into a virtual deep freeze when the Korean War broke out in 1950. When U.S. forces crossed the 38th parallel prompting China to send hundreds of thousands of troops into North Korea, the United States suddenly found itself in a bloody, albeit undeclared, war with the world's most populous country. More than any other single incident, the Korean War is responsible for poisoning Sino-American relations throughout the 1950s and 1960s.[1] Despite the armistice that ended the fighting in Korea in 1953, the United States and China remained irreconcilable foes for years thereafter, with both countries locked in a bitter cycle of mutual recrimination.

Because of U.S. military interventions in Korea and then later in Vietnam, the PRC viewed the United States as one of its greatest threats. As in Korea in the 1950s, the United States sent hundreds of thousands of troops to Vietnam in the 1960s in the name of containing the spread of communism in Asia. While the PRC did not intervene in Vietnam with its own troops the way it did in Korea, Chinese territory became an important supply route for Vietnamese guerrillas fighting U.S. troops and the U.S.-backed South Vietnamese government.

With U.S. troops and installations stationed all around China's periphery, in Taiwan, South Korea, Japan, the Philippines, and Vietnam, Beijing depicted the

Americans as the world's new colonialists who were seeking to establish their hegemony throughout Asia. China denounced the United States as an imperialist power unlawfully intervening in the affairs of other Asian countries. For its part, the United States stubbornly refused to recognize the People's Republic of China and condemned Beijing as the lapdog of the Soviet Union, accusing it of fomenting and aiding violent revolutions throughout the region. Indeed, during the 1950s and into the mid-1960s, some U.S. officials actually considered China a greater threat to American interests than the Soviet Union. Since the Soviets were increasingly seen as practical and willing to work within the bounds of well established and accepted spheres of influence and since China appeared radical, revolutionary, and unstable, Americans viewed Beijing with more caution than Moscow. A 1967 poll found 70 percent of Americans believing that China was the single greatest threat to U.S. security while President Johnson contemplated a nuclear strike against China's growing nuclear weapons stockpile.[2]

Domestic considerations in both countries only worsened matters. In China, revolutionary fervor had reached a feverish pitch; it became impossible to respond positively to anything emanating from Washington. In 1962, for instance, China rejected President Kennedy's modest offer of food aid to help alleviate a severe famine.[3] Moreover, by 1965 the deepening U.S. involvement in Vietnam helped to harden China's position against the United States.[4] In addition, Mao's domestic policies imposed a crushing isolation on China, crippling its ability to take any significant international initiatives. Mao's Great Leap Forward, begun in the late 1950s, was a radical experiment designed to induce rapid, self-sufficient industrialization. But it turned out to be a dismal failure.

In 1966 conditions worsened even more when Mao launched the Cultural Revolution, which was another of his radical experiments, this time designed to wrest control of the country from communist bureaucrats while enshrining Mao's style of fervent communist ideology throughout the country. Revolutionary movements often turn on their own supporters and China's was no different.[5] Radical student and other youth groups were instigated to crack down on anyone who was rightly or wrongly seen as a threat to the revolution. In the ensuing chaos hundreds of thousands are believed to have perished while countless more were left ruined. China withdrew into a cocoon as many of its most talented and industrious people, including many able diplomats, were lost to the zealotry of the Cultural Revolution. At one point, China had no ambassadors located in any country except Egypt.[6]

While not as violent, domestic politics in the United States in the 1950s and most of the 1960s were also not conducive to improved Sino-American relations. During this period, it was politically impossible for a sitting president to seek improved relations with China lest his political adversaries accuse him of being "soft" on communism. At a peace conference in Geneva, Switzerland in 1954, Secretary of State John Foster Dulles even refused to shake Chinese Premier Chou Enlai's hand because he did not want to appear conciliatory in front of the American media. And at the 1955 Bandung Conference, Premier Chou proposed improved relations, but the United States was unresponsive. After President Kennedy assumed office in 1961, former President Eisenhower warned Kennedy that he would oppose any attempt by Kennedy to admit China to the United Nations.[7] As a Congressman and Senator in the late 1940s and early 1950s, Richard Nixon's was one of the loudest anticommunist voices in Washington. Even in 1958, as Eisenhower's vice president, Nixon wrote a memo opposing suggestions that it was time to improve relations with China:

> I wish to have my viewpoint on the record as follows: I am unequivocally opposed at this time to recognition of Red China, admission of Red China to the United Nations, and to any concept of 'two Chinas.'[8]

The "two Chinas" reference dealt with recognizing Mao on the mainland and Chiang on Taiwan.

THE GROUND THAWS

However tortured Sino-American relations were, the diplomatic ice age that existed between the two countries was unnatural and both sides knew it. Surely it made little sense for the world's strongest power to have no diplomatic or economic relations with the world's most populous country, especially given the PRC's strategic location in the heart of Asia. But how could this frozen, decades-old acrimony be altered? What would it take to prompt the capitalist giant in the West and the communist giant in the East to step toward one another? In short, the timing had to be just right for both countries. Not until the late 1960s and early 1970s did a "coincidence of interests" between the United States and China finally emerge.[9] At that time, changes within both countries occurred simultaneously such that each could enhance its own interests by moving toward the other. We turn now to examining those changes.

Changes Pertaining to the United States

From the American side came important shifts in mood and policy, some of which occurred before Nixon's 1968 election. Several factors motivated Washington to moderate its stance toward Beijing. First, policy makers hoped to increase U.S. leverage on the Soviets by improving relations with China, which was increasingly challenging Moscow for leadership in Asia. Second, ever since China's entry into the nuclear weapons club in 1964, the United States had to find a way to account for China's growing strategic strength. Third, U.S. policy makers hoped to entice China to play a stabilizing role in Asia, especially as the United States engaged in difficult negotiations with North Vietnam while reducing its military commitment to South Vietnam. Furthermore, Nixon considered the incredible political victory he would score if he were the one to open relations with China.[10]

Accordingly, members of the foreign policy elite began a campaign to prepare American public opinion to eventually accept a shift in policy. This change would ultimately steer the United States away from Nationalist Taiwan, a close friend and ally for decades and instead establish formal diplomatic relations with the communist regime that had defeated the Nationalists in 1949, and that had also fought the United States to a draw in Korea. In 1959 Dean Rusk, who was an assistant secretary of state and a vocal anti-China hawk during the Truman administration, issued a report that, while not calling for diplomatic recognition of China, nevertheless advised policy makers not to allow "emotion or differences of ideology to stand in the way of improved relations."[11] Meanwhile, a growing chorus of Republican as well as Democratic members of Congress was calling for new ties. In 1960, Sen. Henry Jackson (D-WA), who was influential on foreign affairs, suggested that the United States establish direct communication with China since, in his view, China had progressed significantly. In 1966, the Senate Foreign Relations Committee held hearings to explore how to establish contact with China. In the same year then-President Johnson remarked in a televised speech that eventual reconciliation with China was necessary for U.S. interests.

Even Richard Nixon, that stalwart anti-communist, recognized that American attitudes and policies regarding China had to change. As a presidential candidate in 1960, Nixon was a vocal opponent of admitting China to the United Nations. As a private citizen in 1966, he warned of war with China because of its support for Vietnamese communists. However, by the next year, he displayed a modified position when he wrote in *Foreign Affairs* that, "We simply cannot afford to leave

China forever outside the family of nations."[12] While he still regarded China as an implacable foe and cautioned against moving too fast in improving relations with the PRC, Nixon acknowledged that it was in U.S. interests to see China welcomed back on the world stage, provided that China moderate its radical views on such matters as aiding communist revolutions around the world.

Changes Pertaining to China

The changing attitude in the United States came just as China emerged from its crippling isolation brought on by its domestic policies. Mao realized that the domestic political turmoil created by the Cultural Revolution rendered China vulnerable in world affairs. He concluded that Beijing's stifling self-imposed isolation must end if China was to recover from the failed policies of the Great Leap Forward and the equally disastrous Cultural Revolution. As China emerged from its shell, it had to consider that improved relations with the United States might help China with its economic development. While Chinese leaders disagreed among themselves over whether to engage in international trade with the capitalist West, those favoring such trade eventually gained the upper hand.

Moreover, improved relations with the United States might help China navigate its troubled dealings with powerful regional neighbors, including Japan, India, and Vietnam. Japan had brutalized China in WWII. Now that Tokyo was a close U.S. ally, improved Sino-American relations might give Beijing increased leverage with Tokyo. Additionally, China and India are traditional rivals and even fought a war against each other in 1965. Since India developed a close relationship with the Soviet Union, it might serve China's interest vis-a-vis India to get closer to the United States. And, even though China was helping communist North Vietnam in its fight against the U.S.-backed South Vietnamese regime, Beijing had concerns about a unified Vietnam. Communist or not, Vietnam and China were historic rivals for influence in Southeast Asia.[13] A unified, resurgent Vietnam might pose a threat to China's southern flank. However, while gaining leverage with Japan, India, and Vietnam was important, the primary motivation behind Beijing's decision to move closer to the United States sprung from its worsening relations with its erstwhile friends in Moscow.[14]

A shared communist ideology notwithstanding, the Soviet Union and China were bound to clash over conflicts of interest in Asia. As early as the 1930s, Soviet Premier Joseph Stalin and Mao quarreled over tactics in Mao's struggle to defeat

Chiang Kai Shek in the Chinese Civil War. Mao also resisted Stalin's admonitions to form an alliance with Chiang against Japan during WWII. He then refused Stalin's advice to negotiate with Chiang after the war ended, choosing instead to pursue a military victory over Chiang's forces and establishing himself as the unquestioned leader on the Chinese mainland in 1949.

The Korean War also proved to be a bone of contention between the two communist giants. For one thing, Mao was informed at the last minute, and not consulted, about Stalin having given North Korean leader Kim Il Sung the green light to invade South Korea. Second, after the invasion went badly for Kim, Mao was angry with the Soviets for pressing the Chinese to enter the war while Moscow only provided military aid that was often too little too late.

Even though Mao frequently disagreed with Stalin, he still respected the Soviet leader and considered him a senior partner in their attempts to engineer communist regimes in Asia. However, Sino-Soviet relations deteriorated significantly after Stalin's death in 1953 and with the rise of Soviet Premier Nikita Khrushchev. Mao and his communist cohort in China were suspicious of Khrushchev for a number of reasons. First, in 1956 Khrushchev gave a speech at an important meeting of communist leaders condemning Stalin's policies, which appeared as heresy to the Chinese. Second, Khrushchev refused to side with Beijing in its border dispute with India. Third, Khrushchev promoted what he called "peaceful coexistence" with the capitalist West, which again amounted to heresy to Mao and other radical communists in China who worried that Khrushchev was not sufficiently loyal to the cause of communist revolution.

Relations further deteriorated when Leonid Brezhnev took over for Khrushchev in 1964. Perhaps most troubling for Mao was Brezhnev's use of military force in 1968 to invade another communist country to ensure a pro-Soviet regime there. When Brezhnev sent Soviet tanks into the streets of Prague, Czechoslovakia to crush a homegrown reform movement, he proclaimed a Soviet prerogative to intervene in any "deficient" communist country in order to ensure it remained on the proper path.[15] This Brezhnev Doctrine worried Chinese leaders as they cast a weary eye toward their comrades in Moscow. Ever since their 1949 victory, China's communist leaders were (and remain) highly sensitive to any hint of foreign meddling or interference in China's sovereignty. They wondered if Brezhnev reserved for himself the right to intervene in China, which was especially worrisome in the late 1960s when the Cultural Revolution cast China adrift in turmoil.

By the summer of 1969, U.S. foreign policy makers learned just how severely unhinged Sino-Soviet relations had become. Chinese and Soviet troops were fighting pitched battles along their mutual border, which ran for thousands of miles. A section of the long-disputed border zone erupted into full-scale fighting when a Soviet border patrol came into contact with its Chinese counterpart. At one point, the Soviets had stationed more than a million troops along their border with China while the Chinese condemned the Soviets' "social imperialism" as even worse than American imperialism.[16] The fighting was made all the more serious because both sides possessed nuclear weapons. The Soviets actually consulted the Americans to gauge the Americans' reaction if Moscow launched a limited nuclear strike against China. On the one hand, Kissinger and other top foreign policy makers were encouraged by the opportunities the Sino-Soviet split offered. On the other hand, they surely did not want the two countries exchanging nuclear blows in such a crowded and strategic part of the world.

As the crisis in relations with the Soviet Union worsened, Mao realized that China could not sustain conflicting relations with both superpowers at the same time. But Mao was in luck because, just as the Brezhnev Doctrine indicated a more aggressive period in Soviet foreign policy, the United States was reducing its posture in Asia as it began to draw down in Vietnam. As it happened, therefore, China's image of the United States began to soften as it grew increasingly alarmed by the Soviets, as the "decline in U.S. pressure and the increase in Soviet pressure had reached a point where [Beijing] came to judge that its previous posture toward both superpowers was no longer workable."[17]

PREPARATIONS: NIXON'S PUBLIC AND PRIVATE DIPLOMACY
Although official Sino-American diplomatic relations were long dormant, the two countries had periodic contact through their diplomats in Warsaw, Poland. Between 1955 and 1968, 133 such meetings occurred, although little of consequence was accomplished.[18] In November 1968, shortly after Nixon's election victory, the Americans received an unexpected invitation to renew the talks. The two sides had not spoken for nearly a year. The Americans responded positively hoping for a new chance at a diplomatic breakthrough. However, the renewed talks, scheduled for February 1969, were abruptly canceled over a diplomatic row involving the defection of a Chinese diplomat in the Netherlands. In fact, it would be another year before talks resumed. Nevertheless, Nixon pressed his aides to study how to improve

relations with China. Even though this particular window of opportunity closed rather unexpectedly, the Nixon administration launched a concerted effort to reach out to China. The effort progressed on two tracks: one public; the other, secret.

The Public Track

Publicly, Nixon launched a series of carefully calibrated unilateral changes in policy that he hoped would improve relations with China. In January 1969 Nixon announced that tourists, museums, and similarly interested parties would be allowed to bring noncommercial Chinese products into the United States. In December of the same year, he allowed foreign subsidiaries of American businesses to engage in commerce with communist China. In March 1970 came the announcement that U.S. passports would be validated for travel to the PRC, the first time such travel was permitted. In April, the Nixon administration authorized the *selective* licensing of non-strategic U.S. goods for export to China. In August, the government lifted restrictions on American oil companies operating abroad, permitting them to call on Chinese ports. And in October 1970, during a toast to Rumanian President Nicolae Ceausescu, Nixon deliberately referred to China as the People's Republic of China and not as communist China or even as "Red" China. It was the first time a sitting president referred to the PRC by its official name.[19] Nixon chose the occasion in order to reinforce the secret diplomatic track, in which the Rumanian president played a critical role as go-between, ferrying messages between the Chinese and Americans.[20] To strengthen the weight of his intentions, Nixon also ordered a cessation of patrols by the U.S. Navy's Seventh Fleet in the Taiwan Straits and ended spy flights over China. He even acknowledged that the PRC was the legitimate power on the mainland. In his annual review of foreign policy in early 1971, Nixon reported:

> In this decade there will be no more important challenge than that of drawing the People's Republic of China into a constructive relationship with the world community and particularly the rest of Asia.[21]

Meanwhile, he continued to withdraw American forces from Vietnam, which further helped to ease Sino-American tensions.

By summer 1971, these incremental changes paved the way for the Nixon administration to reveal three fundamental policy shifts on China. In June the administration declared an official end to the trade embargo against China. In July, Nixon stunned the world when he proclaimed that he would visit China the following year. And in August, Secretary of State Rogers signaled that the United States supported seating the PRC at the United Nations even as it tried unsuccessfully to preserve a seat for the Nationalists on Taiwan. U.S. support for Taiwan has always been the key sticking point in Sino-American relations. The PRC long insisted that one prerequisite to normalization was the United States renouncing its recognition of Taiwan, which was difficult for the Americans to do. Relations with Taiwan had grown stronger since 1949 and Taiwan had lots of supporters in the United States, especially in Congress.

One way around this dilemma was the Nixon administration's failed attempt to engineer a two Chinas policy, where both the PRC and Taiwan would be represented at the United Nations. But these efforts fell by the wayside almost as fast as they were proposed, in large part because the United States simply did not have enough U.N. votes to guarantee Taiwan's membership. Even though the Nixon administration knew a two Chinas policy would never work, the diplomatic front had to be carried to its logical conclusion. On October 25, 1971, the United States voted to admit the PRC to the United Nations. On the same day, the United Nations voted to expel Taiwan over only halfhearted American objections. Many members of Congress were angry over Taiwan's expulsion but there was little they could do to prevent it.[22]

China responded positively to these moves. In December 1970 Mao informed *Life* magazine's Edgar Snow that Nixon would be welcome in China as a tourist or as the president.[23] In April 1971 Chinese officials engaged in an unusual, yet attractive, tool of diplomacy when they invited the American table tennis team for a visit. The Americans quickly accepted and became the first to officially visit China in many years.[24] Dubbed "ping pong diplomacy," most observers saw the team's visit as a precursor to more intense high-level government exchanges: the back and forth between the American and Chinese ping pong players was a metaphor for the mutually reinforcing moves by each country's diplomats. These slow but sure bit-by-bit exchanges gradually helped Nixon strengthen ties with Beijing even as he prepared the American people to reach out to an old foe. Public opinion polls in the wake of the ping-pong visit showed that, for the first time, a majority of Americans favored diplomatic recognition of the PRC and its admission to the United Nations.[25]

None of these policy changes, taken on their own, amounted to much. Taken together however, these actions signaled just how serious Nixon was in changing

American policy. This is especially true when these public changes are considered in conjunction with the secret contacts Nixon was nurturing at the very same time.

The Secret Track

When it came to foreign policy, President Nixon worked closely with his right hand man, Henry Kissinger, who served Nixon first as national security advisor (NSA) and later as both NSA and secretary of state. In the late 1960s and early 1970s, as the United States withdrew from South Vietnam, President Nixon announced what came to be called the Nixon Doctrine, which held that the United States would continue to engage in containing the spread of communism but in modified form. Unlike the 1950s and 1960s, when the United States sent American troops overseas to fight the spread of communism (in places like Korea and Vietnam), the Nixon Doctrine called on local government troops to engage communist forces. While the United States would provide military and other support to countries confronting communist challenges, it would no longer provide U.S. troops to fight those battles. In conjunction with the Nixon Doctrine, Kissinger advocated a withdrawal and retrenchment of American power. He wanted to move away from a strictly bipolar system—where the United States squared off against the Soviet Union—toward a multipolar system that included Japan, West Germany, and China as additional key players.[26] So Nixon and Kissinger agreed on the importance of cultivating closer relations with China.

In fact, Nixon and Kissinger were in many ways made for each other. Nixon needed Kissinger because of the latter's reputation as a foreign policy genius, and Kissinger needed Nixon because, as the president's indispensable right hand man on foreign policy, Kissinger would have access to the power he craved so much.[27] Moreover, the two shared the same disdain toward the foreign policy bureaucracy in Washington, D.C., including officials at the Defense Department, the CIA, and the State Department. Both were jealous of the "insider" status of the foreign policy elite, made up of mostly easterners.[28] Nor did they care very much for members of Congress, who were perceived as obstacles and meddlers in affairs of state that rightly belonged in the Oval Office. For both men, maintaining control over foreign policy was paramount. They viewed other officials, whether colleagues in the Executive Branch or elected members of Congress in the legislative branch, as rivals for their control and dominance of foreign policy. Their bitter disdain, combined with a healthy dose of paranoia, degenerated to the point where they actually launched spying operations against some of their own aides in the White House, as well as other administration officials and several journalists.[29]

These shared sentiments contributed to two important and related characteristics of U.S. foreign policy. First, its structure and formulation were centralized in the White House, with Nixon and then Kissinger sitting atop a strictly enforced hierarchy.[30] Important and highly capable officials, such as Secretary of State William P. Rogers, were often bypassed and excluded from many of the most significant policy deliberations.[31] For example, in spring 1970, when U.S. troops massed for the secret and illegal invasion of Cambodia, Nixon's supposed principle advisors on war and peace, the Secretaries of State and Defense, "would be very nearly among the last to know."[32]

A second hallmark of the Nixon-Kissinger team's foreign policy was its shroud of secrecy, where only a few in the administration knew what Nixon and Kissinger were plotting. Even Secretary Rogers, for instance, was not informed of Kissinger's secret visit to China until *after* Kissinger's plane was airborne. When Nixon ordered a series of studies on U.S.-China relations, his own advisors on the National Security Council were kept in the dark about their ultimate purpose.[33] And both Rogers and Vice President Spiro Agnew made public statements on China that were at variance with what Nixon and Kissinger were secretly telling the Chinese.[34]

But Nixon and Kissinger had several reasons for conducting a secret diplomatic track on China that ran parallel to the public one. First, they did not want the conservatives in their own party to find out about the diplomacy for fear the latter might work to scuttle it.[35] Many conservative Republicans had close ties to Taiwan and were loath to see China take Taiwan's place. Second, Nixon and Kissinger knew they would face formidable obstacles from entrenched interests in the State Department, the Defense Department, and the CIA. For twenty years the foreign policy bureaucracy was conditioned to contain a hostile China. Nixon and Kissinger knew they would have difficulty budging this crowd since they were unwilling to endanger their careers on such a risky policy reversal.[36] Third, Nixon and Kissinger did not trust many of the people with whom they worked. Nixon was especially suspicious of his ambitious Secretary of Defense Melvin Laird, who Nixon blamed for just about any leak, true or not.[37] Kissinger worried more about Secretary of State Rogers, who he considered a rival for the president's favor. He need not have worried, though, because Nixon rarely revealed anything to Rogers, despite Rogers's years of loyal service. Fourth, Nixon and Kissinger justified their secrecy because they feared that word of the historic opening would reach the Soviets prematurely and jeopardize efforts at reaching detente with them.

Moreover, they kept it secret because the Chinese preferred secrecy as well. The Chinese utilized Pakistan's ambassador to the United States to deliver a hand written note from Beijing inviting a high ranking official to China for talks. And after Nixon gave his toast referring to the Peoples' Republic of China, the Chinese used secret channels to indicate that Nixon himself would be welcome in China. Both sides relied on secret French intermediaries as well. Through these channels, Nixon sent messages consistently stressing that the United States wanted an expanded dialogue with China, that it no longer wanted an adversarial relationship with China and that it would oppose any Soviet diplomatic or military initiatives that might threaten China's security.[38]

In responding to the secret Chinese invitation, Nixon chose his trusted national security advisor to go to China and lay the groundwork for Nixon's public visit. If it was primarily Nixon's vision to improve relations with China, it was Kissinger's skillful execution that brought that vision to fruition.[39] Indeed, Kissinger's secret July 1971 visit to China reads like a cloak-and-dagger spy novel. While on an official visit to Pakistan, Kissinger feigned severe abdominal pain and canceled a planned state dinner with Pakistan's leader, Gen. Yahya Khan.[40] Since both China and the United States had friendly relations with Pakistan, and since Pakistan bordered China, Pakistan was the natural choice to serve as go-between. General Khan's government announced that Kissinger was going to spend some time convalescing in the mountains, at which point he snuck across the border to meet with Chou Enlai. Kissinger and Chou quickly established a close working relationship as their discussions focused on Taiwan, China's U.N. membership, and the Soviet Union. Despite the drama surrounding Kissinger's secret visit, his main objective was to communicate Nixon's concession on Taiwan. The United States would no longer consider the status of Taiwan as "undetermined" and would neither challenge nor accept that there was one China and that Taiwan was part of it.[41] While Kissinger revealed this concession, the Chinese conceded that the United States would not, at least for the time being, sever diplomatic relations with Taiwan.[42] At that point, Chou issued the formal invitation for Nixon to visit China.

THE HISTORIC OPENING: NIXON'S VISIT

Kissinger's secret visit in 1971, followed by the stunning announcement that Nixon himself would visit China in 1972, shocked the world as much as it shocked the foreign policy community in Washington. Few knew of the secret diplomatic track but fewer still objected once they learned of Nixon's planned visit. As the saying goes, "Only Nixon can go to China." This now famous phrase, which has even entered Hollywood's popular lexicon,[43] illustrates that President Nixon, that famously hardline anti-communist Red Baiter of the 1950s, was the only American politician with sufficient anti-communist credentials to be trusted with the diplomatic opening to China. Surely no one from the Democratic Party was politically capable of such a bold initiative. After all, ever since Mao's 1949 communist revolution, which occurred during President Truman's administration, Democrats were the ones faulted for losing China.

By diplomatic standards, the visit was a great success. Nixon made several stops on his way to China to generate media buzz about the trip. He even timed his arrival to coincide with primetime television on the East Coast to ensure maximum news coverage back home. He made sure to shake hands with Chinese officials, thus making up for the diplomatic snub Eisenhower's secretary of state, John Foster Dulles, inflicted on the Chinese at the 1954 Geneva Conference on Indochina (perhaps because the memory of the Korean War was so fresh or perhaps because he did not want to give U.S. allies like Japan the wrong impression, Dulles refused to even shake hands with the head of the Chinese delegation).

Nixon and his team held hours-long negotiating sessions with Chinese officials regarding the contents of the joint statement that the visit would produce. Nixon had Kissinger, and not Secretary of State Rogers, do the diplomatic heavy lifting during the negotiations. In between the lengthy sessions, Nixon was treated to many warm welcomes as he visited famous Chinese tourist attractions, such as the Great Wall of China.

Although Nixon's visit to China did not lead immediately to normalized relations, the joint statement the two countries released upon the meeting's conclusion signaled that a major shift in the balance of power in Asia was underway. Nixon hailed the so-called Shanghai Communiqué as the hallmark of an exciting new framework of relations between China and the United States since it committed both countries to eventually normalize relations. The communiqué was a masterful diplomatic declaration. While highlighting common interests, such as checking Soviet power in Asia, keeping the Korean Peninsula stable, and promoting cultural and economic ties, it also politely acknowledged continuing policy differences over the fate of Taiwan. The United States pledged to "ultimately" remove its forces from

Taiwan and also acknowledged that Chinese on both sides of the Taiwan Straits hold that there is but one China and that Taiwan is part of that China.[44] This statement amounted to a reversal of policy of only a few months earlier when the United States made its half-hearted attempt at a two Chinas policy. For their part, the Chinese accepted that the United States would, at least in the short run, continue its security relationship with Taiwan.

Back home, Nixon's visit won widespread acclaim including from his Democratic opponents. Sen. Edward Kennedy (D-MA) praised the visit as did Sen. J. W. Fulbright (D-AR), who was a vocal critic of Nixon's Vietnam War policy. On China, Fulbright said, "I completely agree with what [Nixon is] doing."[45] Senator McGovern, who would be soundly defeated by Nixon in the presidential election a few months later, also praised the visit. Even some conservative senators, such as Barry Goldwater, supported the trip. Nevertheless, the visit drew criticism from some of Nixon's other conservative colleagues in Congress. For instance, Rep. John Ashbrook (R-OH), who loathed the PRC and accused it of killing some 34 million people, was angry about the apparent abandonment of millions of Chinese on Taiwan. Ashbrook actually launched a campaign to unseat Nixon as the 1972 Republican presidential candidate. His bid petered out after his dismal showing in the first Republican primary in New Hampshire where he won only 7 percent of the vote.[46]

FORMAL DIPLOMATIC RELATIONS: DEBATES AND DIVISIONS

Nixon's policies generated significant bipartisanship in Washington. In 1974 Kissinger proudly proclaimed that, "no policy of this administration has had greater bipartisan support than the normalization of relations with the People's Republic."[47] That bipartisan support was confirmed by public opinion polls that showed an overwhelming majority of Americans supporting the new policy.

With Nixon's resignation in 1974 due to his involvement in the Watergate scandal, his successor, Gerald R. Ford, came to be seen as a caretaker president until matters could be more definitively settled with the 1976 elections. In fact, unsettled leadership questions in both China and the United States helped cast Sino-American relations adrift in the mid-1970s.[48] President Ford was not in a position to take any bold initiatives in foreign policy so he essentially tried to continue Nixon's policies toward China without taking too many risks. Members of his own party warned him not to abandon Taiwan in the rush to open relations with China, especially so soon after South Vietnam had fallen to the communist North.

House Minority Leader John Rhodes (R-AZ) argued that the United States should not abandon Taiwan to pursue relations with China. Ronald Reagan, who launched a failed bid to defeat Ford in the 1976 Republican presidential primaries, urged Ford not to abandon Taiwan. And more than 200 members of Congress signed a petition advocating that the United States refrain from doing anything that might "compromise the freedom of our friend and ally," Taiwan.[49] Given these sentiments, and Ford's own precarious position, it is not too surprising that Ford was unable to meet the PRC's three longstanding conditions for establishing full diplomatic relations: (1) breaking diplomatic ties with Taiwan; (2) abrogating the Mutual Defense Treaty with Taiwan; and (3) withdrawing all U.S. forces from Taiwan.[50]

It was not until the Carter administration that the United States declared its willingness to meet China's three conditions. While Nixon and Ford were either unable or unwilling to agree to China's conditions, President Carter conceded on all three points even as he convinced the Chinese government to tolerate a significant *un*official U.S. relationship with Taiwan, including the sale of advanced military hardware. On December 15, 1978, President Carter announced that full diplomatic relations would be established with Beijing on January 1, 1979, and that a corresponding severance of relations with Taiwan would be effective simultaneously.

Unlike Nixon's announcement, Carter's generated serious debates and divisions in the foreign policy community, not least because it appeared that Carter broke his 1976 campaign pledge not to "sacrifice or abandon Taiwan."[51] These debates and divisions were especially acute between the Carter administration and members of Congress. Focus was on three related issues. First, there was debate over the depth and breadth of what the new relationship with China should be. How fast should the process progress? Should the United States grant special trading status to China? Should Washington sell military equipment to Beijing? Second, there was debate, and anger, over the secrecy Carter employed in the negotiations. Third was the status of U.S.-Taiwan relations. If the United States abrogated its security treaty with Taiwan, what would happen to the island country? Furthermore, would U.S. allies in Asia come to see the United States as a fair weather friend that could not to be trusted?

Regarding the first debate, National Security Advisor Zbigniew Brzezinski and Secretary of Defense Harold Brown squared off against Secretary of State Cyrus Vance over how fast the process should proceed. Brzezinski and Brown wanted to move quickly on normalizing relations over a wide range of issues, including arms sales to China, because they argued such sales would help establish U.S. influence over China's military while acting as a bulwark against Soviet encroachments. Vance, on the other hand, urged a slower pace. He worried that going faster would not give other countries enough time to react appropriately. He also advised a more evenhanded approach between Moscow and Beijing and held that a quick, broad-based move toward normalization with Beijing might severely damage detente with the Soviets.[52] Would a fast pace, for instance, compel the Soviets to resist U.S. initiatives in the important nuclear weapons talks? Growing Soviet strategic and conventional military power, as well as Moscow's increased influence in the Global South, probably tipped the balance in favor of Brzezinski and Brown[53] as Carter ultimately accepted their argument that rapid normalization would tip the balance of power in Asia away from the Soviets and toward the United States.[54]

Regarding the second area of debate, Carter's use of secret back channels and his exclusion of legislative leaders from the decision-making process angered Congress in ways Nixon's use of secrecy never did. This is probably because Carter failed to build public and congressional support for his policy initiatives. Moreover, Congress was irked because Carter decided *not* to consult congressional leaders even though he had implicitly agreed to when he signed a bill into law that contained a bipartisan amendment requiring congressional consultation on matters pertaining to Taiwan. Congressman Lester Wolff (D-NY) warned of a "divisive debate" if Carter did not uphold his commitment to consult with Congress on China policy.[55] Alas, the Carter administration's nearly complete disregard for Congress opened him to bitter attacks from members of both parties who argued that the president was skirting the legislature's proper role envisioned by the U.S. Constitution.

And in the third area of debate, congressional leaders were also angry with Carter because they did not believe he wrested any significant concessions from China when he agreed to meet China's three conditions. In particular, members of Congress felt that Carter had failed to secure a pledge from China that it would not use force to resolve the Taiwan issue. Nor was Congress convinced that Carter had adequately maintained a residual commitment to Taiwan's security. But the Carter administration defended its actions, arguing that both sides made concessions. For instance, while the United States agreed to China's three conditions, China conceded that the United States would not have to cancel its treaty with Taiwan for another year. Moreover, China also acquiesced to continued U.S. arms sales to Taiwan even after the treaty was canceled.[56]

Carter's treatment of Taiwan was perhaps the sorest bone of contention. Despite his campaign pledge, despite public opinion against normalization with the PRC if that meant abandoning Taiwan, and despite loud and clear messages from Congress demanding consultations before any changes were made to the U.S.-Taiwan Treaty, Carter was undeterred. Bill Brock, chair of the Republican National Committee, called Carter's policy a disgrace. Sen. Jesse Helms (R-NC) accused Carter of selling Taiwan "down the river" and Senator Goldwater called the agreement with China cowardly.[57] Goldwater, who lost to Lyndon Johnson in the 1964 election, had long complained about the United States' "shabby treatment" of Taiwan and warned that if any administration tried to withdraw recognition of Taiwan, he would strongly oppose it.[58] He did just that when he filed a lawsuit against President Carter, charging him with "an outright abuse of presidential power."[59] Goldwater argued that the president did not have the legal authority to unilaterally abrogate the U.S. treaty with Taiwan. Since a U.S. treaty must be ratified by a two-thirds vote in the Senate, Goldwater asserted, the president could not cancel a treaty without the Senate's agreement. As is usually the case with such grandiose lawsuits, Goldwater's attempt to use the federal courts to block the president's foreign policy initiative failed.

Tempers cooled somewhat when the Carter administration worked with the Congress to pass the Taiwan Relations Act, which not only expressed interest in settling the Taiwan issue by peaceful means but also provided Taiwan with significant security assistance in case peaceful means failed. Conservative members of Congress, who opposed Carter's abandonment of Taiwan, were able to get language added to the Act that reiterated a strong American commitment to Taiwan's security.[60] The Act declared that a military assault on Taiwan would be a matter of "grave concern" to the United States, which might launch "appropriate" countermeasures.[61] Further language in the Act gave Congress an explicit oversight role on policy concerning Taiwan, thus showing Congress's anger with President Carter for having earlier ignored the Congress.[62]

AFTERMATH: NIXON'S VISIT TO CHINA AS A TURNING POINT

Nixon's opening to China proved to be a major turning point both domestically as well as internationally. On the domestic front, Americans' image of China changed dramatically. When the United States first established full diplomatic relations with

China in February 1979, American public opinion on China showed that 44 percent held only a neutral opinion toward China. But by the end of that year, nearly two-thirds of the country had a positive impression of China and only 25 percent had a negative view.[63] Moreover, by 1980, 70 percent held a favorable view and 45 percent even favored defending China against a Soviet attack, which was roughly the same percentage that supported defending Taiwan against an attack from the PRC.[64] The opening to China helped establish Nixon and Kissinger's reputations as visionary leaders, their other faults notwithstanding. Both accumulated prestige at home and abroad as the opening helped to stabilize international relations in Asia and throughout the world. Even as the Vietnam War prompted a retrenchment in the projection of American military power, Nixon's bold and risky initiative fundamentally reoriented U.S. foreign policy, giving Washington new options and advantages around the globe.

Internationally, Nixon's visit, which he called "the week that changed the world," had a tremendous impact not only on politics in Asia but on the global balance of power.[65] Countries throughout Asia scrambled to fit the Sino-American friendship into their foreign policy calculations as the end of Sino-American hostility proved to be "one of the most beneficial developments of the post-war era."[66] For instance, Moscow moved quickly to improve relations with India as a counterbalance to growing Chinese-American friendship. As one of China's regional rivals, India was happy to oblige.[67]

Nixon's sudden opening to China shocked Japanese leaders. They felt betrayed by Nixon's surprise announcement, feeling that he was consorting with the enemy.[68] That Nixon kept his China move hidden from Japan created alarm in Tokyo: how could the United States keep such a major turn in its Asia policy a secret from Japan, its closest and most reliable ally in all of Asia? But Nixon and Kissinger were not too worried about Japan's reaction. Tokyo was deferential to American leadership at that time. In addition, Kissinger sent Marshall Green, the Assistant Secretary of State for East Asian and Pacific Affairs, to Japan to smooth the waters.[69] The Sino-American opening marked the first time in the twentieth century that the United States had friendly relations at the same time with both of Asia's main powers.

Japan recovered quickly from its initial shock and actually went further and faster than the United States in establishing formal ties with China. In September 1972, just two months after Nixon's landmark visit, Japan formally recognized the

People's Republic of China, more than six years before the United States. At the same time, Tokyo severed official diplomatic relations with Taiwan although Tokyo retained significant unofficial ties with Taipei. Japan's policy of formally recognizing China while retaining informal ties to Taiwan became known as the Japanese Model, which President Carter essentially copied in 1979.

The communists in Hanoi, North Vietnam were stunned by the news. How could the PRC, one of their main benefactors, welcome the leader of the country that it was fighting against? But the opening helped smooth the way for the United States to withdraw its forces from Indochina.[70] North Vietnam felt pressured into moderating its negotiating position, thus helping the United States conclude an honorable withdrawal agreement.

Perhaps most important of all, the U.S. opening to China enabled the United States to use what is called triangular diplomacy to play one communist power off the other. The Sino-American opening gave the United States enormous advantages in its pursuit of detente with the Soviet Union. For instance, China allowed the United States to establish a monitoring station inside the PRC that could eavesdrop on Soviet missile tests.[71] Faced with the possibility of two nuclear powers arrayed against it, the Soviet Union felt more compelled to reach arms control agreements with the United States.[72] However much American officials publicly disavowed any attempt to isolate the Soviets,[73] it is an undeniable fact that improved Sino-American relations put intense pressure on the Soviet Union to be more conciliatory in its relations with the United States.

Nine

THE OCTOBER 1973 ARAB-ISRAELI
WAR AND THE ENERGY CRISIS

Our attention turns now to a turning point in U.S. foreign policy that is connected to the Middle East, a volatile yet vital region of the world.[1] Not only does the region possess the world's largest proven oil reserves but it is also the birthplace of the world's three great monotheistic religions, Judaism, Christianity, and Islam. For the last century, the Holy City of Jerusalem has been a flashpoint for Jews and Muslims in particular.

Since Israel declared its independence in 1948, the Arabs and Israelis have fought six major wars. In 1948 Arab countries went to war in an unsuccessful attempt to prevent Israel's creation while also failing to create a state for the Palestinian Arabs. In 1956 Israel, together with Britain and France, launched a preemptive war against Egypt only to be compelled by a vehement Eisenhower administration to withdraw from conquered Egyptian territory. In 1967 the Israelis launched another preemptive war and in six days conquered the Sinai Desert from Egypt, the Golan Heights from Syria, and the West Bank and (Arab) East Jerusalem from Jordan. In the October 1973 War, the subject of this chapter, the Egyptians and Syrians launched an attack on Israel. In 1982 the Israelis invaded and occupied Lebanon to prevent Palestinian guerrillas from using Lebanon's territory to launch raids into Israel. In 2006 Israel fought another major war in Lebanon, this time against the militant Islamic Lebanese group Hezbollah. Aside from these wars, the Arabs and Israelis have engaged in other skirmishes, most notably the Egypt-Israel War of Attrition in 1969–1970, Israel's military incursion into Lebanon in 1978, and its military incursion into the Palestinian-controlled Gaza Strip in late 2008–early 2009.

So, out of all these Arab-Israeli wars, why pick the October 1973 War as a turning point in U.S. foreign policy?[2] First, the October War shattered ill-conceived assumptions U.S. foreign policy makers had about how to keep the region stable. Second, the war transformed a regional conflict into one with global implications as the Americans and Soviets engaged in another form of brinkmanship that threatened to engulf them in a dangerous confrontation not seen since the Cuban Missile Crisis (see chapter 6). Third, the war led to an energy crisis, which shocked the world economy worse than anything since the Great Depression. Fourth, Henry Kissinger's diplomacy after the war established the United States as the key playmaker in the Middle East. Finally, the October War forced the Middle East to the top of the U.S. foreign policy agenda where it has remained ever since.

This chapter begins with a look at the Nixon administration's foreign policy agenda prior to the October War, which ranked the Middle East ominously toward the bottom. We also address how the personal rivalries among officials in the Nixon administration, especially between Kissinger and Secretary of State William Rogers, impacted foreign policy. By the time Nixon did turn his attention to the region early in his second term, Egypt's President Anwar Sadat had already set the stage. As such, the chapter moves to examine Sadat's decision to launch the war and the U.S. response, which was dictated almost entirely by Washington's concerns about the Soviet Union's actions on behalf of its client state, Egypt. Next the chapter examines how the oil-rich Arab states, especially Saudi Arabia, changed their mind about using oil as a political weapon when they imposed an embargo on selling oil to the United States for its military support of Israel. Given this international energy crisis and against the war's shaky ceasefire, we explore Kissinger's famous shuttle diplomacy that, while stabilizing the region in the short term, may have helped establish a pattern of diplomacy that lead to long-term deadlock. Finally, we address how the October War is a turning point in U.S. foreign policy as it significantly changed U.S. policy and involvement in the region.

DISTRACTIONS AND DIVISIONS STYMIE DIPLOMATIC PROGRESS

During the Nixon administration's first term (1969–1973), its top foreign policy priorities did not include the Middle East. Neither Nixon nor Henry Kissinger focused on the Middle East. The region had their attention but it remained a low priority as they addressed other issues, such as managing detente with the Soviets, negotiating an end to U.S. military involvement in Vietnam (see chapter 7), and navigating the historic opening to China (see chapter 8).

Furthermore, since Nixon and Kissinger felt little progress could be made on a Middle East peace settlement, neither wanted to invest their time or prestige in what they considered to be a losing proposition.[3] As if to underscore how low on the foreign policy agenda Nixon placed the Middle East, he gave authority for Middle East policy to Secretary of State Rogers, the lone area in Rogers's control. Recall the discussion in chapter 8 regarding Nixon's disdain for the State Department. Giving Rogers authority over Middle East policy, therefore, indicated that Nixon did not consider it a high priority.[4]

Nevertheless, Rogers made several gallant efforts to bring peace to the region, notably his so-called Rogers Peace Plan. The Plan failed in part because it called for a comprehensive peace in the region, which meant pressuring Israel to pull back from conquered Arab lands. Israel was surrounded by more populous, hostile Arab countries, which had staked out a stubborn position just after the 1967 war with their infamous Three Nos: no negotiations, no recognition, and no peace with Israel. Given this hostile environment, Israel saw little benefit in giving up any strategic depth by withdrawing from conquered Arab territory.

But Rogers's attempts at a comprehensive peace plan foundered not only because Israelis and Arabs were unwilling or unable to take risks for peace—he also faced resistance from Nixon and Kissinger. Nixon actually undercut Rogers by informing the Israelis that he did not support Rogers's initiative.[5] In addition, Rogers and Kissinger had serious policy disagreements. They clashed over giving weapons to Israel. Rogers believed that giving arms to Israel not only angered the Arabs but also made Israel less flexible and more likely to launch a preemptive military strike. But Kissinger believed that limited, steady weapons deliveries to Israel would convince the Arabs and their Soviet allies that they could not win using military action. Nixon was more receptive to Kissinger's arguments.[6] As will be shown, arms aid to Israel became a vital, if flawed, tactic in Kissinger's diplomacy.

Rogers and Kissinger also differed over the role the Soviet Union and the Europeans might play in the region. Rogers believed the Soviets should be engaged in a broad-based effort to pressure their clients in the region (notably Egypt) to come to the bargaining table. He also felt that America's European allies, such as France and Great Britain, with their long-standing commercial and diplomatic ties to the region, could help the United States in a multilateral peace effort.[7] But Kissinger disagreed with this assessment. He had little faith that the Europeans would line up with the Americans against the Soviets. Besides, he wanted to find a way to reduce Soviet influence in the region, not help Moscow expand its presence there.

As this rivalry played out, Kissinger worked to weaken Rogers. He held secret meetings with Egyptian diplomats without informing Rogers and presented an initiative at odds with the Rogers Peace Plan. He also remained noticeably silent when the Rogers Plan came under fire in the press. The rivalry became so intense that it led to a confused and inconsistent Middle East policy.[8] By the end of his first term therefore, a "strongly divided policy apparatus" plagued Nixon's Middle East policy.[9]

Early in his second term, however, this confusion was cleared up as Kissinger established unrivaled dominance over foreign policy, including the Middle East. Rogers resigned in mid-August 1973 and Nixon nominated Kissinger to succeed him. Kissinger became the first foreign-born secretary of state and the only person to hold two important foreign policy positions simultaneously—he retained his post as Nixon's national security advisor while becoming secretary of state. As such, Kissinger gained "tight control" over the foreign policy making machinery.[10] Furthermore, Nixon intended to pay more attention to the Arab-Israeli conflict in his second term. He acknowledged that keeping the region on the back burner was dangerous. In a prescient memo he wrote to Kissinger, he said action was needed on the Middle East because "this thing is getting ready to blow."[11] However, while policy debates and divisions were cleared up with Rogers's departure, Nixon became distracted by numerous domestic scandals, the two most serious of which were Vice President Spiro Agnew's resignation and the Watergate scandal that led to Nixon's resignation in August 1974. Agnew resigned amidst bribery charges right in the middle of the October War and as the Watergate scandal consumed his presidency, Nixon was often an absentee president, delegating considerable power to Kissinger as the latter engaged in intense diplomacy.

Kissinger believed diplomatic progress could happen only after Israel's elections in November 1973. He also mistakenly believed that he had more time after having what seemed like a pleasant visit with Ismail Fahmy, the Egyptian National Security Advisor, in February 1973. However, it appears that Egyptian President Anwar al Sadat made the decision to go to war after Fahmy's visit.[12] Sadat was a man of vision, prone to bold moves. In his frustration at the pace of diplomacy, he concluded that war was the only way to jolt the Americans and the Israelis out of their complacency. But Sadat did not go to war to destroy Israel or even to win back all the territory Egypt lost in 1967. Rather, he went to war to restore Arab honor and to force the Americans to pay more attention to the region.[13] In this he succeeded greatly, even though initial Egyptian (and Syrian) military gains were reversed by the end of the war.

THE OCTOBER WAR

Throughout the early 1970s, the Arabs issued public warnings of dire consequences if the Americans failed to win diplomatic concessions from Israel. Little came of these threats, so the Americans and Israelis became tone deaf to Arab rhetoric. When Sadat declared ominously that 1971 was the "year of decision," many observers braced for another Arab-Israeli war. But when that did not happen they concluded it was just another rhetorical bluff coming from the Arab World. When the Egyptians and Syrians mobilized their militaries in early 1973, the Israelis mobilized their own forces, only to draw them down after yet another false alarm. So, when Egyptian and Syrian military moves that fall looked threatening again, both the Israelis and the Americans were caught off guard.

It is not that Israel and the United States had obtained flawed intelligence—they both had ample evidence indicating an attack. It was that neither interpreted the intelligence correctly, perhaps because the previous false alarms had desensitized them to the nature of what was happening in October.[14] Kissinger later remarked that U.S. and Israeli intelligence believed the Egyptians and Syrians were just engaging in their "regular fall maneuvers."[15] Only Ray Cline and his staff at the State Department's Intelligence and Research Bureau (INR) issued a report in May accurately predicting a war but the rivalry between Rogers at State and Kissinger in the White House was so intense, Rogers could not convince Kissinger to take the INR study seriously.[16] Besides, by the summertime, INR had backed away from its earlier prediction.[17] Furthermore, ever since its stunning 1967 victory, the Israeli military was especially confident, evincing a swagger of invincibility. Israeli soldiers held Arab-fighting prowess in disdain. In August 1973, Israeli Defense Minister Moshe Dayan said the Arabs had an inherent weakness derived from "the low level of their soldiers in education, technology, and integrity."[18]

As the attack commenced on October 6, President Nixon was in Florida, contemplating his Watergate troubles and Agnew's impending resignation. Kissinger was asleep in his hotel room in New York City where he was attending a U.N. function. Only fourteen days earlier, he was sworn in as secretary of state. Once it was clear that the fourth Arab-Israeli war had commenced, foreign policy makers realized they had made several incorrect assumptions. First, they incorrectly assumed that, as long as Israel held the military advantage, the Arabs would not resort to war. But when the Egyptian military breached Israel's vaunted Bar Lev Line of Defense in the Sinai Desert and when Syria initially took back nearly all of the Golan Heights, that assumption was burst. Second, Kissinger, the Israelis and even the Soviets mistakenly assumed that the war would end quickly with another crushing Israeli victory. But by the end of the fifth day of fighting, the idea that Israel was unbeatable was shattered.[19] The Egyptians and Syrians demonstrated military capabilities they had not shown before as they advanced and held territory while coordinating a multi-pronged attack. Third, Nixon and Kissinger erred in assuming that the Arab oil states would not impose an oil embargo.[20]

When Kissinger realized that Israel was unable to decisively defeat the Arabs, he saw an opportunity to use the war as a way to simultaneously defuse the crisis while reducing Soviet influence in the region. But the trick to such an outcome would require delicate diplomatic maneuvers that ensured neither side would be victor or vanquished. A battlefield "tie," he calculated, was critical to post-war diplomacy. That is why Kissinger controlled when, and how much, U.S. arms went to Israel.

Both sides depleted their weapons caches at a staggering pace. The Sinai tank battle was the second largest in history after the Battle of Kursk in WWII.[21] By one estimate, the Arabs lost more than 2,000 tanks and 400 planes while the count for Israel was 1,000 tanks and more than 100 aircraft.[22] The Israelis feverishly requested replenishment from the Americans but were infuriated by the slow response. Kissinger was receptive to the idea, but he instructed the Department of Defense to drag its feet. Defense Secretary James Schlesinger was criticized for the delay but he said that blaming the Pentagon was to be the "cover story."[23] Kissinger wanted to prevent Israel from dealing a complete defeat to the Arabs. He kept deliveries modest and secret—at first no U.S. transports were to be used—so that the Arabs would not view the United States as completely allied with Israel.[24] But Schlesinger believed the only way to get Israel enough arms was via U.S. transports. Nixon sided with Schlesinger and formally ordered a full-scale military airlift to Israel on October 13.[25]

Meanwhile, Kissinger worked the diplomatic channels to push both sides to accept a ceasefire, which the Israelis reluctantly and angrily accepted on October 12, but which Sadat rejected. It appears that Sadat, whose own forces were already being re-supplied by the Soviets, was not fully aware that the tide of battle had turned against him. When Kissinger learned that Sadat had rejected the ceasefire and that the Soviets were re-supplying Egypt and Syria, the conflict's contours changed for him. Now, the conflict had *global* implications. Neither he nor Nixon could abide Soviet arms in the hands of Soviet clients defeating American arms in the hands of an American client. Rearming Israel therefore, was done not so much to aid Israel's war with the Arabs as it was to send a signal to the Soviets that the United States could match, even exceed, arms shipments to its client.[26]

As Kissinger flew to the Soviet Union to hastily hash out a ceasefire, Nixon issued a statement granting him complete authority to broker a deal. Kissinger reacted angrily because it denied him a bargaining chip with the Soviets. Since Nixon removed himself from the process, Kissinger could not reject a Soviet proposal on the pretense that Nixon would never accept it. Once Sadat realized that he was losing the war and once he realized the extent of the American airlift, he agreed to a ceasefire. But the Israelis were furious with Kissinger since he had imposed the ceasefire on them without first consulting them. So Kissinger flew to Israel for a visit that some observers believe the Israelis took as a signal that they did not have to strictly observe the ceasefire,[27] which was scheduled to take effect on October 22.

Sadat accused the Israelis of breaching the ceasefire as they encircled Egypt's Third Army, making it vulnerable to annihilation with weapons only recently delivered by the United States. He appealed to the Americans and Soviets to send troops to police the ceasefire, but Nixon and Kissinger agreed that sending U.S. and Soviet troops to the war zone was a dangerous idea. But the Soviets could not stand by and watch Israel destroy their client's military, so Brezhnev sent Nixon a letter imploring him to join the Soviets in policing the ceasefire. Brezhnev said that if the United States refused to join the Soviets in intervening, then he would do so unilaterally. Thus began what looked like a substantial Soviet military buildup, which transformed a regional conflict into a global confrontation as the American and Soviet superpowers engaged in a dangerous form of brinkmanship not seen since the Cuban Missile Crisis.

As Kissinger hastily convened his crisis management team, known as the Washington Special Actions Group (WSAG),[28] he ordered the military to increase its alert status to DefCon III, which is the same level of alert Kennedy ordered during the Cuban Missile Crisis.[29] Kissinger called it a "deliberate overreaction" to demonstrate to the Soviets just how serious the United States was in its opposition to the introduction of Soviet forces in the region.[30] The conflict took yet another ominous turn as it threatened to place American forces in direct confrontation with Soviet troops. Some reporters accused Nixon of exaggerating the threat to distract the country from his Watergate troubles, but Kissinger explained that the DefCon III order had unanimous support in the WSAG. Moreover, nearly all the congressional leaders supported the decision. In fact, Nixon was not even a party to the deliberations. Kissinger convened the WSAG while Nixon slept, and then informed him of the order the next morning.[31]

While they worried about the Soviets, Nixon and Kissinger also worried that Israel's actions would undermine plans for improved relations with Egypt.[32] So Kissinger threatened to abandon the Israelis, proclaiming that they would be on their own in a fight against the Soviet Union.[33] The Israelis held back and the crisis melted away as fast as it had erupted. As of October 26, therefore, the ceasefire held, the war came to an end, and the business of diplomacy resumed.

OIL AND POLITICS DO MIX AFTER ALL

But the diplomacy was seriously complicated by the energy crisis that ensued after the Arab oil states used their petroleum reserves as a weapon in support of Egypt and Syria. U.S. foreign policy makers were wrong about assuming that the Arabs would not use oil as a weapon. They considered the possibility, but the conventional wisdom was that oil-rich Arab states like Saudi Arabia and Kuwait needed to sell the oil as much as the West needed to buy it. With virtually no other source of revenue, the Arabs could not "eat their oil."[34] Besides, after their defeat in both 1956 and 1967, the Arabs tried to use oil as a weapon, but the efforts failed. In 1956 U.S. domestic production was sufficient to compensate and in 1967, the low level of Arab oil imported to the United States rendered that embargo a "farce."[35]

While that may have been true in the 1950s and 1960s, conditions changed markedly by 1970, giving the Organization of Petroleum Exporting Countries (OPEC) increasing control over the oil market. By the early 1970s, OPEC, which is dominated by its Arab member countries,[36] accounted for more than half of the world's oil production[37] and controlled 86 percent of world exports.[38] It turned out that the Arabs did not need to sell their oil as badly as the West needed to buy it. To many Arabs, it became an axiom that the oil was worth more to them in the ground than in a tanker on its way to filling stations overseas.

With the world's largest proven oil reserves, Saudi Arabia dominated OPEC's pricing policy, but Saudi King Faisal resisted attempts by the more radical Arab states, such as Libya and Iraq, to use the Kingdom's oil reserves as a political weapon. Faisal often said, "oil and politics do not mix."[39] However, just as the balance of power in global oil markets was shifting from the *consuming* countries to the *producing* countries, King Faisal was growing more impatient with the Americans. Saudi Arabia had friendly relations with the United States but Faisal had strong feelings about the plight of the Palestinians living under Israeli occupation. He wanted Nixon to do more to pressure Israel to cede the Occupied Territories to Palestinian control. He was also a devout Muslim who felt a personal attachment to Jerusalem. He wanted at least the Arab parts of the Holy City returned to Arab sovereignty so that he could visit the Dome of the Rock before he died.[40] His patience was obviously wearing thin. By 1972, King Faisal, Sheikh Yamani (the powerful Saudi oil minister), and high-ranking members of the royal family issued warnings that they might indeed use oil as a political weapon unless the United States was more "evenhanded" in the Arab-Israeli conflict.[41]

Officials of the big oil companies tried to warn U.S. policy makers of the seriousness of the situation. They urged Washington to take a more fair-minded approach to the Arab-Israeli conflict, but to no avail. U.S. policy makers did not see the change in oil politics for what it was. Shortly after the October War began, a State Department cable to U.S. embassies discounted the likelihood of an oil production cutback.[42] According to one observer, "Use of the 'oil weapon' was largely unanticipated by U.S. officials [who] repeatedly ignored Arab representations . . . [T]he United States did not react decisively to Arab political demands or to growing dependence upon foreign imports."[43]

During the first week of fighting, the oil weapon remained in its sheath. Even after the United States began a modest re-supply effort for Israel, King Faisal remained reluctant. However, by October 16–17, once the full extent of the American re-supply effort became known, the Arab oil ministers, with critical support coming from the Saudis, announced a 70 percent price hike and an oil production cutback of 5 percent for each month the Israelis did not withdraw to their 1967 borders. When Nixon requested a $2.2 billion military aid package for Israel on October 19, the situation reached crisis proportions because the next day the Arab oil states announced a deeper cutback plus a total embargo against the United States.[44] Kissinger later admitted that it was a mistake for Nixon to request so much military aid for Israel right in the middle of the war.[45]

The Arab-Israeli conflict took on yet another global implication, this time threatening world economic stability. The price of oil *quadrupled* in a matter of weeks.[46] Filling stations around the country began rationing gasoline as anxious motorists waited in long lines for a chance to top off their tanks. Kissinger had to scramble to become an expert on energy and international economics. Both he and Nixon knew, and cared, little about the subject. In Nixon's first three years in office, he and Kissinger ordered 144 formal foreign policy reviews, only one of which explicitly addressed international monetary policy.[47] In May 1973, Nixon's annual Foreign Policy Report did not treat energy as a significant *foreign* policy issue.[48] By summer, although a National Intelligence Estimate (NIE) warned that a new Arab-Israeli war might lead to an interruption in the flow of oil, it was not taken too seriously.[49] Energy policy, such as it existed, was spread out and uncoordinated between myriad government agencies, such as the Departments of Interior, Treasury, and Commerce, with each having only partial responsibility.

As Kissinger struggled to craft a policy response to the crisis, he said it should be as profound as the response to Sputnik.[50] The response included creating domestic and international agencies, convening a multilateral conference and even threatening the Arabs. In December 1973, Nixon created the Federal Energy Office (FEO), which sought to unify energy policy among the various government agencies.[51] The same month, Kissinger threatened the Arabs with unspecified "countermeasures," to which Sheikh Yamani responded with a threat to blow up his own oil fields and plunge the planet into a worldwide depression.[52] In January 1974, Defense Secretary Schlesinger spoke openly of the possibility of military action. Next, Kissinger convened the Washington Energy Conference in February 1974. He also sought to coordinate policy with Europe and Japan by forming the International Energy Agency (IEA) in November 1974. In addition, Nixon announced a policy initiative called Project Independence, which had as its goal U.S. energy independence by 1980.

On balance, these efforts did not amount to much. The FEO instituted a stiff rationing program that was blamed for making the energy crisis worse than it actually was.[53] The IEA was a step in the right direction as it sought emergency sharing arrangements in the short term and cooperative ventures to reduce dependence in the long term. But the IEA was unable to wrest control over pricing away from the producing countries.[54] The Washington Energy Conference broke up with only modest progress on establishing a joint response to the energy crisis. The Europeans and Americans found it difficult to forge a unified policy response. While Kissinger criticized the Europeans for striking separate deals with OPEC countries, he did the same thing.[55] Even though he called for coordination, the Europeans and the Americans launched programs and initiatives without consulting the other.[56] As for Nixon's Project Independence, it was little more than a fantasy even though he likened it to the Manhattan Project, the intense government effort to produce a nuclear bomb during WWII. Energy conservation measures were adopted, but reducing speed limits, rationing gas, consolidating airline flights, and lowering thermostats were not enough to make America energy independent. Americans had already grown addicted to imported oil. Besides, once the Arabs lifted the embargo in March 1974, the crisis atmosphere evaporated and the urgency expressed by Project Independence dissolved. As the crisis faded from memory, "the American public reverted to former consumption patterns."[57]

KISSINGER'S SHUTTLE DIPLOMACY: MASTERFUL OR MYOPIC?

The price hike, production cuts, and oil embargo had an immediate impact on Europe and Japan's foreign policy. Tokyo and most western European capitals issued statements sympathetic to the Arabs. Most European countries refused permission to the United States to use their territory to re-supply Israel and some, such as Britain and West Germany, banned arms shipments to the combatants, including Israel. Nevertheless, the crisis hit Europe and Japan, as well as the developing world, very hard.

The challenge for Kissinger and Nixon, therefore, was to conduct U.S. policy under a shaky ceasefire and in the midst of a world energy crisis. This challenge was made all the more daunting first by Nixon and Kissinger's worldview and second, by the constant tension that has long characterized U.S. policy toward the Middle East. In the first instance, Kissinger and Nixon filtered regional conflicts like the Arab-Israeli quarrel through the lens of global competition with the Soviets. Any moves they made in the Middle East were calibrated to reduce Soviet influence there. For example, when the Israelis encircled Egypt's Third Army after the ceasefire, Kissinger compelled them to back off by arguing that they would be responsible for igniting a nuclear war between the Soviets and Americans.

In the second instance, U.S. policy in the region has always suffered from a chronic tension due to incompatible interests. On the one hand, the United States has long been Israel's strongest supporter and for several reasons. First, U.S. policy makers were sympathetic to the plight of the Jews after the Holocaust. Second, U.S. officials considered Israel the only democracy in the region and were thus naturally drawn to it. Third, Israel was a determined opponent of the Soviets during the Cold War. Fourth, there is a strong pro-Israel lobby in Washington that exerts considerable influence on policy makers in Congress and the executive branch. As such, the United States has supported Israel with extensive political, military and economic aid. For decades, Israel has received more American aid, in the form of outright grants, than any other country in the world.

On the other hand, the United States has long sought closer ties with Israel's traditional Arab enemies, particularly those countries that play leadership roles in the Arab World. Egypt, for instance, is the most populous Arab country and remains the political and cultural center of the Arab World. U.S. policy makers feel it is important to maintain good relations with Cairo in hopes that Cairo would use its influence in the Arab World to further U.S. interests. In addition, it is vital for the United States to maintain close relations with oil-rich Saudi Arabia. Against this backdrop Kissinger had to craft peace initiatives that would further American interests. He was adamant that it not appear as if the oil embargo was influencing U.S. foreign policy. Still, Nixon admitted as much when he said that the only way to end the oil crisis was to end the embargo and the only way to end the embargo "is to get the Israelis to act reasonable. I hate to use the word blackmail, but we've got to do some things to get them to behave."[58]

But how should he proceed? Should the United States try for a comprehensive solution by convening an international conference that all the major players, including the Soviets, would attend? Or should the United States opt for a more limited approach? In fact, both approaches were deployed. We begin with the Geneva Peace Conference, which was attended by Egypt, Jordan, Israel, the Soviet Union, and the United States, with U.N. Secretary General Kurt Waldheim presiding. The Conference convened on December 21, 1973 and adjourned the very next day having accomplished little of substance. While the Conference would not have occurred without Kissinger's tireless efforts, he saw it only as a chance to placate the Soviet Union. He did not expect anything significant to come from the Conference.

Shortly after the Geneva Conference adjourned, Kissinger embarked on what is now famously called shuttle diplomacy, which effectively killed the Geneva format. From late December 1973 until late summer 1975 Kissinger logged tens of thousands of miles as he trekked back and forth to the Middle East, hopping from one Arab country to Israel and then back again. Since the Arabs and Israelis did not have formal diplomatic relations, Kissinger had to relay each side's position to the other. It was, by most accounts, a diplomatic tour de force that secured Kissinger's reputation as one of the country's greatest diplomats while it also solidified U.S. influence in the region. Kissinger's diplomatic star rose after he obtained one improbable agreement after another. He was dubbed "Super K" by the press as he seemed indefatigable, sometimes going days with little to no sleep.

He favored this type of diplomacy because it fit well with his sensibilities about moving slowly in a step-by-step fashion. Kissinger hoped that making progress on less important issues would build confidence among the parties to reach agreement on more difficult issues. Moreover, by making himself the only mediator who was acceptable to all the belligerents, Kissinger was able to freeze the Soviets out of the process. He chose to shuttle between Egypt and Israel first for several reasons. First, he believed it would be less difficult to achieve an agreement between these two countries than between Syria and Israel. Second, since Egypt was a leader in the Arab World, Kissinger figured that, once Egypt signed an agreement with Israel, other Arab countries would follow. Third, since Egypt and Israel's militaries were so dangerously entangled in the Sinai, there was a sense of urgency attached to disengaging them.

With only a few trusted aides in tow, Kissinger bounced back and forth between Egypt and Israel, relaying bargaining positions and sometimes offering his own suggestions to keep the negotiations moving forward. He made himself indispensable to the process by ensuring that he was the only person in the room who knew everything about each side's negotiating position. Even his aides did not know the full extent of the Egyptian and Israeli bargaining positions. And if, say, the Israelis offered a series of compromises or concessions, Kissinger would not reveal them to Egypt all at once. Instead, he would hold some in abeyance and then proffer them at times when he felt the talks needed a push.[59]

On January 17, 1974, President Nixon announced that Israel and Egypt had reached an accord. The next day, the two countries signed what came to be called Sinai I, a very complicated and delicate agreement that separated their militaries into more stable positions. It was the first time the Israelis made a withdrawal toward their 1967 borders. Even though this agreement was difficult to achieve, Kissinger actually had an easier time with this one than with the next two. In this case, Israel and Egypt were anxious for an agreement. Egypt wanted an agreement that would relieve pressure on the Third Army and Sadat needed to show his people and the rest of the Arab World that the costly war he launched had resulted in territorial gains. Israel wanted an agreement so that it could stand down its military, which was very expensive to keep mobilized, and to secure the return of Israeli POWs.[60]

To maintain the momentum, Kissinger tried next for an accord between Syria and Israel. He expected the talks to take a week, but they took thirty-two grueling days.[61] The animus between Syrians and Israelis was greater than between the Egyptians and Israelis. Moreover, when the ceasefire took effect, Israeli troops were poised only a few miles from Syria's capital, Damascus, which they could have pummeled with artillery. Compared to the Sinai, which was a much larger chunk of territory that could be used to disentangle the combatants, the Syria-Israel front was more compact. But the Israelis were reluctant to withdraw from the Syrian front. Why, they asked, should the Syrians be rewarded with territory for a war that they started and then lost? Israeli negotiators played tough in order to wring as many concessions as they could from the Syrians. More importantly, the Israelis' tough negotiating style won them commitments of U.S. support in exchange for concessions to the Syrians. The Israelis had leverage over the Syrians as well as the Americans. Damascus was at the mercy of Israeli artillery and the Israelis knew that Nixon needed a diplomatic breakthrough to distract from his Watergate troubles and to improve relations with the Arabs so they would lift the embargo. In fact, the embargo was lifted once the Arabs saw progress in the Syria-Israel talks.

For their part, the Syrians refused any deal that did not match the territorial gains Sadat won for Egypt. More than once, the talks nearly broke down. Nixon and Kissinger blamed the difficulty on Israel's recalcitrance. Kissinger had shouting matches with the Israelis during which he would proclaim that Israel was condemning itself to years of conflict over just a few kilometers.[62] Nixon got so frustrated with Israel that he ordered a halt to arms shipments to the Israelis but Kissinger and high-ranking DOD officials simply ignored the order. In the end, it was Kissinger's stamina, together with U.S. guarantees to Israel that made the difference. On May 31, 1974, Syria and Israel signed a disengagement accord. Syria returned Israeli POWs and Israel withdrew from all the territory it had won in the October War plus a small town it conquered in 1967.[63] Nevertheless, the Israelis continued to occupy most of the strategic Golan Heights, which they had been settling with their own citizens and which they later formally annexed. Kissinger called Israel's actions in the Golan Heights "the worst mistake the Jews have made in 2,500 years."[64]

Achieving this agreement signaled the emergence of an important pattern in U.S. policy toward Israel: to get Israel to agree, the United States had to conclude a side agreement guaranteeing Israel's security and economic prosperity. Known as a Memorandum of Understanding (MOU), this agreement contained provisions for U.S. economic aid, oil assistance, and consultations should the Soviets make any threatening moves in the region. The MOU also committed the United States to being "fully responsive" to Israel's military needs.[65] The most extensive MOU the United States signed with Israel came in the midst of the third, and final, troop disengagement accord to which we now turn.

After the Syria-Israel agreement, U.S. policy makers had to decide what to do next. They had three basic options. First, they could try for a comprehensive political solution that would bring peace to the Middle East, but most observers felt it was too ambitious a plan and doomed to failure. Second, they could try for an agreement between Jordan and Israel over the West Bank, which is where more than a million Palestinians lived but which was under Jordanian control prior to the 1967 war. Although this seemed like the next logical step, the plan fell through when the Arab League unanimously declared the Palestine Liberation Organization (PLO) the sole legitimate representative of the Palestinian people. Kissinger was unprepared for this diplomatic setback as it denied Jordan's King Hussein the chance to negotiate with the Israelis over the West Bank.[66] So, Kissinger chose the third option by default: he returned to shuttle diplomacy to gain another agreement between Israel and Egypt.

Kissinger knew that during this round of talks, Israel's objective was to delay and prolong the negotiations. In December 1974, Israeli Prime Minister Rabin told the Israeli press, "the central aim of Israel should be to gain time."[67] Again, the talks nearly broke down and again Kissinger blamed Israel. He complained that, "I ask Rabin to make concessions and he says he can't because Israel is weak. So I give him more arms, and he says he doesn't need to make concessions because Israel is strong."[68] He later disparaged the Israelis' "excessive caution" and "lack of vision."[69] President Ford, who had taken over the White House after Nixon resigned on August 8, 1974, agreed with Kissinger and carried out his threat to "reassess" U.S.

foreign policy, which amounted to a series of punishments for Israel. The United States suspended arms agreements with Israel and Kissinger held a series of consultations with members of the foreign policy elite known for their critical views of Israel.

But Ford's "reassessment" failed, as Israel only hardened its position, and also because the pro-Israel lobby in Washington succeeded in killing it. Unlike the Arabs, the Israelis benefited from a lobby that wielded considerable influence in Washington, particularly in Congress. While the petroleum industry lobbied the administration to protect its oil interests with the Arabs, it was no match for the pro-Israel lobby.[70] Seventy-six senators signed a letter to President Ford urging him to back away from his policy of reassessment. It was an incredible demonstration of bipartisan unity as liberal Democrats, such as Teddy Kennedy, joined conservative Republicans, such as Barry Goldwater, in signing the letter. Ford resented the pressure but it greatly strengthened Israel's bargaining position.

In the end, Kissinger returned to the region, where he was finally able to obtain a second accord between Egypt and Israel, called Sinai II, but only after signing four more MOUs with Israel that contained so many commitments to Israel that one of Kissinger's aides called them "mind boggling."[71] In addition to the usual pledges of economic and military aid, Kissinger also vowed that the United States would refuse to either recognize or negotiate with the PLO unless it openly accepted Israel's right to exist. Kissinger tied the United States' hands for years to come vis-a-vis the PLO in order to get Israel to agree to a limited troop disengagement accord in the African desert.

Kissinger's shuttle diplomacy resulted in three important, albeit limited, troop withdrawal accords: Sinai I between Egypt and Israel in January 1974, Syria-Israel in May 1974 and Sinai II in September 1975. Although he was able to achieve what few thought was possible, his step-by-step approach did have its critics. His approach was attacked as myopic since it failed to capture the big picture. Princeton University professor Bernard Lewis felt that Kissinger's limited approach focusing on troop disengagement served only to postpone progress on a broader political settlement.[72] By ignoring the bigger political issues, such as the Palestinians, Kissinger undermined long-term progress. Kissinger excluded the Palestinians due to Israel's strident objections to any PLO participation. While this may have been essential to gain Israel's agreement on limited, short-term accords with Egypt and Syria, it prolonged the search for a comprehensive solution since, after all, the Palestinian question remains the core of the Arab-Israeli conflict. Kissinger also bound the Nixon administration, and future presidents, from even talking to the PLO until it accepted Israel's right to exist. In so doing, Kissinger handicapped U.S. officials for years to come. But, as Abba Eban, Israel's Foreign Minister during the October War, liked to say, countries should negotiate with their adversaries, not their friends.

Kissinger's step-by-step approach was also criticized for driving a wedge between Egypt and the other Arabs, who saw Sinai II as a separate peace between Egypt and Israel that favored Israel. Not only did Israel retain the majority of the Sinai but it also furthered Israel's strategic objective of neutralizing Egypt by cleaving it from the Arab fold and by winning Sadat's pledge not to use military force to resolve outstanding issues.

Kissinger was also criticized for using arms as a tactic to hook the Israelis and Arabs. Former Under Secretary of State George Ball worried that this tactic would provoke a regional arms race, which it did, and that arming Israel would tempt it to launch more preemptive strikes, which it also did, first against Lebanon in 1978 and then against Iraq in 1981.[73] The cost to the American taxpayer of meeting these aid commitments was staggering: U.S. aid to Israel from 1970–1973 totaled around $1.6 billion; from 1974–1977, however, the figure jumped to $7.7 billion.[74] U.S. aid to Egypt from 1970–1973 was only $2.3 million but from 1974–1977 the total was more than $2.3 *billion,* a thousandfold increase.[75]

However, in Kissinger's defense, economic and military assistance bound Egypt and Israel closer to the United States than to any other country in the world, which Kissinger believed served U.S. interests in the Cold War against the Soviets. Moreover, these limited agreements were probably all that he could muster. According to Bill Quandt, reaching even these agreements stretched the political systems of the countries involved to the "breaking point."[76] There was little political will left for much else after that. As such, Kissinger had no choice but to pursue short-term gains in hopes that they might lead to long-term progress.

AFTERMATH: THE OCTOBER WAR AS A TURNING POINT

The October War is a turning point because of the significant changes it wrought in U.S foreign policy, in regional politics, and in world affairs. The October War compelled U.S. foreign policy makers to revise their priorities. Resolving the Arab-Israeli conflict and maintaining a stable flow of oil at reasonable prices would remain atop the foreign policy agenda for years to come. When Kissinger first came to power, he saw the Arab-Israeli conflict as little more than a nuisance. But when the October War threatened to suck the United States and the Soviet Union into direct military confrontation, it became clear that resolving the conflict required sustained attention. Consistent, high-level American involvement became the cardinal rule for achieving a settlement in the region. Left to themselves, the Arabs and Israelis were either unwilling or unable to reach an accord. And since the oil crisis produced a sudden shock and a new era in international relations, U.S. officials made securing oil supplies a linchpin of U.S. foreign policy.[77] To this day, Middle East oil remains the lifeblood of transportation and industry around the world. Without it, the world economy would plunge into chaos.

Sadat's decision to attack, despite having inferior military forces, jolted the Middle East. The Israelis could no longer afford to be complacent about their regional dominance. According to Seth Tillman, the October War was to Israel what the Tet Offensive was to the United States.[78] While both countries dominated the battlefield, both suffered a psychological trauma that had its reckoning in the politics of the war's aftermath. No longer could Israel assume that its military superiority could guarantee its security. No longer could the United States rely on Israel's military advantage to keep the region quiet. No longer could the United States ignore the Arabs. While the American press and public retained a negative image of the Arab World, they were at least now more willing to listen to what the Arabs had to say.

Perhaps even more profound was the war's impact on the U.S. position in world affairs. American influence in the region (and globally) skyrocketed while Soviet influence plummeted everywhere except on the fringes, such as Libya. It was the greatest Cold War victory for the Americans since the opening to China.[79] After the October War, Egypt and Syria restored diplomatic relations with the United States, which had been severed after the 1967 war. In 1976 Sadat moved even closer to the United States when he canceled Egypt's Treaty of Friendship with the Soviet Union. Furthermore, although the Saudis helped precipitate the energy crisis, Riyadh and Washington moved closer as Saudi Arabia's growing petrodollar wealth was recycled back into the U.S. economy through arms purchases and development deals. Consequently, the war helped to greatly strengthen America's relations with the two most important Arab countries, Egypt and Saudi Arabia.

The war also helped strengthen U.S.-Iran relations, at least for a time. Although Iran played an important part in raising oil prices, Iran did not participate in the embargo. The Iranians, much like the Saudis, used their newfound wealth to purchase billions of dollars worth of American weapons. In keeping with the Nixon Doctrine of arming anti-communist regimes around the world, the United States was happy to sell weapons to Iran because Washington wanted to prop up the Shah of Iran as its "policeman" in the Persian Gulf. Iran was to be the bulwark of the Nixon Doctrine's anti-communist containment policy in that part of the Middle East. However, as the following chapter discusses, by 1979, U.S.-Iran relations lay in ruins and U.S. interests in the Persian Gulf, as well as American prestige, suffered a devastating blow.

Ten

THE ISLAMIC REVOLUTION IN IRAN AND THE AMERICAN HOSTAGE CRISIS

The year 1979 was a momentous one for U.S. foreign policy makers as they recorded important gains but also critical losses. On the plus side, the United States opened formal relations with China, President Jimmy Carter brokered a historic peace deal between Israel and Egypt, and then he signed a nuclear arms treaty with Soviet Premier Leonid Brezhnev. However, as these issues drew the attention of policy makers, trouble was brewing in the oil-rich Persian Gulf where Iran and its pro-American leader, the shah (king), were facing an anti-American revolution. Few in the American foreign policy bureaucracy predicted that the shah's days were numbered. But on January 16, 1979, when the defeated shah boarded a plane to leave Iran and never return, the linchpin protecting U.S. interests in the Persian Gulf crumbled and U.S. foreign policy in that volatile yet strategic region lay in ruins.

Throughout 1979, U.S. policy makers tried to repair the damage to U.S. interests. However, they turned a bad situation into a humiliating nightmare when their clumsy and monumentally insensitive behavior provoked radical Iranian students into seizing the American Embassy in Tehran and taking its diplomats hostage. When the spiritual leader of Iran's revolution, Ayatollah Ruhollah Khomeini, endorsed the takeover, a prolonged national nightmare ensued. For 444 days, Americans watched in outraged disbelief as Iran thumbed its nose at the United States and world public opinion.

This chapter covers U.S. foreign policy surrounding the Islamic Revolution in Iran as well as the ensuing hostage crisis. We begin by explaining Iran's importance to U.S. interests as we trace the evolution of U.S.-Iran relations since WWII from that of close friend and ally to that of implacable foe. We explain how U.S. intervention in Iran's domestic politics in the 1950s ruined America's image in the eyes of so many Iranians. Next we analyze myriad debates that divided the Carter administration regarding the shah's fall from grace, such as how to respond as the shah's grip on power evaporated, whether or not to admit the shah into the United States, and how to react to the seizure of American diplomats. These debates were the source of so much stress in the Carter administration that they led not only to the very messy resignation of Secretary of State Cyrus Vance but also to competing foreign policies coming out of the nation's capital. Finally, we offer analysis of the impact of the Iranian Revolution and the hostage crisis on American security interests in the Persian Gulf, which even today remain burdened by this turning point in U.S. foreign policy.

U.S.-IRAN RELATIONS AFTER WWII

Ever since WWII, the United States considered Iran a crucial country for several reasons. First, it was part of the Middle East's strategic land bridge joining Europe, Asia, and Africa. Second, it bordered the Soviet Union. Third, it sat on top of 10 percent of the world's proven oil reserves.[1] Consequently, the United States could not resist meddling in Iran's internal affairs, much like the Great Powers, Britain and Russia, who came before it.

For centuries, Iran's rulers were forced to navigate between the competing interests of stronger outside powers. During the nineteenth and early twentieth centuries, Iran, or Persia as it was called back then, was caught up in the Great Game where Great Britain and Russia intervened in Iran as they competed for power and position throughout southwest Asia. In order to gain some maneuverability on the world stage, Iranian leaders engaged in the time-honored tactic of balancing one Great Power against another. For instance, with the rise of Hitler's fascist Germany in the 1930s, Reza Shah, Iran's leader at the time, sought to gain favor with Germany as a counterweight to British and Soviet influence. However, the British could not allow Iran to grow close to Germany, so they ousted Reza Shah in 1941 and installed Reza Shah's son to take his place. Known simply as 'the shah,' Muhammad Reza Shah Pahlavi ruled Iran during WWII in name only. He was a young, insecure leader; the British called most of the shots. When WWII ended in 1945, the shah did what so many Iranian leaders before him did: he cast about for an outside power to help prop up his regime. That power was the United States.

The shah proved to be a trusted ally to the United States for several reasons.[2] First, he allowed the United States to spy on the Soviet Union from Iranian territory. The Americans were keen to exploit Iran's 1,600-mile border with the Soviet Union and in exchange for allowing the Americans to operate advanced electronic listening posts along the border, the shah was allowed to purchase the most advanced military equipment the United States had to offer. In fact, nearly every decision Washington made regarding Iran was influenced by its Cold War rivalry with Moscow. This Soviet-centric perspective dominated policy makers' thinking for so long that few of them were able to see the Iranian Revolution for what it was when it erupted in 1978: an indigenous revolt against domestic corruption and foreign meddling.

Second, the shah supported most of the United States' foreign policies, including the Vietnam War policies of Presidents Johnson and Nixon. Both Johnson and Nixon were buoyed by the shah's support for such an unpopular war. Third, throughout the 1960s and 1970s, the shah was a stable and reliable partner in a region that was engulfed by radical regimes in Egypt, Syria, Iraq, and Libya. As radical Egyptian President Gemal Abdul Nasser's popularity grew, the shah was seen as a bulwark against the spread of Nasserism to the Persian Gulf. Fourth, the shah was the only Middle Eastern leader at the time that had friendly relations with another U.S. ally in the region, Israel. Isolated and surrounded by hostile Arab regimes, Israel found common cause in uniting with Iran (which is not an Arab country) against some of the most radical elements in the Arab World. Finally, and more important than all other strategic considerations save the shah's anti-communist stance, Iran was the world's second largest oil exporter after Saudi Arabia. Although the shah did not always agree with the United States over oil policy, he could be counted on to help keep prices stable, which was vital during the volatile 1970s.

U.S. ties to Iran were not, however, based solely on shared strategic interests. They were also based on close personal relationships that the shah spent years cultivating with the Americans. Few world leaders could boast that they had close personal ties with virtually every American president from Franklin Delano Roosevelt in the early 1940s to Jimmy Carter in the late 1970s. His powerful personal connections ranged from Nelson and David Rockefeller in business to Richard Nixon and Henry Kissinger in government. Just after WWII, the Americans were popular in Iran so the shah's close ties to the United States served him well. American opposition to European colonialism and support for national self-determination won praise throughout Iran. However, the Iranian masses soon changed their minds about the Americans who came to be seen as no different than the British and Russians. Moreover, and more ominously for American interests in the region, as the Iranian masses rose up against the shah's corrupt and brutal rule, they associated anything the royal dictator did with the United States.

AMERICA TARNISHES ITS IMAGE IN IRAN

In 1953 the U.S. image in Iran suffered a blow from which it has yet to recover. That year, the CIA sponsored a coup d'etat that toppled Iran's democratically elected Prime Minister, Muhammad Musaddiq. While few Americans even knew of, much less cared about, the CIA's duplicity in this event, CIA interference is the stuff of legend in Iran. Iranians felt that the United States had unjustly intervened in Iran's internal affairs by overthrowing a popular prime minister in favor of a corrupt monarch. Iranians never forgot how the United States, despite all its rhetoric regarding self-determination, turned out to be as imperial as other outsiders. Under the leadership of agent Kermit Roosevelt (grandson of Theodore Roosevelt), the United States played a key role in Musaddiq's overthrow. Since the memory of this coup heavily influenced the students who seized the American Embassy and took its diplomats hostage in 1979, we shall discuss the events surrounding this turning point in Iranian history.

Musaddiq was elected Prime Minister in 1951 to administer the shah's government. He was a proud Iranian patriot and nationalist who railed against foreign meddling in Iran's internal affairs. His charisma drew widespread support as he amassed power at the expense of the shah. Outraged by what he considered Musaddiq's usurpation of his royal power, the shah dismissed Musaddiq but public outrage forced the shah to reinstate him.[3] Emboldened by this outpouring of popular support, Musaddiq increasingly assailed foreign domination of Iranian politics and economics.

A main target of his criticism was the Anglo Iranian Oil Company (AIOC), which was dominated by the British and which transmitted most of its considerable profits back to Great Britain, leaving the Iranians little to show for their vast oil reserves. In an attempt to gain control over the oil industry, Musaddiq nationalized the AIOC, which meant that the Iranian government would be in control of the AIOC's operations and hence, its revenues. Although this action was popular in Iran, the British reacted harshly by closing down their oil field operations and withdrawing their work crews.[4] Iran's oil revenues plummeted from $400 million to less than $2 million.[5] The economy suffered and instability spread. The shah, fearing for his safety, fled the country. Musaddiq lost many of his supporters and had to rely increasingly on Iran's Communist Party, known as the Tudeh.

U.S. policy makers grew alarmed at these developments for two reasons. First, they feared Musaddiq was steering Iran toward the Soviets even though he was certainly no communist. Second, the United States worried that other developing countries would copy Musaddiq and nationalize *their* industries to the detriment of U.S. business operations. So the CIA authorized Kermit Roosevelt to engineer Musaddiq's ouster and the shah's return. Roosevelt bribed Iranian agents to rise up in protest against Musaddiq and in favor of the shah. Hundreds were killed as Musaddiq was overthrown and the shah returned in triumph to resume his monarchy. Later the grateful shah remarked that he owed his throne to God, the army, and to Kermit Roosevelt.[6] Roosevelt's success in Iran, as well as the CIA-sponsored coup in Guatemala (see chapter 6), gave some U.S. officials the false impression that complex foreign policy problems could be solved by covert operations.

While the Americans considered the coup a great success, they proved incapable of distinguishing between the chimera of a Soviet-inspired communist takeover and a genuine Iranian patriot. In the end, the United States wound up on the wrong side of Iranian nationalism, which permanently tarnished its image in Iran. No longer was the United States viewed favorably. From then on, the United States was seen like all other Great Powers and the shah was seen as Washington's puppet. The CIA became a dirty word in Iran as it trained and equipped the shah's feared and hated secret police, known as SAVAK. The shah's Prime Minister even admitted that SAVAK practiced torture.[7] Anything that happened in Iran that Iranians disliked was attributed to CIA spies or Iranians working for the CIA. Whether this was true or not is beside the point. What matters is the widespread Iranian *perception* that the shah owed his throne to the CIA and that the Americans propped up a corrupt monarch.

After the 1953 coup, the shah's regime established even closer links with the United States. As the U.S. addiction to cheap oil increased, so did the shah's addiction to just about any type of American weapon system. Hundreds, then thousands, of Americans descended upon Iran to take advantage of lucrative business opportunities in the energy and arms industries. At one point in the 1970s, the American embassy employed more than 2,000 people just to help administer all this activity.

Many Iranians objected to the imperious behavior of some of the American expatriates. They also objected to the special privileges granted to Americans stationed in Iran. Perhaps the most outrageous example of these was the Status of Forces Agreement (SOFA) Iran signed with the United States in 1964. In that year, the Iranian Parliament, which served as a rubber stamp for the shah, passed a law that gave all U.S. military personnel *and* their dependents complete immunity from prosecution in Iranian courts for any crimes they might commit in Iran. While diplomats commonly enjoy immunity from prosecution while stationed overseas, the SOFA gave *military* personnel complete immunity—no U.S. soldier could be prosecuted in any Iranian court.

Ayatollah Ruhollah Khomeini, the most outspoken religious leader who despised the shah and his American backers, condemned the SOFA as an affront to Iranian dignity. In one of his typically rousing speeches, Khomeini drew a powerful distinction between American privilege and Iranian restriction when he compared what could happen to an Iranian who ran over an American's dog with an American who ran over the shah:

> They have reduced the Iranian people to a level lower than that of an American dog. If someone runs over a dog belonging to an American, he will be prosecuted. Even if the shah himself were to run over a dog belonging to an American, he would be prosecuted. But if an American cook runs over the shah, the head of state, no one will have the right to interfere with him.[8]

Iranians were outraged at the effrontery. Soon, Khomeini became the leader of the religious opposition. He was joined by many other, albeit secular groups. This fragile and rather tenuous alliance combined to bring down the shah.

RELIGIOUS AND SECULAR OPPOSITION TO THE SHAH

Although Shiite Muslims are the minority branch in Islam, Iran's population is a majority Shiite.[9] Throughout history, Shiites have suffered considerable persecution at the hands of Islam's Sunni majority. The split between Shiite and Sunni Muslims occurred in 632 AD when Islam's founder, the Prophet Muhammad, died and a conflict arose over who should succeed him. Shiites wanted the new leader to come from the Prophet's bloodline while Sunnis wanted the new leader to be the most pious Muslim, regardless of lineage. Violence and bloodshed ensued, during which the Sunnis slaughtered revered Shiite leaders. Over the centuries, Shiites have developed a strong martyr-complex as they commemorate the deaths of their leaders in frenzied moments of self-flagellation.

According to Shiite belief, the last in the line of revered leaders, the so-called Twelfth Imam (a learned religious leader), vanished before the Sunnis could kill him. Shiites refer to this hidden Imam as Mahdi (savior) and believe that he will return one day and establish God's just rule on earth. Iran's Shiite clergy, therefore, believed they should not get involved in politics and government. Instead, government should be left to secular authorities until the Mahdi returned. So they deferred to Iran's secular monarchs and concentrated on pursuing a life of devout worship and submission to the will of God in anticipation of the Mahdi's return.

However, Ayatollah Ruhollah Khomeini's tirades against the shah and his American allies were part of a new political activism among Iran's previously quiescent Shiite clergy. He called on the clergy to resist what he considered the shah's un-Islamic rule. He adopted the name Ruhollah, which means soul or spirit of God. Then the Iranian clergy dubbed him Ayatollah (sign of God). In Shiite Islam, only the most pious Muslims are granted the title Ayatollah. There were only a few hundred ayatollahs in Iran and only about six *grand* ayatollahs, who are considered an even higher cut above the rest. Khomeini earned grand ayatollah status in the early 1960s.[10] As such, it became difficult for the shah or his SAVAK agents to harm or intimidate the Grand Ayatollah Ruholla Khomeini.

In 1963, Khomeini became the first person in ten years to publicly attack the shah, who he compared to Yazid, the ancient Sunni leader who slaughtered Shiites. Khomeini's open opposition landed him in jail, which only increased his legend throughout Iran.[11] He resumed his attacks upon his release, this time condemning the SOFA. Again, Khomeini was arrested but this time forced into exile. He ended up in Najaf, an Iraqi city considered sacred by Shiites.[12] From Najaf, he maintained his attacks on the shah. His sermons, which were recorded on tape cassettes and smuggled into Iran, had a marked influence on rural Iranians who formed the backbone of Khomeini's political support. Many of these traditional-minded folk had moved to the cities in search of work where they confronted a lifestyle they found objectionable. They were offended by what they considered the loose morals of Iran's increasingly westernized urban class. In Khomeini, they found a voice that stressed familiar Islamic themes that they found comforting. Khomeini denounced the urban elite's westernized behavior as "westoxication," as if adopting Western styles of dress and behavior were some kind of disease. Moreover, Khomeini groomed many students who in turn preached and spread his fiery brand of Islam.

But Khomeini and the Shiite clergy were not the only ones resisting the shah. A broad cross-section from secular Iranian society joined the clergy. Working class merchants in Iran's famed bazaars, who had their finger on the pulse of the nation,[13] also resisted the shah. Radical leftists influenced by Karl Marx's communist theory of social equality joined them. In turn, the old members of the liberal, secular National Front, the inheritors of Prime Minister Musaddiq's nationalist movement, joined them. It was easy for these disparate groups to unite against a common foe. But when they ousted the shah in 1979, these groups fought over the contours of the new government. As we shall see below, the American hostages were caught up in the struggle between these various factions, with Khomeini's ultra conservative religious faction using the hostages to seize full control of the revolution.

THE SHAH'S THREATENED THRONE AND THE U.S. POLICY RESPONSE

As this set of broad-based groups increased its resistance to the shah throughout the 1970s, U.S. policy makers confronted a situation for which few were prepared since most had little understanding of political Islam. For years, the shah was considered the bedrock of U.S. security policy in the Persian Gulf, acting as the United States' policeman in the region. As a crucial pillar in the Nixon Doctrine, Nixon envisioned a pivotal role for the shah who would act as his surrogate in the Persian Gulf. When President Nixon visited the shah in 1972, he told the shah to "protect me," which was Nixon's way of asking the shah to look after U.S. interests in the region.[14] Nixon and Kissinger had close personal ties to the shah. Kissinger praised the shah as a rare friend to the Americans. Over the objections of Defense Department officials, Nixon and Kissinger gave the shah carte blanche to purchase any weapons he wanted.[15] From 1972 to 1977, the shah purchased $16 billion in armaments from the United States, a staggering sum at the time.[16] Iran became the world's most lucrative arms market.[17]

By the time Jimmy Carter was inaugurated in January 1977, U.S.-Iran relations were very close, so close in fact, that top policy officials were unable to see that the shah was in danger of losing his throne.[18] Quite the contrary, for as late as August 1978, Carter's key advisors expressed faith in the shah's stability.[19] Moreover, that same month, the CIA reported "Iran is not in a revolutionary or even a pre-revolutionary situation."[20] Six months later, the shah was overthrown as revolutionary fervor consumed Iran.

Even President Carter hopped on the bandwagon. A cornerstone of Carter's foreign policy was the promotion of human rights in other countries, but this was not applied to Iran. In December 1977 prominent opposition leaders in Iran wrote letters praising Carter's human rights policy and beseeched him to apply it to Iran. But when Carter visited the shah only days later, he made no mention of the letters. Instead, he gave a toast to the shah, applauding him for his leadership and proclaiming that Iran was an "island of stability" and that the shah was "beloved by his people."[21] Only days later, the Iranian Revolution broke out in full force. From January 1978 until January 1979 when the shah was overthrown, not a month went by without anti-shah demonstrations, with crowds proclaiming their support for Ayatollah Khomeini while chanting, "God is Great," "Death to the Shah," and "Death to America." Yet, even as late as December 1978, Carter said, "I fully expect the shah to maintain power."[22] Although Carter was trying to shore up a staunch American ally, his public support for the despised despot only worsened the shah's image on the streets or Tehran.

As the revolution progressed and the shah proved unable to bring it under control, Washington failed to respond in a meaningful way. U.S. foreign policy makers, especially Secretary of State Cyrus Vance, were distracted by other pressing matters, such as the opening to China, the Egyptian-Israeli peace talks, and the arms control negotiations with the Soviet Union. Besides, most policy makers were loath to acknowledge that the shah was in danger—they *wanted* to believe that, since he had weathered so many storms during his thirty-seven-year reign, he would ride this one out as well.[23] Moreover, they *had* to believe that the shah would endure. After all, he was the linchpin of U.S. policy in the Persian Gulf. Not until the fall of 1978 did high-ranking officials finally turn their attention to Iran. Part of the reason for that was a cable they received from Ambassador William Sullivan in November titled, "Thinking the Unthinkable." In that cable, Ambassador Sullivan dropped a bombshell on Washington. He reversed his opinion about the shah's prospects, proclaiming now that the shah's days were numbered and that the United States should reach out to the opposition, including Khomeini and the Shiite clergy.

Unlike his predecessors, Ambassador Sullivan had been trying to establish contacts with the shah's opposition ever since he arrived as ambassador in June 1977, but his attempts were thwarted for at least three reasons.[24] First, the shah, given his insecurities, discouraged such contacts. Only after it was too late did the shah urge the Americans to reach out to the opposition. Second, no American official, in the embassy or in Washington, wanted to "make the call" that the shah was on his way out and in turn recommend cultivating relations with his enemies.[25] Besides, making contact with the shah's opponents might embolden them to resist the shah even more. Third, even if U.S. officials did try to reach out to Khomeini, the latter would have nothing to do with the former. For years, Khomeini railed against Western culture in general and the United States in particular. He denounced the United States as 'The Great Satan' and argued that Western-style dress, behavior, and values violated Islam. He called on Iranians to cast off Western influences and adopt strict codes of behavior consistent with Islamic law. For his part, the shah disdained the Islamic clergy, referring to them as "ragheads."[26] He called them a "stupid and reactionary bunch whose brains have not moved . . . for a thousand years."[27] Like his father, the shah worked hard to modernize Iran in part to weaken the clergy's hold on the populace. But, also like his father, he was never able to neutralize the clergy. Accordingly, it was Khomeini, and not the shah, who won the people's hearts and minds.

As the shah teetered on his throne in the fall of 1978, significant debates and divisions among U.S. policy makers emerged and embroiled officials in Washington as well as in the embassy in Tehran. First, there were divisions *within* the State Department, which pitted lower-ranking officials who specialized in Iranian affairs against high-level officers who had broader policy responsibility. For instance, Henry Precht, the State Department's country desk officer for Iran, was one of the first officials to question whether the shah could remain in power. His December report arguing that the shah was finished went ignored by his superiors.[28] In addition, George Griffin, an intelligence analyst at State's small but respected INR, also questioned the prevailing wisdom about the shah's stability, but to no avail.[29] Furthermore, low-ranking officials in the State Department's Human Rights Bureau clashed with Ambassador Sullivan, who wanted the Bureau to take a quieter approach regarding Iran.[30] These debates inside the State Department undermined its ability to manage Iran policy and gave Zbigniew Brzezinski, President Carter's hard-charging national security advisor, the opportunity to seize control, which he did. Even though he had little knowledge of Iran, Brzezinski used his close personal ties to Iran's ambassador in Washington to send messages directly to the shah without going through the State Department.[31] This reflected the broader rivalry for control of U.S. foreign policy between Secretary Vance in the State Department and Brzezinski in the White House.

Second, debates emerged between Ambassador Sullivan in Iran and President Carter and Brzezinski in the White House. Sullivan fretted that his increasingly dire cables to Washington were going unheeded. In his exasperation, he sent a decidedly undiplomatic message to Washington, insisting that the president made a "gross and perhaps irretrievable mistake" in refusing to send an emissary to meet Khomeini.[32] An infuriated President Carter wanted to recall Sullivan, but Secretary Vance convinced him to allow Sullivan to stay in Tehran. Relations between the embassy and the White House grew so strained that Carter and Brzezinski stopped listening to anything Sullivan had to say. Sullivan never received a response from Washington regarding that electrifying cable he sent in November.[33] Instead, Brzezinski sent Gen. Robert "Dutch" Huyser to Tehran to work out of the embassy and report back to him or to the Defense Department, thus bypassing Sullivan and the State Department altogether. While Huyser worked closely with Iran's military and laid the groundwork for a possible military coup, Sullivan continued to work with Iran's Foreign Ministry. Huyser stayed at the ambassador's residence and would actually dine with Sullivan. Each would then send his own cable back to Washington, Sullivan would cable the State Department and Huyser contacted either the defense secretary or the chairman of the Joint Chiefs of Staff.[34] It was as if two competing foreign policies were being implemented in Tehran. According to Sullivan, "there were times when we felt we must have been talking to two different cities."[35]

As if the rift between Sullivan and Brzezinski was not enough to muddle U.S. policy, Brzezinski and Vance clashed over what to do. Brzezinski was nicknamed 'the terrier' for his combative personality.[36] Even after losing a fight, he refused to yield. He consistently pushed for a military response to save the shah partly because he saw the Soviets behind the Iranian revolution.[37] For Brzezinski, a native of Poland who hated to see that country fall under communist domination after WWII, the shah must react forcefully to prevent Soviet inroads.[38] He found support for this stance from Defense Secretary Harold Brown, CIA Director Stansfield Turner, and Energy Secretary James Schlesinger.[39]

Vance countered that a military response by the shah would lead to more Soviet influence, not less. He advocated a more diplomatic approach. Trained as a lawyer, Vance's style emphasized caution. He opposed Brzezinski's aggressive tactics and instead favored the shah taking measures to improve political participation and socio-economic conditions for his people. He worried that a crackdown of the type Brzezinski advocated would make matters worse. Vance won more of these rounds with Brzezinski than he lost since the president sided with him. Moreover, the shah himself did not believe harsher measures would work. He was reluctant to turn the full force of his military against his own people just to save his throne.

Ultimately, however, it appears that by the time policy makers in Washington began paying serious attention to the troubles in Iran, there was little anyone could do to save the shah. So a dejected and beaten shah flew out of Iran and into exile on January 15, 1979, never to return. On February 1, a triumphant Ayatollah Khomeini touched down at the airport and was greeted by millions of adoring Iranians who lined the streets as he made his way to Tehran.

THE DEBATE OVER WHETHER TO ADMIT THE SHAH

As Khomeini established a provisional government, the shah searched for a country that would accept him. This caused yet another debate among U.S. officials. Should they admit the shah or inform him that he was unwelcome? The debate lasted until October 22, 1979, when the shah was admitted to the United States for medical reasons. Resolution of this debate in favor of admitting the shah led directly to the hostage crisis.

On one side of the debate stood Cyrus Vance and virtually the entire State Department, including every diplomat stationed in the American Embassy in Tehran. Admitting the shah was a bad idea for two reasons. First, it would send the wrong signal to revolutionary Iran, thus hindering the prospects for establishing smooth relations.[40] After all, Iran remained a strategically important country. The revolution destabilized the Persian Gulf and sent shock waves through international energy markets. Oil prices doubled and the world economy fell into a recession as it endured its second energy crisis of the decade. The United States needed Iran's cooperation in stabilizing prices no matter who was in charge in Tehran. In addition, the United States needed the provisional government's friendship if only to keep Iran from falling under Soviet influence. Moreover, Vance feared that admitting the shah would damage relations with other important Muslim countries.

Second, Vance worried that admitting the shah might endanger the Americans in the embassy in Iran. On February 14, less than two weeks after Khomeini's return, the embassy was seized by an angry mob. Although the provisional government quickly kicked the mob out of the embassy grounds and freed the diplomats, the seizure made clear the depth of anger and hatred many Iranians felt toward the United States. If the shah was admitted, the February takeover might be repeated, or worse. State Department officials in Washington and the embassy wrote multiple memos arguing against admitting the shah. On September 30, less than a month before the shah was admitted, the embassy cabled Washington arguing that it would be "seriously prejudicial to our interests and to the security of Americans in Iran" if the shah was allowed entry.[41] The embassy received assurances from Washington that the shah would not be admitted. Despite these assurances, the shah was admitted anyway. In Tehran, the faces of embassy officials "went white."[42]

On the other side of this debate stood Brzezinski, who was joined by members of the U.S. foreign policy elite, especially former Secretary of State Henry Kissinger and business tycoon David Rockefeller, both of whom held considerable sway in Washington. For them, the United States must offer the shah safe haven for at least two reasons. First, they argued that refusing the shah entry would send the wrong signal to U.S. allies throughout the world. How would it look, Brzezinski argued, if the United States could not be counted on to support them in *their* time of need?[43] He argued that refusing the shah would be seen as a sign of weakness thus prompting allies to think twice about their friendship with the United States. Second, Brzezinski, Kissinger, and Rockefeller argued that the shah had been a loyal and trusted ally to the United States for thirty-seven years and should therefore be welcomed as a friend. Kissinger complained about how the Carter administration treated the fallen shah. In speeches that were widely reported by the press, he criticized Carter for treating the shah "like a Flying Dutchman looking for a port of call."[44] He also threatened to withhold support for the president's arms talks with the Soviets unless Carter admitted the shah.[45] Kissinger would telephone Brzezinski at the White House who would then bring pressure to bear on Carter. Brzezinski also received calls from Rockefeller to the same effect. Eventually, Brzezinski was able to convince Vice President Walter Mondale into siding with him. Moreover, Carter's political advisors, concerned about his upcoming reelection campaign, also favored admitting the shah in order to avoid attacks from the Republicans.

But President Carter, who grew irritated by the pressure, especially from Kissinger and Rockefeller, exploded with an expletive-laced tirade aimed at the shah. In siding with Vance, Carter, at least for a time, settled the debate in favor of *not* admitting the shah. He said, "I'm not going to welcome him when he has other places where he'll be safe" and he did not like the idea of the shah "playing tennis [in the United States] while Americans in Tehran were being kidnapped or even killed."[46]

However, a sudden development changed Vance and then Carter's mind. Long before the Iranian Revolution, the shah was diagnosed with cancer, but he kept it a closely guarded secret. In October, when word reached Vance that the shah was gravely ill, he changed his mind about admitting the shah. He felt that the medical facilities in Mexico, where the shah had so unhappily landed, could not offer the shah the same quality of care that he could obtain in a U.S. hospital. Admitting the shah therefore, turned into a humanitarian issue for Vance so he urged Carter to admit him. With all his major advisors now arrayed against him, Carter relented. In a somber mood, he asked them, "What are you guys going to advise me to do if they overrun our embassy and take our people hostage?"[47] No one responded.

THE HOSTAGE CRISIS AND THE U.S. POLICY RESPONSE

For nearly two weeks, the shah's admission caused little stir in Iran. Embroiled in revolutionary chaos, Iranians appeared distracted. Besides, Vance received assurances from Iran's provisional government that, although they objected to the shah's entry, they would abide by their international obligations and protect the embassy.[48] However, on October 20, when Henry Precht informed Iranian Foreign Minister Ibrahim Yazdi of the shah's pending arrival, Yazdi said "You are playing with fire."[49] Yazdi's warning proved prophetic when, on November 4, radical students calling themselves "Followers of the Line of the Imam" (out of reverence for Ayatollah Khomeini) entered the embassy and took more than sixty American diplomats hostage.

Although the students demanded the United States return the shah so he could stand trial, the real reason for the takeover was to forestall a perceived attempt by the Americans to reverse the Iranian Revolution and return the shah to power. Well aware of what the Americans had done in restoring the shah's throne in 1953, the students were determined to prevent that from happening again. They believed the shah's entry into the United States, together with a meeting Brzezinski held with secular Iranian leaders in Algeria shortly thereafter, signaled a U.S. attempt to destroy the revolution and deny Khomeini his plans to create an Islamic regime in Iran.

At first, officials in Washington as well as in the embassy expected the takeover to last only a short while. Even the students prepared for just a three-day siege. Entering the grounds peacefully, they carried placards in a way that was eerily reminiscent of 1960s-style civil rights demonstrations in the American South. They even announced, "We do not wish to harm you. We only wish to set-in."[50] At first, Khomeini ordered his aides to expel the students from the embassy, which, under international law, is recognized as sovereign American soil. But when he realized how popular the students' actions were with the Iranian masses, he saw an opportunity to use the takeover to further his plan to establish an Islamic government in Iran. So when he publicly endorsed the takeover a few days later, Khomeini transformed what had begun as an act of piracy by a group of college students into an international incident between the Iranian government and the world's mightiest power.

Denouncing the embassy as a "den of spies," Khomeini declared the students' actions divinely inspired as they led a "second" revolution that amounted to a "struggle between Islam and blasphemy."[51] Once Khomeini sided with the students, any Iranian who opposed the seizure could be labeled un-Islamic. In fact, the secular leaders of Iran's provisional government who vehemently opposed the seizure, resigned in protest. This opened the way for Khomeini to constitute Iran as an Islamic Republic. Khomeini used the hostages as pawns in Iran's domestic politics. Therefore, while the students *seized* the embassy for one reason, to prevent what they saw as an American-sponsored counterrevolution, they *held* it for quite another, to help Khomeini create an Islamic state. This explains why it took 444 days to win the hostages' release. After Precht, the State Department's country desk officer for Iran, heard Khomeini voice support for the students, he correctly predicted that the United States was in for a prolonged standoff.[52]

Emboldened by Khomeini's endorsement, the students blindfolded the hostages and paraded them in front of television cameras with their guns drawn. Shouting "Death to America!" and "Death to the Shah!" they burned Carter's image in effigy and torched the American flag. They threatened to try the hostages and execute them for crimes against Iran. The international media, enthralled by a drama too irresistible to ignore, devoted most of its news coverage to the crisis and the presence of television crews only intensified the students' fury as they seemingly played to the cameras.

Humiliated by a relatively poor and weak country, the American people and the Carter administration were consumed by the crisis. American anger with Iran was compounded by the memory of other recent foreign policy disasters, namely the Vietnam War and the oil embargo (see chapters 7 and 9). Outraged Americans launched counter-demonstrations and tied ribbons around their trees in solidarity with the hostages. Carter made securing the hostages' freedom his own personal mission and declared that he would not leave Washington to campaign for reelection until the crisis was resolved. From November 4, 1979, until the day he left office on January 20, 1981, Carter obsessed over how to win the hostages' freedom.[53]

But how should the Carter administration respond to such a blatant violation of international law? Like the previous debate over whether to admit the shah, the debate over how to respond to the hostage crisis saw Vance again opposing Brzezinski. Also like the previous debate, Vance won the early rounds but Brzezinski got his way in the end. Finally, and again like the previous debate, Brzezinski's ultimate victory here led to disastrous consequences for the United States.

In keeping with his combative style, Brzezinski advocated forceful measures against Iran. While he did not oppose diplomatic efforts, he preferred military force. At various points during the crisis, he considered mining Iran's harbors, imposing a naval blockade, launching a punitive military strike against Iran's oil refineries, militarily occupying strategic portions of Iran, taking Iranians hostage as bargaining chips, and launching a military rescue operation.[54] However, consideration of any military option was shelved after the Soviets invaded nearby Afghanistan on December 27 because policy makers feared a strike against Iran could lead to a confrontation with the Soviets. The Soviet invasion of Afghanistan was yet another blow to U.S. foreign policy interests in the 1970s that reverberates even today (see chapter 12). Nevertheless, preparations to launch an operation to rescue the hostages, which was Brzezinski's preferred option, went forward.

But Vance opposed military force unless the hostages' lives were in danger. He urged Carter to employ diplomatic and economic tools as the means to pressure Iran into negotiating for the hostages' release. Vance convinced Carter to give diplomacy and economic statecraft a chance to succeed. Within days of the seizure, therefore, Carter: (1) ordered many Iranian nationals out of the United States; (2) announced a boycott of Iranian oil; (3) halted delivery of military items for which Iran had already paid; and (4) froze more than $12 billion worth of Iranian assets on deposit in U.S. banks. While Brzezinski accepted these measures, he never ceased pushing for a more forceful response.

As these sanctions were put in place, the United States went to the United Nations and the International Court of Justice (ICJ) in hopes of putting diplomatic pressure on Iran. While the United States won a quick judgment against Iran in the ICJ, Tehran ignored the Court's ruling.[55] And while many of the United States' major allies sympathized with the Americans, none were willing to put much pressure on Iran since they needed Iranian oil for their industries.[56] The United States also engaged multiple back channel negotiating avenues but each time the U.S. negotiators thought they had an agreement, something unpredictable occurred in Tehran to scuttle the deal.

By early April 1980, as yet another negotiation attempt collapsed, the policy ground in Washington shifted away from Vance and toward Brzezinski, who now had the support of nearly all high-ranking officials, including Defense Secretary Brown and Vice President Mondale.[57] Most important, Carter shifted from Vance to Brzezinski. Vance was prepared to wait longer, but the president's patience had run out.[58] Vance's emphasis on cautious diplomacy lost favor as months passed with no resolution in sight. Carter's willingness to dicker with the Iranians over and over made him look weak and indecisive. The media's constant coverage of the crisis eroded confidence in Carter. Walter Cronkite, the famous CBS news anchor known as the "most trusted man in America," ended each broadcast by reminding his audience how many days American diplomats were held captive in Iran. Carter's initial restraint won him sympathy and support in America and the world. His public opinion approval ratings soared from 32 percent in September 1979 to 61 percent in January.[59] However, by the spring of 1980, Carter's approval rating had sunk to 39 percent.[60]

Meanwhile, the elections loomed in November. Carter's Republican challenger, Ronald Reagan, was ahead in the polls. Reagan called Carter's attempts at negotiating a waste of time. When asked what he would do instead, he said he did not know and that he was "waiting for a miracle."[61] Reagan also demanded a congressional investigation of Carter's handling of the crisis but once he was in the White House President Reagan "did not call for an investigation of any kind."[62]

Moreover, Vance's cautious diplomatic style looked anachronistic in the face of a revitalized Soviet threat. The Soviet invasion of Afghanistan, which put thousands of communist troops within striking distance of the oil-rich Persian Gulf, was a "thundering repudiation" of Vance's position.[63] Sensing his chance to convince Carter, Brzezinski wrote the president a memo on April 9 praising the president's restraint but also arguing for a bold rescue operation: "It is time for us to act. Now."[64] Two days later, at a crucial high-level policy meeting, Carter told his senior advisors that the negotiations phase had expired and that the time for bolder action had arrived. But what type of force should be employed? In the end Carter and all his advisors (except Vance) settled on the rescue attempt that Brzezinski had been pushing. Other types of military force, such as a naval blockade or mining Iran's harbors, would not free the hostages and, in fact, might provoke the Iranians into harming them.

Vance was not present at this meeting and was furious that such a decision was made in his absence, especially since this was the first (and only) time President Carter ever authorized the use of military force during his presidency. Vance opposed the operation because: (1) it was so complex something was bound to go wrong; (2) many people, including some hostages, might be killed; (3) the Iranians might take other Americans hostage, such as aid workers; (4) the operation would anger U.S. allies who were promised that no such action was under consideration; and (5) it might lead to attacks on U.S. embassies in other Muslim countries.[65] Embassies in Pakistan and Libya had already been attacked and Vance feared a recurrence.[66] Unconvinced, Carter ordered the operation to proceed. Vance told Carter he would resign no matter the outcome.

On April 25, a visibly shaken President Carter appeared before television cameras to announce to the world that the rescue operation had failed and in a most horrific manner. The plan consisted of two stages, the first of which called for troops to fly by helicopter under cover of darkness to a staging area hundreds of miles inside Iran. Stage Two, the actual assault on the embassy, would occur under cover of darkness the next day. However, the operation had to be aborted in Stage One because bad weather and mechanical malfunctions grounded too many helicopters. As the troops prepared to abandon their desert hideout, a helicopter crashed into a cargo plane, causing a massive fireball that left eight soldiers dead. Although he was not one to gloat, Vance's prediction proved correct. Three days later, he kept his word and resigned. It remains the only time since 1915 (see chapter 2) that a Secretary of State resigned on a matter of principle.[67]

After the failed rescue attempt, Brzezinski, in typical "terrier" fashion, urged Carter to authorize a second operation, but to no avail. The hostage crisis receded from the American political scene. People were fatigued by the whole ordeal. Carter hit the campaign trail. More months passed as the hostages, now scattered throughout Iran, languished in their captivity. It was not until September 1980 that Khomeini, having finally succeeded in putting in place all the instruments of a new Islamic state, signaled he was ready to bargain for the hostages' release. Ironically, "Vance's policy [of negotiation] continued without Vance."[68] However, even that promising opening was curtailed by Iraq's invasion of Iran on September 22, which obviously drew Iran's attention elsewhere.

Nevertheless, Carter's team of negotiators worked tirelessly in hopes of winning the hostages' freedom before November 4, which was not only the one-year anniversary of the crisis but Election Day as well. However, yet another last-ditch effort fell through just before the polls opened and Ronald Reagan trounced Jimmy

Carter. Carter probably would have lost the election anyway since voters blamed him for a broad range of problems ailing America, including the energy crisis, inflation, unemployment, and a general sense of malaise that even Carter unhappily (and unwisely) acknowledged. However, according to his election pollster, Carter was in a dead heat with Reagan in the final days just before the election, then suddenly, "The sky has fallen. . . . I've never seen anything like it in polling. Here we are neck and neck with Reagan up until the very end and everything breaks against us. *It's the hostage thing.*"[69]

Despite his resounding defeat, Carter never gave up trying to get the hostages home. Just before Reagan took the oath of office in January 1981, Carter's team hashed out a deal that boiled down to Iran releasing the hostages in exchange for the United States releasing Iran's frozen assets. Returning the shah to stand trial as a condition for the hostages' release ceased to be a stumbling block long before since the shah had died of cancer while in Egypt the previous July. Khomeini, who had such deep personal hatred for Carter, waited until the moment *after* Reagan was inaugurated to release the hostages. Carter boarded a plane to Germany to welcome the freed hostages, but he did so as a private citizen, not as President of the United States.

AFTERMATH: THE ISLAMIC REVOLUTION AS A TURNING POINT

So, what was the impact of the Iranian Revolution and the American hostage crisis on U.S. foreign policy? We turn first, and perhaps foremost, to the impact on U.S. strategic interests in the region. According to one U.S. official, when the shah's regime collapsed, with it crumbled the security system on which U.S. policy relied in the vital Persian Gulf, and with the sharp decline in Iranian oil production came the second of the 1970s great oil shocks.[70]

Iran's defection from the ranks of U.S. allies altered the balance of power in the region against the United States. For more than thirty-seven years, the shah served as a dependable proxy for U.S. interests in the Persian Gulf. He allowed the United States to establish sensitive electronic listening posts along Iran's border with the Soviet Union. From these posts, the United States could monitor Soviet troop movements as well as nuclear weapons tests and deployments. He helped keep radical regimes in the region in check. For instance, at the behest of President Nixon and Henry Kissinger, he gave weapons to the Kurdish rebellion inside Iraq in order to thwart Iraq's attempt to export its virulent form of pan-Arab nationalism, which the United States saw as a threat. He helped to moderate (at least somewhat) oil prices just when the United States was becoming increasingly dependent on Middle East oil. The shah also helped prop up other conservative monarchies in the Persian Gulf who were friends with the United States. For instance, he sent troops to neighboring Oman to help quell what appeared to be a communist-inspired uprising. In addition, he was a friend to Israel when Israel was surrounded by hostile Arab states pledged to its destruction. Finally, he was an excellent customer, purchasing billions of dollars worth of weapons from U.S. arms manufacturers.

But when the shah was ousted, Khomeini established an anti-American Islamic state. What was once the most stable U.S. friend turned into a vehement foe. Khomeini's deep-seated hatred for the United States transformed a close ally into an arch nemesis, the impacts of which are felt today. Ever since the Iranian Revolution and the hostage crisis, both sides have viewed the other with suspicion, distrust, and hatred. Since 1979, U.S. policy makers have been preoccupied with stopping Iran from spreading its version of political Islam. U.S. policy makers accuse Iran of aiding violent Islamicists in Lebanon, Iraq, and the Palestinian Territories. Washington also claims that Iran is trying to develop a nuclear arsenal. Presidents Clinton, Bush, and Obama have all stated that the United States could not accept a nuclear-armed Iran yet each proved unable to find the correct policy approach to ensure that goal.

The Iranian Revolution also contributed to two major wars in the 1980s. While covering these wars is beyond the scope of this chapter, suffice to say here that the Iranian Revolution destabilized the region by creating a striking fear that radical Islamic movements would spread to other countries. Consequently, the Soviets and then the Iraqis went to war at least in part to stop this spread and check what they perceived to be a growing threat to their own interests. The Soviet Union invaded Afghanistan in December 1979 in part to prevent the spread of radical Islam to its own Muslim-majority republics, such as Turkmenistan and Uzbekistan. And Iraq invaded Iran in September 1980 in part because Ayatollah Khomeini called on Iraq's oppressed Shiite majority to rise up and establish an Islamic state in Baghdad.

Accordingly, this turning point helped contribute to a growing pattern of American activism and intervention in the region that ultimately culminated in the 2003 invasion of Iraq (see chapter 12). After the Iranian Revolution, the Soviet invasion of Afghanistan, and the Iran-Iraq War, the United States felt compelled to increase its military presence in the region. It sent naval armadas to patrol the waters of the Persian Gulf and the Arabian Sea, it pre-positioned huge stockpiles of weapons in nearby countries, and it established the Rapid Deployment Force (RDF), which consisted of lightly armed, highly mobile forces that could respond to fast-emerging threats on short notice. Washington also armed anti-Soviet guerrillas in Afghanistan, some of whom later formed al Qaeda (see chapter 12).

Finally, the Iranian Revolution in general, and the hostage crisis in particular, politically wounded President Carter so severely that it cost him reelection. While he enjoyed a significant boost in his public opinion approval rating during the first weeks of the hostage crisis, his approval rating plummeted as the crisis dragged on for more than a year. Carter was prone to take bold risks in world affairs. These included severing ties to Taiwan, personally mediating the Egypt-Israel peace treaty, negotiating the handover of the Panama Canal to Panama, and concluding a sweeping arms control agreement with the Soviets. The president won widespread acclaim for these accomplishments. But all the gains he amassed were wiped away by the perception that he demonstrated weak and ineffective leadership during the hostage crisis in Iran. Conversely, the crisis emboldened Ronald Reagan and the conservative wing of the Republican Party, which sought to restore the United States to its pre–Vietnam War position of prestige and power in world affairs. In fact, as will be demonstrated in chapter 12, the inheritors of Reagan's vision were prominent in the George W. Bush administration when Osama bin Laden's al Qaeda terrorist network struck multiple targets in the United States on September 11, 2001.

Eleven

THE FALL OF THE BERLIN WALL AND
THE END OF THE COLD WAR

In June 1987, standing in front of the Brandenburg Gate at the center of the Berlin Wall, President Ronald Reagan issued a famous appeal to Soviet Premier Mikhail Gorbachev to "tear down this wall." Within two years of Reagan's speech, the revolutionary changes that Gorbachev had unleashed after coming to power in the Soviet Union in 1985 would result in just that: the demolition of the Berlin Wall. For twenty-eight years the Berlin Wall had stood as the most obvious reminder of the post–WWII division of Europe between the communist Eastern Bloc and the capitalist Western Bloc. Berlin, like Germany as a whole, was divided in two after WWII, with the United States and its allies occupying the western half and the Soviet Union taking control of the eastern half. Its location inside the territory of what would become the Soviet satellite state of the German Democratic Republic made divided Berlin a persistent flashpoint of the Cold War.

West Berlin was both a magnet for refugees fleeing the harsh realities of communist rule in East Germany and a convenient jumping-off point for U.S. spies seeking to penetrate the Iron Curtain. With Moscow's approval, the government of East Germany began construction of the Berlin Wall in 1961 to end this cross-town traffic and compound the isolation of West Berlin. Over the course of the next three decades approximately 150 people died at the hands of East German border guards as they attempted to breach the wall and escape to the West. Many more succeeded using a variety of means from underground tunnels to specially modified cars that enabled passengers to escape scrutiny at designated crossing points along the wall.

Reagan, as John F. Kennedy had done twenty-four years earlier, chose to highlight the wall in his 1987 speech because it was the most visible symbol contrasting the freedoms of Western democracy with the despotism of Eastern communism.

The collapse of the Berlin Wall highlighted a dramatic series of events in 1989 and 1990 that witnessed communist governments throughout Eastern Europe topple in a series of largely peaceful revolts, and that culminated in the once unthinkable reunification of Germany. Since 1947, U.S. foreign policy was built largely around the goal of containing communism, with the aim of destroying it. However, policy makers were surprisingly ill-prepared for the day when that expectation became a reality. Gorbachev's dramatic efforts to reform the Soviet Union and reshape its relationship with the West had initially been met with as much skepticism as support in Washington, but the collapse of the Berlin Wall and the subsequent unification of Germany compelled "even the most hardened cold warriors [in the United States] . . . to acknowledge that the Cold War had ended" before communist rule in the Soviet Union had come to an end.[1] When the Soviet Union did cease to exist in 1991, it served as a somewhat anti-climactic footnote to a decades-long struggle that was already over.

From Harry Truman to Ronald Reagan, successive presidents made confronting the challenge of Soviet communism the cornerstone of U.S. foreign policy. Not since the early Cold War presidencies of Truman and Dwight Eisenhower had any American chief executive done so much to highlight the threat posed by the Soviet Union as Reagan did. During his first term in office, Reagan reversed the politics of detente that had characterized U.S.-Soviet relations in the 1970s and instead reignited the Cold War by abandoning arms control, supporting anti-communist insurgencies throughout the developing world, and hurling a barrage of rhetorical missiles at Moscow. Most of these policy initiatives would be dramatically reversed during his second term, however, as Reagan came to terms with the new Soviet regime of Mikhail Gorbachev. Reagan and Gorbachev would form a close personal relationship and, during a series of historic summits in the latter half of the 1980s, they negotiated agreements that went a long way toward defusing a conflict that on several occasions since the 1940s had threatened the world with nuclear war. While U.S. foreign policy had for so long been built on confrontation in a bipolar world, the greatest challenge facing Washington in these years was reformulating its foreign policy to conform to a world absent the dynamics of the superpower struggle. Symbols like the Berlin Wall had become such integral parts of the United

States' worldview that their sudden disappearance proved somewhat disorienting, and Washington was left scrambling for a clear foreign policy agenda in the post–Cold War world.

This chapter begins by examining Reagan's foreign policy initiatives during his first term in office that led to the abandonment of the policy of detente cultivated during the Nixon-Ford-Carter years and its replacement with a more combative approach to the Soviet Union. The next section of the chapter looks at the revolutionary changes introduced by Mikhail Gorbachev after his accession to power in the Soviet Union in 1985 and the dynamic relationship that he and Reagan formed, leading to a new spirit of detente and cooperation. In this context the fall of the Berlin Wall served as a potent symbol to a radically altered equation in world politics. The final section of the chapter involves a brief examination of foreign policy challenges facing the administration of George H. W. Bush in a world transformed by the end of the Cold War.

RONALD REAGAN AND "THE EVIL EMPIRE"
Ronald Reagan's victory over Jimmy Carter in 1980 marked the first time since Herbert Hoover's defeat in 1932 that a sitting president had failed to win reelection. Carter's defeat was largely a reflection of voter concern over domestic issues, but those concerns were magnified by the domestic impact of the international energy crisis and by the apparent impotence of the United States in the face of the American hostage crisis (see chapter 10). The Reagan campaign successfully portrayed the Carter administration as guilty of perpetuating a culture of national malaise, manifested by stagnation at home and weakness abroad. Reagan's "rhetoric of national assertiveness," replete with promises of economic recovery and renewed international respect, clearly resonated with American voters in 1980.[2] Vietnam had inspired a rethinking of American foreign policy and the Nixon and Carter administrations had abandoned the bipolar framework of early Cold War policy and substituted in its place a multipolar world vision in which traditional East-West concerns had to be balanced against North-South considerations. Reagan, however, returned to the original ideological framework of the Cold War while rejecting the realpolitik detente practiced by Nixon and the human rights–centered idealism favored by Carter.[3] The new president and his foreign policy team reverted to a bipolar vision of the world and rebranded global events in terms of the ideological struggle between communism and capitalism. In contrast to the Nixon-Ford-Carter

years where the emphasis had been on managing world affairs, Reagan adopted from the beginning a confrontational style in foreign policy resting almost entirely on the strategy of opposing the Soviet Union.

Key foreign policy positions in the Reagan administration went to vocal opponents of detente, such as Alexander Haig, who became secretary of state, and Casper Weinberger, who took the post of secretary of defense. Haig and Weinberger, along with other hardliners such as Assistant Secretary of Defense Richard Perle and National Security Council Soviet Expert Richard Pipes, were at the vanguard of a push within the Reagan administration to reverse the policy trend of the 1970s and arrest the perceived decline of American power. These hardliners rejected detente as a naïve policy amounting to a unilateral ceasefire that the Soviets had successfully exploited to their advantage.[4] They rejected the assertion that the world was too diverse for a bipolar foreign policy to succeed, claiming instead that most regional crises and conflicts could and should be addressed within the context of the global struggle between capitalism and communism. The hardliners also charged the Carter administration with having abandoned important friends and allies over issues such as human rights, and they were determined to free the United States from the grip of the Vietnam Syndrome by restoring the use of force as a legitimate tool of foreign policy. Reagan's foreign policy agenda therefore rested on the assumption that American power must be used to put pressure on the Soviet Union and counteract the spread of communism worldwide, and thus constituted "a grand design reminiscent of a world much like the 1950s."[5]

The End of Detente

Reagan's rejection of detente did not represent a completely new departure as Carter had effectively ended it following the Soviet Union's invasion of Afghanistan in 1979. However, whereas Carter employed the stick approach of the Olympic boycott, grain embargo, and suspension of SALT II, he also held out the carrot of reversal of these policies were the Soviets to withdraw from Afghanistan. Reagan's rhetoric hinted at a more fundamental transformation in U.S.-Soviet relations. In a speech before the British parliament in 1982 Reagan predicted that Marxism-Leninism was doomed to "end up on the ash heap of history," and a year later, before an audience of religious conservatives, Reagan famously referred to the Soviet Union as an "evil empire."[6]

The Reagan administration's perception of the Soviet Union was a mixture of optimism and pessimism. On the one hand, the administration espoused a certainty that capitalism would triumph over communism, yet on the other hand Reagan and his foreign policy team routinely represented the Soviet Union as an irrepressible force for evil in the world.[7] This contradiction raises doubts about the degree to which the administration believed its own rhetoric about the imminent demise of communism, yet the evidence does seem to support the conclusion that Reagan and his colleagues recognized that the Soviet Union was weaker than it appeared, and they were convinced that it was susceptible to outside pressure.

One of the primary arenas in which the Reagan administration sought to challenge the Soviet Union was military spending and arms production. While Carter had suspended arms control talks and increased the Pentagon's budget after the Soviets invaded Afghanistan, under Reagan the very future of arms control came into doubt as U.S. defense spending jumped 34 percent between 1981 and 1985.[8] The new administration questioned the premise of the arms control efforts that had formed the centerpiece of detente in the 1970s and hardliners blasted critics who claimed that the United States and the Soviet Union were equally responsible for the arms race. Reagan entered the White House vehemently opposed to continuing the arms reduction program of SALT I and II and his foreign policy team rejected as virtual appeasement the very premise of mutual arms-limitation agreements with the Soviet Union. Instead the emphasis in the first years of the Reagan administration was on reestablishing U.S. supremacy in the arena of strategic nuclear weapons in order to bury the Soviet Union under the weight of an expensive arms race. This logic reflected the early ascendancy of hardliners such as Weinberger and Haig, but in the second half of Reagan's first term the influence of pragmatists such as George Schulz (who replaced Haig as Secretary of State in 1982) pushed the administration back toward considering negotiations with the Soviet Union.[9] Nonetheless, the goal of achieving U.S. nuclear superiority remained, only now the purpose was to facilitate negotiation from a position of strength. The White House sought to change the very language of arms control by replacing SALT (Strategic Arms Limitation Talks) with START (Strategic Arms Reduction Talks). Not only did the proactive tone of START fit better with the Reagan administration's rhetoric of national assertiveness, but by negotiating from a position of strength the United States would be able to promote arms reduction to its particular advantage.

The cornerstone of Reagan's strategic defense policy was known as the Strategic Defense Initiative (SDI). Dubbed "Star Wars" by the press, SDI was a multi-billion dollar project to build a computer-operated, spaced-based program that could de-

stroy incoming nuclear missiles before they reached their intended targets in the
United States. Discounted by critics as science fiction, SDI was Reagan's answer to
the seemingly illogical theory of Mutual Assured Destruction (MAD) that nuclear
strategists had embraced earlier in the Cold War. MAD was based on the premise
that the Soviet Union and the United States would never engage in nuclear war because neither side could possibly hope to survive, let alone win, a conflict in which
both sides deployed their massive nuclear arsenals. By embracing SDI, Reagan rejected MAD and the principle of nuclear deterrence upon which it rested and by so
doing he promoted the concept that the United States could win a nuclear war by
surviving a first-strike attack from the Soviet Union. While SDI would ultimately
wither on the vine of renewed detente in the latter half of the 1980s, setting it as a
goal was part of Reagan's broader strategy to put pressure on Moscow by raising the
possibility that the United States might achieve nuclear superiority.

To Reagan's domestic and international critics SDI resembled the kind of saber
rattling that characterized the Cold War in the run up to the Cuban Missile Crisis.
Having lain dormant for almost two decades, the specter of nuclear war resurfaced
in the 1980s and inspired the anti-nuclear arms movement in Western Europe
and American made-for-TV movies such as *The Day After*. Meanwhile, the administration's claim that it was still serious about arms control failed to counteract
the appearance that its policies "seemed designed to subvert rather than advance
the process."[10] The United States hoped to withdraw obsolete intermediate nuclear
forces (INF) missiles from Western Europe and replace them with the new Pershing
II's and the Tomahawk cruise missile. However, when this proposal met with widespread opposition from NATO allies concerned that it would reignite the arms race
in Europe, Washington responded by proposing what is known as the 'zero-zero
option,' which entailed the removal of all INF from Europe, both American missiles and Soviet SS-20s. Skeptics doubted the sincerity of the U.S. proposal, which
amounted to offering the cancellation of American missiles that had not yet been
deployed in return for the dismantling of perhaps the most important weapons in
the Soviet Union's strategic arsenal. Neither the zero-zero option nor START had
any realistic chance of gaining traction in Moscow and they both appear to have
been more important as rhetorical clubs with which to beat the Soviet Union rather
than serious efforts at arms control.

Another key element of the Reagan administration's foreign policy was the
Reagan Doctrine, "a low risk, low cost [effort] to roll back Soviet power" and in-

fluence in the developing world.[11] Hardliners believed that for too long the Soviet Union had enjoyed a monopoly on the tactic of promoting insurgency around the world in an effort to promote its global agenda. Whereas on numerous occasions throughout the Cold War the Soviet Union had successfully frustrated U.S. interests by supporting left wing insurgencies, the Reagan administration now began to actively support right wing insurgencies in places where it perceived Soviet influence to be vulnerable. During the Reagan years the United States actively supported insurgencies against the Soviet occupation in Afghanistan and against leftist forces or regimes in Angola, Cambodia, and Nicaragua. The extent of U.S. involvement in these conflicts was often masked by secrecy, either to avoid compromising important allies such as Pakistan through which U.S. aid to insurgents in Afghanistan was funneled, or to hide extralegal activities such as mining Nicaragua's harbors and the arms-for-hostages deal that the Reagan administration struck with Iran in order to funnel money to the Contra rebels in Nicaragua despite a congressional prohibition on such aid. The goal of the Reagan Doctrine was clearly more geostrategic than ideological as many of the recipients of American aid, such as the radical Islamist mujahideen (holy warriors) in Afghanistan and the communist Khmer Rouge in Cambodia, harbored goals radically inconsistent with the administration's professed support for spreading democracy around the world. The Reagan Doctrine had its greatest success in Afghanistan where the mujahideen, recipients of $100 million annually in U.S. aid, battled the Soviet Union to a standstill. Pakistani intelligence, aided by the CIA, carried out covert operations inside the Soviet Union to disrupt supply lines to Afghanistan, and the introduction of U.S. stinger anti-aircraft missiles proved decisive in robbing the Soviets of air-superiority in the conflict.[12] Moscow was eventually forced to announce its withdrawal from Afghanistan in 1988 and the disastrous war left deep economic and psychological scars on the Soviet Union very much akin to the U.S experience in Vietnam.

In addition to fighting communism through proxy wars, the Reagan administration eagerly sought to demonstrate its willingness to directly deploy U.S. forces in support of its foreign policy agenda. Secretary of State Schulz contended that American diplomacy could only be effective if the United States was willing to back it up with force. On this count Schultz was at odds with Secretary of Defense Weinberger who outlined a series of conditions—such as the existence of vital national security interests and the guarantee of strong public support, most of which were lessons from Vietnam—that must be met before the United States committed forces overseas.[13] While Reagan tended to side with his secretary of defense on this issue, he proved less reluctant than his immediate predecessors to resort to the use of force. In 1982 Reagan dispatched U.S. troops to Lebanon as part of a peacekeeping mission to stabilize a region thrown into turmoil by civil war and an Israeli invasion aimed at crushing the Palestine Liberation Organization operating from refugee camps inside Lebanon. The mission ended in disaster when the U.S. troops were quickly withdrawn after hundreds of marines died at the hands of a suicide bomber who drove a truck laden with explosives into their barracks in Beirut. The withdrawal from Lebanon, however, was somewhat overshadowed by the 1983 U.S. invasion of Grenada, which resulted in the toppling of the tiny island nation's leftist regime that had seized power in 1979. The White House ostensibly claimed that the troops were dispatched to protect American medical students in Grenada in the wake of a coup on the island, but the larger goal was to send a clear message that the United States would not tolerate any new "Cubas" in the Caribbean. The other occasion on which the United States resorted to force was the bombing of Tripoli, the capital of Libya, by U.S. warplanes in 1986 in retaliation for the Libyan orchestrated terrorist attacks against Americans in Europe. Both the invasion of Grenada and the Libyan bombing raids were designed to send a message to America's adversaries that Washington was not squeamish when it came to using force. Some Reagan officials also hoped these actions "would rehabilitate military power as an instrument of American foreign policy" and lift the shadow of Vietnam from "the American psyche."[14] Grenada and Libya represented relatively safe and limited uses of force and both proved popular with the American public and useful in cementing a mood of "new nationalism."[15]

The Reagan administration's abandonment of detente, together with increased defense spending, support for anti-communist insurgencies and a limited but purposeful use of force, were the constituent parts of the larger policy goal of increasing American power at the Soviet Union's expense and advancing the cause of Western liberal-capitalism over communism. In this global struggle between capitalism and communism, which the Reagan administration consistently portrayed in stark terms of good and evil, the White House employed the additional tactics of economic warfare, in particular the exploitation of the mounting gap in industrial technology between East and West and rhetorical support for anti-communist elements behind the Iron Curtain such as the Solidarity Movement in Poland. In the early 1980s, however, none of these strategies appeared to have any noticeable impact on Soviet policies. Built on the principle of expanding American military power and global influence, Reagan's foreign policy offered little incentive for the Soviet Union to reevaluate its policies.

Meanwhile Soviet leadership was atrophied and there was no momentum toward dialogue or negotiation.[16] The death of Leonid Brezhnev in 1982, in power since 1964, precipitated a leadership crisis in the Soviet Union that exposed the stagnation in which the communist superpower had become mired. His immediate successors, seventy-year-old Yuri Andropov, who died just fifteen months after succeeding Brezhnev, and seventy-three-year-old Constantine Chernenko, who succumbed to pneumonia just thirteen months after taking office, were neither willing nor able to inject new life into the Soviet system. The Soviet economy had begun to buckle under the weight of massive military spending in the 1970s, a situation exacerbated by the growing gap between East and West in the crucial new industrial arena of high technology. Andropov and Chernenko were the last in the line of Stalinist leaders who had dominated the Soviet Communist Party since the Great Purges of the 1930s and so it was left to a new generation of Soviet leaders to attempt the first major overhaul of the communist system since Khrushchev's short-lived reform efforts in the immediate post-Stalin era.

The accession to power in the Soviet Union of Mikhail Gorbachev in 1985 decisively altered the course of the Cold War. Many scholars contend that Gorbachev's reform movement precipitated the end of the Cold War by transforming the Soviet system, dismantling the Iron Curtain, and injecting new life into detente.[17] This thesis stands in stark contrast to the school of thought that credits Reagan's aggressive anti-communist foreign policy with creating the conditions under which Gorbachev's reforms became necessary, ultimately triggering the implosion of the Soviet system.[18] There are also those scholars who contend that Reagan's foreign policy had undergone a subtle transformation in 1984, a year before Gorbachev came to power, with the hardline anti-communism of his early presidency giving way to an emphasis on cooperation and understanding with the Soviet Union, thus creating a receptive environment for the renewal of detente.[19] By taking the offensive in the Cold War in the early 1980s, Reagan's foreign policy brought pressure to bear on the Soviet Union in a number of key areas and thus compounded the atmosphere of crisis that had begun to envelope the communist superpower in the 1970s. Only when Gorbachev took the reins of power, however, was there any serious endeavor inside the Soviet Union toward addressing this crisis and by that point

Reagan had already begun to moderate his Cold War tactics. The leadership of both men would ultimately prove critical in terminating the forty-year struggle between the United States and the Soviet Union. Gorbachev created the environment in which the dramatic events that brought the Cold War to an end took place, while Reagan demonstrated great skill and nerve in embracing the new Soviet leader's initiatives, even when many hardliners in his own administration remained skeptical about Moscow's intentions.

THE GORBACHEV REVOLUTION AND THE FALL OF THE BERLIN WALL
From the beginning of 1984 Ronald Reagan began to replace his antagonistic rhetoric toward the Soviet Union with a more conciliatory approach emphasizing common interests among the two superpowers. This shift highlighted an important division in the Reagan administration between, on the one hand, hardliners opposed to any softening of U.S. policy toward the Soviet Union—such as Secretary of Defense Weinberger, CIA Director Casey and the staff of the National Security Council—and those, on the other hand, who increasingly favored a more open approach—such as Secretary of State Schulz and the president himself.[20] According to historian Beth Fischer, the motivation for the shift in Reagan's perception of the Soviet Union was his realization that Moscow and Washington shared a common enemy in the shape of "inadvertent nuclear war" and that only improved relations could neutralize this threat.[21] Another explanation for Reagan's new rhetoric lies in the administration's avowed support for the principle of "negotiation from strength." Having taken action to strengthen the power of the United States vis-a-vis the Soviet Union, Reagan was now seriously interested in engaging Moscow.[22] However, Reagan's earlier antagonism had convinced the Soviet old guard that Washington had completely abandoned detente in its search for military superiority and neither side now had the requisite vision to defuse the confrontational air that had characterized Soviet-American relations since 1979. The catalyst for the dramatic transformation of Cold War politics in the latter half of the 1980s was the change in Soviet leadership in 1985.[23] Gorbachev's vision, while ultimately flawed in terms of domestic reform, transformed the landscape of U.S.-Soviet relations and found a receptive audience in the new pragmatic approach of Ronald Reagan.

Gorbachev's accession to power represented a generational shift inside the Soviet Union. By the mid-1980s the Stalinist generation was giving way to a new cohort of leaders and educated professionals who questioned the politics of the status quo and who were anxious to inject new life into the Soviet system.[24] It was in this context that Gorbachev's "new thinking" found a receptive home. Gorbachev's twin reform agenda of glasnost (political openness) and perestroika (economic restructuring) was introduced with the intent of strengthening the Soviet Union and modernizing its communist system. Glasnost was Gorbachev's answer to the stifling secrecy of the Brezhnev era, while perestroika aimed at modernizing the decrepit Soviet economy. What Gorbachev had intended as piecemeal reform, however, quickly snowballed into a revolution over which its originator eventually lost control. The problem for Gorbachev was that glasnost outpaced perestroika.[25] By allowing for greater openness and freedom of expression in the Soviet Union, Gorbachev exposed the Kremlin to criticism heretofore unseen, much of which now centered on the painful process of perestroika. Soviet conservatives charged that Gorbachev was moving too quickly and undermining socioeconomic certainties such as access to housing and jobs that had been a hallmark of the old Soviet system. On the other hand, exposure for the first time to the material wealth of the West led to charges from more radical critics that Gorbachev's reforms were moving too slowly. Gorbachev's domestic reform agenda would fail in the face of mounting opposition from the left and the right, and eventually his "new thinking" would be left behind as a more radical vision swept through the Soviet Union. Gorbachev ultimately proved to be a much more popular figure outside the Soviet Union than he was with his own people.

The simple explanation for this is that his reform of Soviet foreign policy would dramatically alter the course of the Cold War and have short-term implications that were positive for people across Europe and in the United States to an extent that was not matched by his domestic reforms. In Gorbachev's "new thinking," domestic and foreign policy reform were inextricably linked from the outset. In order to effectively restructure the Soviet economy, Gorbachev recognized that Moscow needed to reduce the burden of empire. Long before Gorbachev took office, the Soviet economy had begun to crumble under the weight of spiraling nuclear arms costs, maintaining the largest standing army in the world, continuing to exercise control in Eastern Europe, providing aid to communist allies in the developing world, fighting a war in Afghanistan, and funding proxy wars in several other parts of the world. One of Gorbachev's first foreign policy priorities therefore was to revive detente and push for a significant breakthrough in arms reduction and a general demilitarization of the Cold War. Gorbachev's arms control agenda was "not merely to stabilize a perpetual deterrent balance," which had been the hallmark of detente in the 1970s, but rather to end the arms race altogether.[26]

Reagan and Gorbachev

Reagan's first term emphasis on establishing U.S. nuclear superiority as a precursor to negotiations on the principle of arms reduction—exemplified by the SDI initiative, the zero-zero option in Europe, and the replacement of SALT (arms limitation) with START (arms reduction)—succeeded in altering the status quo of the 1970s, which hardliners rejected as an unnecessary concession to the Soviets. Rather than entice the Soviet Union to embrace arms reduction, however, these policies served only to reignite the arms race, an eventuality embraced by hardliners as a means of crippling the Soviet economy.[27] Arguably one of the most important implications of Reagan's arms policy, and one not anticipated by hardliners, was the growing concern it caused in the United States Congress and among NATO allies, resulting in pressure from both of these constituencies for a renewal of arms control negotiations with the Soviets. As noted above, in 1984 President Reagan too became increasingly concerned about the dangers of the renewed arms race and as a result adopted a more conciliatory approach toward the Soviets.[28] Nonetheless arms control was largely a moribund issue before Gorbachev came to power in 1985. From that time on, it was the Soviet Union that established the parameters of future arms control negotiations by seizing the initiative in new talks with United States.[29]

Gorbachev's early public pronouncements on foreign policy indicated a strong desire to resurrect detente and hinted at the new Soviet leader's enthusiasm for arms control. Reagan's willingness to reciprocate is evident in his insistence on proceeding with a proposed summit meeting with the new Soviet leader, despite calls from Secretary of Defense Weinberger that the summit be cancelled following the controversial shooting death of an American official in East Germany in March 1985.[30] The Geneva Summit in the fall of 1985 marked the first in a series of historic meetings between Gorbachev and Reagan that would have profound implications for East-West relations. The Geneva Summit witnessed little in the way of substantive agreement on arms reduction, largely because Gorbachev made little headway in convincing Reagan to reevaluate the future of SDI. Geneva nonetheless hinted at a new relationship as the two leaders agreed in principle to a 50 percent cut in strategic forces and reopened cultural exchange programs between the United States and the Soviet Union. Perhaps the most significant consequence of the Geneva Summit was that it marked the beginning of a strong personal bond between Reagan and Gorbachev that would soon come to replace the deep mutual distrust that had characterized U.S.-Soviet relations in the first half of the 1980s.

The next meeting between the two leaders in Reykjavik, Iceland, in the fall of 1986, was the most remarkable U.S.-Soviet summit since the Cold War began.[31] Gorbachev and Reagan emerged from fourteen hours of talks with the stunning news that they had agreed to eliminate all intermediate range missiles from Europe, which to that point had been one of the most intense arenas of U.S.-Soviet competition. The Reykjavik agreement marked a major turning point in the Cold War in that the Soviet Union and the United States for the first time agreed to a mutual reduction of a specific area of their strategic arsenals. At the time this was undoubtedly the most far-reaching arms reduction deal of the Cold War.[32] Incredibly Reagan and Gorbachev came close to going a great deal further at Reykjavik. Only Reagan's insistence that SDI was necessary to protect the United States from other nuclear powers prevented the American president from embracing Gorbachev's suggestion that the United States and the Soviet Union agree to disband their whole nuclear arsenals within ten years. Reykjavik created significant momentum toward future arms reduction, however, and when Reagan and Gorbachev next met in Washington in 1987 they signed a sweeping INF Treaty eliminating all medium- and short-range missiles, thus marking "the first time an entire class of U.S. and Soviet nuclear weapons was not merely limited, but eliminated."[33] Despite the fact that administration hardliners such as Weinberger continued to caution that U.S. security concerns should not be abandoned in the face of an overly-optimistic assessment of East-West relations, Reagan was clearly committed to working with Gorbachev to defuse the Cold War.[34]

In 1988 Reagan visited Moscow and in the same year Gorbachev returned to the United States, this time visiting New York where he made the stunning announcement before the United Nations that the Soviet Union was to withdraw 200,000 troops from Eastern Europe. Reagan and Gorbachev continued to cultivate a close personal bond and their frequent summits took on characteristics that were once unthinkable in U.S.-Soviet relations, most notably when Gorbachev stopped in the middle of traffic in Washington to meet and greet the public. But it was the substantive headway made on arms reduction that most clearly illustrates the extent to which U.S.-Soviet relations had been transformed in three short years. These agreements were so significant that by the time Reagan left office in 1989 the threat of nuclear war had receded to a point that had seemed unimaginable in the previous four decades.[35] Nonetheless, hardliners in both countries had a hard time embracing the new relationship forged by Reagan and Gorbachev and its implications for U.S.-Soviet relations. Gorbachev continued to overhaul Soviet foreign policy despite the misgivings of the Communist Party old guard, and his actions confounded skeptics in the United States who did not quite know what to make of this Soviet maverick. His public disavowal of wars of national liberation, reduction of aid to communist states such as Cuba, intervention to end the war in Angola, and decision to withdraw Soviet troops from Afghanistan were all important steps in defusing the Cold War, but proved extremely disorienting to officials in both Moscow and Washington for whom the East-West standoff had for so long been the yardstick of international affairs. Unlike many other old Cold Warriors, however, Ronald Reagan proved both willing and able to embrace this new direction in Soviet leadership.

The End of the Cold War

In early 1989 when George H. W. Bush replaced Reagan in the White House, the United States no longer had to grapple with the issue of how to fight the Cold War but instead faced the dilemma of deciding whether the Cold War was over or not.[36] Most of the impetus for the dramatic pace of arms reduction over the preceding four years had come from the Soviets and Moscow had made "the lion's share of concessions," indicating perhaps that Gorbachev's intent was not simply to stabilize the arms race but rather to completely demolish the edifice of U.S.-Soviet military confrontation.[37] Gorbachev's rhetoric, such as his call before the Council of Europe in Strasbourg in 1989 to create "a new European home," pointed to a seismic shift in the Soviet Union's perception of itself in the world. Gorbachev appeared to be intent on terminating the East-West paradigm and on repositioning the Soviet Union within the context of a Europe being dramatically transformed by the growth of the European Economic Community (EEC). It was in this context that Gorbachev renounced the Brezhnev Doctrine, dating from Moscow's 1968 military intervention in Czechoslovakia, which held that the Soviet Union was committed to preventing any of the communist states in Eastern Europe from breaking free from the Soviet orbit. In its stead Moscow now began to champion the Sinatra Doctrine, named for the Frank Sinatra song *My Way,* which signaled to the countries of Eastern Europe that they were free to leave the Warsaw Pact and to go their own way politically.[38]

This set the stage for the dramatic transformation of the political landscape of Europe in the summer and fall of 1989 that proceeded at a pace few people in the East or West had ever imagined possible and that no one in Washington, Moscow, or the various capitals of Europe was fully prepared to deal with.

The Bush administration was somewhat perplexed by the rapidity of the changes taking place in Europe and adopted an extremely cautious approach, dubbed "status quo plus," that amounted to little more than passive observation.[39] Criticism of the Iron Curtain and the ideological division of Europe had long been a staple of American Cold War rhetoric, but rapid disintegration of the old Eastern Bloc compelled a complete reevaluation of U.S. policy.[40] The White House's cautious response to Gorbachev's reforms reflected significant divisions within the administration regarding the Soviet leader's intent. While Bush and Secretary of State James Baker tended to accept Gorbachev as a genuine reformer, National Security Advisor Brent Scowcroft, Secretary of Defense Dick Cheney, and CIA Director Robert Gates all suspected that perestroika, glasnost, and the changes in Soviet foreign policy were feints disguising a more sinister Soviet agenda.[41] The administration's apparent indecisiveness also reflected the fact that the momentum for change was coming from Moscow or, after the Kremlin's renunciation of the Brezhnev Doctrine, increasingly from populist movements across Eastern Europe. The dizzying pace of change put the White House in a reactive stance. European members of NATO moved much more quickly than the United States to embrace the breakdown of the post–WWII order, in the process significantly reducing American leverage in Western Europe and intensifying the atmosphere of disorientation in Washington. Perhaps the most constructive assessment that could be offered of the United States' role in the changes that swept Europe in 1989 is that President Bush facilitated the Sinatra Doctrine by not seeking to affect the pace of change or adopt a posture of triumph.[42]

Without the continued active support of the Soviet Union, the communist governments in Eastern Europe proved untenable. One by one, during the summer and fall of 1989, they began to collapse in the face of mounting public protest. In Poland, the Solidarity Movement that had shaken the communist regime to its roots in 1981 only to be driven underground, resurfaced in 1988 and successfully pushed for free elections, which it won resoundingly in late 1989. At roughly the same time the Communist Party in Hungary voted itself out of existence and in Czechoslovakia hundreds of thousands of peaceful protestors took to the streets of

Prague compelling the Communist Party to relinquish power, a process dubbed the Velvet Revolution because of its smoothness. The once iron grip of communist rule in Bulgaria would also melt away in the face of sustained public protests. Only the Romanian communist ruler Nicolae Ceausescu attempted to resist this tide of change, a futile exercise that ended when he was summarily executed after the military joined the massive public protests against him.

Perhaps the most dramatic developments, however, occurred in East Germany, a country whose very existence symbolized the East-West divide. Spurred on by the changes taking place in other East European communist countries, hundreds of thousands of East Germans took to the streets to press for change and to pressure the government to open its border with the West, across which free movement had been largely prohibited since the early Cold War. When the East German regime hesitated, thousands of people defied the communist authorities and crossed the border into Austria and Hungary (which had opened its borders with the West) essentially making the closed border between the two Germanys irrelevant. The subsequent decision of the East German government to bow to the inevitable and begin dismantling the Berlin Wall sparked incredible scenes that were shown live on television around the world. Huge crowds from both sides of the city gathered in a celebration of destruction as they took over the process of razing this hated artificial symbol of German division. A festive atmosphere prevailed as myriad music concerts along the Wall paid tribute to its demise.

The destruction of the Berlin Wall symbolically ended the Cold War, sparking jubilation in Germany and across Europe. The sudden, dramatic demise of the East-West world order, however, created a great deal of uncertainty for both the United States and the Soviet Union. Moscow initiated the process of change but as the anti-communist wave that had swept aside the regimes of Eastern Europe began to wash over the westernmost Soviet republics, the Kremlin was faced with challenges it had not anticipated and would now prove powerless to control. Washington, for its part, could take a great deal of comfort from the fact that the people of Eastern Europe had overwhelmingly rejected their communist rulers and embraced pro-Western leaders intent on initiating liberal-capitalist reforms. However, while the terms on which the Cold War was coming to an end were almost exclusively in accordance with principles espoused by the United States, Washington was largely removed from the process of reshaping post–Berlin Wall Europe. The unilateral decision of West German Chancellor Helmut Kohl to call for the unification of

Germany in November 1989 exemplified the degree to which the superpowers had been marginalized in this process of change. Since its division in the aftermath of WWII, German reunification had been one of the rhetorical cornerstones of U.S. policy, yet in reality "both American and Soviet leaders had grown comfortable with its division."[43] The Soviets expressed alarm about what amounted to the absorption of East Germany by West Germany with the likelihood that the reunified Germany would become a member of NATO. The Bush administration found itself in the awkward position of not wanting to undermine Gorbachev by publicly endorsing a unification process anathema to hardliners in the Soviet Communist Party. Yet it was unthinkable for the White House to take any position other than to embrace what had become a virtual article of faith in U.S. foreign policy over the previous four decades. Ultimately American and Soviet opinion proved somewhat incidental as the Germans pushed the process to its conclusion in 1990.

As the 1990s began George Bush was faced with a radically different international scene than when he had entered office just two years earlier, and things were set to change even more dramatically with the collapse of the Soviet Union. Beginning with the Baltic republics of Latvia, Lithuania, and Estonia, and then spreading across Belarus and Ukraine and into the Caucasus and central Asian republics, perestroika released a pent-up surge of national, ethnic, and religious sentiment that would tear the Soviet Union apart. Gorbachev proved powerless to stop the process as he faced a growing tide of opposition from within the traditional power centers of the Soviet system, the Russian Republic, and the Communist Party. In Russia, free elections resulted in a defeat for the Communist Party. The new president of the Russian Republic, Boris Yeltsin, emerged as a powerful critic of the Soviet system and an exponent of a more radical push toward democracy and a free market economy. Meanwhile hardliners within the Communist Party resented Gorbachev's failure to prevent the departure of the Baltic states from the Soviet Union and the general decline in the party's power. Ironically only the intervention of the populist Yeltsin prevented Gorbachev from being overthrown in a hardline coup in August 1991. From this point on, however, the architect of perestroika and glasnost, along with the Soviet system he had sought to reform, was only marginal to the unfolding process. In December 1991, Yeltsin joined the leaders of the Ukraine and Belarus in voting the Soviet Union out of existence and Gorbachev, bowing to the inevitable, resigned as president of the now-defunct state and handed the reins of power to Yeltsin, the new Russian president.

Throughout this remarkable process the Bush administration struggled to find a consistent position. Bush continued to cultivate the strong personal relationship with Gorbachev that Reagan had initiated, resulting in further milestones in arms reduction such as a production ban on chemical weapons and the signing of the historic and comprehensive START in 1991. While the White House favored a policy of facilitating Gorbachev's gradual reform agenda and looked with some suspicion on the populist Yeltsin, Bush's ability to provide financial aid for the Soviet transition was severely limited by the alarming increase in the U.S. national debt resulting from Reagan's 1980s arms buildup (combined with his extensive tax cuts). Bush, however, failed to enact less costly measures that might have facilitated Gorbachev's economic and, by extension, political reforms. For example, Washington did not extend most-favored-nation trading status to the Soviet Union, though communist China continued to enjoy that important benefit even after its brutal crackdown on pro-democracy demonstrators in Beijing's Tiananmen Square in 1989.[44] Meanwhile Bush's indecisive approach to the events in the Soviet Union was evident during the August coup, when the White House briefly contemplated reaching out to the coup leaders before Yeltsin took to the streets of Moscow and initiated a course that the United States was compelled to follow. When the Soviet Union finally collapsed under the weight of internal forces of change, wistful uncertainty about the future tempered the sense of triumph that would only gradually come into focus in Washington.

AFTERMATH: THE FALL OF THE BERLIN WALL AS A TURNING POINT

The fall of the Berlin Wall in 1989 marked the culmination of a four-year period during which the East-West confrontation that had dominated world affairs for almost half a century was completely turned on its head. Mikhail Gorbachev's domestic reform agenda precipitated an unprecedented revision in Soviet foreign policy that entailed massive strategic and conventional arms reductions, retreat from Moscow's global commitments and, most surprisingly of all, abandonment of the Soviet foothold in the once strategically vital region of Eastern Europe. The transformation of U.S. foreign policy in this same period was equally remarkable. Ronald Reagan, the same president whose policies had so markedly intensified the Cold War in the early 1980s, embraced the initiatives for arms reduction coming from Moscow after 1985 and fostered a personal relationship with Gorbachev that was a vital ingredient in cementing the Soviet leader's credibility as a genuine reformer. The tangible fruit of a series of dramatic summit meetings between the two men created a viable context in which many people from the East and West could really start to believe that the Cold War was coming to end. Thus, when Gorbachev renounced the Brezhnev Doctrine the people of Eastern Europe were ready to take Moscow at its word and embrace the invitation to go their own way. In this sense Reagan and Gorbachev, working together, made the destruction of the Berlin Wall possible.

Neither the United States nor the Soviet Union, however, was fully prepared for what happened when the Cold War came to an end and awkwardly reassuring symbols such as the Berlin Wall vanished. Indeed for some officials in the administration of George H. W. Bush, it took two more years, and the eventual collapse of the Soviet Union, for the end of the Cold War to sink in as a reality. During these two years U.S. foreign policy was marked by hesitation and uncertainty as Washington struggled to come to terms with its place in the world without a monolithic nemesis against which it could contrast its values. However, there were clear signs, such as a 73 percent favorable rating for Mikhail Gorbachev in a 1990 *Washington Post-ABC* poll, that a dramatic mood shift had taken place in the United States with regard to the Soviet Union. By 1991 the Bush administration had finally come to terms with the fact that the end of the Cold War had ushered in a new world order, but as the planet's sole remaining superpower, the United States would struggle to define its role in a world that lacked the clear dynamic of the bipolar Cold War. The atmosphere of drift that permeated U.S. foreign policy through much of the 1990s would come to an end in September 2001, when a new nemesis emerged on the world stage (see chapter 12).

The first major post–Cold War foreign policy test for the United States was the Iraqi invasion of Kuwait in 1990. Since the 1940s U.S. policy toward the Middle East was shaped within the milieu of the global struggle between capitalism and communism, resulting in the United States often taking contradictory positions in the region. For example, fear of the Soviet Union gaining influence and leverage in the Middle East goes a long way toward explaining how the United States could make both Israel and Egypt, once mortal enemies, major recipients of American military aid and how the United States could justify funneling arms and material support to the radical Islamist mujahideen in Afghanistan while at the same time seeking to contain the spread of political Islam from post–revolutionary Iran. As part of this strategy of preventing the Iranians from spreading their brand of Islamic revolutionary politics, the United States had given significant material support to the Iraqi dictator Saddam Hussein during the long Iran-Iraq War in the 1980s. With that war ending in a stalemate and the Cold War coming to an end, U.S. policy in the region began to develop a sharper focus. In August 1990, Hussein's aggressive push into the Persian Gulf state of Kuwait raised alarm bells in Washington where fear mounted that the Iraqi leader had designs on expanding into the other oil-rich states in the region, including perhaps Saudi Arabia.

Iraq's invasion of Kuwait posed a significant challenge for the Bush administration in a number of respects. Iraqi expansion posed a direct threat to the vital oil reserves of the Persian Gulf and Saddam Hussein's pan-Arab and anti-Israel rhetoric threatened to fan anti-American flames throughout the region. Meanwhile the lingering effect of Vietnam raised doubts as to whether the American public would support a major U.S. military commitment overseas, despite successful and relatively painless interventions in Grenada and Panama (the latter resulted in the U.S. ouster of Manuel Noriega in 1989 and allowed Bush to counteract critics in his own party who feared he lacked Reagan's resolve when it came to using force). Another major challenge for the White House was to test the extent to which the Cold War was truly over by inviting the Soviet Union (still in existence at this point) to join a U.S.-led international effort to pressure Iraq to withdraw from Kuwait. Washington's success in securing Moscow's support for a joint communiqué condemning Iraqi aggression and for a united front against Iraq in the UNSC represented another historic juncture in U.S.-Soviet relations and served as an important building block for a successful U.S. effort to build a broad international coalition against Hussein. It is hard to imagine that this could have happened had the Berlin Wall not come down. With echoes of Munich and appeasement in his head, Bush was determined to prevent unchecked aggression from becoming a characteristic of the post–Cold War world and the U.S. campaign to remove Iraq from Kuwait quickly took on the strong moral overtones of a struggle between "good and evil."[45]

What was at stake for President Bush was not just the fate of one small country but rather the stability of the post–Cold War world, what he dubbed "the new world order."[46] The resulting Gulf War represents a major diplomatic and military triumph for the United States. Having first isolated Iraq in the eyes of world opinion, the U.S.-led military coalition decisively drove Iraqi forces from Kuwait. The precision of U.S. bombing and the apparent ease with which highly sophisticated U.S. forces routed the Iraqi army served as a powerful exclamation of the United States' new status as the world's sole remaining superpower. The Gulf War appeared to offer a hopeful pattern for the future of Bush's new world order. Most of the nations of the world had joined the United States in punishing a volatile aggressor and the efficiency and power of the military operation led President Bush to confidently conclude that the United State had finally kicked the Vietnam Syndrome. This new spirit of international cooperation, backed by the awesome power of the United States, appeared to offer an ideal environment for consolidating the global triumph of liberal capitalism over communism and other forms of tyranny. The warm afterglow of the Gulf War, however, proved to be short lived. The collapse of the Soviet Union and the uncertainty it caused was the first major blow to the new world order.

The United States could not publicly lament the collapse of the Soviet Union, but the demise of the once mighty "evil empire" was nonetheless a cause of some concern in Washington. The nuclear arsenal of the former Soviet Union was now dispersed among four states, Russia, Ukraine, Belarus, and Kazakhstan, whose leaders Washington either viewed with skepticism, such as Yeltsin, or who were unknown quantities. While Russia, Ukraine, and several other former Soviet republics sought to forge a common purpose through the creation of the Commonwealth of Independent States (CIS), the passing of the Soviet Union nonetheless left a major power vacuum in the region. Many of the same forces that had toppled Gorbachev, such as ethnic conflict, nationalism, and economic drift, threatened to undermine Russia and the other members of the CIS. Ukraine, Belarus, and Kazakhstan were successfully induced to give up their nuclear arsenals as Bush and Yeltsin pushed ahead with the implementation of START and then went on to sign START II in 1993. However, as had been the case with Gorbachev, the United States' domestic economic woes made it difficult for Washington to provide sufficient aid to smooth the transition of Russia and other members of the CIS to free market economies, deemed a necessary prerequisite for their future political stability. Yeltsin was feted during a visit to Washington in 1992, but he returned to Russia having failed to secure the level of assistance from the United States he deemed vital to his country's economic transformation.[47] Widespread unemployment and homelessness, problems largely unknown during the Soviet era, created nostalgia for the communist past among many older Russian citizens, while the younger generation was impatient to begin reaping the rewards of capitalism. Russia also faced a series of internal crises, including increased organized crime and violent regional independence movements, most notably in the oil-rich region of Chechnya where the presence of a large Muslim population proved a further complicating factor.

A similar explosive mix of religion and nationalism was at the heart of Europe's most serious post–Cold War crisis, the disintegration of Yugoslavia. Much like the Soviet Union, Yugoslavia was a federation of states long held together by the authoritarian rule of the Communist Party. With communism in retreat across Eastern Europe in the late 1980s, only nationalists in the largest of the Yugoslav republics, Serbia, remained committed to maintaining the unity of the state. Beginning with Slovenia's declaration of independence in 1990, Yugoslavia began to fracture in much the same way the Soviet Union had. When Croatia sought to follow suit a year later, its Serbian minority, backed by the Serb dominated Yugoslav government in Belgrade, sought to block the secession. While Croatia would successfully fight its way to independence, the decision of the neighboring republic of Bosnia-Herzegovina to declare its independence in 1992 would have even more tragic consequences. Here the Serb minority was larger and more entrenched and even a Croat minority in Bosnia resisted the process in the hope that Croatia might annex part of the territory. The ensuing Bosnian War pitted supporters of an independent Bosnia against a Serb militia backed by the government in Belgrade. Inflamed by religious animosity between the Christian Orthodox Serbs and Bosnian Muslims that had deep roots in the long history of Ottoman Turkish rule in the region, the Bosnian War sparked brutal tactics of ethnic cleansing and the mass slaughter of civilians that resurrected painful memories of the dark days of WWII. As was the case with the peaceful revolutions that had toppled communism in Eastern Europe, the painful disintegration of Yugoslavia unfolded live on satellite television screens across the world and public pressure mounted in Europe and the United States for a response similar to the one that had quashed Saddam Hussein's ambitions in the Middle East. Driven by emotive media coverage, humanitarian pressure mounted for military intervention by the United States and NATO, the police arm of the new world order.[48] However, in the words of Secretary of State James Baker, the United States "had no dog in this fight," and the lack of a clear national security concern for the United States in the region resulted in a policy of equivocation.[49]

The contrasting reactions of the United States to aggression in Kuwait and Bosnia brought into focus a major foreign policy dilemma in the post–Cold War era, the lack of a consistent standard by which to measure American interests. During the Cold War that standard had been containing the spread of communism and counteracting the global influence of the Soviet Union. The very existence of the superpower rivalry between the United States and the Soviet Union had often served as a stabilizing force by keeping proxy forces and regional powers in check and diminishing the propensity for ethnic and religious conflict to occur in regions under their respective influence. Without a global paradigm against which to gauge regional crises, U.S. foreign policy was often inconsistent in the aftermath of the Cold War, shifting between a narrow emphasis on vital strategic interests and a broader, humanitarian-driven worldview. This tension is evident in the wavering response of the Bush administration to Bosnia and in Somalia, where Bush committed U.S. troops in 1992 as part of a U.N. mission to provide security for food distribution to starving people amid a chaotic civil war. It was a decision that would prove politically disastrous for his successor, Bill Clinton, who was forced to withdraw American troops several months later in the face of significant public pressure following the death of eighteen American soldiers at the hands of heavily armed militias in Mogadishu. The tension between humanitarian concerns and vital interests would prove to be an ongoing concern for Clinton during his two terms in office as he struggled with a series of similar crises, including the ongoing war in Bosnia, a genocidal civil war in Rwanda, a mass exodus of refugees from Haiti following the overthrow of its democratically elected government, and the spread of the Serbian ethnic cleansing campaign from Bosnia to Kosovo. Without a uniform global agenda such as the one that guided U.S foreign policy during the Cold War, each separate crisis was addressed on an ad hoc basis often resulting in an inconsistent American approach to world affairs. The collapse of communism in Europe had certainly ushered in a new world order, but for U.S. foreign policy makers, it may have been new, but it was far from ordered.

Twelve

THE SEPTEMBER 11, 2001,
TERRORIST ATTACKS

As discussed in the previous chapter, after the Soviet Union collapsed in December 1991, U.S. foreign policy suffered from a lack of clarity. Before then, it was clear that the enemy was the Soviet Union. For decades U.S. foreign policy was guided by an overarching strategy to contain the Soviets and either prevent or retard the spread of communism. But after the Berlin Wall fell in 1989, U.S. foreign policy entered a period of drift and confusion. At one point the U.S. commander of nuclear forces in Europe confessed to a congressional committee that he did not know where to aim his weapons.

However, U.S. foreign policy took on a new focus on September 11, 2001 when nineteen terrorists hijacked four fuel-laden jetliners and crashed them into the World Trade Center in New York City, the Pentagon in Washington, D.C., and a field outside of Pittsburgh, Pennsylvania. Thousands were killed by this heinous act of violence, which was perpetrated by Islamic extremists from Osama bin Laden's al Qaeda terrorist network. People all over the world were simultaneously fearful, hurt, and enraged by this murderous act. In response, the Bush administration engineered a radical shift in U.S. foreign policy that included, among other things, launching a preemptive war against Iraq, a country that did not pose an imminent threat to the United States.

This chapter begins by discussing the 9/11 attacks in the context of al Qaeda's grievances against the United States. Contrary to what President George W. Bush claimed in his public rhetoric, al Qaeda did not attack the United States because it hates America's freedom. Rather, al Qaeda's quarrel with the United States stems from its vehement opposition to U.S. policy in the Arab and Islamic worlds. Next, the chapter covers the policy consensus on invading Afghanistan. After that, the chapter goes into detail about the debates and divisions over the controversial decision to invade Iraq. In launching this war of choice, President Bush, who was heavily influenced by the so-called neoconservatives in his administration, fundamentally reoriented U.S. foreign policy by adopting a controversial strategy known as preemption. The final sections give a reckoning of the neoconservative-dominated foreign policy in the Bush White House and a brief discussion of U.S foreign policy since 9/11.

AL QAEDA, BLOWBACK, AND THE TERRORIST THREAT

Al Qaeda's has its origins in the anti-Soviet guerrilla war in Afghanistan in the 1980s. Recall that U.S. policy was designed to prevent the spread of Soviet influence. Toward that end, the United States armed and trained the anti-Soviet guerrillas, or mujahideen, fighting the Soviet occupation of Afghanistan. But it was not just Afghans the United States aided. Muslims from all over the world, but mostly from Arab countries, flocked to Afghanistan to engage in a Holy War against the *kuffar* (nonbelieving, infidel) communist Soviets who had invaded a Muslim country. But when these same Arabs attacked the United States, the country suffered blowback.

Among those Arabs who received U.S. weapons and training, albeit indirectly, was a wealthy Saudi named Osama bin Laden. He created a network of mostly Arab resistance fighters known as al Qaeda. He kept a list of members in a computer database, which came to be referred to simply as al Qaeda or "the base." Like most Saudis, bin Laden adheres to a conservative form of Islam known as Wahhabism, which views non-Muslims and even other Muslims, especially Shiites, as kuffar. He advocates overthrowing Arab leaders and replacing them with an Islamic caliph (ruler) who would govern according to a strict and intolerant interpretation of Islamic law. He also calls for the spread of this caliphate first to non-Arab, Muslim countries like Afghanistan and Indonesia and then eventually to the rest of the world.

By 1988, the U.S.-backed mujahideen helped compel the Soviet Union to withdraw from Afghanistan in defeat. Bin Laden returned to Saudi Arabia and turned his attention toward the United States and its close ally, the Saudi royal family. He was incensed by two components of U.S. policy in the Middle East. First, he objected to U.S. support for Israel at the expense of the Palestinians, with whom he identified as part of the Arab and Muslim cohort. Bin Laden blamed the United States, which gives Israel billions of dollars in economic and military aid every year, for Israel's oppression of the Palestinians. Second, he objected to the presence of U.S. troops on Saudi soil, the birthplace of Islam. When Saddam Hussein invaded Kuwait in 1990, the Saudis invited U.S. troops to Saudi Arabia for protection and as a base from which to repulse Hussein from Kuwait. For bin Laden, the Saudi rulers committed apostasy for allowing kuffar soldiers to set foot on holy Muslim land. He called for the overthrow of the Saudi monarchy and the removal of U.S. troops. The Saudi government expelled bin Laden and he eventually returned to Afghanistan, where he found kindred spirits in the new Taliban regime, which had taken over in Afghanistan. The Taliban (which means "students") practiced the virulent form of Islamic law bin Laden was calling for in the Arab World. From his hideout in the mountains along the rugged, inaccessible border between Pakistan and Afghanistan, bin Laden and his al Qaeda network planned attacks on U.S. targets. In 1993 terrorists connected to al Qaeda detonated a truck bomb in the underground parking garage of the World Trade Center, killing six and wounding more than a thousand. In 1998 al Qaeda terrorists were responsible for simultaneous suicide truck bombings on the U.S. embassies in Tanzania and Kenya resulting in hundreds dead and thousands wounded.[1] In 2000 al Qaeda suicide bombers rammed a bomb-laden boat into the USS *Cole* near the Persian Gulf, killing seventeen American sailors.

By the end of the 1990s, al Qaeda became *the* priority for the Clinton administration, as Clinton identified terrorism as the single most important post–Cold War threat. In 1996, he gave a speech effectively declaring war on terror, saying, "this will be a long, hard struggle."[2] After George W. Bush won the 2000 election, Sandy Berger, Clinton's outgoing NSA, told Condoleezza Rice, Bush's incoming NSA, "you're going to spend more time during your four years on terrorism generally and al Qaeda specifically than [on] any other issue."[3] The week before Bush's inauguration on January 20, 2001, CIA Director George Tenet met with President Bush and Vice President Dick Cheney and told them that al Qaeda was one of the three gravest threats facing the United States,[4] and that the threat was "tremendous" and "immediate."[5] However the Bush administration had other priorities.

POLICY CONSENSUS AND THE CONQUEST OF AFGHANISTAN
Even before the dust from the collapsed Twin Towers had settled, people wondered how such an attack could occur. How could a man, hiding in a cave so far away,

orchestrate such a spectacular assault on the world's greatest power? In short, the hijackers were able to inflict the worst terrorist attack on U.S. soil because of a combination of errors.

First, there was lax airport security. Some of the hijackers' names were known and considered suspicious, but they passed through passenger screening anyway. Second, this was an intelligence failure of historic proportions. The hijackers benefited from poor coordination between disparate law enforcement and intelligence agencies. For instance, in June 2001 an FBI agent in Phoenix sent a memo to Washington warning of the danger posed by some Middle Eastern students at Arizona flight schools.[6] The memo reported concern among the flight school instructors that a few of the students (of Middle Eastern extraction) expressed interest only in learning how to fly an aircraft but not how to land or take off. Then on August 6, an intelligence report was sent to President Bush entitled, "Bin Laden Determined to Strike in U.S." But those who had written this briefing had not seen the June FBI memo.

Third, there was a critical lack of attention paid to the terrorist threat by Bush, Cheney, Rice, and other senior officials. Tenet would later say the system was "blinking red," but he could not convince senior officials to drop what they were doing.[7] When the Bush administration assumed office in January 2001, counterterrorism chief Richard Clarke spent months trying unsuccessfully to convince policy makers to focus on al Qaeda. He repeatedly requested a principals meeting on the subject, which would include Secretary of State Colin Powell, Secretary of Defense Donald Rumsfeld, and NSA Rice, among others. After several delays, the meeting finally took place on September 4 but was largely uneventful.[8] CIA Director Tenet's daily briefing for the president mentioned al Qaeda on no less than forty occasions before September 11, "often with great urgency," but again, to little affect.[9] In February 2001 Tenet testified before the Senate that "Osama bin Laden and his global network of lieutenants and associates are the most immediate and serious threat" to the United States.[10] But Bush and other senior officials were preoccupied with what they considered more important issues. Bush focused on national missile defense and announced plans to cancel U.S. membership in the Anti-Ballistic Missile Treaty with Russia. Rumsfeld focused on military transformation, his pet project to reform military doctrine to emphasize speed, mobility, and high-tech gadgetry. Vice President Cheney focused on energy and other domestic issues and Rice focused on relations with Russia.[11] Al Qaeda and terrorism were placed on the back burner. Bush later admitted that he "did not feel a sense of urgency" regarding the terrorist threat.[12]

Testifying before Congress after 9/11, Rice defended the administration's lack of preparation, asserting that no one expected terrorists to use a plane as a weapon. But there is evidence to the contrary. In 1994 an Algerian hijacked an Air France plane and threatened to crash it into the Eiffel Tower. In addition, one of Ramzi Yousef's[13] collaborators told intelligence officials that he earned his pilot's license in an American flight school and was planning to seize a small plane, fill it with explosives, and crash it into the CIA's headquarters.[14] Furthermore, in 1996, Richard Clarke, while helping oversee security precautions at the 1996 Olympics in Atlanta, asked at one of the planning sessions: "What if somebody blows up a 747 over Olympic Stadium or even flies one into the stadium?"[15] In 2000 the Federal Aviation Administration said that al Qaeda posed "a significant threat to civil aviation."[16]

In the weeks and months after the attack, the United States enjoyed an outpouring of support from all over the world. *Le Monde,* a French paper often critical of the United States declared, "we are all Americans."[17] NATO, the world's largest and most powerful military alliance, invoked Article 5 of its charter, which enabled a collective military response by the entire organization. The United Nations passed a resolution authorizing "all necessary steps," i.e., military force, to respond to the attacks. Even in Iran thousands held candlelight vigils for the victims and their families.

Nearly everyone agreed that al Qaeda was directly responsible and that the Taliban regime in Afghanistan was indirectly responsible since it gave al Qaeda safe haven. In a rare display of unity, Congress overwhelmingly passed a bipartisan resolution giving the president power to wage war in Afghanistan. President Bush used stark, albeit simplistic, language as he prepared the country for war. He said the United States would make no distinction between the terrorists and any state that provided them safe haven. In television appearances, Bush demanded the Taliban turn over bin Laden "dead or alive." He said that the country was now engaged in a long battle of good vs. evil and announced to the world, "You're either with us or you're with the terrorists." On October 7, 2001, the United States launched a war against the Taliban regime in Afghanistan. By mid-November, the Taliban were routed and withdrew, with their al Qaeda allies, into the impenetrable Tora Bora Mountains along the Afghanistan-Pakistan border. However, the military failed to capture or kill bin Laden because it did not commit enough troops. Bush authorized fewer forces for the effort than the number of police officers assigned to patrol Manhattan.[18] This was in large part because American forces were being pulled out of Afghanistan in preparation for a second war, this time in Iraq. In December 2002, more than a year after the Taliban were ousted but still four months before the war in Iraq began, Rumsfeld appeared on CNN's *Larry King Live* and gave an upbeat assessment of the war in Afghanistan.[19] In fact, Osama bin Laden had not been captured, al Qaeda was still able to mount attacks, and the Taliban remained a force in many parts of the country.

As the administration proved unable to kill or capture Osama bin Laden, it began downplaying his significance, especially as it directed attention to Iraq. Critics charged that the Bush administration let Osama bin Laden and the Taliban leaders slip away because they got distracted by Iraq, a country that had nothing to do with 9/11. Indeed, al Qaeda and the Taliban are resurgent in Afghanistan. In July 2007 the Bush White House admitted that its strategy to fight al Qaeda had failed and that the United States was in fact losing ground.[20] By December of that year, worried officials began a major policy review of this "forgotten war," as they began shifting troops from Iraq *back to* Afghanistan, a process intensified by the Obama administration when it took over in January 2009. Part of the problem lay in President Bush's opposition to nation-building, which helps explain why his interest in Afghanistan was sporadic at best and neglectful at worst. For instance, in April 2002, the president gave a major speech promising a Marshall Plan for Afghanistan similar to the massive aid effort the United States launched in Europe after WWII. But the promise went largely unfulfilled as the United States spent an average of only $3.4 billion a year reconstructing Afghanistan, which is less than half of what it spent in Iraq.[21]

POLICY DISSENSUS AND THE CONQUEST OF IRAQ

While consensus prevailed on Afghanistan, the opposite prevailed regarding Iraq. The domestic unity and international goodwill that existed in the wake of 9/11 evaporated as Bush launched a controversial war against Iraq. Profound debates erupted over the administration's doctrine of preemption, an offensive strategy that called for attacking potential enemies before they could become immediate threats. The neoconservatives in the Bush administration were the primary authors of this new doctrine, which left its mark on Iraq and in fact the whole world. They were often opposed by the more moderate and cautious voice of Secretary of State Colin

Powell and his aides. Hostility between officials in the Defense and State Departments sometimes degenerated into shouting matches; at other times officials behaved like high school cliques refusing to even look at each other much less engage in discussions. Under Secretary of Defense Douglas Feith and Deputy Secretary of State Richard Armitage loathed each other so much that they could be found arguing in the White House Situation Room. Relations between their bosses, Defense Secretary Rumsfeld and Secretary of State Powell, were also strained—while briefing the president, each refused to look at or even acknowledge the other. And Rice's relationship with Rumsfeld bordered on the juvenile. At times Rumsfeld would not even return Rice's phone calls so she had to go to the president in order to compel Rumsfeld to call her back.[22]

The Neoconservative Agenda

The neoconservatives, or neocons as they are known, were a group of high-ranking officials who held considerable influence, especially during the Bush administration's first term. They are new conservatives because they used to be aligned with the Democratic Party, from which they broke in the 1970s over disputes regarding the Cold War. Many of the neocons in the Bush administration were also the hardliners in the Reagan administration who had shaped the confrontational policy toward the Soviets during Reagan's first term (see chapter 11).

The neocons were especially prevalent in the Bush administration's Department of Defense, which dominated the planning, or the lack thereof, for the Iraq War. Key among them included Deputy Secretary of Defense Paul Wolfowitz and Under Secretary of Defense for Policy Douglas Feith. Neocons also sat on the Pentagon's influential Defense Policy Board, including Richard Perle and Kenneth Adelman, who wrote that toppling Hussein would be a "cakewalk."[23] Rice, who headed the White House's National Security Council in Bush's first term, and then served as Secretary of State in the second term, is also a neoconservative. I. Lewis "Scooter" Libby, who served as Vice President Cheney's chief of staff, is also a neocon. And while Cheney and Defense Secretary Rumsfeld are not considered formal neocons, their views are similar to the neocons, so they played a crucial role in helping the neocons win important policy debates.

Neoconservative ideology is a mixture of idealism and realism. Neocons are idealists insofar as they see America as a force for good in the world. The United States can and *should* work to transform countries into free-market democratic societies reflecting American values.[24] But neocons are also realists since they advocate building a military so powerful that no country would ever think of challenging America.[25] They also share the realists' disdain for international institutions like the United Nations, which is something they have in common with Bush. Neocons are also willing to ignore, and even disparage, America's traditional allies, preferring to act unilaterally, again something they share with Bush. But they differ with Bush regarding the issue of nation building. Unlike traditional realists, who oppose using the military for nation-building and peacekeeping operations, neocons argue that America's unrivaled military power should be applied in places like Afghanistan and Iraq to not only defeat enemies but to rebuild and transform societies. As a presidential candidate in 2000, Bush criticized Clinton's use of the military for nation-building operations in Somalia, Haiti, and Kosovo as a fool's errand. However, after 9/11, the neocons convinced President Bush to commit the military to do exactly the kind of nation-building missions he vilified while campaigning.

The neoconservatives, together with Cheney and Rumsfeld as their supporters, went up against Secretary of State Powell. At first, Powell won some of the policy debates but in the end, it was Cheney, Rumsfeld, and Wolfowitz who convinced the president to adopt their policies on Iraq. Overall, four major areas of contention arose concerning the Iraq War. First was the intense debate over whether the United States should even go to war against Iraq. This debate, which began in January 2002, consumed not only the Bush administration but the country and the global community as well. It is one of the greatest foreign policy debates in U.S. history, comparable to the Great Debate that occurred during the Korean War (see chapter 4). In fact, this issue remains unresolved and continues to split the country. Second, there was a bitter debate over whether or not the United States should seek diplomatic approval from the United Nations to launch the war against Iraq. This debate pitted Cheney against Powell. Third, policy makers disagreed about the tactics and size of the military force that should be used to topple Saddam Hussein. Civilian leaders in the Pentagon (Rumsfeld, Feith, and Wolfowitz) clashed with the military leadership as well as Secretary of State Powell, most of whom wanted a much larger force than Rumsfeld would agree to. Finally, there was a debate over the troop increases that the president ordered in the fall of 2006 after more than three years of failed attempts to subdue Iraq. While the military leadership opposed the escalation, the White House pushed hard for it. We begin with the debate over the decision to go to war in Iraq, which represents the neocons' greatest triumph.

The Debate Over Going To War Against Iraq

While not part of the U.S. foreign policy making bureaucracy under Clinton in the 1990s, the neocons remained influential among the foreign policy elite. They were out of power but not out of ideas. They advocated finishing the job against Saddam Hussein that they felt the elder President Bush had left undone in 1991. In 1997 they founded The Project for the New American Century, which laid out an ambitious foreign policy vision to reshape the world in America's image. In 1998 they published a letter to Clinton calling on him to adopt a policy of regime change in Iraq. They won enough support to pressure Clinton into signing the Iraq Liberation Act, which provided $97 million to train and equip Iraqi opposition groups but with little effect.

When George W. Bush was inaugurated in January 2001, the neocons' time had come as many of the signatories of the Project's 1998 letter, including Wolfowitz, Rumsfeld, and Perle, became key policy makers. Wolfowitz used 9/11 to make the case for toppling Hussein, claiming that there was up to a 50 percent chance that Hussein was involved. He did not believe al Qaeda was able to launch such an attack without help from a state sponsor, namely Iraq. He also believed Iraq helped al Qaeda's 1993 bombing of the World Trade Center,[26] although no evidence of this ever emerged. In a major policy meeting at Camp David just after 9/11, Wolfowitz made the case for attacking Iraq. However, nearly everyone else dismissed his argument and instead agreed with Powell who argued that the United States must strike against al Qaeda and the Taliban. Powell warned that international support would vanish if the United States attacked Iraq. Bush agreed and said the initial focus would be on Afghanistan. Nevertheless, Iraq remained a focus of the president's attention as he ordered officials to probe for even the smallest connection between Saddam Hussein and 9/11 even though they had told him there was no operational link. He also directed Rice to oversee plans for a possible military attack against Iraq.[27] Moreover, Vice President Cheney, who increasingly sided with Wolfowitz and the neocons, steered the foreign policy bureaucracy in the direction Wolfowitz had long advocated: confrontation with Iraq.

Even before the Taliban were defeated, the neocons looked for other targets. They considered Sudan and Somalia, but neither was considered important enough to demonstrate American resolve. So they focused on three countries: North Korea, Iran, and Iraq. Bush labeled them an "axis of evil" and alleged that their nuclear ambitions, combined with their connections to terrorist groups, made them an especially lethal threat. Although "axis of evil" was an attractive catchphrase, it was too simplistic a slogan because it falsely implied strategic and tactical coordination between three disparate countries, two of which (Iran and Iraq) were actually mortal enemies.

After the president's January 2002 State of the Union address, in which he first unveiled the axis of evil metaphor, the administration spent the next fourteen months articulating a new foreign policy doctrine as Bush singled out Iraq even though it was not an immediate threat. Bush used fearful language to enunciate the doctrine of preemption, which was a significant departure from the traditional doctrines of deterrence and containment. Deterrence and containment were the cornerstones of U.S. policy during the Cold War through which the United States sought to prevent attacks by threatening adversaries with unacceptable costs if they launched a strike against the United States. The 9/11 attacks reinforced the preexisting antipathy the neocons held for deterrence and containment, which in their minds had been effectively discredited under President Reagan. For his part, President Bush rejected deterrence because he did not think it would work against amorphous, suicidal actors like al Qaeda, which, he believed, Iraq might supply with weapons of mass destruction (WMD). Given this potential threat, Bush argued that the United States could no longer rely on deterrence and then sit back and wait while threats materialized. Instead, he adopted an offensive strategy that called for preemptively eliminating threats before they could fully emerge.[28] In January Bush declared, "I will not wait on events while dangers gather. I will not stand by as peril draws closer and closer. The United States of America will not permit the world's most dangerous regimes to threaten us with the world's most destructive weapons."[29]

Then on June 1, the president told the graduating class at West Point, "We must take the battle to the enemy," and "confront the worst threats before they emerge."[30] In September, the Bush administration made the policy official with its release of a National Security Strategy, which called for using military power in a policy of preemption that would also promote American values overseas.[31] That same month, Condoleezza Rice used another fearful metaphor when she raised the issue of nuclear terrorism to reinforce the argument: "We don't want the smoking gun to be [in the form of] a mushroom cloud."[32]

Critics found the doctrine of preemption fraught with analytical holes. Who was to say what sort of *potential* threat appearing sometime in the unknown future would justify a preemptive strike now? What if other countries used the same principle to justify a preemptive strike against the United States? And why was Iraq the first choice against which to implement this bold new doctrine and not the other members of the presumptive axis of evil? After all, Iran also had nuclear ambitions and was more clearly linked to terrorist groups in Lebanon and the Palestinian territories than was Iraq. And although President Bush proclaimed that the United States would not tolerate a nuclear-armed North Korea, he did very little to stop North Korea's program even after it was clear that Pyongyang had actually built several nuclear bombs.[33] Iraq, on the other hand, "was an inviting target for preemption not because it was an immediate threat but because it was thought to be a prospective menace that was incapable of successfully defending itself."[34]

Iraq, which had been severely weakened by the 1991 Gulf War and by more than a decade of crippling economic sanctions, had always been the neocons' focus since they saw regime change in Baghdad as central to their dream of reshaping the Middle East. It was not that Iraq was the greatest threat, therefore, but the most attractive target.

As the country debated the merits of preemption and whether the doctrine should be applied to Iraq, President Bush had apparently made up his mind. Even though he did not share his decision with the country in a formal announcement, it was clear to members of the National Security Council that, at least by March 2002—a full year before hostilities were launched—the president had decided on war with Iraq.[35] At a gathering of senators who Rice was briefing at that time, he cursed Saddam Hussein and said, "We're taking him out."[36] Despite this conviction, however, he repeatedly told the press, "I have no plans to attack [Iraq] on my desk."[37] While this was technically true—the plans actually sat on the desks of Secretary Rumsfeld and General Tommy Franks, the war's chief architects—Bush's denials obscured the "direct and personal nature of his involvement in the war planning."[38]

Meanwhile, many observers were unconvinced that Iraq posed a serious threat to the United States. While Hussein may have used WMD against Iranians and Kurds in the 1980s, that did not justify a preemptive attack by the Americans more than fifteen years later. After all, when Hussein gassed his regional opponents, the United States did not do anything. In fact, although Washington publicly condemned Saddam Hussein's use of chemical and biological weapons against Iran, the United States provided valuable military intelligence to Iraq in its war with

Iran. Even prominent Republicans opposed the doctrine of preemption. House Majority Leader Dick Armey (R-TX) said that as long as Saddam Hussein was contained within his own borders "we should not address any attack or resources against him."[39] Furthermore, Republicans in the foreign policy elite who served in the elder Bush administration, especially former NSA Brent Scowcroft and former Secretary of State Lawrence Eagleburger, similarly spoke out against invading Iraq. Opponents questioned Bush's claim that Hussein possessed WMD, which was the main reason he gave for going to war.

Shortly before the war started, Cheney declared "there is no doubt" Hussein had WMD.[40] After the war started on March 19, 2003, U.S. officials expressed certainty that they would find WMD. On March 30, Rumsfeld told reporters un- equivocally, "we know where they are," and cited the region around Tikrit, Saddam Hussein's hometown. White House spokesman Ari Fleischer said, "there is no ques- tion" that chemical and biological weapons would be found and reminded reporters that this was the main reason Bush felt so strongly about going to war in Iraq.[41] On May 29, nearly a month after Bush declared an end to major combat operations, he proclaimed, "we have found the weapons of mass destruction" in a desperate and feeble attempt to vindicate his war policy. He cited the discovery of two tractor trailers that Powell had earlier claimed were mobile weapons labs. But weapons in- spectors had examined the trailers *before* Bush's declaration and concluded that they had nothing to do with WMD.[42] In July 2003, Bush again proclaimed, "There's no doubt in my mind when it's all said and done, the facts will show the truth. There's absolutely no doubt in my mind."[43] Of course, no WMD were ever found and the administration quietly changed its rhetoric from finding actual *weapons* to finding weapons *programs,* a huge difference they tried to downplay. But Bush remained defiant and unrepentant. At an August 2004 press conference he said, "Let me just say this to you: knowing what I know today, we still would have gone into Iraq."[44] When a *Washington Post* reporter interviewed Bush for a book he was writing, he noted that it took five minutes "of back and forth simply for Bush to acknowledge the *fact*" that WMD were never found.[45]

The Debate Over Diplomatic Strategy and the United Nations
The second major area of debate involved Secretary Powell and Vice President Cheney squaring off over whether or not the United States should present its case before the United Nations to build international support. Powell supported going to the United Nations but Cheney was opposed.

Cheney opposed going to the United Nations for several reasons. First, he believed that the United Nations had already passed numerous resolutions regarding Iraq and felt another was unnecessary. Second, he worried that Saddam Hussein would take advantage of the United Nations' diplomatic processes to prevaricate and forestall any real progress. He also opposed going to the United Nations because he felt renewed weapons inspections were a waste of time. Finally, he resisted going to the United Nations because he did not believe gaining international support through the world body was necessary. Like the neocons he supported, Cheney held the United Nations in disdain.

Powell on the other hand, argued that the United States needed as many allies as it could find and that the United Nations was the ideal place for building such a coalition. He wanted to assemble as broad-based a coalition against Iraq as the elder President Bush had done in 1991. Powell also argued that it would be impossible to go after Saddam Hussein without diplomatic progress in the Arab-Israeli dispute.[46] He was convinced that movement in the peace process would lessen Hussein's appeal among other Arab countries. By contrast, Cheney was prepared to deal with Iraq unilaterally and to make it a test case of the Bush Doctrine of preemption.[47] He argued that the Arab states would be pressured into making peace with the Israelis once Saddam Hussein was weakened or toppled.[48] Bush sided with Powell mostly because it was the only way to convince British Prime Minister Tony Blair to join him. Bush needed Blair to show the world that he was not alone in viewing Hussein as a threat and Blair needed the United Nations for his own domestic political reasons. So, first Bush and then Powell made strong, convincing speeches at the United Nations as they sought to mount international pressure on Iraq. Powell's presentation was quite convincing. He even held up a simulated vial of anthrax to dramatize his position that Iraq was a threat.

On November 8, 2002, just after Bush's U.N. speech, the UNSC passed resolution 1441 calling for weapons inspections to resume. Since Cheney could not convince Bush to bypass the United Nations, he fought to get tough language inserted in the resolution promising "serious consequences" if Iraq failed to comply. Feeling the pressure, Iraq acceded to resumed weapons inspections. However, it was clear that Hussein was not cooperating fully. In February 2003 after Powell gave his speech, the United States, Great Britain, and Spain introduced a resolution declaring Iraq had failed to meet its requirements. This resolution failed to pass however, because France declared its intention to veto. Cheney's fears had been realized: "For

American diplomacy, the six-month venture at the United Nations was a remarkable failure."[49] Nevertheless, Bush and Blair agreed that the language of resolution 1441 gave them authority to launch the war, which began on March 19. By April 9, Saddam Hussein's regime was history as jubilant Iraqis toppled his statue with the help of American soldiers. On May 1 the president helped pilot a military jet just before it landed on the USS *Abraham* stationed off the coast of San Diego. Wearing a flight suit and standing on the carrier deck beneath a huge banner proclaiming "Mission Accomplished," the president proudly declared an end to major combat operations as the *Abraham*'s sailors cheered wildly. Unfortunately, the president did his victory dance just as Iraq's sectarian strife and the anti-American insurgency were heating up.

Debate Over Troop Levels

In addition to the diplomatic debate over the role of the United Nations, there was an intense debate over war-fighting strategy that centered on troop levels. This was one of the most serious debates because its resolution in Rumsfeld's favor had disastrous consequences. Most of the Pentagon's military leaders wanted to apply the Powell Doctrine, which called for an invasion force of several hundred thousand troops in a display of overwhelming force.[50] Although he had no combat experience, Rumsfeld rejected the Powell Doctrine. He overruled his generals and insisted that they fight the war using speed and mobility, which called for much smaller troop levels. Each time General Franks submitted his war plan to Rumsfeld, the Secretary ordered that force levels be trimmed down further.

When Army Chief of Staff General Eric Shinseki testified before Congress that it would take hundreds of thousands of troops to subdue Iraq, he was publicly criticized by Wolfowitz and Rumsfeld, with the former declaring Shinseki's estimate "widely off the mark."[51] Wolfowitz argued that it was unlikely that it would take more troops to secure Iraq after the war than it would take to topple Saddam Hussein's dictatorship. It turned out, however, that Shinseki was right and Wolfowitz and Rumsfeld were wrong. Obsessed with controlling troop levels *for* the war, Rumsfeld paid little attention to how many troops it would take to secure the country *after* the war. Indeed, he spent most of his time on the easiest task, toppling Saddam Hussein, and the least amount of time on the hardest task, securing and rebuilding a deeply divided and traumatized country that had been devastated by years of war, sanctions, and brutal dictatorship.[52]

Once Baghdad fell, the country degenerated into lawlessness, looting, and re-venge killings. It seemed clear to everyone except Rumsfeld and Bush that there were not enough troops to secure the country. Rumsfeld dismissed the chaos with a wave of his hand, saying "freedom is untidy" and "stuff happens."[53] At one news conference, he complained that the media were showing the same man steal the same vase from the same building over and over, giving an exaggerated impression of the chaos. It was an astonishingly ignorant statement about what was really hap-pening. In fact, looters ransacked everything from nearly every unattended build-ing, including the Iraqi National Museum, which housed artifacts from some of the world's oldest civilizations. Office furniture, doors, windows, toilets, and even electric wiring were stolen. One looter was seen tugging a luxury boat down a Bagh-dad street without a trailer, unmindful of the damage he was causing to the boat's hull. The only government building U.S. troops *did* secure was the Oil Ministry while the nearby Ministry of Irrigation (the water authority) was left burning.[54] The symbolism did not escape the Iraqi people. While Rumsfeld won the debate about troop levels, his small, speedy task force was simply insufficient to secure the country. The security vacuum that emerged after the regime collapsed was filled—not by the thinly spread U.S. military, but by vengeful Iraqi militias, suicidal insur-gents, and criminal gangs. Moreover, had there actually been WMD caches, there were not enough troops to find and secure them.

By fall 2006, the Bush administration's policy was clearly a failure. Bush had appointed L. Paul "Jerry" Bremer to head up the Coalition Provisional Authority (CPA) to oversee Iraq's reconstruction. Bremer had never been to Iraq before, did not speak Arabic, and had no experience in post-conflict societies.[55] As head of the CPA, however, he made two key decisions that had serious unintended conse-quences. First, he disbanded the top four levels of Saddam Hussein's Baath Party. While most Iraqis welcomed this decision, the Baathists were the only ones who knew how to run the government ministries. Second, Bremer issued an order dis-solving Iraq's entire military and its security service. While this also seemed like a good idea, it left no one to help secure the country and provide law and order. Since there were too few U.S. troops to address Iraq's massive security and reconstruc-tion needs, ordinary Iraqis found themselves worse off under the CPA than they were under Hussein's Baath Party. Electricity, for instance, was often unavailable for hours or days at a time and clean water was hard to find. Iraqis began referring to the CPA as "Can't Provide Anything."[56]

Iraq degenerated into a Hobbesian state of civil war. Insurgency spread and suicide killings, previously unheard of in Iraq, became almost a daily scourge. In July, 2003, speaking to reporters at the White House, Bush taunted the insurgents by saying "Bring 'em on."[57] The insurgents did, in fact, "bring it," killing thousands of Americans and wounding tens of thousands more. Moreover, hundreds of Iraqis turned up dead each week as a result of ethnic and religious factions attacking each other. This bleak picture ran counter to the image promoted by the administration. In May, 2005, for instance, Cheney told CNN's Larry King that the insurgents "are in the last throes,"[58] which subsequent violence proved was far from the truth.

Administration allies began to turn against the president. Kenneth Adelman, who supported the war and even toasted its initial success, grew disenchanted with Bush's foreign policy team and said that it was "the most incompetent" group of foreign policy makers in the last fifty years.[59] Adelman broke with the administration when President Bush awarded the Medal of Freedom, the country's highest civilian honor, to the officials Adelman blamed most for the Iraq mess: CPA head Bremer, CIA chief Tenet, and General Franks. David Kay, the chief weapons inspector who admitted to his own failure on the WMD question, said Rice was the worst NSA since the position was created.[60] Several retired generals, who were closely involved in the invasion or occupation of Iraq, called for Rumsfeld's resignation, citing his ignorance of counterinsurgency techniques, his decision to send troops into combat without proper equipment, and his abrasive management style.

Debate Over the Troop Surge

In December 2006, the Republican Party suffered a crushing defeat in the congressional elections, which prompted a change in Bush's rhetoric. Only days before the election, the president boasted, "Absolutely, we're winning" in Iraq.[61] But after the mid-term elections saw control of both the House and Senate shift to the Democrats, the president reversed position and conceded that America was not winning the war. The new Democratic majority in Congress promised to pressure the president into bringing the troops home. This reflected not only widespread public sentiment regarding the unpopular war but also the conclusions reached by the Baker-Hamilton Report, which was released by the bipartisan Iraq Study Group. However, rather than accede to these recommendations, President Bush instead favored escalating force levels by more than 30,000 troops. Again, the decision in this, the fourth major area of debate, caused a split within the Bush administration.

The JCS unanimously opposed the surge, arguing that it would have little impact in the short run and only provide more targets for anti-American insurgents. They worried that the surge would not have any long-lasting impact since the insurgents would simply melt away and return when the Americans deescalated.[62] They also argued that it would stretch the armed forces too thin and bring the army to the breaking point. Already, the army was under severe stress, falling short of recruitment goals, and having to extend tours of duty and shorten soldiers' leaves. Nevertheless, President Bush ordered an escalation of troops that took place during the winter and spring of 2007. Critics were perplexed by the decision given the election results and also since Rumsfeld had resisted calls for a bigger force for years.

Perhaps this new direction in policy is why Bush finally agreed to jettison Rumsfeld, who resigned right after the Republicans' electoral debacle. Until that time, Bush had resisted firing Rumsfeld even though his Chief of Staff Andrew Card urged him to do so. Bush resisted because he feared it would be seen as an admission that his Iraq policy was failing. But most people believed that anyway. Sticking with Rumsfeld only made Bush look stubborn, incompetent, and isolated from reality, especially given his public statements insisting that Rumsfeld was a great defense secretary. It also opened Bush to charges that he kept with an unpopular defense secretary, risking more U.S. casualties, just to protect his political fortunes. Indeed, 2007 proved to be the bloodiest year for U.S. forces in Iraq.

Nevertheless, violence has declined in Iraq. Bush and his supporters argued that the surge worked. However, other factors contributed to the lessening of violence. For instance, many of Iraq's tribal leaders rose up against foreign insurgents and kicked them out of their towns and villages. This happened in areas where the surge of U.S troops did not occur. Another reason why violence declined was that, by late 2007 and early 2008, many of Iraq's religious and ethnically mixed towns had finished violently cleansing their populations of unwanted people. Whether the surge or other factors were responsible, the fact remains that U.S. casualty rates for 2008 were nearly two-thirds less than they were for 2007.[63] The trend continued for 2009 and 2010. However, while U.S. casualties have significantly declined in Iraq, the *New York Times* reports that Iraqi and American troops come under attack "almost daily" and that "an intermittent pattern of major attacks continues to wreak havoc."[64] This continued violence reflects the fact that the competing Iraqi factions have had considerable difficulty in ironing out their differences.[65]

WMD AND THE NEOCON REPORT CARD

Throughout this book, we have examined instances where the U.S. intelligence community failed to anticipate or prevent a number of significant developments in world affairs, such as the attack on Pearl Harbor, the launch of Sputnik, the fall of the Berlin Wall, and the failure to discover and prevent the 9/11 attacks. In this section, we focus on the intelligence fiasco regarding allegations that Saddam Hussein possessed WMD and that he had operational ties to al Qaeda. In some cases, the intelligence on Iraq was deeply flawed while in others, senior officials either ignored or twisted it to fit their own preconceived agendas. Either way, the United States justified its conquest of another country based on false premises.

A critical area where the intelligence was flawed concerns the administration's (incorrect) charge that Hussein possessed WMD. On at least two occasions, CIA Director Tenet told President Bush that it was a "slam dunk" case that Iraq possessed WMD. The problem, however, was that the list the intelligence community compiled of Iraq's 900 suspected WMD cites was five years old. When Hussein kicked weapons inspectors out of Iraq in 1998, the United States lost the ability to obtain accurate information on Iraq's military programs. By 2003, no one could really say whether the 900 cites on the 1998 list were in fact real.[66] In September 2002 General Franks informed Bush that he was having difficulty locating suitable bombing targets, such as Scud missile emplacements. But if the intelligence was so poor in finding good bombing targets, how could it be good enough for Cheney to insist that there was "no doubt" that Saddam Hussein had WMD?[67] In fact, "nobody pored or labored over the details of the list where the stuff was supposed to be stored."[68] Moreover, in June 2003, when Bush asked Bremer and Rumsfeld who was in charge of the WMD hunt, each indicated that the other was, meaning that, more than a month *after* Bush had declared an end to major combat operations, there was no clear chain of responsibility for locating the very items Bush cited as the main cause for war.[69]

On some occasions, policy makers distorted the intelligence in hopes of finding a result that fit their preconceived notions about Iraq. Cheney and his Chief of Staff Scooter Libby put so much pressure on intelligence officials that it "created an environment in which some analysts felt pressured to make their assessments fit with the Bush administration's policy objectives."[70] The most egregious case involves the neocons in the Pentagon who created their own intelligence wing because they were dissatisfied by the intelligence community's reluctance to declare a clear operational link between al Qaeda and Iraq. Wolfowitz created the Defense Department's Office of Special Plans in order to find evidence of what he, Rumsfeld, and Feith already believed to be true, that Saddam Hussein had close ties to al Qaeda. But this office was "cherry-picking" bits of incomplete and raw information that had not been properly vetted by trained intelligence professionals.[71]

On other occasions, policy makers simply disregarded the conclusions reached by their own intelligence professionals. The most infamous example of this occurred with President Bush's 2003 State of the Union address in which he claimed that Iraq sought nuclear weapons material from Niger. However, this turned out to be a myth that had been debunked by intelligence officials before the president's speech.[72] There were other instances as well. A fall 2001 report from the State Department's INR concluded there was no persuasive evidence that Iraq's nuclear weapons program had been reconstituted but it went largely ignored.[73] A fall 2002 NIE poked a "gaping hole" in Bush's case for war since it raised serious doubts about Iraq's nuclear weapons program but Bush gave a speech in Cincinnati ignoring these doubts and stated categorically that Iraq was pursuing nuclear weapons.[74] He also made a speech at the White House stating flatly that Saddam Hussein "possesses biological and chemical weapons," but this contradicted a widely circulated intelligence report issued at the time which said there was "no reliable information on whether Iraq was producing or stockpiling" chemical weapons.[75] A Defense Intelligence Agency report, completed in September 2002, but not released until June 2003 (nearly four months after the war started) said there was no reliable information on whether Iraq was producing stockpiles of chemical weapons.[76] In fall 2006, Bush continued to insist that an al Qaeda-linked terrorist named Abu Musab al-Zarqawi, who was active in Iraq, had close ties to Saddam Hussein even though the CIA had repudiated such claims a year earlier.[77] And, despite the lack of evidence linking Saddam Hussein to al Qaeda, Cheney continued to make the claim long after virtually everyone else in Washington believed otherwise.

Policy makers mentioned al Qaeda, 9/11, WMD, and Iraq in the same breath so often that, by the time the war began, a public opinion poll showed that more than half of the country mistakenly held Saddam Hussein responsible for 9/11.[78] Another poll, taken six months after the war began, found that 70 percent of Americans thought Saddam Hussein had played a part in the 9/11 attacks and that Americans were even led to believe that WMD were found in Iraq and that Hussein had used them against U.S. forces during the war.[79]

Many of the predictions Bush, Cheney, Rumsfeld, and the neoconservatives made on Iraq failed to materialize. Bush predicted that, once the United States committed to a military operation, its allies would fall in line but only Britain followed suit as the Bush Doctrine generated increased opposition—even from Washington's closest and oldest allies—to U.S. policies around the globe.[80] Cheney insisted that American troops would be greeted as liberators, but few Iraqis were happy to see them. Rather, Iraq declared a national holiday on June 30, 2009, marking the U.S. troop redeployment from Iraq's urban areas as jubilant Iraqis celebrated the withdrawal. And in May 2005, Cheney claimed that the insurgency was in its "last throes," yet more Americans have been killed in Iraq after that statement than before it. Both Rumsfeld and Cheney predicted the war would last weeks, not months, but that claim was obviously widely off the mark. Wolfowitz insisted that a show of American force would immediately trigger a widespread revolt against Saddam Hussein but that did not happen either.[81] He also claimed that the Iraq War would pay for itself by using Iraq's oil riches. Since the war began, however, Iraq's oil revenues have not come close to paying for the war. Before the invasion, Iraq produced 2.6 million barrels of oil per day (mbd) but in December 2005, that figure had dropped to 1.1 mbd.[82] By January 2006, Iraq actually had to import oil to meet its energy needs.[83] By 2010, the Iraq War had cost the American taxpayer close to a *trillion* dollars. Bush and the neocons also predicted that inspectors would find huge stockpiles of WMD, but none were ever found. They said investigators would uncover evidence of links between Saddam Hussein and al Qaeda, but none existed. They also predicted that Iraq would be reborn as a democracy and serve as a model for other Arab countries but that has not happened either. Despite registering a slight improvement in its democratic ranking, Freedom House still rates Iraq "not free" along with the vast majority of Arab states.[84]

AFTERMATH: 9/11 AS A TURNING POINT

Much like the surprise attack on Pearl Harbor in 1941, the 9/11 tragedy also wrought significant changes in U.S. foreign policy. Earlier we discussed the Bush Doctrine of preemption. Here we discuss two other issues. First is the intensification of the growth of executive power. From Teddy Roosevelt to Franklin Roosevelt to Richard Nixon, the expansion of presidential power in U.S foreign policy has been a fairly constant trend. In recent times, no other president has interpreted executive power more broadly than George W. Bush.

Since the 9/11 attacks, President Bush and Vice President Cheney sought to strengthen the executive branch in hopes of better fighting terrorism. Less than seven weeks after 9/11, Congress passed the president's anti-terrorism legislation with very little debate and few significant changes. The USA PATRIOT Act (United and Strengthening America by Providing Appropriate Tools Required to Intercept and Obstruct Terrorism) gives the president sweeping new powers without providing the checks and balances that the other two branches of government normally perform. For instance, the Act allows for secret searches of terror suspects' computers, library records, or Internet activity, all without court review to show probable cause.[85] Bush and Cheney also argued that the executive does not need judicial warrants to monitor communications between suspected terrorists abroad and people inside the United States. The FBI and the intelligence community can now conduct roving electronic wiretaps that follow a suspect no matter whose phone, computer, or email address is used. The PATRIOT Act also gives the U.S. attorney general the power to arrest and indefinitely detain immigrants suspected of terrorism. Conservatives as well as liberals have challenged it as a violation of civil liberties protections contained in the U.S. Constitution's Bill of Rights. In fact, the Supreme Court struck down the provision that enabled the FBI to forbid librarians from discussing FBI searches of library records on the grounds that such a gag violated First Amendment Rights.

Bush also issued emergency orders giving him sweeping power to set up secret military courts to try aliens suspected of terrorism. Conservative columnist William Safire condemned the president's actions in the *New York Times* saying that, "Misadvised by a frustrated and panic-stricken attorney general, a president of the United States has just assumed dictatorial power to jail or execute aliens."[86] Inmates at the infamous prison on Guantanamo Bay in Cuba languished in jail for years without a charge or a trial. When the media uncovered secret detention facilities located in foreign countries outside American jurisdiction, there was an international outcry and U.S. officials, or their contracted agents, have been accused of torturing suspects held in these facilities. The most infamous example occurred in Baghdad's notorious Abu Ghraib prison, which ultimately led to the conviction of several low-ranking American soldiers.

The Bush administration consistently opposed an increased role for Congress in overseeing its conduct in the war against terrorism. Bush and Cheney insisted that the president alone, as commander-in-chief, can set the rules for surveilling, detaining, and interrogating terrorist suspects. During Bush's first term, Vice President Cheney bypassed Congress altogether when it came to policy on issues like detention and interrogation of terrorist suspects.[87] In Bush's second term, however, Congress and the courts began to push back in what amounts to a typical pattern of give and take between the executive, legislative, and judicial branches. In June 2006, the Supreme Court ruled that terror suspects have a right to basic legal protections under the Geneva Conventions, which Cheney and Bush had previously denied them. For its part, while the Obama administration works much more closely with Congress, it continues the tradition of asserting executive power as evidenced by its continued use of secret surveillance tactics.[88] Moreover, despite his campaign promise, Obama has still proved unable or unwilling to close the prison at Guantanamo Bay two years into his administration.

The 9/11 attacks also led to the single greatest restructuring of the federal bureaucracy since passage of the National Security Act in 1947, which further strengthened executive power. The two most important changes are the creation of the Department of Homeland Security (DHS) in 2002 and the establishment of the Director of National Intelligence (DNI) in 2005. After 9/11 the president established the *Office* of Homeland Security, which had a small staff. Initially, President Bush opposed elevating the office to a full-fledged department in his Cabinet, but he dropped his opposition amidst public demands and when Republicans and Democrats in Congress agreed on a bill to create the DHS. Creation of the DHS affected more than 170,000 federal employees as their agencies were swallowed up by DHS, including the Federal Emergency Management Agency, the Coast Guard, the Secret Service, the Customs Service, the Immigration and Naturalization Service, and the newly created Transportation Security Administration, which handles airport security. DHS is experiencing growing pains. Job satisfaction among employees is dismal: employee turnover is among the highest in the government. To date, the public has been unimpressed with its performance. For instance, the DHS color-coding scheme, which was designed for marking terrorist threat levels, was ridiculed as meaningless and perhaps little more than a political tool to increase public support for the government's anti-terrorism policies. Its recommendation that people stock up on duct tape in case of a chemical attack was scorned by the public and mocked on late-night talk shows. And its sluggish response to Hurricane Katrina severely damaged its reputation as critics questioned DHS ability to respond to a national crisis that is, unlike Katrina, unexpected.

The new director of national intelligence (DNI) replaces the CIA director as head of the entire intelligence community, which is composed of sixteen separate agencies, some of which include the CIA, the National Security Agency, the Defense Intelligence Agency, and the State Department's INR. It is the DNI's job to ensure proper sharing of intelligence information between the disparate intelligence agencies as well as with policy makers in the White House. The DNI is also responsible for overseeing the release of National Intelligence Estimates, which are major studies and predictions that represent the consensus of all sixteen intelligence agencies. However, Mike McConnell, President Bush's last DNI, complained that his office lacked sufficient authority needed to effectively run the vast intelligence bureaucracy. And Adm. Dennis Blair (ret.), the DNI for the Obama administration, found his early tenure consumed by a public debate between President Obama and former Vice President Cheney about whether or not the United States should engage in torture in its efforts to stop terrorist acts.

The second change concerns the dissolution of American unity at home and of U.S. prestige abroad. When George W. Bush campaigned for office in 2000 he proclaimed, "I'm a uniter, not a divider." However, President Bush's foreign policy caused division and bitterness throughout the country, not least because of his administration's use of what officials called "enhanced interrogation techniques," but what most everyone else calls torture. Despite Bush's public denial that the "United States does not torture," there is compelling evidence to the contrary, including graphic pictures of abuse by U.S. soldiers at Abu Ghraib prison in Iraq and numerous government reports documenting the use of such techniques as sleep deprivation, extreme stress positions, punching, open handed slapping, and waterboarding.[89] Ironically, the Japanese soldiers who waterboarded American POWs during WWII were later placed on trial for war crimes. Overall, President Bush's anti-terrorism policies, like the USA PATRIOT Act and the use of torture, intensified the country's political cleavages, weakened his standing in the polls and severely damaged the U.S. image abroad. In a dramatic reversal, the president's post–9/11 public approval rating of 90 percent plummeted at one point to 28 percent, which is among the lowest of any president since WWII.

Unlike his father, who refused to politicize the war against Iraq in 1991, the younger President Bush deliberately politicized the 2003 Iraq War in an effort to win electoral support. For instance, the president forced a vote in Congress giving him authority to wage war in Iraq just before the November 2002 congressional elections so that Democrats who voted against the resolution could be targeted in the campaign as being soft on terrorism. Karl Rove, the president's chief political strategist, urged Republicans to "run on the war" by attacking Democrats who did not support Bush's policies as unpatriotic, defeatist, and unsupportive of American troops. When the 2002 elections were held, Republicans increased their majority in the House and retook control of the Senate. Rove also wrote a memo suggesting that the war could help the president win reelection in 2004. He counseled Bush to remind voters that he is a "war president." Robert D. Blackwill, who served as a special assistant to the president on Iraq from 2003–2004, noted that whenever Iraq came up in meetings, it was always filtered through the prism of winning the 2004 election.[89] When Cheney was campaigning, he engaged in fear mongering by implying that voting for the Democrats would aid the terrorists. He said that voters must "make the right choice. Because if we make the wrong choice, then the danger is that we'll get hit again."[91] And when the Iraq Study Group examined what went wrong in Iraq, the president delayed the report's release until *after* the 2006 elections, claiming he did not want the report twisted for political purposes. In fact, delaying the report's release served the *president's* political purposes since the voters deserved to know the report's conclusions and recommendations *before* the election so they could make an informed decision. Moreover, even though policy makers knew North Korea broke its agreements in 2002 and was on the verge of deploying a nuclear weapon, they kept this information secret until after Congress held its vote authorizing war against Iraq,[92] fearing that developments in North Korea might derail their plans for Iraq.

While campaigning in 2000, candidate Bush promised a modest U.S. foreign policy. He said, "If we're an arrogant nation, they'll resent us," but if the United States instead acts with humility, it would be welcomed all over the world.[93] But Bush's foreign policy proved to be anything but humble. With an emphasis on offensive military power and unilateralism, the Bush Doctrine of preemption not only increased anti-Americanism throughout the world but also "counter-Americanism," which seeks to deliberately weaken the United States by, say, voting against U.S. interests at the United Nations or refusing to purchase American goods.[94] Many Europeans even consider the United States as much a threat to world peace as they do North Korea. American prestige throughout the world was at an all-time low as President Bush wound down his presidency.

Interestingly, it is Barack Obama who is carrying out *candidate* Bush's recommendation for the United States to act with humility on the world stage. Obama gave his very first formal television interview to *Al Arabiya*, the Arabic-language network based in Dubai in the Persian Gulf. And in June 2009 he went to Cairo, Egypt to give a major speech seeking to mend the rift between the Islamic and Western worlds.

Having said that, Obama's foreign policy team has not had much better success than Bush's. Since President Obama completed his promised drawdown of U.S. troops in Iraq to 50,000 and declared an official end to major combat operations there in September 2010, the country remains on edge and politically unstable. Meanwhile, U.S. success in Afghanistan remains elusive. Despite Obama pouring thousands more troops into Afghanistan and despite ordering increased Predator drone attacks in Afghanistan and Pakistan, the Taliban and their al Qaeda allies have won control of large portions of Afghanistan. Indeed, before September ended, the year 2010 had already proved to be the bloodiest year for U.S. casualties in Afghanistan.

Moreover, the Obama administration has, like the Bush administration, experienced serious internal divisions that have proved embarrassing. For instance, Obama fired Gen. Stanley McChrystal, the Commander of U.S. and NATO forces in Afghanistan, after *Rolling Stone* magazine published an interview McChrystal gave that openly and contemptuously disparaged both President Obama and Vice President Biden. Like Truman before him, Obama relieved McChrystal to ensure civilian control of the military and war-fighting policy. And *Washington Post* reporter Bob Woodward's book, *Obama's War*, paints Obama's foreign policy team as deeply divided on Afghanistan as was Bush's on Iraq. Perhaps these divisions are inevitable byproducts of the frustrations that come with the decade-long effort of trying to bring stability to Afghanistan, a country that has never in its history been fully subdued by an outside power.

Conclusion

The case studies in this book offer several lessons and conclusions about United States foreign policy. These lessons are not exhaustive, but they do point out some important elements that students of U.S. foreign policy must keep in mind.

The first element is that political and historical context matter. No event or development in U.S. foreign policy can be fully understood without first examining the historical milieu in which it occurs. For instance, eight of the twelve turning points examined in this book occurred at some point during the Cold War struggle between the United States and the Soviet Union. As such, it is vital to comprehend this global superpower rivalry as it ebbed and flowed through several decades. Consider the North Korean invasion of South Korea, for instance, which occurred at the height of early Cold War tensions. By first understanding the incredibly high stakes of the U.S.-Soviet rivalry that extended from Europe to the Global South, we get a clear picture of how serious a threat communist North Korea's invasion appeared to U.S. policy makers. South Korea was initially of limited strategic interest to the United States, but since the 1949 communist victory in nearby China and that country's subsequent close ties to Moscow, U.S. policy makers were terrified that the entire Asian landmass was going to fall under communist domination. They were particularly fearful about the danger a communist Korea would pose to neighboring Japan, the linchpin in the U.S. policy of promoting capitalism and democracy in Asia. In light of these broader considerations, American officials felt compelled to respond forcefully to North Korea's invasion.

The same holds for the other turning points examined in this book that occurred during the Cold War, from the Soviet launch of Sputnik to the fall of the Berlin Wall. As U.S. foreign policy makers weighed their responses to each of these turning points, they had to filter their decisions through the prism of the U.S.-Soviet Cold War rivalry. In two of the case studies, the Cuban Missile Crisis and the 1973 Arab-Israeli War, Washington and Moscow came perilously close to exchanging blows that likely would have resulted in a nuclear exchange. Both in terms of the context and consequences, several of these Cold War turning points spanned the administrations of more than one president. For example, while the Tet Offensive proved to be a critical turning point in the presidency of Lyndon Johnson, it can be understood only in the context of policies pursued by his three predecessors. Moreover, Tet surely influenced the policy of Johnson's successor, Richard Nixon, whose Nixon Doctrine reflected the shift in America toward distaste for foreign military adventures. And for the turning points examined in the first three chapters of this book, the context is obviously different in each case, although some common themes such as Great Power rivalries and the American tradition of isolation provide important foundations for understanding these cases.

Second, Americans generally pay little attention to foreign policy, which usually leaves the foreign policy elite—officials inside the upper echelons of the national security bureaucracy as well as those well-connected parties outside the government—free to chart a course of their own liking. In those circumstances, foreign policy can be distorted by the narrow self interests of various sectors among the foreign policy elite vying for dominance. For example, the United States was deeply entrenched in Vietnam long before American involvement in the conflict there began to draw widespread public scrutiny in the late 1960s. Reaction in the United States to the Tet Offensive destroyed the monopoly over Vietnam policy the foreign policy elite had enjoyed going back to 1945. Similarly, Iran was very much off the public radar, despite decades of deep U.S. involvement there, before the hostage crisis in 1979. The taking of U.S. hostages in Tehran placed U.S. policy in Iran under a public microscope for the first time.

The onset of crises, like the ones covered in this book, tends to draw the attention of the general American populace to matters of foreign policy. Intensified public scrutiny during these turning points can either hinder or enable policy makers in their pursuit of American national interests. For example, press coverage of the conflict with Spain stoked anti-Spanish sentiment among the American people, which in turn laid the foundation for popular support of the Spanish-American War. U.S. officials' bellicose statements after the 9/11 terrorist attacks, together with the media's coverage thereof, helped enable President Bush to manipulate a majority of the American public into the mistaken beliefs that Iraq and Saddam Hussein possessed WMD and also that they were behind the attacks on the Twin Towers, which then helped stir up support for the American invasion and conquest of Iraq. On the other side of the ledger, popular sentiment regarding Europe and isolationism prior to World War II made it especially difficult for President Franklin Roosevelt to prepare the country for what he considered the inevitable U.S. entry in WWII on the side of the Allies. Only the outrage felt over Pearl Harbor was sufficient to swing public support behind FDR's position. Public opinion on China was so negative during the Kennedy administration that it prevented JFK from launching any serious policy initiative to improve Sino-American relations. Such an initiative would have to wait until the Nixon administration nearly ten years later, and even then it caught the American public, not to mention the foreign policy elite, completely off guard. In other examples, the American public's intensely negative response to President Truman's handling of the Korean War as well as President Johnson's handling of the Vietnam War prompted both incumbents to declare their intention *not* to run for reelection.

Third, and related to number two above, is a central irony that characterizes the American presidency. As they campaign for the White House, presidential candidates emphasize domestic issues, such as jobs, healthcare, and education. However, once in office their historical legacies are often determined by how well they manage a foreign policy crisis that seems inevitably to befall every presidency. Consider just a few of the crises or turning points covered in this book as evidence. Woodrow Wilson's response to the attack on the *Lusitania* and German violations of American neutrality led to American entry into WWI and helped define Wilson's presidency and cement his place in history as the architect of the League of Nations. President Kennedy's successful management of the Cuban Missile Crisis left an enduring impression of JFK as a forceful leader. And although the Watergate scandal led to President Nixon's resignation and seriously tarnished his overall legacy, there is no denying that his adroit opening to China along with his response to the 1973 Arab-Israeli War established him as one of the most visionary chief executives in terms of shaping American foreign policy. Meanwhile, President Carter's legacy will forever be marred by what many consider his inept handling of the American hostage crisis in Iran. The tragic failure of the rescue attempt, together with the overall duration of the humiliating hostage crisis, contributed heavily to Carter's defeat to Ronald Reagan in 1980. And President George W. Bush's historical legacy will be tied not only to his failure to properly detect and prevent the 9/11 tragedy in the first place, but also to his controversial decision to invade Iraq on flimsy evidence, alleging Iraq's possession of WMD and its direct connection to terrorism in general and to al Qaeda in particular.

Fourth, these case studies illustrate the fact that debates and divisions among top ranking officials are an integral, and often revealing, element of the foreign policy making process. Given the disparate personalities of these towering individuals (most often with egos to match) it is no small wonder that the president's chief foreign affairs advisors will clash over the issues. William Jennings Bryan's disagreements with Woodrow Wilson over the issue of neutrality during WWI became so deep that the former resigned his post as secretary of state. Henry Kissinger, President Nixon's national security advisor, was so suspicious of Secretary of State William Rogers, that he kept Rogers in the dark about important foreign policy developments in China, the Middle East, and elsewhere in which Rogers' expertise could surely have been put to good use. The two rivals in President Carter's administration—Secretary of State Cyrus Vance and National Security Advisor Zbigniew Brzezinski—got along so poorly that there appeared to be competing foreign policies emanating from Washington at the same time. And dysfunction so plagued the relationship between Defense Secretary Donald Rumsfeld, Secretary of State Colin Powell, and National Security Advisor Condoleezza Rice in President George W. Bush's administration that these principle parties could barely look at or even talk to each other in meetings.

Fifth, by focusing on these crises as turning points, we illustrate a seemingly permanent characteristic of U.S. foreign policy, which is that American officials are often caught off guard by fast paced, unexpected developments in international relations. Often times, they find themselves reacting to events that are not fully under their control. Of course the United States regularly takes the lead in shaping world events, but, as we have sought to demonstrate in this book, the direction of U.S. foreign policy is sometimes shaped by crises and unanticipated developments on the world stage. The sinking of the *Maine* and of the *Lusitania,* along with the Japanese attack on Pearl Harbor, all serve as examples where U.S. foreign policy makers were compelled to reshape or alter the course of existing policies in response to unexpected developments. The North Korean invasion of South Korea, the Soviet launch of Sputnik, and Soviet-Cuban placement of nuclear missiles ninety miles off the coast of the United States all placed U.S. leadership on the back foot and required bold responses and new initiatives on the part of Washington. The shock of the Tet Offensive forced a dramatic reassessment of U.S. policy in Vietnam, while the fall of the Berlin Wall and the rapid collapse of the communist bloc in Eastern Europe in the late 1980s proved disorienting to a U.S. foreign policy establishment that had become accustomed to a confrontational relationship with the Soviet Union. And as the current preemptive war in Iraq so clearly illustrates, even when the United States seeks to shape world events to its advantage the results can prove quite unexpected.

Perhaps nowhere has U.S. foreign policy appeared to be so reactive as in the Middle East. In the 1973 Arab-Israeli War the United States was caught off guard by Egypt and Syria's well-coordinated attack on Israel and the Nixon administration was compelled to forge new initiatives to stabilize a region that was quickly becoming Washington's primary geostrategic concern. Nowhere was this more evident than during the energy crisis that rocked the world economy in the wake of the Arab oil embargo and which once again appeared to place American policy makers on the back foot. The Iranian Revolution and the hostage crisis show, yet again, how senior U.S. foreign policy makers found themselves in reactive mode when they faced serious, unforeseen, and shocking developments in the Middle East. The September 11, 2001, terrorist attack was reminiscent of the attack on Pearl Harbor and echoes how poor intelligence left the country wholly unprepared for and stunned by this devastating attack on American soil.

Richard Nixon's historic opening to the People's Republic of China is really the only case study in this book where a proactive U.S. initiative set the stage for a sudden turning point in U.S. foreign policy. Once Washington comprehended the extent of the fissure between China and the Soviet Union, Kissinger and Nixon devised a bold plan to strengthen Washington's hand in its Cold War with Moscow. Nixon's visit to Beijing compelled Moscow to take a conciliatory approach in its relations with the United States in order to counteract the impact of the Sino-American rapprochement. This event fits the pattern of the book in that Nixon and Kissinger conducted the opening to China largely in secret and as such it came as a major surprise to both the American political establishment and the public at large and required a significant reorientation of American thinking in the Cold War.

Of course Nixon's opening to China required a reciprocal gesture on the part of the Chinese, and this underlines the important point that the United States does not act alone on the world stage and what we call U.S. foreign policy necessarily involves a complex interplay between states. Also, as the world's strongest power for much of the twentieth century, the United States was far from a passive bystander to world events but rather through its own policies helped to shape the environment in which all the turning points examined in this book occurred. These points have been worked into the narrative in each case study examined in this volume. The primary goal of this book, however, has been to examine how U.S. policy makers deal with sudden crises or unforeseen developments and to illustrate how, in the very public climate that these surprise events engender, significant shifts or turning points in U.S. foreign policy are likely to result. Despite the increase in the power of the executive branch in the political system over the last one hundred years, Congress, public opinion, the media, and the election cycle all continue to act as a brake on presidential prerogative in matters of foreign policy. This is particularly true in moments of crisis when foreign policy becomes a priority on the national political agenda and it is in such a climate that major turning points in U.S. foreign policy are likely to occur.

Notes

Introduction

1. See, for instance, Frank L. Klingberg, "The Historical Alternation of Moods in American Foreign Policy," *World Politics* 4 (January 1952), 239–73; Jack E. Holmes, *The Mood Interest Theory of American Foreign Policy* (Lexington: University Press of Kentucky, 1985); Brian Pollins and Randall L. Schweller, "Linking the Levels: The Long Wave and Shifts in U.S. Foreign Policy, 1790–1993," *American Journal of Political Science* 43 (April 1999), 431–464; Dexter Perkins, *The American Approach to Foreign Policy* (Cambridge, MA: Harvard University Press, 1953); and Geir Lundestad, "Uniqueness and Pendulum Swings in US Foreign Policy," *International Affairs* 62 (Summer, 1986), 405–21.
2. Detente is a French word describing the "relaxation of tensions" that characterized improved U.S.-Soviet relations for much of the 1970s. See chapter 8.

Chapter 1. The Sinking of the *Maine* and the War of 1898

1. These principles of isolation and expansion were first clearly established by George Washington in his famous Farewell Address of 1796.
2. Issued by President James Monroe in his annual address to Congress in 1823, this doctrine claimed the Western Hemisphere to be off limits to the imperial powers of Europe and sowed the seeds for the principle of American hegemony in the region.
3. Paul T. McCartney, *Power and Progress: American National Identity, the War of 1898 and the Rise of American Imperialism* (Baton Rouge: Louisiana State University Press, 2006), 47.
4. While a strong case could be made that American foreign policy throughout the nineteenth century—with its emphasis on continental expansion and manifest destiny—was imperialist, the term here applies to those who favored territorial expansion beyond the contiguous United States and who believed that American in-

terests should not be limited to the Western Hemisphere. "Isolationist" here refers to those Americans who favored a limited American foreign policy consistent with the parameters set by George Washington and other leaders of the early Republic.

5. Frank Ninkovich, *The United States and Imperialism* (Malden, MA: Blackwell Publishing, 2000), 10.
6. David Healy, *U.S. Expansionism: The Imperialist Urge in the 1890s* (Madison: University of Wisconsin Press, 1970), 38.
7. Ernest May, *Imperial Democracy: The Emergence of America as a Great Power* (New York: Harcourt Brace, 1961).
8. Thomas G. Paterson, "United States Intervention in Cuba, 1898: Interpretation of the Spanish-American-Cuban-Filipino War," *The History Teacher* 29 (May 1996), 350.
9. Healy, *U.S. Expansionism*, 215–17.
10. Ninkovich, *The United States and Imperialism*, 12.
11. May, *Imperial Democracy*, 133–47.
12. Ninkovich, *The United States and Imperialism*, 22.
13. Ibid., 26.
14. Ibid., 24.
15. Ibid.
16. May, *Imperial Democracy*, 120.
17. Ibid., 79.
18. Ibid., 120.
19. Ibid., 126.
20. Ibid., 137.
21. John Offner, *Unwanted War: The Diplomacy of the United States and Spain over Cuba, 1895–1898* (Chapel Hill: University of North Carolina Press, 1992), 123.
22. Ibid., 126.
23. The cause of the explosion that sunk the *Maine* remains an issue of controversy. The report of the 1898 naval board stopped short of accusing the Spanish of deliberate sabotage and intimated that a floating mine was responsible for the explosion. More recent investigations of the *Maine* incident, however, point to the strong possibility that the ship sank following a boiler room explosion.
24. The concept of American exceptionalism—a consistent theme in American history from John Winthrop's vision of "a city upon a hill" in colonial Massachusetts to Manifest Destiny in the nineteenth century—refers to the belief that there is a qualitative difference between New World America and Old World Europe, with the New World considered special and preferable.
25. Offner, *Unwanted War*, 134.
26. May, *Imperial Democracy*, 158.
27. Ninkovich, *The United States and Imperialism*, 26.
28. Paterson, "United States Intervention in Cuba," 351.
29. Frank L. Klingberg, "The Historical Alternation of Moods in American Foreign Policy," *World Politics* 4 (January 1952), 239.
30. May, *Imperial Democracy*, 253.
31. Ninkovich, *The United States and Imperialism*, 34.

32. May, *Imperial Democracy*, 252–53.
33. See Michael Roskin, "From Pearl Harbor to Vietnam: Shifting Generational Paradigms and Foreign Policy," *Political Science Quarterly* 89 (Autumn 1974), 563–88.
34. McCartney, *Power and Progress*, 2.

Chapter 2. The *Lusitania* Crisis and U.S. Entry into World War I
 1. John Milton Cooper, *The Vanity of Power: American Isolation and World War I, 1914–1917* (Westport, CT: Greenwood Press, 1969), 37.
 2. Cooper, *The Vanity of Power*, 17, 69.
 3. Ibid., 19.
 4. H. W. Brands, *Woodrow Wilson* (New York: Macmillan, 2003), 51.
 5. Cooper, *The Vanity of Power*, 20–21.
 6. Akira Iriye, *The Cambridge History of American Foreign Relations, Volume III: The Globalizing of America, 1913–1945* (West Nyack, NY: Cambridge University Press, 1993), 23.
 7. Thomas J. Knock, *To End All Wars: Woodrow Wilson and the Quest for a New World Order* (Princeton, NJ: Princeton University Press, 1992), 33.
 8. John W. Coogan, *The End of Neutrality: The United States, Britain and Maritime Rights, 1899–1915* (Ithaca, NY: Cornell University Press, 1981), 180.
 9. Ross Gregory, *The Origins of American Intervention in World War I* (New York: W. W. Norton, 1971), 41.
10. Coogan, *The End of Neutrality*, 205.
11. Ernest May, *The World War and American Isolation, 1914–1917* (Cambridge, MA: Harvard University Press, 1959), 34–35, and Coogan, *The End of Neutrality*, 205.
12. Cooper, *The Vanity of Power*, 28–32.
13. Ibid., 32.
14. Gregory, *The Origins of American Intervention in World War I*, 54.
15. Knock, *To End All Wars*, 60.
16. Cooper, *The Vanity of Power*, 37.
17. Gregory, *The Origins of American Intervention in World War I*, 65.
18. Ibid., 66.
19. Cooper, *The Vanity of Power*, 107, and Gregory, *The Origins of American Intervention in World War I*, 72.
20. Knock, *To End All Wars*, 61, and Cooper, *The Vanity of Power*, 108.
21. Michael H. Hunt, *Crises in U.S. Foreign Policy* (New Haven, CT: Yale University Press, 1996), 34–35.
22. Gregory, *The Origins of American Intervention in World War I*, 79.
23. Ibid., 90.
24. Knock, *To End All Wars*, 77.
25. Iriye, *The Cambridge History of American Foreign Relations*, 30.
26. Knock, *To End All Wars*, 103.
27. Gregory, *The Origins of American Intervention in World War I*, 116.
28. Godfrey Hodgson, *Woodrow Wilson's Right Hand: The Life of Colonel Edward M. House* (New Haven, CT: Yale University Press, 2006), 136.
29. Cooper, *The Vanity of Power*, 176–77.

30. Hunt, *Crises in U.S. Foreign Policy*, 52–53.

31. Iriye, *The Cambridge History of American Foreign Relations*, 30.

32. In 1917 the Bolshevik Party successfully overthrew the pro-western government of Russia and established the Soviet Republic. The decision of the new government to withdraw from World War I and sign a separate peace treaty with Germany in 1917 was bitterly resented by the western allies. This, together with western fears of the spread of communism, led to the post-war isolation of Soviet Russia.

Chapter 3. The Attack on Pearl Harbor and World War II

1. Daniel Snowman, *America Since 1920* (London: Heinemann Educational Books, 1978), 64.

2. Bernard Fensterwald Jr., "The Anatomy of American 'Isolationism' and Expansionism, Part II," *Journal of Conflict Resolution* 2 (December 1958), 307.

3. Snowman, *America since 1920*, 64.

4. Bernard Fensterwald, Jr., "The Anatomy of American 'Isolationism' and Expansionism, Part I," *Journal of Conflict Resolution* 2 (June, 1958), 117.

5. Burt Solomon, "Isolationism be Damned," *National Journal* 31 (April 17, 1999), 1006–1008.

6. Roskin, "From Pearl Harbor to Vietnam," 577.

7. Fensterwald, Jr., "The Anatomy of American 'Isolationism' and Expansionism, Part I," 121.

8. Shortly before his death in 1924, President Wilson predicted prophetically, "The great tragedy of the last six years is the fact that American failure to accept world responsibility means that the job will have to be done again within twenty years and at ten times the cost" (Fensterwald, Jr. 1958a, 122 fn).

9. Foster Rhea Dulles, *America's Rise to World Power: 1898–1945* (New York: Harper and Brothers, 1954), 160.

10. Selig Adler, *The Isolationist Impulse: Its Twentieth Century Reaction* (New York: Collier, 1961), 269.

11. World War II officially began in September 1939 after Hitler invaded Poland and France and Great Britain declared war in response.

12. Dan Scroop, "September 11th, Pearl Harbor and the Uses of Presidential Power," *Cambridge Review of International Affairs* 15 (2002), 322.

13. Fensterwald, "The Anatomy of American 'Isolationism' and Expansionism, Part I," 124.

14. Herbert Feis, *The Road to Pearl Harbor* (Princeton, NJ: Princeton University Press, 1971), 7–8.

15. Feis, *The Road to Pearl Harbor*, 60.

16. Fensterwald, "The Anatomy of American 'Isolationism' and Expansionism, Part I," 125.

17. Paul Duke, "The Greatest Generation?" *Virginia Quarterly Review* 78 (Winter 2002), 23.

18. Duke, "The Greatest Generation?" 23.

19. Snowman, *America since 1920*, 66.

20. Dulles, *America's Rise to World Power*, 175.

21. Ibid., 188.
22. John C., Chalberg, ed., *Isolationism: Opposing Viewpoints* (San Diego: Greenhaven Press, 1995), 137.
23. In exchange for fifty refitted American warships, Britain issued ninety-nine year leases to the United States so it could establish military bases on British possessions such as Jamaica, Bermuda and Trinidad. Roosevelt concluded the deal acting on his own authority, leading to charges that it was an illegal act of war.
24. Snowman, *America since 1920*, 67.
25. Dulles, *America's Rise to World Power*, 204 and Adler, *The Isolationist Impulse*, 257.
26. Dulles, *America's Rise to World Power*, 189.
27. Ibid., 195.
28. Duke, "The Greatest Generation?" 23.
29. Adler, *The Isolationist Impulse*, 252–53.
30. Some two million copies of the book were purchased, illustrating internationalism's growing popularity.
31. Dulles, *America's Rise to World Power*, 210.
32. Adler, *The Isolationist Impulse*, 308.
33. Dulles, *America's Rise to World Power*, 212.
34. Ibid.
35. Adler, *The Isolationist Impulse*, 312.
36. Japan's defeat of Russia marked the first time an Asiatic power defeated a European power.
37. Hunt, *Crises in U.S. Foreign Policy*, 57.
38. Dulles, *America's Rise to World Power*, 163.
39. Fensterwald, "The Anatomy of American 'Isolationism' and Expansionism, Part I," 123.
40. Ronald H. Spector, *Eagle Against the Sun: The American War with Japan* (New York: Free Press, 1985), 63.
41. Feis, *The Road to Pearl Harbor*, 6.
42. John Toland, *Infamy: Pearl Harbor and its Aftermath* (New York: Berkeley Books, 1972), 331.
43. Hunt, *Crises in U.S. Foreign Policy*, 59.
44. Stimson was Secretary of State in Hoover's Cabinet and Secretary of War under Taft.
45. Feis, *The Road to Pearl Harbor*, 72.
46. Snowman, *America since 1920*, 75.
47. Spector, *Eagle Against the Sun*, 64.
48. John C. Zimmerman, "Pearl Harbor Revisionism: Robert Stinnett's *Day of Deceit*," *Intelligence and National Security* 17 (Summer 2002), 134.
49. Feis, *The Road to Pearl Harbor*, 252.
50. Ibid., 269.
51. The NEI included Java, Sumatra and Borneo, in present-day Indonesia.
52. Feis, *The Road to Pearl Harbor*, 277.
53. Ibid., 109.
54. Hunt, *Crises in U.S. Foreign Policy*, 67.
55. Zimmerman, "Pearl Harbor Revisionism," 131.

56. Spector, *Eagle Against the Sun,* 3.
57. Its hull is now an underwater memorial to the event.
58. While the Senate voted unanimously, one member in the House, Montana pacifist Jeanette Rankin, dissented.
59. Snowman, *America since 1920,* 77.
60. Arthur Krock, "Unity Clicks into Place: Capital Dissensions Fade Out in Necessities of Common Cause," *New York Times,* December 8, 1941.
61. Arthur Krock, "Six Months after Pearl Harbor," *New York Times,* June 7, 1942.
62. Ralph Barton Perry, "Care Held Needed to Preserve Unity Under Adversity," *New York Times,* February 1, 1942.
63. Perry, "Care Held Needed to Preserve Unity Under Adversity."
64. Adler, *The Isolationist Impulse,* 289.
65. Laurence Goldstein, "The Legacy of Hiroshima," *Michigan Quarterly Review* 38 (Summer 1999), 473, 478.
66. Roger Daniels, "Incarcerating Japanese Americans," *Magazine of History* 16 (Spring 2002), 19.
67. Adler, *The Isolationist Impulse,* 294.
68. Dulles, *America's Rise to World Power,* 207.
69. Zimmerman, "Pearl Harbor Revisionism," 127.
70. Snowman, *America since 1920,* 98–99.
71. Dulles, *America's Rise to World Power,* 207.
72. Adler, *The Isolationist Impulse,* 294.
73. Ibid., 315.
74. Solomon, "Isolationism be Damned," 1008.
75. Dulles, *America's Rise to World Power,* 219.
76. Roberta Wohlstetter, "Cuba and Pearl Harbor: Hindsight and Foresight," *Foreign Affairs* 43 (1965), 698.
77. Zimmerman, "Pearl Harbor Revisionism," 130.

Chapter 4. The Korean War and the Cold War in Asia

1. Communist efforts were defeated in Greece, Turkey, and Berlin.
2. Adam B. Ulam, "Washington, Moscow and the Korean War," in *Korea: Cold War and Limited War,* 2nd edition, ed. Allen Guttman (Lexington, MA: D. C. Heath and Company, 1972), 277.
3. Kim was mistaken when he convinced Soviet Premier Josef Stalin, on whom Kim was totally dependent, that the invasion would be quick and that the United States would not intervene. See Paul Wingrove, "Who Started Korea?" *History Today* 50 (2000), 44–46.
4. David Rees, *Korea: The Limited War* (New York: St. Martin's Press, 1964), 22–23.
5. Walter LaFeber, "Crossing the 38th: The Cold War in Microcosm," in *Reflections on the Cold War: A Quarter Century of American Foreign Policy,* eds. Lynn H Miller and Ronald W. Preussen (Philadelphia: Temple University Press, 1974), 79.
6. Arnold A. Offner, "'Another Such Victory:' President Truman, American Foreign Policy, And the Cold War," *Diplomatic History* 23 (Spring 1999), 144.
7. LaFeber, "Crossing the 38th," 39.

8. Michael Hickey, *The Korean War: The West Confronts Communism* (Woodstock, NY: Overland Press, 1999), 40.

9. Rees, *Korea: The Limited War,* 28. This from the same president who made the decision to drop atomic bombs on Japan in 1945 and who then risked World War III by conducting the Berlin Airlift in 1948–1949.

10. Hunt, *Crises in U.S. Foreign Policy,* 175. The United States was able to get the Security Council resolution passed because the Soviets, who would surely have vetoed the measure, were boycotting the Council as a protest against communist China's exclusion from the United Nations. The Soviets would never make the mistake of boycotting the UNSC again.

11. Offner, "'Another Such Victory,'" 148.

12. Although the vast majority of the U.N.-authorized force consisted of U.S. troops, its official name was the United Nations Command and that is how it is referred to in this chapter.

13. Several mock landings were staged elsewhere as diversionary feints.

14. Burton I. Kaufman, *The Korean War: Challenges in Crisis, Credibility, and Command* (Philadelphia: Temple University Press, 1986), 57–59.

15. LaFeber, "Crossing the 38th," 83.

16. Rosemary Foot, *The Wrong War: American Policy and the Dimensions of the Korean Conflict, 1950–1953* (Ithaca, NY: Cornell University Press, 1985), 73.

17. Kaufman, *The Korean War,* 9.

18. Offner, "'Another Such Victory,'" 131.

19. Rees, *Korea: The Limited War,* 100.

20. Allen Guttman, *Korea: Cold War and Limited War,* 2nd ed. (Lexington, MA: D. C. Heath and Company, 1972), 14. Although those same orders carried precautions in case he provoked Soviet or Chinese entry in the war, MacArthur paid more attention to the "unhampered" part of the message and ignored the cautionary parts.

21. Rees, *Korea: The Limited War,* 108.

22. LaFeber, "Crossing the 38th," 74–75.

23. Offner, "'Another Such Victory,'" 150.

24. Michael H. Hunt, "Beijing and the Korean Crisis: June 1950–June 1951," *Political Science Quarterly* 107 (1992), 464.

25. Frederick F. Siegel, *Troubled Journey: From Pearl Harbor to Ronald Reagan* (New York: Hill and Wang, 1984), 83.

26. Robert Leckie, *Conflict: The History of the Korean War, 1950–53* (New York: G. P. Putnam's Sons, 1962), 212.

27. LaFeber, "Crossing the 38th," 84.

28. Leckie, *Conflict: The History of the Korean War, 1950–53,* 246.

29. Interestingly, to this day, China has been able to win only the last of these three items but not until a quarter century after the Korean War ended and for reasons unconnected to Korea (see chapter 8).

30. Offner, "'Another Such Victory,'" 151.

31. Rees, *Korea: The Limited War,* 201.

32. Guttman, *Korea: Cold War and Limited War,* 15.

33. Adler, *The Isolationist Impulse,* 381.

34. Walter Mills, "Truman and MacArthur," in *Korea: Cold War and Limited War*, 2nd edition, ed. Allen Guttman (Lexington, MA: D.C. Heath and Company, 1972), 78–79.

35. Guttman, *Korea: Cold War and Limited War*, 24.

36. Leckie, *Conflict: The History of the Korean War, 1950–53*, 278–79.

37. Hickey, *The Korean War*, 99.

38. Leckie, *Conflict: The History of the Korean War, 1950–53*, 214.

39. He also used "police action" to underscore his determination to keep the war limited.

40. Hunt, "East Asia in Henry Luce's 'American Century,'" *Diplomatic History* 23 (Spring 1999), 328.

41. John E. Mueller, *War, Presidents, and Public Opinion* (New York: John Wiley and Sons, 1973), 51, 202.

42. The Democratic majority in the House shrank from ninety-two to thirty-six and from twelve to two in the Senate. Powerful Democrats were defeated, including Majority Leader Scott Lucas, Majority Whip Francis Myers and Millard Tydings, who suffered payback for his critical report of Senator McCarthy's communist witchhunt.

43. John Edward Wiltz, "The Korean War and American Society," in *The Korean War: A 25-Year Perspective*, ed. Francis H. Heller (Lawrence, KS: Regents Press, 1975), 130.

44. Wiltz, "The Korean War and American Society," 130.

45. Ibid., 132.

46. Dulles, *America's Rise to World Power*, 264.

47. Kaufman, *The Korean War*, 128.

48. Other factors contributed to Truman's sagging poll numbers, including the constant drumbeat of Republican charges that Truman's government, especially Secretary Acheson's State Department, was riddled by corruption and communist infiltration.

49. Kaufman, *The Korean War*, 292.

50. Foot, *The Wrong War*, 34, 205.

51. Adler, *The Isolationist Impulse*, 383.

52. Dulles, *America's Rise to World Power*, 271.

53. Foot, *The Wrong War*, 34, 205.

54. Kaufman, *The Korean War*, 319.

55. Mueller, *War, Presidents, and Public Opinion*, 105.

56. Dulles, *America's Rise to World Power*, 271–72.

57. Kathryn Weathersby, "The Korean War Revisited," *Wilson Quarterly* (Summer 1999), 95.

58. David Ekbladh, "How to Build a Nation," *Wilson Quarterly* (Winter 2004), 12.

59. Kaufman, *The Korean War*, 349.

60. Lawrence S. Kaplan, "The Korean War and U.S. Foreign Relations: The Case of NATO," in *The Korean War: A 25-Year Perspective*, ed. Francis H. Heller (Lawrence, KS: Regents Press, 1975), 40–41.

61. Offner, "'Another Such Victory,'" 149.

62. Kaufman, *The Korean War*, 28, 61.

63. Kaplan, "The Korean War and U.S. Foreign Relations," 69.

Chapter 5. The Sputnik Crisis and the Nuclear Age

1. Paul Dickson, *Sputnik: Shock of the Century* (New York: Berkeley Publishing Group, 2003), 108.

2. Robert A. Divine, *The Sputnik Challenge: Eisenhower's Response to the Soviet Satellite* (New York: Oxford University Press, 1993), vii.

3. John Lewis Gaddis, *We Now Know: Rethinking Cold War History* (New York: Oxford University Press, 1997), 226–31.

4. Divine, *The Sputnik Challenge,* 4.

5. Ibid., xiv.

6. Walter A. McDougall, *The Heavens and the Earth: A Political History of the Space Age* (Baltimore, MD: Johns Hopkins University Press, 1997), 148.

7. Melvin Small, *Democracy and Diplomacy: The Impact of Domestic Politics on U.S. Foreign Policy, 1789–1994* (Baltimore: Johns Hopkins University Press, 1996), 103.

8. Divine, *The Sputnik Challenge,* xv–xvi.

9. Gaddis, *We Now Know,* 183.

10. Divine, *The Sputnik Challenge,* 44–45.

11. John Lewis Gaddis, *Strategies of Containment: A Critical Appraisal of American National Security Policy During the Cold War* (New York: Oxford University Press, 1982), 183.

12. Donald L. Michael, "The Beginning of the Space Age and American Public Opinion," *The Public Opinion Quarterly,* 24 (Winter, 1960), 577.

13. Dickson, *Sputnik,* 139.

14. McGeorge Bundy, *Danger and Survival: Choices about the Bomb in the First Fifty Years* (New York: Random House, 1998), 342.

15. Divine, *The Sputnik Challenge,* 43.

16. Bundy, *Danger and Survival,* 73.

17. Ibid., 338.

18. Ibid., 339.

19. Divine, *The Sputnik Challenge,* 62.

20. Ibid., 73.

21. Bundy, *Danger and Survival,* 336.

22. Gaddis, *Strategies of Containment,* 184.

23. Bundy, *Danger and Survival,* 336.

24. Divine, *The Sputnik Challenge,* 73.

25. McDougall, *The Heavens and the Earth,* 156.

26. Divine, *The Sputnik Challenge,* 92.

27. The very existence of Explorer is illustrative of the depth of interservice rivalry in the field of missile production in the American armed forces. Gen. John Medaris, head of the Army Ballistic Missile Agency, and his chief engineer, former Nazi rocketeer Verner Von Braun, had at times concealed their work on this project after the Navy was given control of the Vanguard program while all the while using public and private pressure to secure funding from the White House.

28. Divine, *The Sputnik Challenge,* 96.

29. Ibid., 110.

30. Ibid., 165.
31. John A. Douglass, "A Certain Future: Sputnik, American Higher Education, and the Survival of a Nation," in *Reconsidering Sputnik: Forty Years Since the Soviet Satellite*, ed. Roger Launus (New York: Routledge, 2000), 29.
32. Divine, *The Sputnik Challenge*, 125.
33. McDougall, *The Heavens and the Earth*, 176.
34. Bundy, *Danger and Survival*, 47.
35. Divine, *The Sputnik Challenge*, viii.

Chapte 6. The Cuban Missile Crisis and the Brink of Nuclear War
1. John Lewis Gaddis, *We Now Know: Rethinking Cold War History* (New York: Oxford University Press, 1997) 260.
2. Gaddis, *We Now Know*, 261.
3. Thomas G. Paterson, "Fixation with Cuba: The Bay of Pigs, Missile Crisis and Covert War Against Fidel Castro," in *Kennedy's Quest for Victory: American Foreign Policy 1961–1963*, ed. Thomas G. Paterson (New York: Oxford University Press, 1989), 127.
4. Gaddis Smith, *The Last Days of the Monroe Doctrine, 1945–1993* (New York: Hill and Wang, 1994), 91.
5. Gaddis, *We Now Know*, 178.
6. James A. Nathan, *Anatomy of the Cuban Missile Crisis* (Westport, CT: Greenwood Press, 2000), 50.
7. White, *The Cuban Missile Crisis*, 32.
8. Ibid., 25.
9. Paterson, "Fixation with Cuba," 123–25.
10. Nathan, *Anatomy of the Cuban Missile Crisis*, 67.
11. Anna Kasten Nelson, "President Kennedy's National Security Policy: A Reconsideration," *Reviews in American History* 19 (March 1991), 11.
12. Paterson, "Fixation with Cuba," 130.
13. Kennedy's decision not to provide air support was driven primarily by his strong desire to distance the United States from the invasion so he could plausibly deny American culpability.
14. Nathan, *Anatomy of the Cuban Missile Crisis*, 67–68.
15. Ibid., 71.
16. Lawrence Freedman, *Kennedy's Wars: Berlin, Cuba, Laos, and Vietnam* (New York: Oxford University Press, 2000), 153.
17. James G. Blight, Bruce J. Allyn, and David A. Welch, eds., *Cuba on the Brink: Castro, the Missile Crisis, and Soviet Collapse* (Lanham, MD: Rowan and Littlefield, 2002), 344.
18. Smith, *The Last Days of the Monroe Doctrine, 1945–1993*, 99.
19. Robert Dallek, *An Unfinished Life: John F. Kennedy, 1917–1963* (Boston: Little, Brown and Co., 2003), 536.
20. Don Munton and David A. Welch, *The Cuban Missile Crisis: A Concise History* (New York: Oxford University Press, 2007), 30–31.
21. Munton and Welch, *The Cuban Missile Crisis*, 33–40.

22. Ibid., 40–1.
23. Nathan, *Anatomy of the Cuban Missile Crisis,* 84–85.
24. James T. Graham, "Kennedy, Cuba, and the Press," *Journalism History* 24 (Summer 1998), 63.
25. Munton and Welch, *The Cuban Missile Crisis,* 46.
26. Freedman, *Kennedy's Wars,* 168.
27. Nathan, *Anatomy of the Cuban Missile Crisis,* 90.
28. See for example Graham T. Allison, and Philip Zelikow, eds., *Essence of Decision: Explaining the Cuban Missile Crisis* (New York: Pearson Longman, 1999).
29. Mark J. White, *The Cuban Missile Crisis* (New York: McMillan, 1996), 160.
30. Nathan, *Anatomy of the Cuban Missile Crisis,* 94.
31. Munton and Welch, *The Cuban Missile Crisis,* 52.
32. Graham, "Kennedy, Cuba, and the Press," 64.
33. Nathan, *Anatomy of the Cuban Missile Crisis,* 94.
34. Munton and Welch, *The Cuban Missile Crisis,* 64–65.
35. Graham, "Kennedy, Cuba and the Press," 63–64.
36. Munton and Welch, *The Cuban Missile Crisis,* 69–70.
37. Freedman, *Kennedy's Wars,* 209.
38. Munton and Welch, *The Cuban Missile Crisis,* 78–79.
39. Dallek, *An Unfinished Life,* 574.
40. Nathan, *Anatomy of the Cuban Missile Crisis,* 96.
41. Dallek, *An Unfinished Life,* 620.
42. Munton and Welch, *The Cuban Missile Crisis,* 100.
43. Smith, *The Last Days of the Monroe Doctrine, 1945–1993,* 111.
44. Graham, "Kennedy, Cuba, and the Press," 67.
45. Ibid., 66–67.
46. Nathan, *Anatomy of the Cuban Missile Crisis,* 119, 125.
47. Gaddis, *We Now Know,* 279.
48. Nathan, *Anatomy of the Cuban Missile Crisis,* 115–20.

Chapter 7. The Tet Offensive and the Vietnam War

1. James W Mooney, and Thomas R. West, eds., *Vietnam: A History and Anthology* (Rancho Cucamonga, CA: Brandywine Press, 1994), 172.
2. Marilyn B. Young, *The Vietnam Wars, 1945–1990* (New York: Harper Collins, 1991), 220.
3. *Indochina* in this context refers to present-day Vietnam, Cambodia, and Laos.
4. The Atlantic Charter was a joint British and American declaration outlining a vision for a post–WWII world where, among other things, subject peoples would have the right to self-determination.
5. Gaddis, *We Now Know,* 156.
6. George C. Herring, *America's Longest War: The United States and Vietnam, 1950–1975* (New York: McGraw Hill, 2002), 11.
7. Patrick Hearden, *The Tragedy of Vietnam* (New York: Pearson Longman, 2004), 31.
8. Herring, *America's Longest War,* 29.
9. Gaddis, *We Now Know,* 163.

10. Young, *The Vietnam Wars, 1945–1990*, 31.
11. This policy would eventually result in the creation of the Southeast Asian Treaty Organization (SEATO) with a membership comprised of the United States, Great Britain, France, Australia, New Zealand, the Philippines, Pakistan, and Thailand. SEATO never materialized as a major factor in the politics of Southeast Asia partly because key states such as India and Indonesia refused to join and partly because its members were far from united on their policies in the region (for example, only Australia, New Zealand, and the Philippines would actively support American intervention in Vietnam).
12. Young, *The Vietnam Wars, 1945–1990*, 38.
13. Hearden, *The Tragedy of Vietnam*, 55.
14. Herring, *America's Longest War*, 53–54.
15. Ibid., 68–70.
16. Gaddis, *We Now Know*, 190.
17. Herring, *America's Longest War*, 102.
18. Hearden, *The Tragedy of Vietnam*, 80.
19. Lloyd C. Gardner, *Pay Any Price: Lyndon Johnson and the Wars for Vietnam* (Chicago: Ivan R. Dee, 1995), 65.
20. Herring, *America's Longest War*, 123.
21. Ibid., 129.
22. David Kaiser, *American Tragedy: Kennedy, Johnson, and the Origins of the Vietnam War* (Cambridge, MA: Belknap Press, 2000), 289.
23. Melvin Small, *Antiwarriors: The Vietnam War and the Battle for America's Hearts and Minds* (Lanham, MD: SR Books, 2004), 30.
24. Herring, *America's Longest War*, 138.
25. Kaiser, *American Tragedy*, 307.
26. Significant controversy surrounds the second of these two incidents as the evidence indicates that the *Maddox* was not fired upon on this occasion and that the Pentagon made no effort to publicly correct initial reports to the contrary.
27. Hearden, *The Tragedy of Vietnam*, 99.
28. Herring, *America's Longest War*, 147–48.
29. Kaiser, *American Tragedy*, 311.
30. Herring, *America's Longest War*, 149.
31. Ibid., 158.
32. Hearden, *The Tragedy of Vietnam*, 109–11.
33. Ibid., 156.
34. Kaiser, *American Tragedy*, 443.
35. Hearden, *The Tragedy of Vietnam*, 201.
36. Small, *Antiwarriors*, 50.
37. Herring, *America's Longest War*, 205.
38. Hearden, *The Tragedy of Vietnam*, 131.
39. Young, *The Vietnam Wars, 1945–1990*, 214–15.
40. Ibid., 215–16.
41. Ronald H. Spector, *After Tet: The Bloodiest Year In Vietnam* (New York: The Free Press, 1993), xvi.

42. Larry Berman, "The Tet Offensive" in *The Tet Offensive*, eds. Marc Jason Gilbert and William Head (Westport, CT: Praeger, 1996), 19.

43. Herring, *America's Longest War*, 232–33.

44. Small, *Antiwarriors*, 90 and Herring, *America's Longest War*, 243.

45. Robert Buzzanco, "The Myth of Tet: American Failure and the Politics of War" in *The Tet Offensive*, eds. Marc Jason Gilbert and William Head (Westport, CT: Praeger, 1996), 231.

46. Spector, *After Tet*, 5.

47. Berman, "The Tet Offensive," 31.

48. Herring, *America's Longest War*, 241.

49. Spector, *After Tet*, 311–12.

50. Young, *The Vietnam Wars, 1945–1990*, 230.

51. Eugene McCarthy's quest to win the Democratic nomination had been eclipsed by the entry of Robert Kennedy into the campaign. But RFK's assassination after the California primary threw the Democratic race into turmoil and ultimately the party bosses maneuvered Vice President Humphrey into the nomination, alienating antiwar activists many of whom protested in Chicago.

52. Herring, *America's Longest War*, 271.

53. Small, *Antiwarriors*, 162.

54. Young, *The Vietnam Wars, 1945–1990*, 241.

55. Ibid., 243.

56. Buzzanco, "The Myth of Tet," 248.

Chapter 8. The U.S. Opening to China and Detente

1. A. Doak Barnett, *China Policy: Old Problems and New Challenges* (Washington, D.C.: The Brookings Institution, 1977), 2.

2. Harry Harding, *A Fragile Relationship: The United States and China since 1972* (Washington, D.C.: The Brookings Institution, 1992), 3.

3. Tad Szulc, *The Illusion of Peace: Foreign Policy in the Nixon Years* (New York: Viking Press, 1978), 109–10.

4. Szulc, *The Illusion of Peace*, 64.

5. After the 1917 Bolshevik Revolution in Russia, Lenin, and to a much greater degree Stalin, turned against many revolutionary allies. The same holds for the other great revolution of the twentieth century, the Islamic Revolution in Iran, where Ayatollah Khomeini's radical allies quashed moderate supporters of the Revolution (see chapter 9).

6. John Robert Greene, *The Limits of Power: The Nixon and Ford Administrations* (Bloomington: Indiana University Press, 1992), 108.

7. Robert G. Sutter, *The China Quandary: Domestic Determinants of U.S. China Policy, 1972—1982* (Boulder, CO: Westview Press, 1983), ix.

8. Stephen E. Ambrose, *Nixon: The Education of a Politician 1913–1962*, vol. 1 (New York: Simon and Schuster, 1987), 460.

9. Richard C. Thornton, *The Nixon-Kissinger Years: Reshaping America's Foreign Policy* (New York: Paragon House, 1989), 11.

10. Greene, *The Limits of Power*, 108.

11. Claude A. Buss, *China: The People's Republic of China and Richard Nixon* (San Francisco: W. H. Freeman, 1974), 83.

12. Buss, *China,* 68.

13. In 1979, only four years after communist North Vietnam militarily united South Vietnam, China launched military operations against Vietnam along their common border to teach Vietnam a lesson. Interestingly, it was China that was taught a lesson. The experienced and battle-tested Vietnamese soldiers got the better of the Chinese.

14. Barnett, *China Policy,* 3.

15. Greene, *The Limits of Power,* 107.

16. Michael Schaller, *The United States and China in the Twentieth Century* (New York: Oxford University Press, 1979), 163.

17. Sutter, *The China Quandary,* 102.

18. Szulc, *The Illusion of Peace,* 111.

19. Kwan Ha Yim, ed., *China & the U.S., 1964–1972* (New York: Facts on File, Inc., 1975), 216–17. While Nixon was the first president to make such a reference, his Undersecretary of State, Elliot L. Richardson, made the same reference at a conference nearly a year earlier. See Seyom Brown, *The Crises of Power: An Interpretation of United States Foreign Policy During the Kissinger Years* (New York: Columbia University Press, 1979), 34.

20. Leonard A. Kusnitz, *Public Opinion and Foreign Policy: America's China Policy, 1949–1979* (Westport, CT: Greenwood Press, 1984), 132.

21. Buss, *China,* 94.

22. On October 13, Nixon received a petition signed by more than three-fourths of the members of the House of Representatives strongly opposing Taiwan's expulsion; twelve days later, Taiwan was expelled anyway.

23. Schaller, *The United States and China in the Twentieth Century,* 168.

24. The Chinese, who are perhaps the best ping-pong players in the world, roundly trounced the Americans.

25. Kusnitz, *Public Opinion and Foreign Policy,* 135.

26. Thornton, *The Nixon-Kissinger Years,* 145–46.

27. Robert D. Schulzinger, *Henry Kissinger: Doctor of Diplomacy* (New York: Columbia University Press, 1989), 3.

28. Roger Morris, *Uncertain Greatness: Henry Kissinger and American Foreign Policy* (New York: Harper and Row: 1977), 63. Nixon was from California and Kissinger is from Germany and speaks English with a heavy accent.

29. Szulc, *The Illusion of Peace,* 189.

30. Patrick J. Haney, "The Nixon Administration and Middle East Crises: Theory and Evidence of Presidential Management of Foreign Policy Decision Making," *Political Research Quarterly* 47 (December 1994), 942.

31. Szulc, *The Illusion of Peace,* 12–13.

32. Morris, *Uncertain Greatness,* 92–93.

33. Szulc, *The Illusion of Peace,* 111.

34. Harding, *A Fragile Relationship,* 40.

35. Greene, *The Limits of Power,* 108.

36. Schaller, *The United States and China in the Twentieth Century*, 165.
37. Morris, *Uncertain Greatness*, 185.
38. Harding, *A Fragile Relationship*, 37–38.
39. Morris, *Uncertain Greatness*, 205.
40. Even though the state dinner was a ruse all along, General Khan made sure his kitchen personnel prepared a sumptuous meal in case a curious reporter called to inquire about the menu. See Szulc, *The Illusion of Peace*, 406.
41. See Greene, *The Limits of Power*, 112 and Harding, *A Fragile Relationship*, 43.
42. Szulc, *The Illusion of Peace*, 410–11.
43. In the movie *Star Trek: The Undiscovered Country*, Spock convinces Kirk that Kirk is the only man for the job of opening relations with the dreaded Klingons despite, and *because* of, Kirk's personal and well known loathing of the Klingon Empire. "We have a saying on Vulcan," says Spock, "Only Nixon can go to China."
44. Kusnitz, *Public Opinion and Foreign Policy*, 138.
45. Schulzinger, *Henry Kissinger*, 94.
46. Ibid., 100.
47. Barnett, *China Policy*, 13.
48. Sutter, *The China Quandary*, 21.
49. Barnett, *China Policy*, 14–15.
50. Kusnitz, *Public Opinion and Foreign Policy*, 139.
51. Ibid., 141.
52. Harding, *A Fragile Relationship*, 72, 88.
53. Sutter, *The China Quandary*, 73.
54. Kusnitz, *Public Opinion and Foreign Policy*, 144.
55. Sutter, *The China Quandary*, 90–91.
56. Harding, *A Fragile Relationship*, 82–83.
57. Ibid., 72–73, 83–84.
58. Barnett, *China Policy*, 14.
59. Kusnitz, *Public Opinion and Foreign Policy*, 146.
60. Harding, *A Fragile Relationship*, 6.
61. Schaller, *The United States and China in the Twentieth Century*, 192.
62. Sutter, *The China Quandary*, 80.
63. Harding, *A Fragile Relationship*, 102.
64. Ibid.
65. Harding, *A Fragile Relationship*, 4.
66. Ibid., 325.
67. Indo-American relations have improved considerably in the new century. President Bush's March 2006 visit led to a landmark agreement on nuclear energy.
68. Greene, *The Limits of Power*, 112.
69. Having been part of the team that joined Nixon in China, Green was one of the few State Department hands Kissinger trusted.
70. Sutter, *The China Quandary*, 2.
71. Ibid., 141.
72. Ibid., 3.
73. Brown, *The Crises of Power*, 32.

Chapter 9. The October 1973 Arab-Israeli War and the Energy Crisis

1. The Middle East spans North Africa, the Eastern Mediterranean, and the Persian Gulf. Except for Turkey, Israel, and Iran, all the other countries in the Middle East contain majority Arab populations, including Egypt in North Africa, Lebanon, and Syria in the Eastern Mediterranean, and Iraq and Saudi Arabia in the oil-rich Persian Gulf.
2. To most Israelis, this war is known as the Yom Kippur War because the Arabs attacked on Yom Kippur, the Jewish Day of Atonement. To most Arabs, this war is called the Ramadan War because it occurred during Ramadan, the Muslim Holy Month of Fasting. Here, we refer to it as the October War.
3. Schulzinger, *Henry Kissinger,* 148.
4. Greene, *The Limits of Power,* 120.
5. Steven L. Spiegel, *The Other Arab-Israeli Conflict: Making America's Middle East Policy, from Truman to Reagan* (Chicago: University of Chicago Press, 1985).
6. Spiegel, *The Other Arab-Israeli Conflict,* 212–13.
7. Thomas Parker, *The Road to Camp David: U.S. Negotiating Strategy Toward the Arab-Israeli Conflict* (New York: Peter Lang, 1989), 17.
8. William B. Quandt, *Peace Process: American Diplomacy and the Arab-Israeli Conflict Since 1967,* 3rd ed. (Washington, D.C.: Brookings Institution, 2005), 103.
9. Spiegel, *The Other Arab-Israeli Conflict,* 181, 185.
10. Quandt, *Peace Process,* 28.
11. Spiegel, *The Other Arab-Israeli Conflict,* 237.
12. Edward R. F. Sheehan, *The Arabs, Israelis, and Kissinger: A Secret History of American Diplomacy in the Middle East* (New York: Reader's Digest Press, 1976), 26; Joe Stork, *Middle East Oil, and the Energy Crisis* (New York: Monthly Review Press, 1975), 218; and Thornton, *The Nixon-Kissinger Years,* 240.
13. Harold H. Saunders, *The Other Walls: The Politics of the Arab-Israeli Peace Process* (Washington, D.C.: American Enterprise Institute for Public Policy Research, 1985), 11.
14. T. G. Fraser, *The USA and the Middle East since World War II* (New York: St. Martin's Press, 1989), 102.
15. G. Matthew Bonham, Michael J. Shapiro, and Thomas L. Trumble, "The October War: Changes in Cognitive Orientation Toward the Middle East Conflict, *International Studies Quarterly* 23 (March 1979), 6.
16. Szulc, *The Illusion of Peace,* 706.
17. Bonham, et. al., "The October War," 7.
18. Abraham Rabinovich, *The Yom Kippur War: The Epic Encounter that Transformed the Middle East* (New York: Schocken Books, 2004), 8.
19. Spiegel, *The Other Arab-Israeli Conflict,* 249.
20. Ibid., 245.
21. Walter Laquer, *Confrontation: The Middle East and World Politics* (New York: Quadrangle/New York Times Book Co., 1974), 126.
22. Rabinovich, *The Yom Kippur War,* 496–97.
23. Sheehan, *The Arabs, Israelis, and Kissinger,* 33.
24. Brown, *The Crises of Power,* 95.

25. Quandt, *Peace Process,* 114.

26. Ibid.

27. Thornton, *The Nixon-Kissinger Years,* 248–49.

28. WSAG members included White House Chief of Staff Al Haig, Chairman of the Joint Chiefs of Staff Adm. Thomas Moorer, Kissinger's deputy Brent Scowcroft and CIA Director William Colby.

29. Brown, *The Crises of Power,* 99.

30. Seth Tillman, *The United States in the Middle East: Interests and Obstacles* (Bloomington: Indiana University Press, 1982), 256.

31. Haney, "The Nixon Administration and Middle East Crises," 948.

32. Greene, *The Limits of Power,* 127.

33. Laquer, *Confrontation,* 216.

34. Szulc, *The Illusion of Peace* Szulc, 212.

35. Joe Stork, *Middle East Oil and the Energy Crisis* (New York: Monthly Review Press, 1975), 211.

36. The Arab members of OPEC are Algeria, Iraq, Kuwait, Libya, Qatar, Saudi Arabia, and the United Arab Emirates. The non-Arab members are Angola, Ecuador, Iran, Nigeria, and Venezuela.

37. Vo Xuan Han, *Oil, the Persian Gulf States, and the United States* (Westport, CT: Praeger, 1994), 23.

38. Richard Chadbourn Weisberg, *The Politics of Crude Oil Pricing in the Middle East, 1970–1975* (Berkeley, CA: Institute of International Studies, 1977), 146.

39. Weisberg, *The Politics of Crude Oil Pricing in the Middle East, 1970–1975,* 86.

40. When the Prophet Muhammad died in Jerusalem in 632 AD, Muslims believe that he left his footprint on a boulder as he ascended into heaven. Followers then built a mosque adorned with a golden dome around this rock to commemorate the Prophet's ascension into heaven. This Dome of the Rock is the Old City of Jerusalem's most striking architectural feature. Faisal was assassinated in 1975 never having made a trip to Jerusalem.

41. Sheehan, *The Arabs, Israelis, and Kissinger,* 67.

42. Weisberg, *The Politics of Crude Oil Pricing in the Middle East, 1970–1975,* 89.

43. Ibid.

44. The embargo was later expanded to include the Netherlands, Portugal, and South Africa. The Netherlands and South Africa were embargoed for official government statements that were critical of the Egyptian and Syrian attack; Portugal was embargoed for allowing the United States to use territory it controlled as a way station in resupplying the Israelis.

45. Sheehan, *The Arabs, Israelis, and Kissinger,* 69.

46. Schulzinger, *Henry Kissinger,* 156. Compare that to the aftermath of Hurricane Katrina in 2005, which saw retail gas prices increase by less than half.

47. Morris, *Uncertain Greatness,* 102.

48. Joseph Szyliowicz, "The Embargo and U.S. Foreign Policy," in *The Energy Crisis and U.S. Foreign Policy,* eds. Joseph S. Szyliowicz and Bard E. O'Neill (New York: Praeger, 1975), 216.

49. Szyliowicz, "The Embargo and U.S. Foreign Policy," 217.

50. Stork, *Middle East Oil and the Energy Crisis,* 248. Also see chapter 5.
51. Nixon also called on Congress to create a cabinet-level Department of Energy, but that did not happen until the Carter administration in 1977.
52. Szyliowicz, "The Embargo and U.S. Foreign Policy," 204.
53. Richard B. Mancke, "The Genesis of the U.S. Oil Crisis," in *The Energy Crisis and U.S. Foreign Policy,* eds. Joseph S. Szyliowicz and Bard E. O'Neill (New York: Praeger, 1975), 63.
54. Weisberg, *The Politics of Crude Oil Pricing in the Middle East, 1970–1975,* 128.
55. Ibid., 127.
56. Szyliowicz, "The Embargo and U.S. Foreign Policy," 191.
57. Ibid., 183.
58. Spiegel, *The Other Arab-Israeli Conflict,* 271.
59. Parker, *The Road to Camp David,* 63.
60. Sheehan, *The Arabs, Israelis, and Kissinger,* 112.
61. Fraser, *The USA and the Middle East since World War II,* 124.
62. Spiegel, *The Other Arab-Israeli Conflict,* 279.
63. Parker, *The Road to Camp David,* 6.
64. Sheehan, *The Arabs, Israelis, and Kissinger,* 118.
65. Naseer H. Aruri, "U.S. Policy Toward the Arab-Israeli Conflict," in *The United States and the Middle East: A Search for New Perspectives,* ed. Hooshang Amirahmadi (Albany, NY: SUNY Press, 1993). 101.
66. Quandt, *Peace Process,* 159.
67. Sheehan, *The Arabs, Israelis, and Kissinger,* 155.
68. Ibid., 199.
69. Tillman, *The United States in the Middle East,* 152.
70. Spiegel, *The Other Arab-Israeli Conflict,* 170–71 and 241–43.
71. Sheehan, *The Arabs, Israelis, and Kissinger,* 190.
72. Parker, *The Road to Camp David,* 95.
73. Ibid., 92.
74. Clyde Mark, *Israel: U.S. Foreign Assistance,* Congressional Research Service Issue Brief, April 26, 2005, www.fas.org/sgp/crs/mideast/IB85066.pdf, 13.
75. Clyde Mark, *Egypt-United States Relations,* Congressional Research Service Issue Brief, April 2, 2003, www.fas.org/asmp/resources/govern/crs-ib93087.pdf, 13.
76. Quandt, *Peace Process,* 155.
77. Weisberg, *The Politics of Crude Oil Pricing in the Middle East, 1970–1975,* 95.
78. Tillman, *The United States in the Middle East,* 22. Also see chapter 7.
79. Sheehan, *The Arabs, Israelis, and Kissinger,* 205. Also see chapter 8.

Chapter 10. The Islamic Revolution in Iran and the American Hostage Crisis

1. James A. Bill, *The Eagle and the Lion: The Tragedy of American-Iranian Relations* (New Haven, CT: Yale University Press, 1988), 6.
2. Ibid., 176.
3. Richard Cottam, "U.S. Policy in the Middle East," in *The United States and the Middle East: A Search for New Perspective,* ed. Hooshang Amirahmadi (Albany, NY: SUNY Press, 1993), 100.

4. Don Lawson, *America Held Hostage: The Iran Hostage Crisis and the Iran-Contra Affair* (New York: Franklin Watts, 1991), 31.
5. Bill, *The Eagle and the Lion*, 66.
6. David Farber, *Taken Hostage: The Iran Hostage Crisis and America's First Encounter with Radical Islam* (Princeton, NJ: Princeton University Press, 2005), 37.
7. Bill, *The Eagle and the Lion*, 186.
8. Ibid., 160.
9. The only other countries in the Middle East with Shiite majorities are Iraq and Bahrain.
10. David Harris, *The Crisis: The President, the Prophet, and the Shah-1979 and the Coming of Militant Islam* (New York: Little, Brown and Co., 2004), 33.
11. Harris, *The Crisis*, 41.
12. Although most Arabs are Sunni Muslims, the Shiite branch began in Iraq, an Arab country, and then became most popular in Iran, a Persian country often at odds with its Arab neighbors.
13. William H. Sullivan, *Mission to Iran* (New York: W. W. Norton and Company, 1981), 100.
14. Farber, *Taken Hostage*, 69.
15. Gary Sick, *All Fall Down: America's Tragic Encounter with Iran* (New York: Random House, 1985), 14–15.
16. Lawson, *America Held Hostage*, 36.
17. Sick, *All Fall Down*, 44.
18. Cottam, "U.S. Policy in the Middle East," 153.
19. Farber, *Taken Hostage*, 93.
20. Sick, *All Fall Down*, 92.
21. Cottam, "U.S. Policy in the Middle East," 163.
22. Bill, *The Eagle and the Lion*, 3.
23. Hunt, *Crises in U.S. Foreign Policy*, 377.
24. Cottam, "U.S. Policy in the Middle East," 173.
25. Sick, *All Fall Down*, 43.
26. Sullivan, *Mission to Iran*, 90.
27. Farber, *Taken Hostage*, 61.
28. Harris, *The Crisis*, 130.
29. Bill, *The Eagle and the Lion*, 246.
30. Ibid., 247.
31. Harris, *The Crisis*, 65.
32. Farber, *Taken Hostage*, 101.
33. Harris, *The Crisis*, 105.
34. Sullivan, *Mission to Iran*, 230.
35. Ibid.
36. Farber, *Taken Hostage*, 46.
37. Cottam, "U.S. Policy in the Middle East," 48.
38. Hunt, *Crises in U.S. Foreign Policy*, 378.
39. Bill, *The Eagle and the Lion*, 251.

40. Mansour Farhang, "U.S. Policy Toward the Islamic Republic of Iran: A Case of Misperception and Reactive Behavior," *The United States and the Middle East: A Search for New Perspectives,* ed. Hooshang Amirahmadi (Albany, NY: SUNY Press, 1993), 153.

41. Bill, *The Eagle and the Lion,* 323–24.

42. Ibid., 326.

43. Farhang, "U.S. Policy Toward the Islamic Republic of Iran," 154.

44. Sick, *All Fall Down,* 180.

45. Harris, *The Crisis,* 189.

46. Farber, *Taken Hostage,* 125.

47. Harris, *The Crisis,* 193.

48. Warren Christopher, et al., *American Hostages in Iran: The Conduct of a Crisis* (New Haven, CT: Yale University Press, 1985), 57.

49. Farhang, "U.S. Policy Toward the Islamic Republic of Iran," 155.

50. Mark Bowden, *Guests of the Ayatollah: The First Battle in America's War with Militant Islam* (New York: Atlantic Monthly Press, 2006), 34.

51. Warren, et al., *American Hostages in Iran,* 149.

52. Bowden, *Guests of the Ayatollah,* 124.

53. Edward R. Drachman, et al., *Presidents and Foreign Policy: Countdown to Ten Controversial Decisions* (Albany, NY: SUNY Press, 1997), 221.

54. David Patrick Houghton, *U.S. Foreign Policy and the Iran Hostage Crisis,* Cambridge Studies in International Relations (Cambridge: Cambridge University Press, 2001), 81, and Bowden, *Guests of the Ayatollah,* 379, 481.

55. Warren, et al., *American Hostages in Iran,* 93–94.

56. Bowden, *Guests of the Ayatollah,* 407.

57. Harris, *The Crisis,* 43.

58. Houghton, *U.S. Foreign Policy and the Iran Hostage Crisis,* 124.

59. Sick, *All Fall Down,* 18.

60. Houghton, *U.S. Foreign Policy and the Iran Hostage Crisis,* 3–4.

61. Bowden, *Guests of the Ayatollah,* 378.

62. Sick, *All Fall Down,* 171. Gary Sick, who was Brzezinski's Iran specialist on the National Security Council, argues forcefully that William Casey, Reagan's campaign manager, reached a secret deal with the Iranians to delay the hostages' release in order to guarantee Reagan's November victory. See Gary Sick, *October Surprise: America's Hostages in Iran and the Election of Ronald Reagan* (New York: Times Books, 1991).

63. Sick, *All Fall Down,* 291.

64. Farber, *Taken Hostage,* 171.

65. Sick, *All Fall Down,* 293.

66. Bowden, *Guests of the Ayatollah,* 216.

67. Houghton, *U.S. Foreign Policy and the Iran Hostage Crisis,* 9.

68. Ibid., 139.

69. Harris, *The Crisis,* 410 (emphasis added).

70. Warren, et al., *American Hostages in Iran,* 38.

Chapter 11. The Fall of the Berlin Wall and the End of the Cold War

1. Raymond L. Garthoff, *The Great Transition: American-Soviet Relations at the End of the Cold War* (Washington, D.C.: The Brookings Institution, 1994), 757.
2. Richard A. Melanson, *American Foreign Policy since the Vietnam War: The Search for Consensus from Nixon to Clinton,* 3rd ed. (New York: M. E. Sharpe, 2000), 135.
3. H. W. Brands, *Since Vietnam: The United States in World Affairs, 1973–1995* (New York: McGraw Hill, 1996), 82.
4. Ibid., 84.
5. Melanson, *American Foreign Policy since the Vietnam War,* 138.
6. Walter LaFeber, *America, Russia, and the Cold War, 1945–2000,* 9th ed. (New York: McGraw Hill, 2002), 317.
7. John Lewis Gaddis, *The United States and the End of the Cold War: Implications, Reconsiderations, Provocations* (New York: Oxford University Press, 1992), 123.
8. Brands, *Since Vietnam,* 85.
9. Gaddis, *The United States and the End of the Cold War,* 125.
10. Ibid., 121.
11. Peter Schweizer, ed., *The Fall of the Berlin Wall: Reassessing the Causes and Consequences of the End of the Cold War* (Stanford, CA: Hoover Institution Press, 2000), 15.
12. Schweizer, ed., *The Fall of the Berlin Wall,* 19–21.
13. Brands, *Since Vietnam,* 87–89.
14. Ibid., 91.
15. LaFeber, *America, Russia, and the Cold War, 1945–2000,* 324.
16. Garthoff, *The Great Transition,* 758.
17. See, for example, Garthoff, *The Great Transition* and LaFeber, *America, Russia, and the Cold War, 1945–2000.*
18. See, for example, Schweizer, ed., *The Fall of the Berlin Wall.*
19. See, for example, Beth A. Fischer, *The Reagan Reversal: Foreign Policy and the End of the Cold War* (Columbia: University of Missouri Press), 1997, and Gaddis, *The United States and the End of the Cold War.*
20. Barbara Farnham, "Reagan and the Gorbachev Revolution: Perceiving the End of Threat," *Political Science Quarterly* 116 (Summer 2001), 233.
21. Fischer, *The Reagan Reversal,* 148.
22. Gaddis, *The United States and the End of the Cold War,* 125.
23. Garthoff, *The Great Transition,* 766.
24. LaFeber, *America, Russia and the Cold War, 1945–2000,* 334.
25. Brands, *Since Vietnam,* 111.
26. Garthoff, *The Great Transition,* 766.
27. Schweizer, ed., *The Fall of the Berlin Wall,* 28.
28. Fischer, *The Reagan Reversal,* 110.
29. Gaddis, *The United States and the End of the Cold War,* 127.
30. Garthoff, *The Great Transition,* 210.
31. Gaddis, *The United States and the End of the Cold War,* 128.
32. Brands, *Since Vietnam,* 117.
33. LaFeber, *America, Russia, and the Cold War, 1945–2000,* 339.
34. Farnham, "Reagan and the Gorbachev Revolution," 238.

35. Gaddis, *The United States and the End of the Cold War,* 130.
36. Ibid., 131.
37. Garthoff, *The Great Transition,* 775.
38. Established by the Soviet Union in 1955 as a military alliance to counteract NATO, the Warsaw Pact's members were Albania, Bulgaria, Czechoslovakia, East Germany, Hungary, Poland, Romania, and the Soviet Union. Arguably the least important from a Soviet strategic point of view, Albania was allowed to withdraw in 1968.
39. LaFeber, *America, Russia, and the Cold War, 1945–2000,* 351.
40. Brands, *Since Vietnam,* 108.
41. Warren I. Cohen, *America's Falling Empire: U.S. Foreign Relations since the Cold War* (Malden, MA: Blackwell Publishing, 2006), 13.
42. Garthoff, *The Great Transition,* 777.
43. Cohen, *America's Falling Empire,* 21.
44. LaFeber, *America, Russia, and the Cold War, 1945–2000,* 353–54.
45. Cohen, *America's Falling Empire,* 23.
46. LaFeber, *America, Russia, and the Cold War, 1945–2000,* 359.
47. Cohen, *America's Falling Empire,* 36.
48. Joseph Nye, *The Paradox of American Power: Why the World's Only Superpower Can't Go It Alone* (New York: Oxford University Press, 2002), 87.
49. Cohen, *America's Falling Empire,* 33.

Chapter 12. The September 11, 2001, Terrorist Attacks

1. These multiple, simultaneous bombings became a trademark of al Qaeda attacks, with the hijackings of four jetliners on 9/11 demonstrating just how sophisticated, and deadly, al Qaeda's organizational prowess had become.
2. Richard A. Clarke, *Against All Enemies: Inside America's War on Terror* (New York: Free Press, 2004), 129.
3. Ivo H. Dalder and James M. Lindsay *America Unbound: The Bush Revolution in Foreign Policy* (Washington, D.C.: Brookings Institution Press, 2003), 75.
4. The other two threats were the proliferation of weapons of mass destruction and China's rising power.
5. Dalder and Lindsay, *America Unbound,* 75.
6. Seymour M. Hersh, *Chain of Command: The Road from 9/11 to Abu Ghraib* (New York: Harper Collins, 2004), 87–88.
7. Bob Woodward, *State of Denial: Bush at War, Part III* (New York: Simon and Schuster, 2006), 80.
8. Clarke, *Against All Enemies,* 237.
9. Ibid., xiii.
10. John Newhouse, *Imperial America: The Bush Assault on the World Order* (New York: Alfred A. Knopf, 2003), 7.
11. Dalder and Lindsay, *America Unbound,* 129. Soviet/Russian studies was Rice's specialty when she was in academia.
12. Bob Woodward, *Plan of Attack* (New York: Simon and Schuster, 2004), 24.

13. Ramzi Yousef, who had strong ties to al Qaeda before his 1995 arrest in Pakistan, was one of the key planners of the 1993 World Trade Center bombing.
14. Hersh, *Chain of Command,* 96.
15. Clarke, *Against All Enemies,* 106.
16. Hersh, *Chain of Command,* 96.
17. Newhouse, *Imperial America,* 3.
18. Clarke, *Against All Enemies,* 245.
19. Hersh, *Chain of Command,* 147.
20. Mark Mazzetti, and David E. Sanger, "Bush Aides See Failure in Fight with Al Qaeda in Pakistan," *New York Times,* July 18, 2007, nytimes.com/2007/07/18/washington/18intel.html?hp.
21. David Rohde and David E. Sanger, "How a 'Good War' in Afghanistan Went Bad," *New York Times,* August 12, 2007, nytimes.com/2007/08/12/world/asia/12afghan.html?hp#.
22. Woodward, *State of Denial,* 109–110, 241.
23. Peter Baker, "Embittered Insiders Turn Against Bush," *Washington Post,* November 19, 2006, washingtonpost.com/wp-dyn/content/article/2006/11/18/AR2006111801076.html.
24. Quandt, *Peace Process,* 387.
25. James Mann, *Rise of the Vulcans: The History of Bush's War Cabinet* (New York: Viking Press, 2004), 363
26. Clarke, *Against All Enemies,* 30.
27. Michael R. Gordon and General Bernard E. Trainor, *Cobra II: The Inside Story of the Invasion and Occupation of Iraq* (New York: Pantheon Books, 2006), 17.
28. Quandt, *Peace Process,* 395.
29. Dalder and Lindsay, *America Unbound,* 120.
30. Mann, *Rise of the Vulcans,* 327.
31. Ibid., 329.
32. Woodward, *State of Denial,* 97.
33. Peter W. Galbraith, *The End of Iraq: How American Incompetence Created a War Without End* (New York: Simon and Schuster, 2006), 10.
34. Gordon and Trainor, *Cobra II,* 64.
35. Hersh, *Chain of Command,* 188.
36. Dalder and Lindsay, *America Unbound,* 132.
37. Woodward, *Plan of Attack,* 120.
38. Ibid.
39. Dalder and Lindsay, *America Unbound,* 137.
40. Woodward, *Plan of Attack,* 164.
41. Dalder and Lindsay, *America Unbound,* 160.
42. Joby Warrick, "Lacking Biolabs, Trailers Carried Case for War: Administration Pushed Notion of Banned Iraqi Weapons Despite Evidence to Contrary," *Washington Post,* April 12, 2006, washingtonpost.com/wp-dyn/content/article/2006/04/11/AR2006041101888.html.
43. Ibid., 166.
44. Hersh, *Chain of Command,* 367.

45. Woodward, *State of Denial,* 489.
46. Mann, *Rise of the Vulcans,* 323.
47. Quandt, *Peace Process,* 399.
48. Mann, *Rise of the Vulcans,* 322.
49. Ibid., 357.
50. Powell's doctrine became famous for its success against Hussein in the 1991 Gulf War when he was Chairman of the Joint Chiefs of Staff, which is the country's highest-ranking military officer.
51. Stefan Halper and Jonathan Clarke, *America Alone: The Neo-Conservatives and the Global Order* (Cambridge: Cambridge University Press, 2004), 222.
52. Gordon and Trainor, *Cobra II,* 503.
53. Sean Loughlin, "Rumsfeld on Looting in Iraq: 'Stuff happens': Administration Asking Countries for Help with Security," April 12, 2003, cnn.com/2003/US/04/11/sprj.irq.pentagon.
54. Galbraith, *The End of Iraq,* 112.
55. Ibid., 121–22.
56. Ibid., 130.
57. Woodward, *State of Denial,* 229.
58. Galbraith, *The End of Iraq,* 179.
59. Peter Baker, "Embittered Insiders Turn Against Bush."
60. Woodward, *State of Denial,* 330.
61. Peter Baker, "U.S. Not Winning War in Iraq, Bush Says for 1st Time," *Washington Post,* December 20, 2006, washingtonpost.com/wp-dyn/content/article/2006/12/20/AR2006122000268.html.
62. Robin Wright, and Peter Baker, "White House, Joint Chiefs at Odds on Adding Troops," *Washington Post,* December 19, 2006, washingtonpost.com/wp-dyn/content/article/2006/12/18/AR2006121801477.html.
63. "U.S. Casualties in Iraq," http://www.globalsecurity.org/military/ops/iraq_casualties.htm (no date).
64. Steven Lee Myers, "Truck Bomb Kills Dozens in Northern Iraq," *New York Times,* June 20, 2009, http://www.nytimes.com/2009/06/21/world/middleeast/21iraq.html?hp.
65. Iraq's three main factions are split along religious and ethnic lines. Shiite Muslims are in the majority but were historically oppressed by the Sunni Muslim minority, led by Saddam Hussein. Besides the Shiite vs. Sunni religious rivalry, there is also the Kurdish ethnic minority in the north which opposes any Iraqi Arabs (whether Sunni or Shiite) intervening in their now self-governing province of Kurdistan.
66. Woodward, *State of Denial,* 102.
67. Ibid., 173.
68. Gordon and Trainor, *Cobra II,* 81.
69. Woodward, *State of Denial,* 212.
70. Newhouse, *Imperial America,* 158.
71. Hersh, *Chain of Command,* 210.
72. Newhouse, *Imperial America,* 71.
73. Hersh, *Chain of Command,* 225.

74. Gordon and Trainor, *Cobra II,* 130.

75. Newhouse, *Imperial America,* 158.

76. Dalder and Lindsay, *America Unbound,* 165,

77. Mark Mazzetti, "CIA Said to Find No Hussein Link to Terror Chief," *New York Times,* September 9, 2006, nytimes.com/2006/09/09/world/middleeast/09intel.ht ml?hp&ex=1157860800&en=6b11a9b2ce4125ad&ei=5094&partner=homepage.

78. Newhouse, *Imperial America,* 69–70.

79. Halper and Clarke, *America Alone,* 193 and 201.

80. James Mann, *Rise of the Vulcans* 357.

81. Hersh, *Chain of Command,* 182.

82. Galbraith, *The End of Iraq,* 129.

83. Woodward, *State of Denial,* 440.

84. Freedom House, "Freedom in the World 2010: Global Erosion of Freedom," January 12, 2010, http://www.freedomhouse.org/template.cfm?page=70&release=1120.

85. Douglas Kellner, *From 9/11 to Terror War: The Dangers of the Bush Legacy,* (Oxford: Rowman & Littlefield, 2003), 100–101.

86. Kellner, *From 9/11 to Terror War,* 101.

87. Noah Feldman, "How Different is Obama from Bush on Terrorism?" *Foreign Policy,* September 3, 2010.

88. David E. Sanger, and Eric Schmitt, "Cheney's Power No Longer Goes Unquestioned," *New York Times,* September 10, 2006, nytimes.com/2006/09/10/washington/10cheney.html.

89. Shane Scott, "Waterboarding Used 266 Times on 2 Suspects," *New York Times,* April 19, 2009, http://www.nytimes.com/2009/04/20/world/20detain.html?scp= 2&sq=waterboarding&st=cse.

90. Woodward, *State of Denial,* 335.

91. Ibid., 354.

92. Hersh, *Chain of Command,* 309.

93. Mann, *Rise of the Vulcans,* 257.

94. Halper and Clarke, *America Alone,* 237.

Bibliography

Adler, Selig. *The Isolationist Impulse: Its Twentieth Century Reaction.* New York: Collier, 1961.

Allison, Graham T. and Philip Zelikow, eds. *Essence of Decision: Explaining the Cuban Missile Crisis.* New York: Pearson Longman, 1999.

Ambrose, Stephen E. *Nixon: The Education of a Politician 1913–1962,* volume 1. New York: Simon and Schuster, 1987.

Aruri, Naseer H. "U.S. Policy Toward the Arab-Israeli Conflict." In Hooshang Amirahmadi, Ed. *The United States and the Middle East: A Search for New Perspectives.* Albany, NY: SUNY Press, 1993.

Baker, Peter. "Embittered Insiders Turn Against Bush." *Washington Post.* November 19, 2006, washingtonpost.com/wp-dyn/content/article/2006/11/18/AR2006 111801076.html.

———. "U.S. Not Winning War in Iraq, Bush Says for 1st Time." *Washington Post.* December 20, 2006, washingtonpost.com/wp-dyn/content/article/2006/12/20/AR2006122000268.html.

Barnett, A. Doak. *China Policy: Old Problems and New Challenges.* Washington, D.C.: The Brookings Institution, 1977.

Beisner, Robert. *Twelve Against Empire: The Anti-Imperialists, 1898–1900.* New York: McGraw Hill, 1968.

Berman, Larry. "The Tet Offensive." In Marc Jason Gilbert and William Head, eds. *The Tet Offensive.* Wesport, CT: Praeger, 1996.

Bill, James A. *The Eagle and the Lion: The Tragedy of American-Iranian Relations.* New Haven, CT: Yale University Press, 1988.

Blight, James G., Bruce J. Allyn and David A. Welch, eds. *Cuba on the Brink: Castro, the Missile Crisis, and Soviet Collapse.* Lanham, MD: Rowan and Littlefield, 2002.

Bonham, G. Matthew, Shapiro, Michael J. and Trumble, Thomas L. "The October War: Changes in Cognitive Orientation Toward the Middle East Conflict." *International Studies Quarterly* 23:1 (March 1979): 3–44.

Bowden, Mark. *Guests of the Ayatollah: The First Battle in America's War with Militant Islam.* New York: Atlantic Monthly Press, 2006.

Brands, H. W. *Since Vietnam: The United States in World Affairs, 1973–1995.* New York: McGraw Hill, 1996.

———. *Woodrow Wilson.* New York: MacMillan, 2003.

Brown, Seyom. *The Crises of Power: An Interpretation of United States Foreign Policy During the Kissinger Years.* New York: Columbia University Press, 1979.

Bundy, McGeorge. *Danger and Survival: Choices about the Bomb in the First Fifty Years.* New York: Random House, 1998.

Burner, David. *John F. Kennedy and a New Generation.* New York: Pearson Longman, 2005.

Buss, Claude A. *China: The People's Republic of China and Richard Nixon.* San Francisco: W. H. Freeman, 1974.

Buzzanco, Robert. "The Myth of Tet: American Failure and the Politics of War." In Marc Jason Gilbert and William Head, eds. *The Tet Offensive.* Westport, CT: Praeger, 1996.

Chalberg, John C., ed. *Isolationism: Opposing Viewpoints.* San Diego: Greenhaven Press, Inc., 1995.

Christopher, Warren, et al. *American Hostages in Iran: The Conduct of a Crisis.* New Haven, CT: Yale University Press, 1985.

Clarke, Richard A. *Against All Enemies: Inside America's War on Terror.* New York: Free Press, 2004.

Cohen, Warren I. *America's Falling Empire: U.S. Foreign Relations since the Cold War.* Malden, MA: Blackwell Publishing, 2006.

Coogan, John W. *The End of Neutrality: The United States, Britain, and Maritime Rights, 1899–1915.* Ithaca, NY: Cornell University Press, 1981.

Cooper, John Milton. *The Vanity of Power: American Isolation and World War I, 1914–1917.* Westport, CT: Greenwood Press, 1969.

Cottam, Richard. "U.S. Policy in the Middle East." In Hooshang Amirahmadi, ed. *The United States and the Middle East: A Search for New Perspectives.* Albany, NY: SUNY Press, 1993.

Dalder, Ivo H. and James M. Lindsay. *America Unbound: The Bush Revolution in Foreign Policy.* Washington, D.C.: Brookings Institution Press, 2003.

Dallek, Robert. "National Mood and American Foreign Policy: A Suggestive Essay." *American Quarterly,* 34:4 (Autumn, 1982): 339–361.

———. *An Unfinished Life: John F. Kennedy, 1917–1963.* Boston: Little, Brown and Co., 2003.

Daniels, Roger. "Incarcerating Japanese Americans." *Magazine of History* 16:3 (Spring 2002): 19–23.

Devlin, Patrick. *Too Proud to Fight: Woodrow Wilson's Neutrality.* New York: Oxford University Press, 1975.

Dickson, Paul. *Sputnik: Shock of the Century.* New York: Berkeley Publishing Group, 2003.

Divine, Robert A. *The Sputnik Challenge: Eisenhower's Response to the Soviet Satellite.* New York: Oxford University Press, 1993.

Dockrill, Saki Ruth. *The End of the Cold War Era.* New York: Oxford University Press, 2005.

Douglass, John A. "A Certain Future: Sputnik, American Higher Education and the Survival of a Nation." In Roger Launus, ed. *Reconsidering Sputnik: Forty Years Since the Soviet Satellite.* New York: Routledge, 2000.

Drachman Edward R., et. al. *Presidents and Foreign Policy: Countdown to Ten Controversial Decisions.* Albany, NY: SUNY Press, 1997.

Duke, Paul. "The Greatest Generation?" *Virginia Quarterly Review* 78:1 (Winter 2002): 19–25.

Dulles, Foster Rhea. *America's Rise to World Power: 1898–1945.* New York: Harper and Brothers, 1954.

Ekbladh, David. "How to Build a Nation." *Wilson Quarterly* (Winter 2004): 12–20.

Farber, David. *Taken Hostage: The Iran Hostage Crisis and America's First Encounter with Radical Islam.* Princeton, NJ: Princeton University Press, 2005.

Farhang, Mansour. "U.S. Policy Toward the Islamic Republic of Iran: A Case of Misperception and Reactive Behavior." In Hooshang Amirahmadi, ed. *The United States and the Middle East: A Search for New Perspectives.* Albany, NY: SUNY Press, 1993.

Farnham, Barbara. "Reagan and the Gorbachev Revolution: Perceiving the End of Threat," *Political Science Quarterly* 116:2 (Summer 2001): 225–52.

Feis, Herbert. *The Road to Pearl Harbor.* Princeton, NJ: Princeton University Press, 1971.

Fensterwald, Bernard, Jr. "The Anatomy of American 'Isolationism' and Expansionism, Part I." *Journal of Conflict Resolution* 2:2 (June, 1958a): 111–39.

———. "The Anatomy of American 'Isolationism' and Expansionism, part II." *Journal of Conflict Resolution* 2:4 (December 1958): 280–309.

Fischer, Beth A. *The Reagan Reversal: Foreign Policy and the End of the Cold War.* Columbia, MO: University of Missouri Press, 1997.

Foot, Rosemary. *The Wrong War: American Policy and the Dimensions of the Korean Conflict, 1950–1953.* Ithaca, NY: Cornell University Press, 1985.

Fraser, T. G. *The USA and the Middle East Since World War II.* New York: St. Martin's Press, 1989.

Freedman, Lawrence. *Kennedy's Wars: Berlin, Cuba, Laos, and Vietnam.* New York: Oxford University Press, 2000.

Freedom House. "Freedom in the World 2010: Global Erosion of Freedom." January 12, 2010, http://www.freedomhouse.org/template.cfm?page=70&release=1120.

Gaddis, John Lewis. *Strategies of Containment: A Critical Appraisal of American National Security Policy During the Cold War.* New York: Oxford University Press, 1982.

———. *The United States and the End of the Cold War: Implications, Reconsiderations, Provocations.* New York: Oxford University Press, 1992.

———. *We Now Know: Rethinking Cold War History.* New York: Oxford University Press, 1997.

Galbraith, Peter W. *The End of Iraq: How American Incompetence Created a War Without End.* New York: Simon and Schuster, 2006.

Galloway, Eilene. "Organizing the U.S. Government for Outer Space." In Roger Launus,

ed. *Reconsidering Sputnik: Forty Years Since the Soviet Satellite.* New York: Routledge, 2000.

Gardner, Lloyd C. *Pay Any Price: Lyndon Johnson and the Wars for Vietnam.* Chicago:
Ivan R. Dee, 1995.

Garthoff, Raymond L. *The Great Transition: American-Soviet Relations at the End of the
Cold War.* Washington, D.C.: The Brookings Institution, 1994.

Goldstein, Laurence. "The Legacy of Hiroshima." *Michigan Quarterly Review* 38:3
(Summer 1999): 471–486.

Gordon, Michael R. and Trainor, General Bernard E. *Cobra II: The Inside Story of the
Invasion and Occupation of Iraq.* New York: Pantheon Books, 2006.

Graham, James T. "Kennedy, Cuba, and the Press." *Journalism History* 24:2 (Summer
1998): 60–71.

Greene, John Robert. *The Limits of Power: The Nixon and Ford Administrations.* Bloomington IN: Indiana University Press, 1992.

Gregory, Ross. *The Origins of American Intervention in World War I.* New York: W.W.
Norton, 1971.

Guttman, Allen. *Korea: Cold War and Limited War,* second ed. Lexington, MA: D.C.
Heath and Company, 1972.

Halper, Stefan and Clarke, Jonathan. *America Alone: The Neo-Conservatives and the
Global Order.* Cambridge: Cambridge University Press, 2004.

Han, Vo Xuan. *Oil, the Persian Gulf States and the United States.* Westport, CT: Praeger,
1994.

Haney, Patrick J. "The Nixon Administration and Middle East Crises: Theory and Evidence of Presidential Management of Foreign Policy Decision Making." *Political
Research Quarterly* 47:4 (December 1994): 939–959.

Harding, Harry. *A Fragile Relationship: The United States and China Since 1972.* Washington, D.C.: The Brookings Institution, 1992.

Harris, David. *The Crisis: The President, the Prophet, and the Shah—1979 and the Coming of Militant Islam.* New York: Little, Brown and Co., 2004.

Healy, David. *U.S. Expansionism: The Imperialist Urge in the 1890s.* Madison: University of Wisconsin Press, 1970.

Hearden, Patrick, *The Tragedy of Vietnam.* New York: Pearson Longman, 2004.

Herring, George C. *America's Longest War: The United States and Vietnam, 1950–1975.*
New York: McGraw Hill, 2002.

Hersh, Seymour M. *Chain of Command: The Road from 9/11 to Abu Ghraib.* New York:
Harper Collins, 2004.

Hickey, Michael. *The Korean War: The West Confronts Communism.* Woodstock, NY:
Overland Press, 1999.

Hodgson, Godfrey. *Woodrow Wilson's Right Hand: The Life of Colonel Edward M. House.*
New Haven, CT: Yale University Press, 2006.

Holmes, Jack E. *The Mood Interest Theory of American Foreign Policy.* Foreword by Frank
L. Klingberg. Lexington: University Press of Kentucky, 1985.

Houghton, David Patrick. *U.S. Foreign Policy and the Iran Hostage.* Cambridge Studies
in International Relations. Cambridge: Cambridge University Press, 2001.

Hunt, Michael H. "Beijing and the Korean Crisis: June 1950–June 1951." *Political Science Quarterly* 107:3 (1992): 453–77.

———. *Crises in U.S. Foreign Policy.* New Haven, CT: Yale University Press, 1996.

———. "East Asia in Henry Luce's 'American Century.'" *Diplomatic History* 23 (Spring 1999): 321–53.

Iriye, Akira. *The Cambridge History of American Foreign Relations, Volume III: The Globalizing of America, 1913–1945.* Cambridge, MA: Cambridge University Press, 1993.

Kaiser, David. *American Tragedy: Kennedy, Johnson, and, the Origins of the Vietnam War.* Cambridge, MA: Belknap Press, 2000.

Kaplan, Lawrence S. "The Korean War and U.S. Foreign Relations: The Case of NATO." In Francis H. Heller, ed. *The Korean War: A 25-Year Perspective.* Lawrence, KS: Regents Press, 1975.

Kaufman, Burton I. *The Korean War: Challenges in Crisis, Credibility, and Command.* Philadelphia: Temple University Press, 1986.

Kellner, Douglas. *From 9/11 to Terror War: The Dangers of the Bush Legacy.* Oxford: Rowman & Littlefield, 2003.

Klingberg, Frank L. "The Historical Alternation of Moods in American Foreign Policy." *World Politics* 4 (Jan., 1952): 239–273.

Knock, Thomas J. *To End All Wars: Woodrow Wilson and the Quest for a New World Order.* Princeton, NJ: Princeton University Press, 1992.

Krock, Arthur. "Six Months after Pearl Harbor." *New York Times,* June 7, 1942, SM3.

———. "Unity Clicks into Place: Capital Dissensions Fade Out in Necessities of Common Cause." *New York Times,* December 8, 1941, 6.

Kusnitz, Leonard A. *Public Opinion and Foreign Policy: America's China Policy, 1949–1979.* Westport, CT: Greenwood Press, 1984.

LaFeber, Walter. *America, Russia, and the Cold War, 1945–2000,* ninth edition. New York: McGraw Hill, 2002.

———. *The Cambridge History of American Foreign Relations: Volume 2, The American Search for Opportunity, 1865–1913.* New York: Cambridge University Press, 1993.

———. "Crossing the 38th: The Cold War in Microcosm." In Lynn H Miller and Ronald W. Preussen, eds. *Reflections on the Cold War: A Quarter Century of American Foreign Policy.* Philadelphia: Temple University Press, 1974.

Laquer, Walter. *Confrontation: The Middle East and World Politics.* New York: Quadrangle/New York Times Book Co., 1974.

Lawson, Don. *America Held Hostage: The Iran Hostage Crisis and the Iran-Contra Affair.* New York: Franklin Watts, 1991.

Leckie, Robert. *Conflict: The History of the Korean War, 1950–53.* New York: G.P. Putnam's Sons, 1962.

Loughlin, Sean. "Rumsfeld on Looting in Iraq: 'Stuff happens': Administration Asking Countries for Help with Security." April 12, 2003, cnn.com/2003/US/04/11/sprj.irq.pentagon.

Lundestad, Geir. "Uniqueness and Pendulum Swings in US Foreign Policy." *International Affairs* 62: 3 (Summer, 1986): 405–21.

Mancke, Richard B. "The Genesis of the U.S. Oil Crisis." In Joseph S. Szyliowicz and Bard E. O'Neill, eds. *The Energy Crisis and U.S. Foreign Policy.* New York: Praeger, 1975.

Mann, James. *Rise of the Vulcans: The History of Bush's War Cabinet.* New York: Viking Press, 2004.

Mark, Clyde. *Israel: U.S. Foreign Assistance.* Congressional Research Service Issue Brief for Congress, April 26, 2005, www.fas.org/sgp/crs/mideast/IB85066.pdf.

———. *Egypt—United States Relations.* Congressional Research Service Issue Brief, April 2, 2003, www.fas.org/asmp/resources/govern/crs-ib93087.pdf.

May, Ernest. *Imperial Democracy: The Emergence of America as a Great Power.* New York: Harcourt Brace, 1961.

———. *The World War and American Isolation, 1914–1917.* Cambridge, MA: Harvard University Press, 1959.

Mazzetti, Mark. "CIA Said to Find No Hussein Link to Terror Chief." *New York Times.* September 9, 2006, nytimes.com/2006/09/09/world/middleeast/09intel.html?hp &ex=1157860800&en=6b11a9b2ce4125ad&ei=5094&partner=homepage.

Mazzetti, Mark and David E. Sanger. "Bush Aides See Failure in Fight with Al Qaeda in Pakistan." *New York Times.* July 18, 2007, nytimes.com/2007/07/18/washington/18intel.html?hp.

McCartney, Paul T. *Power and Progress: American National Identity, the War of 1898, and the Rise of American Imperialism.* Baton Rouge: Louisiana State University Press, 2006.

McDougall, Walter A. *The Heavens and the Earth: A Political History of the Space Age.* Baltimore: Johns Hopkins University Press, 1997.

Melanson, Richard A. *American Foreign Policy since the Vietnam War: The Search for Consensus from Nixon to Clinton,* third ed., New York: M.E. Sharpe, 2000.

Michael, Donald L. "The Beginning of the Space Age and American Public Opinion." *The Public Opinion Quarterly,* 24:4 (Winter, 1960): 573–82.

Miller, Richard H., ed. *American Imperialism in 1898: The Quest for National Fulfillment,* Hoboken, NJ: Wiley and Sons, 1970.

Mills, Walter. "Truman and MacArthur." In Allen Guttman, ed. *Korea: Cold War and Limited War,* second ed. Lexington, MA: D.C. Heath and Company, 1972.

Mooney, James W., and Thomas R. West, eds. *Vietnam: A History and Anthology.* Rancho Cucamonga, CA: Brandywine Press, 1994.

Morris, Roger. *Uncertain Greatness: Henry Kissinger and American Foreign Policy.* New York: Harper and Row: 1977.

Mueller, John E. *War, Presidents, and Public Opinion.* New York: John Wiley and Sons, 1973.

Munton, Don, and David A. Welch. *The Cuban Missile Crisis: A Concise History.* New York: Oxford University Press, 2007.

Myers, Steven Lee. "Truck Bomb Kills Dozens in Northern Iraq." *New York Times,* June 20, 2009, http://www.nytimes.com/2009/06/21/world/middleeast/21iraq.html?hp.

Nathan, James A. *Anatomy of the Cuban Missile Crisis.* Westport, CT: Greenwood Press, 2000.

Nelson, Anna Kasten. "President Kennedy's National Security Policy: A Reconsideration." *Reviews in American History* 19:1 (March 1991): 1–14.

Newhouse, John. *Imperial America: The Bush Assault on the World Order.* New York: Alfred A. Knopf, 2003.

Ninkovich, Frank. *The United States and Imperialism.* Malden, MA: Blackwell Publishing, 2000.

Nye, Joseph. *The Paradox of American Power: Why the World's Only Superpower Can't Go It Alone.* New York: Oxford University Press, 2002.

Offner, Arnold A. "'Another Such Victory:' President Truman, American Foreign Policy, and the Cold War." *Diplomatic History* 23:2 (Spring 1999): 127–55.

Offner, John. *Unwanted War: The Diplomacy of the United States and Spain over Cuba, 1895–1898.* Chapel Hill: University of North Carolina Press, 1992.

Parker, Thomas. *The Road to Camp David: U.S. Negotiating Strategy Toward the Arab-Israeli Conflict.* New York: Peter Lang, 1989.

Paterson, Thomas G. "Fixation with Cuba: The Bay of Pigs, Missile Crisis, and Covert War Against Fidel Castro." In Thomas G. Paterson, ed. *Kennedy's Quest for Victory: American Foreign Policy 1961–1963.* New York: Oxford University Press, 1989.

———. "United States Intervention in Cuba, 1898: Interpretation of the Spanish-American-Cuban-Filipino War." *The History Teacher* 29:3 (May, 1996): 341–61.

Perez, Louis. A. *The War of 1898: The United States and Cuba in History and Historiography.* Chapel Hill: University of North Carolina Press, 1998.

Perkins, Dexter. *The American Approach to Foreign Policy.* Cambridge, MA: Harvard University Press, 1953.

Perry, Ralph Barton. "Care Held Needed to Preserve Unity Under Adversity." *New York Times,* February 1, 1942, E6.

Pollins, Brian and Randall L. Schweller. "Linking the Levels: The Long Wave and Shifts in U.S. Foreign Policy, 1790–1993." *American Journal of Political Science* 43:2 (April 1999): 431–64.

Quandt, William B. *Peace Process: American Diplomacy and the Arab-Israeli Conflict Since 1967,* 3rd ed. Washington, D.C.: Brookings Institution, 2005.

Rabinovich, Abraham. *The Yom Kippur War: The Epic Encounter that Transformed the Middle East.* New York: Schocken Books, 2004.

Rees, David. *Korea: The Limited War.* New York: St. Martin's Press, 1964.

Rohde, David and David E. Sanger. "How a 'Good War' in Afghanistan Went Bad." *New York Times.* August 12, 2007, nytimes.com/2007/08/12/world/asia/12afghan. html?hp.

Roskin, Michael. "From Pearl Harbor to Vietnam: Shifting Generational Paradigms and Foreign Policy." *Political Science Quarterly* 89:3 (Autumn 1974): 563–588.

Sanger, David E. and Eric Schmitt. "Cheney's Power No Longer Goes Unquestioned." *New York Times,* September 10, 2006, nytimes.com/2006/09/10/washington/ 10cheney.html.

Saunders, Harold H. *The Other Walls: The Politics of the Arab-Israeli Peace Process.* Washington, D.C.: American Enterprise Institute for Public Policy Research, 1985.

Schaller, Michael. *The United States and China in the Twentieth Century.* New York: Oxford University Press, 1979.

Schoonover, Thomas. *The War of 1898 and the Origins of Globalization.* Lexington: University of Kentucky Press, 2003.

Schulzinger, Robert D. "The End of the Old World Order." *Diplomatic History* 20:4 (Fall 1996): 689–693.

———. *Henry Kissinger: Doctor of Diplomacy.* New York: Columbia University Press, 1989.

Schweizer, Peter, ed. *The Fall of the Berlin Wall: Reassessing the Causes and Consequences of the End of the Cold War.* Stanford, CA: Hoover Institution Press, 2000.

Scroop, Dan. "September 11th, Pearl Harbor and the Uses of Presidential Power." *Cambridge Review of International Affairs* 15:2 (2002): 317–27.

Shane, Scott. "Waterboarding Used 266 Times on 2 Suspects." *New York Times,* April 19, 2009, http://www.nytimes.com/2009/04/20/world/20detain.html?scp=2&sq=waterboarding&st=cse.

Sheehan, Edward R. F. *The Arabs, Israelis, and Kissinger: A Secret History of American Diplomacy in the Middle East.* New York: Reader's Digest Press, 1976.

Sick, Gary. *All Fall Down: America's Tragic Encounter with Iran.* New York: Random House, 1985.

———. *October Surprise: America's Hostages in Iran and the Election of Ronald Reagan.* New York: Times Books, 1991.

Siegel, Frederick F. *Troubled Journey: From Pearl Harbor to Ronald Reagan.* New York: Hill and Wang, 1984.

Small, Melvin. *Democracy and Diplomacy: The Impact of Domestic Politics on U.S. Foreign Policy, 1789–1994.* Baltimore: Johns Hopkins University Press, 1996.

———. *Antiwarriors: The Vietnam War and the Battle for America's Hearts and Minds.* Lanham, MD: SR Books, 2004.

Smith, Gaddis. *The Last Days of the Monroe Doctrine, 1945–1993.* New York: Hill and Wang, 1994.

Snowman, Daniel. *America since 1920.* London: Heinemann Educational Books, 1978.

Solomon, Burt. "Isolationism be Damned." *National Journal* 31:16 (April 17, 1999): 1006–1008.

Spector, Ronald H. *After Tet: The Bloodiest Year In Vietnam.* New York: The Free Press, 1993.

———. *Eagle Against the Sun: The American War with Japan.* New York: Free Press, 1985.

Spiegel, Steven L. *The Other Arab-Israeli Conflict: Making America's Middle East Policy, from Truman to Reagan.* Chicago: University of Chicago Press, 1985.

Stork, Joe. *Middle East Oil and the Energy Crisis.* New York: Monthly Review Press, 1975.

Sullivan, William H. *Mission to Iran.* New York: W.W. Norton and Company, 1981.

Sutter, Robert G. *The China Quandary: Domestic Determinants of U.S. China Policy, 1972—1982.* Boulder, CO: Westview, 1983.

———. *China-Watch: Toward Sino-American Reconciliation.* Baltimore: Johns Hopkins University Press, 1978.

Szulc, Tad. *The Illusion of Peace: Foreign Policy in the Nixon Years.* New York: Viking Press, 1978.

Szyliowicz, Joseph. "The Embargo and U.S. Foreign Policy." In Joseph S. Szyliowicz and Bard E. O'Neill, eds. *The Energy Crisis and U.S. Foreign Policy.* New York: Praeger, 1975.

Thornton, Richard C. *The Nixon-Kissinger Years: Reshaping America's Foreign Policy.* New York: Paragon House, 1989.

Tillman, Seth. *The United States in the Middle East: Interests and Obstacles.* Bloomington: Indiana University Press, 1982.

Toland, John. *Infamy: Pearl Harbor and its Aftermath.* New York: Berkeley Books, 1972.

Ulam, Adam B. "Washington, Moscow, and the Korean War." In Allen Guttman, ed. *Korea: Cold War and Limited War,* 2nd ed. Lexington, MA: D.C. Heath and Company, 1972.

"U.S. Casualties in Iraq." http://www.globalsecurity.org/military/ops/iraq_casualties .htm.

Van Dyke, Gretchen J. "Sputnik: A Political Symbol & Tool in 1960 Campaign Politics." In Roger Launus, ed. *Reconsidering Sputnik: Forty Years since the Soviet Satellite.* New York: Routledge, 2000.

Warrick, Joby. "Lacking Biolabs, Trailers Carried Case for War: Administration Pushed Notion of Banned Iraqi Weapons Despite Evidence to Contrary." *Washington Post,* April 12, 2006, washingtonpost.com/wp-dyn/content/article/2006/04/11/ AR2006041101888.html.

Weathersby, Kathryn. "The Korean War Revisited." *Wilson Quarterly* (Summer 1999): 91–95.

Weisberg, Richard Chadbourn. *The Politics of Crude Oil Pricing in the Middle East, 1970–1975.* Berkeley, CA: Institute of International Studies, 1977.

White, Mark J. *The Cuban Missile Crisis.* New York: McMillan, 1996.

Wiltz, John Edward. "The Korean War and American Society." In Francis H. Heller, ed. *The Korean War: A 25-Year Perspective.* Lawrence, KS: Regents Press, 1975.

Wingrove, Paul. "Who Started Korea?" *History Today* 50:7 (2000): 44–46.

Wohlstetter, Roberta. "Cuba and Pearl Harbor: Hindsight and Foresight." *Foreign Affairs* 43 (1965): 691–707.

Woodward, Bob. *Plan of Attack.* New York: Simon and Schuster, 2004.

———. *State of Denial: Bush at War, Part III.* New York: Simon and Schuster, 2006.

Wright, Robin and Peter Baker. "White House, Joint Chiefs at Odds on Adding Troops." *Washington Post,* December 19, 2006, washingtonpost.com/wp-dyn/content/article/2006/12/18/AR2006121801477.html.

Yim, Kwan Ha ed. *China and the U.S., 1964–1972.* New York: Facts on File, Inc., 1975.

Young, Marilyn B. *The Vietnam Wars, 1945–1990.* New York: Harper Collins, 1991.

Zimmerman John C. "Pearl Harbor Revisionism: Robert Stinnett's *Day of Deceit.*" *Intelligence and National Security* 17:2 (Summer 2002): 127–46.

Index

Schlesinger, James, 170, 174, 195
Schulz, George, 211, 213, 216
Schurz, Carl, 5, 16
Scowcroft, Brent, 221, 242, 279
SDI. *See* Strategic Defense Initiative
Second Hague Peace Conference, 21
Secret Service, 252
Senate, U.S., 234; and Cuba, 11, 13; and
    Cuban Missile Crisis, 105–106; and Iraq
    War, 246; 254; and Korean War, 70, 270;
    and NATO Treaty, 53; and Sputnik, 86;
    and Taiwan, 162; and Treaty of Versailles,
    5, 36, 41; and Vietnam War, 127–28; and
    WWI, 25, 26, 33; WWII, 268
Senate Foreign Relations Committee, 11,
    132, 133, 137, 149
September 11, xii, xxiv, 143, 205, 231, 234, 261
Serbia, 228
Seventh Fleet, 60, 72, 153
Shah of Iran, xv, xvi, xvii, xxiv, 183, 204;
    admission to U.S., 196–200; death of, 203;
    downfall of, 185, 186; exile and return to
    power, 188–89; and Khomeini, 190–92;
    ties to U.S., 183, 187, 192–95; as U.S. ally,
    187. *See also* Pahlavi, Muhammad Reza Shah
Shanghai Communique, 158
Sherman, Forrest, 62
Shinseki, Eric, 244
Sinai Desert, 165, 170, 177, 178, 181
Sinai I, 177, 180
Sinai II, 180, 181
Sinatra Doctrine, 220–21
Singapore, 48
Slovenia, 288
Snow, Edgar, 154
SOFA. *See* Status of Forces Agreement
Solidarity Movement, 221, 241
Somalia, xxi, 143, 229, 238, 239
Sorenson, Theodore, 107, 111, 114
Southeast Asia, 49, 101, 121, 150; U.S.
    policy in, 123, 125, 133, 138; containment
    of communism in, 117, 118, 120–21, 126,
    128, 139; and Japan, 49, 119, 120
South Korea, 146; and Acheson speech, 59;
    evacuation of U.S. nationals, 60; and
    MacArthur, 60, 67; North Korea's attack
    on, xviii, xxii, 57, 59, 63–65, 151, 257,
    261; and Truman, 60, 61, 64, 65, 66; and
    U.S. policy toward, 60, 61, 73, 259. *See
    also* Republic of Korea, Korea
South Vietnam, 159, 276; and Geneva Ac-
    cords, 121–22; instability in, 126–30, 132;
    and Nixon, 140, 141; and Tet Offensive,
    117, 127, 134–38; U.S. aid to, 122–23,
    124, 132, 142; U.S. counterinsurgency in,
    102, 124, 129, 130, 131; U.S. involvement
    in, 124; U.S. policy toward, 124–25, 126.

See also Vietnam
Southeast Asia Treaty Organization (SEATO), 75
Soviet Union, 108, 113, 157, 193, 218,
    219; and Castro, 97; and China, xviii,
    xxiii, 147, 150, 152, 261;Cold War with
    U.S., xxii, 57–59, 79–80, 103, 145, 187,
    203, 213, 219, 225, 226, 257; collapse
    of, xvii, xxiv, 208, 223, 224, 227, 228,
    231; containment of, 119; and Cuba, 101,
    102, 103, 104, 105; and Cuban Missile
    Crisis, xv, xxiii, 95–96, 106–112, 114; and
    detente, 143, 145, 164, 210; and Eastern
    Europe, 220, 221, 261, 284; and fall of
    Berlin Wall, 207, 208, 216, 222, 226, 258,
    261; and Gorbachev reforms, 216–27;
    Hungary uprising, 81–82; invasion of
    Afghanistan, 204, 213, 232; and JFK,
    99, 113; and Korea, 64, 66; leadership
    changes in, 215, 216; and Middle East,
    166, 167, 171, 172, 176, 182, 225; missile
    capabilities of, 85, 86, 87, 103; Open
    Skies, 80–81; and Reagan, 208–16; and
    Sputnik, xxii, 77–78, 82–83, 89, 93, 101,
    103, 258; U-2 spy plane incident, 106; and
    Vietnam, 120, 126, 132, 140
Spain, xvii, 1, 5, 16, 21, 243; dispute with
    U.S. over Cuba, 7–10, 13; and *Maine*
    incident, 11; U.S. defeat of, 1, 2, 3, 20;
    war with U.S., 12, 14, 15, 258
Spanish-American War, xiii, xxii, 2, 15, 96,
    259. *See also* War of 1898
Spanish Civil War, 42
Sputnik, xxiii, 81, 101, 103, 174; Eisenhower
    response to, 78, 82–92; impact of, 83, 84,
    89–93; launch of, xv, xvii, xx, xxii, 77, 248,
    258, 261; Senate hearings on, 88–89
Sputnik II, 85
SS-20, 212
Stalin, Joseph, 72, 80, 102, 150, 268, 275
Stark, Harold R., 47
START, 211, 212, 218, 224, 227
START II, 227
"Star Wars." *See* Strategic Defense Initiative
State, Department of, 23, 73, 87, 104,
    155, 270, 277; clashes with Defense
    Department, xvi, 58, 63, 156, 195,
    237; and hostage crisis, 194, 196, 199;
    Intelligence and Research Bureau, 169,
    194, 249, 253; and Nixon, 167; and
    October War, 169, 173
Status of Forces Agreement (SOFA), 190, 191
Stevenson, Adlai, 71, 78, 79, 108, 110, 111, 114
Stimson, Henry L., 25, 46, 47
Stimson Doctrine, 46
Strategic Air Command (SAC), 83, 87, 88
Strategic Defense Initiative (SDI), 211, 212,
    218, 219

About the Authors

Michael J. Nojeim is program coordinator and associate professor of political science at Prairie View A&M University in Prairie View, Texas. He has published articles on U.S. foreign policy, international relations, and nonviolent resistance. He is the author of *Gandhi and King: The Power of Nonviolent Resistance* (Praeger, 2004). He lives in Tomball, Texas.

David P. Kilroy is an associate professor of history and chair of international studies at Nova Southeastern University in Ft. Lauderdale, Florida. He has published articles on U.S. foreign relations and U.S. military history. He is the author of *For Race and Country: The Life and Career of Colonel Charles Young* (Praeger, 2003). He lives in Davie, Florida.